COFFEELAND

COFFEELAND

ONE MAN'S DARK EMPIRE AND THE MAKING OF OUR FAVORITE DRUG

AUGUSTINE SEDGEWICK

THORNDIKE PRESS
A part of Gale, a Cengage Company

**LIBRARY OF CONGRESS CIP DATA ON FILE.
CATALOGUING IN PUBLICATION FOR THIS BOOK
IS AVAILABLE FROM THE LIBRARY OF CONGRESS**

ISBN-13: 978-1-4328-8094-1 (hardcover alk. paper)

Published in 2020 by arrangement with Penguin Press, an imprint of Penguin Publishing Group, a division of Penguin Random House, LLC

Printed in Mexico
Print Number: 01   Print Year: 2020

For my family,
and especially for my boy

You get up in the morning and go to the bathroom and reach over for the sponge, and that's handed to you by a Pacific islander. You reach for a bar of soap, and that's given to you at the hands of a Frenchman. And then you go into the kitchen to drink your coffee for the morning, and that's poured into your cup by a South American. And maybe you want tea: that's poured into your cup by a Chinese. Or maybe you're desirous of having cocoa for breakfast, and that's poured into your cup by a West African. And then you reach over for your toast, and that's given to you at the hands of an English-speaking farmer, not to mention the baker. And before you finish eating breakfast in the morning, you've depended on more than half the world.

— Martin Luther King Jr.

CONTENTS

PROLOGUE:
ONE HUNDRED
YEARS OF COFFEE

Many years later, Jaime Hill would think back to the afternoon of his kidnapping and blame his father. It was late in the day on October 31, 1979, and Jaime had just settled at his desk to write to his daughter Alexandra.[1] At that time Halloween was still a new holiday in El Salvador, arriving with the surge of diplomatic families who moved in after Castro's 1959 revolution in Cuba. Trick-or-treating had caught on quickly in the upscale neighborhoods of the capital, San Salvador, where the forty-two-year-old businessman lived and worked as an executive in his family's company. Each year there were more and more costumed children going door-to-door, usually by car, for safety. Even so, Halloween paled in importance next to the upcoming Day of the Dead, celebrated at the beginning of November, and marking the start of the harvest season.

Jaime always looked forward to the harvest season, when six months of steaming down-

11

pours finally gave way to blue skies and cool breezes, and his excitement said a good deal about the country's history. Lacking an Atlantic coastline, El Salvador had been something of a "backwater" when it won independence from Spain in 1821 — a land of subsistence farmers with four lawyers and four physicians among its 250,000 citizens. Only two or three ships a year called at its primary port.[3] That is not to say its citizens were poor, exactly, for "poor" is a relative term, and the other side of the country's commercial isolation was economic equality. Travelers from Europe who disembarked in El Salvador in the middle of the nineteenth century were struck by "the absence of all extreme poverty" and the obvious richness of the soil.[4] Indigo and balsam, profitable exports, flourished in the countryside, and even the towns were "literally embowered in tropical fruit-trees," including palms, oranges, and "broad-leaved plantains, almost sinking beneath their heavy clusters of golden fruit."[5] While foreign visitors marveled at the natural abundance and saw a place "eminently adapted for the production of tropical staples," the majority of Salvadorans lived by farming communal land.[6] They had little incentive to produce new and unfamiliar cash crops for distant markets, and even less to work for someone who did. Traditionally, the region's subsistence farmers dreaded the arrival of the dry season. Every November, with months of drought ahead, Salvadorans, like their neighbors, prayed for the return of the rains on which they depended.

Deep into the nineteenth century, life for many people in the Salvadoran countryside went on much as it had for hundreds of years. As the sun came up, men carried farm tools along narrow dirt paths that ran from small villages to remote garden plots, and when work was done they returned home with whatever was ready to eat or sell in local markets.[7] Parents taught their children everything they needed to know to live this way.[8] And once a year, when the weather changed, Salvadorans, like their neighbors across Central America, honored their families' ancient debts to the earth and called out to the protective spirits of their ancestors by decorating graves, dancing, singing, drinking, and feasting.[9]

Yet there were also those Salvadorans for whom this deep continuity with the past was not a comfort — those who looked out into the wider world of combustion engines, telephones, and electric lights and feared their country was falling behind — and this group wielded disproportionate political power. Subtly at first, but then radically after 1879, the agrarian foundation of Salvadoran life was uprooted to clear the way for a different future.

By 1889, when Jaime Hill's grandfather James, then a young man of eighteen, arrived in El Salvador from Manchester, England, a profound transformation was under way. Within two generations, El Salvador was a different place. "The first thing that strikes the visitor," wrote an American traveler in 1928, "is the apparent unanimity of thought: COFFEE. Everything is coffee, everyone is directly or indirectly engaged in coffee." "Salvador is a country which should live as a unit with but one theme, a single subject: COFFEE," said the Salvadoran minister of agriculture, a coffee planter himself, in the same year.[10]

Though he settled in El Salvador a decade into the coffee boom, and though, as an immigrant, he was barred from holding political office, James Hill arguably did more than anyone else to transform his adopted country into one of the most intensive monocultures in modern history. By the second half of the twentieth century, due in part to practices Hill introduced on his plantations and in his coffee mill, coffee covered a quarter of El Salvador's arable land and employed a fifth of its population. Salvadoran plantations generated per-acre yields 50 percent higher than Brazil's, producing an annual coffee crop that made up a quarter of the country's GDP and more than 90 percent of its exports. Significantly — and due in part, again, to

14

relationships Hill helped to forge — most of those exports ended up inside brightly colored tin cans lining supermarket shelves in the United States, which had, over the same period, become far and away the world's leading coffee-drinking country.[11] In a century, the harvest in El Salvador had taken on a new meaning — picking and milling coffee bound for American cups — and its bounty had changed hands.

In the Hill family, as a result, the start of the coffee harvest normally meant rewards close at hand, but 1979 was not a normal year. The weather, as usual, had changed right on time, bringing sunny skies and dry air ideal for picking and milling coffee. Yet these favorable conditions were clouded by developments within the family and in the country at large. Jaime, the oldest of three brothers, had recently been demoted from his position in the family business, which had expanded since World War II from coffee into real estate, construction, finance, and insurance. More troubling, the renewal of old political conflicts had put the success of the year's harvest seriously in doubt.

One hundred years of coffee had split El Salvador in two. At the same time as the country had achieved extraordinary levels of economic productivity, it had also become poor in the most fundamental ways. Eighty percent of the nation's children were malnourished.[12] "Extreme poverty," once nowhere to be seen, had become one of the two basic facts of Salvadoran life — the other being the extraordinary wealth of the legendary "Fourteen Families," including the Hill family, who had started in coffee and kept going until they achieved a near monopoly over the country's land, resources, economy, and politics. There was the oligarchy — educated abroad, driven around in the backseats of armored European cars, their power in business and government secured by the military, private bodyguards, and high walls around their gated homes — and there was everyone else. The fracturing of El Salvador into very rich and very poor had not gone unchallenged, but historically opposition to coffee capitalism had met fearsome repression, and for a time the popular resistance, once fearsome in its own right, had been driven underground.

Despite the danger, the revolutionary spirit had come back to life after Castro's victory in Cuba. In turn, the Salvadoran government — backed up by the United States, on high alert against communism in the hemisphere — responded with escalating demonstrations of deadly force, amplified by the arrival on the scene of a menacing new presence: shadowy "death squads" made up of moonlighting soldiers and funded by the oligarchy.

Throughout the 1970s, a rash of kidnappings, disappearances, and assassinations led to bloody retaliation and widespread terror. Then, on October 15, 1979, there was a coup. Not for the first time in Salvadoran history, the forcible change in government failed to translate directly into clear changes in policy and daily life. Even by Halloween, its consequences were not entirely clear.

Jaime Hill had much to say to his daughter Alexandra, who was away for her senior year at the Foxcroft School in Virginia and hoping to go on to study political science at college in Boston. As a boy Jaime himself had been sent to boarding school in Rhode Island, and the whole time he was there he dreamed of returning home and working on the coffee plantations, just as his grandfather James had. Then one day his father, also named Jaime, showed up at the school unannounced and explained to his son that he was losing his eyesight and would need someone to take over the administration of the family business. Jaime Hill went on to college at the Wharton School in Philadelphia. After graduation he worked for a few years on Wall Street before moving back to El Salvador to fulfill his father's wishes.[13]

The hands of the grandfather clock in the corner of Jaime's office turned past 4:15. He reached for his typewriter and tapped out a greeting to Alexandra, just as a jeep and a pickup truck sped up to his building and braked to a quick halt in front. Men dressed in police and army uniforms piled out of the jeep and cleared the street, directing traffic with military-issue Heckler & Koch G3 assault rifles. A second crew in dark masks and olive fatigues jumped down from the pickup and stormed the entrance, carrying Uzis. Bursts of gunfire dropped a guard and tore a hole in the steel security door. The gunmen charged inside, past a stunned secretary, and up the stairs.

When Jaime heard commotion below his office window, his first thought was that the police were chasing a thief. When he heard shots and screams downstairs, he knew he was mistaken. Eight years earlier a hit squad disguised as a road crew had stopped a car carrying Ernesto Regalado Dueñas, Jaime's cousin by marriage. Three days later, Ernesto Regalado's corpse was dumped in the street. Jaime's father made him buy a bulletproof vest, and fear began to follow him everywhere.[14]

Panicking now, Jaime grabbed for the .45 he kept in his desk and ran to hide in the bathroom — and there he found himself trapped, holding a pistol that now felt like an iron dumbbell in his hand. A voice called his name from the other side of the door. Jaime laid his gun down, inched out of the bath-

18

room, and faced the masked intruders. Immediately a hood swept down over his head, handcuffs clamped around his wrists, and unseen hands grabbed at his arms and dragged him down the stairs, past his helpless secretary, past his lifeless bodyguard, and out into the street. "Tell my family I am not hurt," Jaime cried behind him, and he was thrown facedown into the back of the idling pickup underneath a green tarp that snapped in the wind as the truck sped away from the building and out of the city to the west, toward the place once known as "Coffeeland."[15]

Half a century earlier, the road to Santa Ana was small and rough, winding downhill into the wide basin of the Lempa River valley. On the plain below, the white stucco walls of tidy buildings shone brilliantly against the dense jungle surrounding the settlement on three sides, and red tile roofs toasted gently under the warm sun. At a distance, Santa Ana was "the prettiest little town" in all of Central America, decided one American journalist who stopped for the night in the 1920s.[16]

By then Santa Ana was also El Salvador's second-largest city, the center of an economic boom that had begun in the 1880s and was still going strong, thanks especially to the increasing commerce with California conducted since the start of the Great War in

19

1914. And if the city proper, laid out on an orderly grid around a central plaza, seemed somewhat "less animated" than might be expected of a global boomtown, that was due to the nature of the boom itself.[17] Most of the real business was done beyond the edge of town, on the furrowed slopes of the eight-thousand-foot Santa Ana Volcano, the tallest in El Salvador and long thought to be extinct.

All across the broad face of the volcano, from the foothills most of the way up its steep truncated cone, spread a lush green patchwork of coffee plantations. Every day during the harvest season, from November to February, tens of thousands of people worked on these plantations, picking coffee from dawn to dusk, six in the morning to late afternoon. At the end of the workday, mule trains overloaded with bulging brown sacks and teams of oxen pulling carts overflowing with red ripe coffee cherries staggered down the volcano and through the dusty streets of Santa Ana on their way to one of the city's many coffee mills, where the freshly picked cherries would be processed into export-ready beans.

Among the busiest streets during this time of year was a narrow road that led north from the center of town, through a stand of Spanish oaks whose branches had grown together to form a dark-green tunnel. On the outskirts of the city, just before the road began to

20

climb off the valley floor, the way turned slightly to the right, and on the left appeared the gate of a modern coffee mill called Las Tres Puertas, The Three Doors.

Beyond the gate, drivers led their work animals up to a utilitarian receiving station, where crews of men worked quickly to feed the fresh coffee cherries into the mill. Over the next several days, the seeds would be extracted from the cherries, washed clean, and conveyed through water channels toward the sunbaked drying patios stretching out behind the mill. In one corner of the patios, bold white lines had been painted on the brown bricks, marking out a regulation tennis court, with doubles alleys.

On the other side of the tennis court, atop a small rise, stood an elegant two-story house of recent construction. The house had been built in the style called Spanish Colonial Revival, popular after the Panama-Pacific International Exposition of 1915, the San Francisco fair celebrating the opening of the Panama Canal — sharp white walls, sweeping exterior stairs, columned entry, trim red tile dormers and roof. Inside, with his petite, dark-eyed wife and their brigade of children — ten born, seven surviving — lived James Hill, the spindly six-foot-tall Englishman with wire-framed eyeglasses who by the 1920s had established himself as "the coffee king of El Salvador."[18]

The title was sincere, and deserved, but nonetheless it carried an unintended irony that its bearer sometimes relished and sometimes tried to conceal. James Hill had been born in Queen Victoria's England in 1871, in the slums of industrial Manchester, a neighborhood infamous around the world for its poverty and pollution. He sailed for El Salvador in 1889 with hardly a shilling to his name, and not for coffee at all, but rather to escape the gloomy skies and prospects that hung over his life in Manchester, by selling textiles abroad.

In many ways, the textile business could not have been more different from coffee. Cloth was an unglamorous but steady trade, which did after all provide a basic necessity. Coffee by comparison was a high-wire act of agriculture and finance. The fragile and temperamental trees demanded years of hard labor and delicate tending before giving a real harvest. Worse, the value of whatever coffee crop finally arrived depended entirely on an international market of such notorious volatility that it served as the setting and subject of popular melodramatic novels of the day, parables of risk and ruin.[19]

Yet from this unlikely beginning James Hill built a coffee empire that came to be considered by many, including his neighbors and rivals on the Santa Ana Volcano, perhaps the very finest in El Salvador — and therefore in the world. By the time he died in 1951, Hill ruled an archipelago of eighteen plantations that fed his mill Las Tres Puertas, together comprising over 3,000 acres planted in coffee, employing nearly 5,000 people at the height of the season, yielding an annual harvest of perhaps 2,000 tons of export-ready coffee beans, and netting, in a good year, a profit of hundreds of thousands of dollars. And as impressive as these totals were, the full reach of James Hill's coffee empire could not be calculated in acres, trees, employees, tons, or dollars — for it also served as a kind of "showplace" for coffee drinkers thousands of miles away who, for one reason or another, wanted to know where their coffee came from, and what it was like there.[20]

Arthur Ruhl had been everywhere. He left his boyhood home in Rockford, Illinois, for Harvard in 1895, and four years later he began a reporting career in New York that took him around the world. He was underneath Manhattan for the excavation of the subway in 1902; he was on the beach in Kitty Hawk with the Wright brothers in 1908; he was in scorching Reno on Independence Day in 1910 to see Jack Johnson knock out Jim Jeffries, the "Great White Hope"; he was in Veracruz, Mexico, when U.S. Marines took the city in 1914; he was on the front lines of the Great War in Gallipoli in 1915; he was in

23

Russia just before the Bolshevik Revolution in 1917; and from each place he sent thoughtful, amiable dispatches back to readers of *Harper's, Collier's,* and *The Century.*[21]

Ruhl's adventures taught him that the world was not so big as it looked from a fixed point, and was only getting smaller every day. "The motor-car, radio, and newspaper syndicate, let alone cables and modern steamships, are shrinking the world faster than many stay-at-home people think," he wrote. As a matter of personal preference, he was all for nice hotels, "sport and health," good manners, "clean streets," competent traffic policemen, and cocktails at a "well-regulated" country club, but Ruhl was not so naive as to confuse comfort with progress. He didn't object to change in principle, he just wanted to find out what it meant.

One morning in 1927, Ruhl went down to the southern tip of Manhattan and boarded a big white banana boat belonging to the United Fruit Company, bound for Central America. In "Nice Little Costa Rica," "Troubled Nicaragua," Honduras, Guatemala, and "Busy Salvador," he hoped to get a close-up view of the "profound changes" under way in the "once pastoral and patriarchal republics" as they were "drawn into the general stream of the modern world" — where, for better or worse, virtue was measured in numbers ("speed, height, population, profits!") and efficiency ("energy, time-saving, sanitation, the magic of machinery") was celebrated as genius.

Arthur Ruhl found what he was looking for in El Salvador. Conduits for telephone and power lines ran under "new and very perfect" city streets. High-level government officials promised highways and airports coming soon. The "soldierlike" police force had been trained by an American and convincingly outfitted with pith helmets and military-dress belts. And the large, hardworking, mixed-race peasant class, if not so "white" and "democratic" as Costa Rica's, was neither so "Indian" and difficult as Guatemala's. There were moments during his stay in the capital when Ruhl felt as if he had been transported to southern California, yet he could not completely forget that he was "in a land where most workers receive less than half a dollar a day," and where some of the new iron manhole covers above the utility conduits had been stolen and sold for scrap. After a few pleasant days in the city — and well aware that "everything in El Salvador revolves around coffee" — Ruhl boarded the train to Santa Ana, where he had made some contacts in advance.

Waiting for him at the railway station in Santa Ana was one of James Hill's three sons, recently returned from college in California and driving his father's car. When they pulled

25

up to Las Tres Puertas, Ruhl stepped out of the car and greeted the "calm, capable, and polite" Englishman who was to be his host and guide. James Hill, then nearing sixty, led a tour of the "experimental plantation" adjoining his house and mill, probing the "black loam" around the trees with his "stout walking-stick" as they went. All the while, Hill talked convivially in his Manchester accent about coffee life and lore, soil and trees, prices and wages, coups and revolutions, his fellow planters and "his work-people," doling out wisdom from his four decades in El Salvador.

After the tour, the two men settled in the immaculate office Hill had furnished in the style of a City of London counting house. With a "casual air," Hill ventured again into serious subjects: the complicated political and economic questions facing El Salvador, the dramatic measures that had been and could be taken to secure the health of the country's coffee industry, the important role the younger generations of his own family would certainly play therein, and the good he hoped they would do. It was all very businesslike, and yet as Arthur Ruhl listened to James Hill go on calmly predicting El Salvador's future, an uneasy feeling crept over him. He could not help thinking that the whole scene, if on the one hand so representative of the changing world, was also, actually, distinctly "odd."[22]

■ ■ ■ ■

James Hill lived eighty years and two lives. Born into the world's first industrial working class, he would be recognized as a true Salvadoran, a native member of one of the world's most entrenched oligarchies, before he died in 1951. By then Manchester and Santa Ana were not as far apart as they had been when Hill first left home. In the eight decades of James Hill's life — the years between the end of the U.S. Civil War and the beginning of the Cold War — the world, as Arthur Ruhl observed, got smaller. Railroads, steamships, automobiles, airplanes, telegraphs, telephones, radios, moving pictures, together with other novel forms of fuel, power, and governance, brought together people, places, and things that had once been distant, if not isolated from one another. It was not only the age when what we now call " 'globalization' first became clearly manifest" — it was also the time when the word "global" was first applied to phenomena that seemed to encompass the whole of the earth.[23] It was an age of "ever greater global interconnectedness," when the word "interconnected" was first used to describe the sense that individual connections were themselves linked together into something greater.[24] The "densely knit web of global

27

connections" that took shape during these decades, many historians contend, forms the "basic fact" of the modern world.[25]

The history of coffee runs through the middle of this larger story of global connection and transformation. Four hundred years ago, coffee was a mysterious Ottoman custom, and there was no word for it in English; today "coffee" is perhaps the most widespread word on the planet.[26] Three hundred years ago, coffee was cultivated commercially in only one place, Yemen, its supply controlled by a small group of merchants. Today it is a cash crop for more than twenty-five million people in over seventy countries.[27] Two hundred years ago, coffee was a luxury for society's privileged classes, enjoyed in coffeehouses that were centers of ideas, conversation, art, politics, and culture. Today it is the unrivaled work drug, filling billions of cups around the world each day and consumed by nearly two-thirds of Americans.[28] A hundred years ago, planters in Latin America and merchants in the United States concerned about the consequences of low coffee prices began to try to teach American coffee drinkers about conditions on plantations and why they mattered. Today coffee is by far the leading "fair trade" product, the commodity we use more than any other to think about how the world economy works and what to do about it.[29]

For all these reasons, it has often been said that "coffee connected the world."[30] It is true that the transformation of coffee from a mysterious Muslim custom to a cultured European luxury to a ubiquitous daily necessity tells a story about the world becoming what it is. And certainly, following James Hill from Manchester to the Santa Ana Volcano, tracking coffee from his plantations and mill into the San Francisco roasting plants and vacuum-sealed cans of major American coffee brands, and on to grocery stores, kitchens, break rooms, and cafés across the U.S., reveals distant people, places, and things being geared together with increasing precision: "a world connecting," in the words of a recent landmark book on the period.[31] But that is only half the story.

Modern history moves in two directions at once. New connections bred deep new divisions. In the nineteenth century, the world economy grew forty-four times larger. Between 1850 and 1914, world trade increased by 1,000 percent — "the world had never seen such a dizzying creation of wealth."[32] Yet the income gap between people who lived in regions with temperate climates and industrial economies and those who lived in regions with tropical climates and agricultural economies widened in step with increasing global connection.[33] In 1880 per capita income in "developed" industrial societies was double that of the rest of the world; by 1914 it was triple; by 1950 it was five times greater.[34]

The division of the world into rich and poor paralleled the division of the world into coffee drinkers, overwhelmingly concentrated in the industrialized global north, and coffee workers, even more concentrated in the predominantly agricultural and perpetually "developing" global south. As the most valuable agricultural product of the world's poorest regions, coffee has played a central role in shaping this divide.[35] In the last 150 years, coffee has become an exceptionally valuable commodity — exports are now worth over $25 billion a year, and retail sales many times more — that is a virtual monopoly of the world's poorest nations.[36] Coffee is not just one of the most important commodities in the history of global capitalism, as is commonly claimed — it is one of the most important commodities in the history of global inequality.

Coffee did not simply "connect the world." What it did, instead — what it does — is raise a question with no easy answer, one as consequential as it is complex: What does it mean to be connected to faraway people and places through everyday things?

1.
THE PERFECT
SYMBOL OF ISLAM

In 1554, two Syrians went into business together in their adopted hometown of Constantinople. Schems had come from Damascus, Hekim from Aleppo. Amid the stalls of the busy market district near the Bosporus, they opened a coffee shop, the city's first. The shop was furnished "with very neat Couches and Carpets," and it became known as an upstanding social place, "very proper to make acquaintances in." Many of the patrons were students and other "studious Persons," unemployed professionals searching for jobs, "Lovers of Chess," and professors.[1] At that point, coffee had entered the written historical record about fifty years earlier.[2]

Coffee is native to Ethiopia, where the first commercial harvests were gathered from wild plants in the fifteenth century. Early cultivation took place on terraced hillsides in sixteenth-century Yemen, while consumption spread across the Arabian Peninsula and around the Mediterranean through trade and war. A coffeehouse was often one of the first things Ottoman emperors built upon conquering a new city, "to demonstrate the civility of their rule."[3] Given this mode of diffusion, the meanings of the drink were contested. According to many etymologies, the word "coffee" derives from the Arabic *qahwah,* meaning wine: coffee was "the wine of Islam," and this raised some questions.[4]

In 1511, a policeman in Mecca, returning soberly from prayers one evening, observed a group of his coreligionists preparing themselves for a night of worship by drinking coffee. Suspicious of coffee's intoxicating effects, Mecca's police torched the city's supplies, though that hardly settled the matter. A pamphlet published in 1587 surveyed the history of the drink in the hope of determining "What ought to be sincerely and distinctly believ'd concerning Coffee, that is, if it be lawful for a Mussulman to drink it."[5]

By then European men had also discovered coffee. In 1573, Leonhard Rauwolf, a German scholar, traveled to Aleppo, where he noticed a group gathered around a drink "black as Ink": "Without any fear or regard out of *China* Cups, as hot as they can, they put it often to their Lips but drink but little at a time, and let it go round as they sit." In 1596 a Dutch physician, Bernard ten Broeke, described the process of coffee making he had seen in the Levant: "They take of this fruite one pound and a half, and roast them a little in the fire, and then sieth them in twentie poundes of water, till the half be consumed away: this drinke they take every morning fasting in their chambers, out of an earthen pot, being verie hote . . . and they say it strengtheneth and maketh them warme, breaketh wind, and openeth any stopping."[6]

"They" werc the Turks. So strong was the association that coffee appeared in Europe as "the sign of Turkish difference" and "the perfect symbol of Islam." Viewed across this symbolic distance, the European discovery of coffee was also an encounter with a foreign body, and many early depictions of coffee drinking were inflected with suspicion and disgust. In 1609, William Biddulph, an English minister who had been employed in Aleppo, described "a blacke kind of drinke made of a kind of Pulse like Pease, called *Coava;* which being grownd in the Mill, and boiled in water, they drinke it as hot as they can suffer it." In 1610, the poet and translator George Sandys tried coffee for himself and found it "blacke as soote, and tasting not much unlike it."[7]

Even when they doubted coffee's appeal, Europeans recognized its power. Like alcohol and opium, coffee changed the people who consumed it, though there was no consensus on exactly how or why. In 1632 the philosopher-librarian Robert Burton likened

Turkish coffeehouses to "our Ale-houses or Taverns" and described coffee as an "alterative," a cure for melancholy.[8] In 1640, London apothecary John Parkinson wrote that "the Turkes berry drinke hath many good Physicall properties therein: for it strengtheneth a weak stomacke, helping digestion, and the tumours and obstructions of the liver and spleene."[9]

As Parkinson's endorsement suggests, coffee was often used as medicine. The medical thinking of the age emphasized balancing the body's four humors — blood, phlegm, black bile, and yellow bile — by using foods as drugs, with bloodletting and surgery performed as needed. Foods were classified within one of four categories: hot, cold, wet, and dry. Yet coffee, along with tea and chocolate, did not seem to fit within a single category. It was hot and stimulating, but also cooling and diuretic, confounding ideas of the human body that had been fixed in place for about 1,500 years.[10] Nor was there agreement about coffee's basic effects. Many of its proponents said that coffee was fortifying, but its opponents blamed coffee for a variety of ailments, especially impotence.[11]

The "Turkes berry drinke" became English, and then European, by way of the coffeehouse.[12] The first coffeehouse in London opened in the early 1650s, bankrolled by agents of the Levant Company who had acquired the taste for coffee while trading spices, wool, tin, and gunpowder in the East. One merchant, Daniel Edwards, employed a domestic servant from Smyrna, Pasqua Rosée, who made coffee for him every day in his London home. When Edwards's friends began dropping by regularly to get a bowlful, he saw a business opportunity. Selling coffee at retail was below his station, so he set up his servant Rosée as a proxy.[13]

Rosée's coffee stall, built of "thick planks of pine or fir" and wedged in among the shops and offices that lined the narrow St. Michael's Alley in the City of London, lacked the comforts Schems and Hekim had provided, though he did hang a sign featuring an image of himself dressed as a Turk. The stall flourished, but soon Rosée suffered a fate familiar to pioneers of new foods in the West. Alehouse keepers in the neighborhood, worried that he was taking their customers, tried to drive him out of business by using his alien status against him. By law only citizens of London could do business in the City, so Rosée's merchant backers got him a native partner, a farm boy named Christopher Bowman. Together Rosée and Bowman moved into a bigger storefront and carried on, but before long Rosée's name was off the lease. Then the coffee shop, along with the other makeshift wooden structures jammed

35

into the market district, burned in the fire of 1666.[14]

Nevertheless, coffee was catching on in London, and many of the new coffee shops opening around the city were more than market stalls. Offering ample seating and reading material, they became "penny universities," open forums for the discussion of news and ideas. Visiting London coffeehouses in 1660, diarist Samuel Pepys recorded talk of the weather, the sex lives of insects, and the proper distribution of wealth.[15] Philosopher Jürgen Habermas suggests that such coffeehouse conversations gave rise to a new social class free from old hierarchies of title and wealth — a nascent civil society beyond the court, church, and state, with far-reaching implications for politics and governance.[16]

In mid-seventeenth-century London a lot was happening in the way of governance: the execution of King Charles I in 1649, the establishment of a republican Commonwealth under Oliver Cromwell, and the subsequent restoration of the monarchy and the Church of England under Charles II in 1660. As "the primary social space in which 'news' was both produced and consumed," London's coffeehouses embodied emergent democratic norms of freedom of speech and assembly, nurturing "the public" that was increasingly questioning the authority of the royal court.[17] Registering the threat, Charles

II tried to snuff out dissent by getting rid of the coffeehouses, which were condemned as "seedbeds of political unrest" and hives of "false news" — talk of affairs of state that diverged from the authorized accounts of the court.[18] Charles's fears were not assuaged when, in response to his campaign to clean up the coffeehouses, London reached "a mutinous condition." Trying a new approach, the king issued licenses to coffeehouses on the condition that they not allow subversive literature or talk. To escape surveillance, some coffeehouses recast themselves as pubs.[19]

The shadow of foreignness heightened suspicions hanging over coffeehouses. Patriotic ale-drinkers were supposed to hate coffee "as *Mahomatizm.*" Still, London employers could see the benefits. "Whereas formerly apprentices and clerks with others, used to take their mornings draught in ale, beer or wine," one scholar wrote at the time, "which by the dizziness they cause in the brain, make many unfit for businesse, they use now to play the good-fellows in this wakefull and civill drink." Coffee seemed to have none of alcohol's dulling effects: it was "a drink at once to make us sober and merry." The use of the first-person pronoun is striking. By the turn of the century, a hundred years after the first mention of coffee in English, London had several hundred coffeehouses. By comparison, Amsterdam had thirty-two.[20]

In a century, coffee drinking had gone from unknown to epidemic in England. Especially in light of the physiological questions coffee raised, overconsumption had become a concern. In June 1699, John Houghton, a druggist and commodity trader, gave a "Discourse of Coffee" before England's most distinguished learned society, whose members often gathered in a coffeehouse called the Grecian. Largely in the tone of local gossip, the paper describes the introduction of coffee into an entire culture and way of life. Houghton dared not put forward an answer to the question of coffee's effects on health and wakefulness, for he did not have what he judged to be a sound "Theory of Sleep." But he did note that coffee had made "all sorts of People sociable" and so "improved useful knowledge very much."[21]

Given its popularity, there was strong interest in planting coffee across the Atlantic in Britain's New England, Virginia, and Caribbean colonies.[22] Yet British merchants couldn't get past the Arab traders working out of Yemeni ports on the Red Sea who had all but monopolized the world supply of coffee. In this regard, British trading companies were more successful with tea than with coffee. Tea had been introduced to the British consumer market after coffee, and it was initially more expensive, for the tea trade was controlled by the Dutch, who used their island colony of Java as a transshipment point.[23] But then, in the first quarter of the eighteenth century, the British East India Company at last gained access to Chinese ports, and cheap tea flooded the British market. British tea imports increased by perhaps 4,000 times in the eighteenth century, while the Dutch shifted the focus of Java to coffee.[24] As a result, it was tea, not coffee, that was destroyed in protest in Boston Harbor in 1773, and it was East Indian tea, taken with West Indian sugar, that fortified the workers who powered the industrial revolution that took off in the North of England shortly after.

2.
COTTONOPOLIS

Before he was Karl Marx's benefactor and coauthor, Friedrich Engels was the poet son of a rich Prussian textile-manufacturing family. In 1842, when Friedrich was twenty-two, his father sent his idealistic heir across the North Sea to Manchester, England, where the family had recently opened a large mill for the manufacture of cotton thread, called the Victoria Mill, after the queen.

The mill was in Salford, a rural district just then beginning to be swallowed up by the fast-growing city. Scarcely half a century earlier, Manchester was a provincial market town in the riverine northwest of England, home to about 30,000 people and a single tall chimney. By the time Friedrich Engels arrived, Manchester had become the capital of what historian Eric Hobsbawm called "the most important event in world history," the Industrial Revolution.[1] The city's lone chimney had sprouted into a defoliated forest of smokestacks, below which lived 300,000 people and above which bloomed a bruise-colored canopy of smoke so thick it extinguished sunlight, the result of the coal-burning, steam-powered mills that were turning more cotton into cloth than in any other city on earth. In tribute to its leading industry, Manchester had been popularly renamed "Cottonopolis." Likewise, in markets far from England, things made of cotton were called simply "Manchester goods," and from distant corners of the earth the curious traveled to see where their stuff was made.

To arrive in Cottonopolis in the age of Queen Victoria was to suffer insults to every sense. "As I entered your city, a sort of hum, a prolonged, continuous vibration struck my ear, as if some irresistible and mysterious force was at work," wrote the American railroad baron Richard B. Kimball, who would not have been unacquainted with great noises, in 1858.[2] At street level, the city was terrifying and exhilarating, "monstrous and awe-inspiring."[3] To Scottish writer Thomas Carlyle, the sound of the mills starting up at 5:30 each morning was "like the boom of an Atlantic tide."[4] Others had never heard anything like it. "A thousand noises disturb this damp, dark labyrinth, but they are not at all the ordinary sounds one hears in great cities," observed the French journalist Alexis de Tocqueville, not long returned from his tour of the United States when he traveled to

41

Manchester in 1835. "The crunching wheels of machinery, the shriek of steam from boilers, the regular beat of the looms, the heavy rumble of carts, those are the noises from which you can never escape."[5]

Down each alley, "largely hidden from public view," people lived in "almost unimaginable" squalor. The smells were "excrementitious."[6] Exhaust from the mills displaced the air and reduced the sun to "a disc without rays."[7] In 1872, a worried scientist who had been studying Manchester's "chemical climatology" coined the term "acid rain" to describe the sulfuric dilute falling from the sky.[8]

The clangor, the stench, the poverty, the gloom, and the acid rain were by-products of the accumulation of an immense fortune. Factories in and around Manchester generated around half of the value of the trade of Great Britain in the second half of the nineteenth century, when the British Empire was growing to encompass a quarter of the planet's population and land, and when British factories were taking almost a third of the world's raw materials and producing almost 40 percent of the world's manufactured exports each year.[9] Sometimes the capitalists get the credit for this dynamism, seeking profit, shaping policy, setting armies into motion, ruling their global empire of cotton from well-appointed merchant houses and banquet halls.[10] Sometimes the machines do: steam engines, mechanical looms and frames, locomotives, steamships, telegraphs.[11] Yet all the powerful new forms of governance and technology that combined to remake Manchester into Cottonopolis, the center of industrial capitalism in the nineteenth century, were at bottom tools for the extraction of unprecedented quantities of hard labor. There were the distant laborers, many enslaved and others simply coerced, who worked to supply the raw materials — the coal, the cotton, and the food — that Manchester turned into finished goods. And there was also, for the first time, an industrial working class, an innovation as important as the steam engine. Before Manchester became Manchester, "the world had seen extreme poverty and labor exploitation for centuries, but it had never seen a sea of humanity organizing every aspect of their lives around the rhythms of machine production."[12] Though perhaps an organized sea is not the best metaphor in this case.

In the words of one nineteenth-century French politician who visited Manchester to figure out how his country could avoid the city's problems: "Amid the fogs which exhale from this marshy district, and the clouds of smoke vomited forth among the numberless chimneys, Labour presents a mysterious activity, somewhat akin to the subterraneous action of a volcano."[13] The foremost historian of British industry approved of the description. "The city was a volcano," Eric Hobsbawm wrote, "to whose rumblings the rich and powerful listened with fear, and whose eruptions they dreaded."[14]

Once he got to Manchester, Friedrich Engels was no longer content with metaphor, no matter how poetic. The city had indeed sparked his curiosity about the business of manufacturing, though not precisely as his father intended, and Engels was to spend the rest of his life trying to figure out how it all worked. When not busy in the office of his family's cotton mill, Engels attended scientific lectures around Manchester, many of which probed the invisible inner workings of the great steam engines at the heart of the mills. At the same time, he began to investigate what the mills made of the people who worked in them. With Mary Burns, a working-class Irish woman with whom he would live on and off for twenty years, Engels went into the slums.

The book Engels wrote about what he found there, *The Condition of the Working Class in England,* strains at the limits of language to capture the "perfection" of industrial Manchester's horrors. Engels was especially fascinated by a street called Long Millgate, and he included a map of it in his book, because he thought it would be "impossible to convey an idea" of the chaos with mere words: "the irregular cramming together of dwellings in ways which defy all rational plan, of the tangle in which they are crowded literally one upon the other." Long Millgate, Engels promised his readers, was "not the worst spot and not one-tenth of the whole Old Town." But its "heaps of rubbish, garbage, and offal" were bad enough to stand in for the "entire district."

> Right and left a multitude of covered passages lead from the main street into numerous courts, and he who turns in thither gets into a filth and disgusting grime, the equal of which is not to be found — especially in the courts which lead down to the [River] Irk, and which contain unqualifiedly the most horrible dwellings which I have yet beheld. In one of these courts there stands directly, at the entrance, at the end of the covered passage, a privy without a door, so dirty that the inhabitants can pass into and out of the court only by passing through foul pools of stagnant urine and excrement.[15]

For Engels, who published *The Communist Manifesto* with Marx four years later, Long Millgate was the stage of a great struggle for equality and justice. For James and Alice Hill, the parents of James, future coffee king, Long Millgate was the street below their marital bed.

James Hill, son of the slater Ralph Hill, was twenty-one when he married twenty-year-old Alice Greenway, daughter of the carter Thomas Greenway, in a group wedding in Manchester Cathedral on April 26, 1869.[16] James signed his name to the marriage certificate, and Alice made her mark. Their first home together was at 41 Long Millgate, a boardinghouse owned by a woman named Boardman.[17]

Mrs. Boardman's would not have been the worst place on the street. James worked for the Lancashire and Yorkshire Railway, a busy combination of lines spidering out from central Manchester across the hinterlands to the north and east. The route began and ended at Victoria Station, just across the street from Mrs. Boardman's. For his wage, James rode the railway from Victoria Station into the countryside, drumming up business for the railroad from people who needed to move things to market.

The first child of James and Alice was born two years after the wedding, on May 13, 1871, and given his father's name. He was baptized a month later on a feast day at St. Barnabas, Church of England, its brick nave boxed in by mills on three sides. After the baptism, James and Alice carried their infant son James through the city's most crowded

46

mill district, Ancoats, across the busy Oldham Road, and into a neighborhood called Collyhurst, where they settled after leaving Mrs. Boardman's.

Before the turn of the nineteenth century, Collyhurst had been home to a church called St. George's-in-the-Fields. By the time James and Alice Hill moved out of Mrs. Boardman's, the name of the church had been shortened to St. George's. New railroad tracks ran where the fields had been, drawing behind them new enterprises: the Cable Street Finishing Mills, the Livesey Street Mills, a glassworks, an ironworks. Then James Sr.'s employer, the Lancashire and Yorkshire Railway, sited a new goods station in Collyhurst, and the sharp angle formed by the depot and the tracks began to fill up with people. Newcomers crowded into low "jerry-built houses [that] shared a common back wall," constructed from the cheapest materials and meant to hold as many people as possible — in form and function, the barracks of Manchester's industrial army. To say that comforts were scarce misses the point. In such districts "a single communal privy . . . might serve as many as forty multi-family dwellings." The overflow ran so thickly into the nearby canals and streams that birds often perched on what appeared to be the surface of the water.[18]

At best, Collyhurst was considered a place

"to pass through on the way to somewhere else," though that was often easier said than done.[19] The Hill family moved around but never out of the neighborhood during James's childhood. The three of them, then the four of them, the five, the six, the seven of them lived on Clegg Street, then next to a draper's shop on Rome Street, then on Apollo Street, and finally on Reather Street, mixing with millworkers and tradesmen of all kinds, cotton ballers and umbrella makers, orbiting the goods station of the Lancashire and Yorkshire Railway in a tight arc shaped by the strong gravity of the problem of hungry mouths to feed.[20]

Bitter hardship and acid rain notwithstanding, 1871 was an auspicious year to be born in the gloomy middle of the world economy. In August 1870, the nationwide Elementary Education Act made provisions for the public schooling of children ages five to thirteen. The previous requirements had mandated part-time schooling for children working in factories, but because factory owners were effectively the schoolmasters, practice matched principle only when the boss made it so. In contrast, under the Education Act, thousands of new schools opened in poor neighborhoods, and "education in England transitioned from a charity to a right upheld by the state."[21]

48

In September 1875, James Hill entered school in Collyhurst only a few blocks from his house.[22] The school was affiliated with St. George's Church, and on many mornings it filled up with more than two hundred children. An inspector from the Anglican Diocese of Manchester visited in the same year Hill began and gave his cautious approval: "The infants answer well on the life of Moses and the leading incidents of the life of Christ. The upper class also knows something of Joseph + Samuel. Repetition is good and the Babies are nicely taught. The discipline under the present mistress seems to be quite satisfactory."[23]

The state had an interest in making a sound education a right. One by-product of steam-powered manufacturing in Manchester was a great population of young people who stood virtually no chance of inheriting property, the children of millworkers who were just scraping by. For years, most of these children had followed their parents into the mills, but by 1870 "it was clear to many that the future of the nation was ultimately served best, not by making children work, but by educating them."[24] Especially in light of increasing overseas economic competition from industrializing Germany and the United States, serving the future of Victoria's England meant serving the empire.[25] School was a training ground for the business of empire, and a door into the world beyond Manchester.

As a boy, James Hill found work delivering milk door-to-door.[26] On sodden mornings, as he walked the mucky streets of his neighborhood — some, such as Oldham Road, named for the next town over; others, such as Rome and Apollo, named for distant capitals and mythic gods — his mind ranged across wider, sunnier territory. Hill idolized Alexander the Great, who at eighteen led his Macedonian cavalry through Greece, ultimately extending his rule all the way to the Indian frontier.[27] Alexander — also Napoleon's hero — was an extraordinarily popular figure among Victorians, who viewed their sooty age through gilded historical analogies, the most important of which was ancient Greece.[28] The timeless accomplishments of the Greeks cast a flattering light on Britain's relentless overseas expansionism, and the Hellenic ideal of the "warrior-citizen" held special appeal for "the ambitious citizens of Victoria's empire," who did the work that made that empire thrive.[29] Though Alexander the Great had never made it there, James Hill dreamed of exploring the brightly colored maps of the Americas he had studied in school.[30]

If the ancient world gave Victorian England an ennobling sense of purpose, it was the "new world" that provided the tingle of possibility. The crumbling of Spain's empire had created one of history's great business opportunities. "Spanish America is free," announced the British foreign secretary and future prime minister George Canning in 1824, "and if we do not mismanage our affairs sadly, she is *English.*"[31]

That was also the premise of the most popular story of James Hill's day: Robert Louis Stevenson's *Treasure Island,* serialized in 1881 and 1882.[32] Set in the mid-eighteenth century, *Treasure Island* is the story of a boy named Jim who works to help his widowed mother run a struggling inn on the west coast of England, the Admiral Benbow. After the death of a lodger, Captain Billy Bones, Jim's mother opens his sea chest and discovers among his belongings some gold pieces and a map. From these she takes what she is owed for room and board, and "not a farthing over." Jim curses his mother's rectitude and raises a party not similarly afflicted to go see about the map. At the opportunity of joining this enterprise, Jim's acquaintances Dr. Livesey and Squire Trelawney give up their "wretched practice[s]" — physician, magistrate — in an instant.[33]

By no accident, the principal themes of the children's literature of the first great industrial empire were adventure and ambition, pursued overseas.[34] Jim, Dr. Livesey, Squire

51

Trelawney, and the crew they hire sail forth from England not to claim what is rightly theirs but to take whatever they can get. Their venture is both motivated and justified by the principle that buried treasure is fair game until someone says otherwise, pulls it out of the earth, and beats back whoever would disagree. In the world beyond the shabby propriety of the Admiral Benbow, everyone kills for treasure. In the world James Hill knew as a boy, Treasure Island was a place it was possible to go, and the story was a guidebook to this place. It held "nothing back but the bearings of the island" — for there was "still treasure not yet lifted."[35]

It would have been impossible for James Hill to imagine setting out for Spanish America in the late nineteenth century without wondering about its people. After all, it was there, in 1832, that Charles Darwin first encountered the "untamed savage" who set him meditating on the differences among creatures great and small. "The sight of a naked savage in his native land is an event which can never be forgotten," Darwin testified in his 1887 autobiography.[36] By that time it was necessary to specify "in his native land," for there were savages to be seen in Darwin's own native land, too.

Two in particular had caused a minor sensation in Victorian Britain. Máximo and

Bertola were not, though they were sometimes advertised to be, "a new type of humanity," nor were they "Aztec Lilliputians." Instead they were very small Salvadorans with very small heads, microcephalics. Their "live shows," the basis for a profitable career that extended from the 1850s into the 1890s, consisted primarily of allowing themselves to be kissed and petted on the head.[37]

It mattered that they were small. The popularity of Máximo and Bertola reflected a Victorian enthusiasm for the foreign: the unusual, the freakish, the distant and ancient, whatever made the familiar domestic world look like the high ground. Decline and fall — first ancient, then Spanish — was the frame in which the Victorians viewed Latin America, clearing the way for the superior British Empire to rule over the territories and peoples lesser empires could not hold. "Nothing but Anglo-Saxon energy will ever stir this sluggish pool into life," Charles Dickens's magazine *Household Words* wrote of Central America in 1851. "The present inhabitants of Central America — Spanish, mixed, or coloured — know no more of the use which they might make of their unlimited resources, than a baby knows what it can buy with half-a-crown. . . . Who is to fell the trees . . . to form the roads, to work the mines, to make the cultivated soil yield its best treasures in their full abundance?"[38] The answer was implied.

Beneath the chauvinism was uncertainty and anxiety about the place of Central and South Americans in the history and hierarchy of the races, for despite the reach of British power in the world, or because of it, there was considerable doubt that British travelers would be welcomed everywhere they ventured. American explorer John Stephens reported in his *Incidents of Travel in Central America, Chiapas, and Yucatan,* a bestseller in England, that on the Salvadoran leg of his trip he had found the mood "furious against strangers," with special enmity reserved for "los Ingleses, their usurpation and ambition, and their unjust design of adding to their extended dominions . . . Central America."[39]

At the least, James Hill knew that he needed to learn Spanish, a second language of British business in the nineteenth century. And it was with the hope of finding a job and Spanish lessons that, in 1888, he went out the door of his family home, turned his back on Collyhurst, and set out on his own for London, the largest city in the world.[40]

In London, Hill settled in Clerkenwell, where he would have felt at home. Like Collyhurst, Clerkenwell was a working-class district outside the old center of the city that had become crowded with Catholic immigrants and shaded with disrepute. In the popular imagination its streets were full of "Italians and thieves," including a few marauding "pistol gangs" that came out at night.[41] Its landmarks included a prison and a public green notorious for hosting political rallies: the Chartists in the first half of the nineteenth century, then the Socialists, Marxists, and anarchists in the second. It was in Clerkenwell that Vladimir Lenin would settle in 1902–1903 during his exile from Russia, and it was to Clerkenwell that many young men came to apprentice themselves in a trade.[42]

With the exception of a large envelope factory, working life in Clerkenwell was not confined within giant mills as it was in Manchester. Instead the neighborhood was a honeycomb of small workshops occupied by tradesmen and artisans, including watchmakers, jewelers, and tailors, described in the title of a novel published in 1889 and celebrated for its "terrible realism": *The Nether World.* The author, George Gissing, had studied in Manchester, and his favorite urban pastime was to stroll the streets of London observing the poor. Gissing's plot, "unutterably sad, because . . . so disastrously true," unfolds in Clerkenwell's cell-like warrens, which the characters, doomed by their creator's fascination with poverty's follow-on tragedies, never manage to escape.[43]

Go where you may in Clerkenwell, on every hand are multiform evidences of toil, intolerable as a nightmare. . . . . Here every alley is thronged with small industries; all but every door and window exhibits the advertisement of a craft that is carried on within. . . . Workers in metal, workers in glass and in enamel, workers in weed, workers in every substance on earth, or from the waters under the earth, that can be made commercially valuable. In Clerkenwell the demand is not so much for rude strength as for the cunning fingers and the contriving brain. The inscriptions on the house-fronts would make you believe that you were in a region of gold and silver and precious stones. In the recesses of dim byways, where sunshine and free air are forgotten things, where families herd together in dear-rented garrets and cellars, craftsmen are for ever handling jewellery, shaping bright ornaments for the necks and arms of such as are born to the joy of life.[44]

James Hill, who had grown up next to a draper's shop, found work as a clerk in a fabric store, taking most of his salary in the form of food and a small attic room above the shop. Yet he did not get pulled along with the throngs that headed out into the streets at the end of the workday toward the public houses and political clubs. Instead he worked

56

to do what Gissing's characters could not do, and get out.

Hill arranged for Spanish lessons, which he undertook in the evenings after work at the fabric shop.[45] After a year's study, he secured a job as a textile salesman in El Salvador. He booked transatlantic passage, likely on a ship operated by the Royal Mail Steam Packet Company, departing Southampton with the Empire's post twice a month. And on September 3, 1889, eighteen-year-old James Hill boarded his ship and sailed out into the wishes and fears he carried in the colorful region of his mind called Central America.

3.
A STATE OF
CONSTANT ERUPTION

"Few persons go to Central America for pleasure," observed the *New York Times* in 1888.[1] But plenty went for business. A large-scale commercial migration from the United States and Europe, and from the United Kingdom especially, had begun after Latin American independence in the 1820s. At the outset, Britain's jump-start on industrialization made it Latin America's leading supplier of cotton goods, its banker, its shipper, its railroad engineer, its power company, and its technical school, just as British interests had hoped. In economic terms, the nineteenth century — the century of Latin American independence — was the "British Century" in Latin America.[2]

Yet even in the second half of the "British Century," rival industrial empires, Germany and the United States in particular, were moving aggressively into Latin America to claim a share of the proceeds of the region's historic "export boom." Spanning eight decades between 1850 and 1930, the export boom has also been described as "the second conquest of Latin America," and with reason. In this conquest, the laws of prices, wages, and profits replaced the old principles of gold, God, and glory. Not long after independence, Latin American commercial elites partnered with foreign investors, entrepreneurs, shippers, bankers, and brokers to channel the resources of their new nations into the production of commodities destined for markets an ocean away, especially the fast-industrializing empires on both shores of the North Atlantic: coffee, wheat, bananas, sugar, hides for leather, henequen fiber for burlap, cinchona for quinine, and nitrates for fertilizer, to list just a handful of the most important ones. Between 1850 and 1900 exports from Latin America into the world market grew 1,000 percent.[3] European and American capitalists were rewarded richly for funding the construction of ports, rail lines, and roads, stringing telegraph cables, founding banks and brokerages, and developing plantations, ranches, and mines. And even after the necessary infrastructure had been built, the loans serviced, and the freight costs and brokerage commissions paid, there was still an unprecedented pile of cash left over for the rising Latin American upper and middle classes to spend on goods produced by manufacturers in Europe and the United

States, and it was up to young men like James Hill to do the selling.

Hill's ship steamed southwest across the Atlantic from Southampton toward the busy Mexican port of Veracruz, five thousand miles and several weeks distant from England. Veracruz was said to be the first place Hernán Cortés's army had landed on the American continent in 1519, and nearly four centuries later it was still a perilous and rather unwelcoming point of entry. Even in good weather, ships wrecked on the narrow approach to the harbor, and storms led to delays that could stretch on for days. The port facilities themselves were primitive, so once large ocean liners calling at Veracruz had negotiated the mouth of the harbor, they dropped anchor well offshore, where they were met by a logjam of small launches staffed by "dark, ragged boatmen" and offering taxi to shore.[4]

Glimpsed from the water, Veracruz appeared as a fantasy of conquest. Its Spanish castles and "shining domes and spires" were fringed with shaggy coconut palms, and above the city swirled a dark cloud of hundreds of turkey vultures. Yet ashore the romance often dissolved into fear and confusion. Helen Sanborn, daughter of the founder of the Boston-based coffee company Chase & Sanborn, traveled through Mexico and

Central America with her father in 1885 and found the streets of Veracruz crowded with "strange and curious" scenes: "Mexicans in their striking costumes, with broad sombreros; the Indians with their burdens . . . the packs of 'burros,' poor, thin, wretched little donkeys, carrying great loads of charcoal, 'zacate,' or barrels of water . . . three mules harnessed side by side, with the driver riding on the back of one of the mules instead of sitting in the wagon." Sanborn had studied Spanish with the idea of translating for her father on his coffee-buying trips. On many of the "villainous faces" she encountered in Veracruz she thought she read "the word desperado . . . plainly written."

In truth, the greatest danger was yellow fever, epidemic especially in the hot and rainy months between May and November. The worst outbreaks were known to kill up to forty of the city's ten thousand people each day. No one wanted to stop over in Veracruz, but everyone had to, for there was one train out a day, and it left at dawn.[5]

It was this train that James Hill boarded before six o'clock one morning in September 1889 to travel 263 miles and thirteen hours from Veracruz to Mexico City.[6] The line was called "the English road" in tribute to the $40 million and the battalion of British engineers who built it over the course of sixteen years — the reason for the extravagant cost and duration of the project being the "almost insuperable" peaks of the Sierra Madre that lay between the Atlantic coast and the Mexican capital.

Starting from the steamy coastal plain, a double-ended locomotive pulled its cars up the sides of mountains over eight thousand feet tall "like a fly crawling up a wall." As the train climbed, the day brightened, the temperature dropped, the humidity lifted, and seaside palms gave way to bananas, oranges, tobacco, coffee, corn, wheat, oaks, and pines. The line bored through rocky tunnels, spanned gaping crevasses, and skirted cliffs around curves so sharp that "the whole train is visible from one end to the other, and the winding road itself can be seen traversing the mountains by a sinuous path, like the trail of a serpent." Rushing waterfalls put the peril of the route in high relief. Inside the cars passengers leaned toward the windows, hoping for a glimpse of the distant peak of Orizaba, a volcano more than eighteen thousand feet tall and crowned with glaciers. On the way up, the laboring locomotive stopped at several way stations where Indians sold fruit, "hideous, ragged, and dirty" beggars crowded in, and state police stood guard against "thieves and cut-throats." But once the height of the land had been crested, the descent into the Valley of Mexico toward Mexico City was gentle.[7]

In Mexico City, the elegant colonial capital and teeming metropolis of half a million people, Hill arranged to travel two hundred miles by mule to Acapulco. In Acapulco, he boarded a Colombian steamer headed south down the Pacific coast of the Central American isthmus.[8]

Whether he arrived by day or night, James Hill could have sighted his first view of El Salvador when his ship was still miles offshore, thanks to what sailors called "the lighthouse of the Pacific" — Izalco, a 5,000-foot-tall volcano that spat flame and rock into the sky every twelve to fifteen minutes "with extraordinary regularity."[9] At night its internal fire "glowed steady against the sky," presenting "a most weird appearance," and Izalco was hardly less striking in the light of day, its cone rising from a base of "the densest green" and tapering by degrees into the "bare, burned, and rugged rocks" at the top. Above its peak a "smoky plume" writhed in the air, "ever changing in color with sunlight and crater fire." From a safe distance it was "difficult to conceive a grander natural object" — closer up Izalco seemed a "monster," its eruptions thundering like "the discharge of heavy artillery."[10]

Even in an age when mass travel on steamships and passenger railways made it newly possible to see things that had once been known primarily from the pages of books, volcanoes were sites of special fascination. Many Europeans imbued volcanoes with a "strange and exceptional" power because they seemed so different from the steady ground of home. "It is only when actually gazing on an active volcano that one can fully realize its awfulness and grandeur," wrote the naturalist Alfred Russel Wallace in 1869.

The inhabitant of most parts of northern Europe, sees in the earth the emblem of stability and repose. His whole life-experience, and that of all his age and generation, teaches him that the earth is solid and firm, that its massive rocks may contain water in abundance but never fire; and these essential characteristics of the earth are manifest in every mountain his country contains. A volcano is a fact opposed to all this mass of experience, a fact of so awful a character that, if it were the rule instead of the exception, it would make the earth uninhabitable; a fact so strange and unaccountable that we may be sure it would not be believed on any human testimony, if presented to us now for the first time, as a natural phenomenon happening in a distant country.[11]

To put this awful strangeness into terms Europeans could comprehend, nineteenth-

64

century geologists began to describe volcanoes as a type of "natural steam-engine."[12]

El Salvador's Izalco in particular was celebrated as perhaps "the most remarkable volcano on earth."[13] It was renowned not only for the frequency and regularity of its eruptions, but also because it had risen from the ground in the same time as Manchester's chimneys: from a crack in the middle of a cattle estate to a perfectly formed five-thousand-foot cone in a century. Geologists hypothesized that Izalco was born from "a deviation of the subterranean fire which animated the neighboring system of extinct volcanoes clustered around the great peak of Santa Ana," less than three miles away.[14] "About the close of 1769," reported author and diplomat E. G. Squier,

the dwellers on this estate were alarmed by subterranean noises and shocks of earthquakes, which continued to increase in loudness and strength until the twenty-third of February following, when the earth opened . . . sending out lava, accompanied by fire and smoke. The inhabitants fled, but the *vaqueros* or herdsmen, who visited the estate daily, reported a constant increase in the smoke and flame, and that the ejection of lava was at times suspended, and vast quantities of ashes, cinders, and stones sent out instead, forming an increasing cone around the vent or crater. This process was repeated for a long period, but for many years the volcano has thrown out no lava. It has, however, remained in a state of constant eruption.[15]

Squier's description fit the entire country. "During my residence of four years at San Salvador," recorded the French seismologist Ferdinand de Montessus in 1886, "I have been able to write the detailed history of twenty-three hundred and thirty-two earthquakes, one-hundred and thirty-seven volcanic eruptions, twenty-seven ruins of important towns, and the formation of three new volcanoes." That record made Central America, Montessus concluded, "probably the region of the globe in which the manifestations of volcanic and seismic phenomena are most frequent and continuous."[16]

In El Salvador, volcanoes were the rule rather than the exception — and yet, far from being a wasteland, as Alfred Russel Wallace had predicted, the country was a verdant hothouse. "For days the traveler within its borders journeys over unbroken beds of lava, scoriae, and volcanic sand," E. G. Squier wrote, "constituting, contrary to what most people would suppose, a soil of unbounded fertility, and densely covered with vegetation."[17] The volcanic soil was so rich that it seemed as if "no amount of misgovernment" could exhaust it.[18] And from this exceptional soil, in greater and greater quantities, grew the second thing James Hill would have seen as he approached El Salvador for the first time: coffee trees climbing the hills that seemed to rise straight from the shore, and coffee beans that had been packed into rough fiber bags, loaded onto the train at the foot of Izalco, rolled down to the port, transferred onto lighters, and launched into the roiling harbor to meet the passing steamers.

Of all the commodities shipped out of Latin America during the export boom, coffee was the most important, sweeping through the Americas so convincingly that it appeared as if the coffee tree had found its "true habitat" an ocean away from its origin.[19]

The species name of the plant *Coffea arabica,* native to Ethiopia, derives from the fact that Arab traders in Yemen, across the Red Sea from Ethiopia, dominated commercial coffee production during the sixteenth and seventeenth centuries, the age in which Europeans gave plants Latin names. European empires of the day, including the British, the French, and the Dutch in particular, tried unsuccessfully to establish coffee plantations in places where other rare and valuable commodities thrived — for example, in Ceylon (now Sri Lanka), proprietary home of the world's cinnamon, and on the Malabar

67

Coast of India, home to much of the world's black pepper. The Dutch finally succeeded in establishing coffee cultivation outside Arab control in 1699, when they introduced coffee into Java, an island colony taken from Portugal and formerly used as a base for the tea trade with China. Coffee production in Java quickly caught up to and surpassed the trade from the Yemeni port of Mocha, and the Arab monopoly was broken.[20]

From Java coffee spread along a path cut by empire and slavery. In 1714 the Dutch gave a coffee tree to Louis XIV for the royal botanical garden in Paris. The following year French colonial administrators took coffee plants to Bourbon, an island off the southeast coast of Africa later renamed Réunion, where every planter was required by law to plant 200 coffee trees for every enslaved person he owned. By 1718 the Dutch had brought coffee to Surinam, their colony on the northeast coast of South America. Five years later, in 1723, Gabriel de Clieu, a former French colonial official who had fallen out of favor, is said to have stolen a seedling from the royal botanical garden in Paris and smuggled it to Martinique. In 1727 a Portuguese official smuggled coffee seedlings from French Guiana into Brazil and established plantings on the Amazon. The British were cultivating coffee in Jamaica by 1730, and the Spanish, whose preferences ran to cacao, established coffee in Cuba by 1748. Over the second half of the eighteenth century, coffee spread virtually everywhere in the Americas where there was sufficient sun, rain, and forced labor to make it pay. But in no corner of the Western Hemisphere did coffee take root as it did in Saint-Domingue — Haiti. By the end of the eighteenth century, the French island colony, home to 40,000 white settlers and 500,000 enslaved laborers, was producing half of the world's annual coffee crop.[21]

The height of coffee production in Haiti was also its demise. A creation of empire and slavery, coffee become a casualty of the Haitian Revolution, which began as a slave rebellion in 1791 and led to the abolition of slavery and the overthrow of the French colonial government by 1804. After losing Haiti, France's most valuable Caribbean colony, Napoleon refocused his ambitions on Europe, invading Portugal in 1808 with the idea of taking the port of Lisbon. Overmatched, the Portuguese court fled across the Atlantic to Rio de Janeiro. To increase commerce in Rio, the Portuguese king opened Brazilian ports to ships from the United States, many of which arrived carrying cargoes of slaves and departed loaded with coffee. Soon Brazilian planters were burning hillsides clear to make way for more coffee — nearly 3,000 square miles of forest went up in smoke so thick that gray ash fell in the center of Rio, and the sun's rays reached the earth as if through smoked glass. In 1790, the state of Rio produced only a single ton of coffee for local consumption.[22] Yet by the 1830s, Brazilian coffee production surpassed that of Java, and by the middle of the nineteenth century, hundreds of thousands of enslaved laborers in Brazil were producing 50 percent of the world's annual supply, which was only the beginning.

Coffee came to Latin America through empire and slavery, but it spread and flourished there through liberalism. Latin American liberalism was the classical political liberalism of freedom, equality, and brotherhood — ideals that informed Latin American independence movements in the 1820s, just as they had informed the U.S., French, and Haitian revolutions before — crossed with the economic liberalism of Adam Smith and David Ricardo, which cast the health and wealth of a nation as a function of its place in the system of international trade. The result was a vision of market-based national progress tailored to fit the difficult question of what independence would look like in practice, an especially complicated problem in a small commercial "backwater" such as El Salvador.

Within a year of gaining independence from Spain in 1821, Salvadoran elites, doubting the economic viability of nationhood, decided

70

to petition the U.S. for statehood.[23] If the U.S. government, then in the midst of a hungry and far-reaching territorial expansion, ever debated the proposal, that record has been lost. Left alone with the ambitions of the British and their richer Guatemalan neighbors, Salvadoran liberals, like their counterparts across the region, sought national progress through economic development. For decades they chased viable export crops, "the fruits of more hope," including cacao, balsam, rubber, wheat, tobacco, vanilla, agave, and coffee.[24] To build the necessary infrastructure, they granted concessions to foreign banks, steamship companies, and railways.[25] And they sealed the country's first major trade agreement with the United States, which became not only an important trading partner but also an example of what was possible for a new nation, having "transformed deserts . . . into very beautiful cities" by encouraging business to flourish.[26]

In 1840, Antonio Coelho, a Brazilian who had come to El Salvador to work as a teacher, bought some land outside the capital, San Salvador, planted it with coffee seeds he had brought with him from Brazil, and named the plantation "La Esperanza," Hope.[27] Many of Coelho's new compatriots shared his feeling. Commercial agriculture in El Salvador had centered on indigo, much of it sold across the Atlantic in Manchester, where

71

it enlivened cotton goods before they were shipped back out around the world. Yet by the mid-nineteenth century, the future of El Salvador's indigo industry was in doubt as a result of competition with new sources of the dye that came from Asia and, later, from German laboratories.[28]

Still, it was far from obvious that coffee would supplant indigo. Compared with indigo, coffee was a temperamental and expensive crop, requiring abundant rain on a consistent schedule, enough sun to keep frosts at bay, and plenty of labor, especially in the early going. Even under the best conditions, coffee trees yield mature harvests only after four to seven years of attentive cultivation.[29] And on top of all this, in El Salvador more than anywhere else in Latin America, the liberal hope for economic development through exports, and particularly through coffee, ran into the additional problem of scarce land.[30] The country was small — about the size of Massachusetts — and perhaps a quarter or more of its arable land was already under the control of Indian and peasant subsistence farmers, the legacy of a system of communal land tenure held over from the colonial period.[31] In many cases, it simply wasn't clear who owned a particular plot of land, and this ambiguity discouraged investment in risky commercial crops. If coffee was going to transform El Salvador, it would have to take over.

The Salvadoran government first backed coffee in 1846, offering tax breaks to anyone who planted more than 5,000 trees and exempting workers employed on coffee plantations from national military service.[32] These early incentives produced scant results, but in 1859, under President Gerardo Barrios, whose travels in Europe as a young man had inspired him to "regenerate" his home country through economic development, the government began to distribute parcels of land to those who agreed to cultivate coffee there.[33] Later, the state also gave tens of thousands of coffee seedlings to large landowners and peasants alike.[34] Thanks to such subsidies, the area of land planted in coffee increased steadily, and a wide swath of Salvadoran society got in on it: merchants, artisans, teachers, professionals, commercial farmers — in the beginning, "even the poorest people had their plantings."[35] The state-led campaign for coffee centered in the western highlands around the Santa Ana Volcano. By the early 1860s there were more than three million coffee trees growing in and around Santa Ana, and President Barrios predicted that within two years El Salvador would be the coffee capital of Central America.[36]

Yet well after time ran out on that prediction, much of what appeared to be the country's best coffee land remained in the hands of Indian and peasant farmers and was planted largely, though not exclusively, with food crops.[37] In particular, the slopes of the Santa Ana Volcano, where Indians had settled after being displaced from the plains by Spanish conquest and colonization, were extensively cultivated with corn.[38] This overlap brought those who had the most hope for coffee into conflict with those who had long relied on the land to survive.

Through this conflict, the problem of economic development was recast as a racial problem. Indians were labeled "backward" and blamed for the "evils" that had resulted in commercial stagnation. Liberal elites, many of whom claimed European descent, dreamed of using the land to produce coffee and cash and civilization. They credited themselves, in advance, with all the promise of the future, and moved to "cut . . . with a firm hand, the chains that enslave agriculture."[39]

The politics of coffee shifted from incentives to commands. The liberal government began to act more aggressively in favor of coffee and against the owners and occupants of "virgin fertile lands" — "virgin" meaning that the government had deemed them unproductive, no matter how many meals had grown there. Particularly targeted were communal landholders who seemed "content to grow crops of maize and beans that will never raise this miserable people above their sorry position, but will remain in the same wretched state as they endured in colonial times."[40] After 1874, Indian and peasant communities in the volcanic highlands were ordered to build coffee nurseries, and to pay for the construction of these nurseries by levying a tax on dogs.[41] The liberal government was "determined to transform the Republic, to make each one of the villages into centers of work, wealth, and comfort."[42] There is no reason to doubt the sincerity of the liberal vision of widespread work, wealth, and comfort, but there is the question of why only the first part — work — became reality for the great majority of Salvadorans.

Over two decades, the hope for economic development in El Salvador through coffee exports built toward the "emancipation" or "liberation" of the country's land from the "backward" people — peasant farmers, especially Indians — who appeared to be "removed from all progress and activity," caught in the trap of eating what they grew.[43]

In 1879, after a state-mandated land census that put the extent of the problem and opportunity into focus, El Salvador's liberal government began the legal process of freeing the land from the past for the future. At first, individual parcels of what had been communal lands were to be granted to those who planted coffee there, and there was evidence to suggest that many Indians were willing to make a "substantial effort" to plant coffee to avoid losing their land.[44] But perhaps that was not exactly what liberal elites had in mind, for three years later, in 1882, the system of communal landownership in El Salvador was abolished entirely by a legislative decree authored by a senator from Santa Ana. Those without a land title in hand were instructed to go to local authorities with proof that they had been cultivating a particular plot, pay a fee, and secure the title. If they did not or could not do so within six months, the land would be put up for auction.[45]

Haltingly, unevenly, snagging everywhere on legitimate confusion, bureaucratic incompetence, local conflicts, and bald corruption, the process of land privatization stretched on for years, even decades.[46] Yet by the time it was complete, a quarter or more of El Salvador's land was rezoned from communal to private.[47] Access to land, long a social right, became a market commodity, sold to the savviest buyer.

Privatization was concentrated in the western highlands around the Santa Ana Volcano, where it transformed long-standing patterns of land use. As coffee displaced food crops, it grew from scorched earth. "We were surrounded by fires on all sides," wrote a French traveler of his journey through western El Salvador during the rise of coffee. "Fields of grain were being burnt over and parts of the forest were being burnt also to clear them, so that the mountains around us seemed to be illuminated and glowing red."[48] Even where coffee did not take over cultivated communal lands, it took over woodlands that had been an important factor in subsistence economies: a source of game, fruit, fuel, and medicine.[49]

With these changes in the land came new ways of life. Some Indians and peasants who lost access to land picked up and moved, leaving the coffee districts for northern and eastern regions of the country, where they sought to resume subsistence farming on marginal land.[50] Many of those who stayed, their ability to feed themselves compromised if not destroyed, went to work on the coffee plantations, where they became subject to "a new and more strict regulation of rural life."[51] Lists were made of all day workers, to track those who failed to fulfill their obligations.[52] An 1882 nationwide mandate required local officials to crack down on laborers who skipped out on work contracts. The next year a quarter of the nearly eight hundred arrests in Santa Ana were for work breaking, while arrests for that offense outside the coffee zones were rare.[53] An 1884 law targeted squatters, an increasingly common obstacle to the "effective" ownership of private property.[54] In 1888, as opposition to privatization increased in the western part of the country, a new tax was placed on coffee to expand rural police forces.[55] In 1889 a new mounted police force was created, and it operated primarily in the western regions where the hope for coffee was strongest: the area around the Santa Ana Volcano and the area between the volcano and the Pacific coast ports.[56]

The results were impressive. The amount of land under coffee in El Salvador had increased from 2,100 acres in 1860 to more than 110,000 in 1890, while the value of exports had increased by a factor of sixty over the same period.[57] Coffee production tripled between 1880 and 1890 alone, and there was good reason to expect more.[58] A British firm had begun to lay track for an extension of the railroad around the base of the Santa Ana Volcano, a line that would finally connect the coffee capital, Santa Ana, to the Pacific ports. And while the country had no banks of its own before 1880, it had three by 1890, including the Banco Occidental, founded by San Francisco merchants and based in Santa Ana.[59]

Even so, the new economic and social order that Salvadoran liberals were building around coffee was not yet completely stable. Some Indian and peasant producers held on to their land for decades after privatization, even in coffee-rich areas such as the town of Chalchuapa, just outside Santa Ana.[60] At the same time, many of those who lost their lands did not simply give them up quietly. There was no broad-based rebellion or revolution in the immediate aftermath of land privatization in El Salvador, but for virtually every new liberal law that was passed there was a counterpoint of resistance in the volcanic highlands. Some of the dispossessed set fire to coffee plantations and mills, while others were reported to have cut off the hands of officials in charge of writing new land titles.[61] Yet "there was an army to deal with them, and it did," without much difficulty. "Indian communities could not match the weapons, the numbers, the organization, or the mobility of the army," writes historian Héctor Lindo-Fuentes. "Moreover, they had nobody to turn to for support."[62]

The privatization of land; the militarization of commerce; the strict policing of work and social life: collectively these laws were the "liberal reforms." They were liberal to the extent that they concealed their core racism behind the principle of equality of opportunity in the marketplace — a principle that applied, of course, only to those who had money.

In 1885, in response to a request from the U.S. State Department, the U.S. consul in San Salvador, an Englishman named Maurice

Duke, described the business landscape in the aftermath of land privatization: "There are at this present time very first-rate opportunities offering to men of industry and sobriety who will put a little intelligent work into the land; men of this description, with a moderate capital of, say, five to fifteen thousand dollars, are the men required here; at the same time others with a much smaller capital have very great advantages of making money from the outset; but those who come merely seeking work will find themselves hopelessly miserable."[63] There were already plenty of workers — what El Salvador needed was bosses.

This was not only a business opportunity but also a civilizing mission and a whitening process that altered the makeup of the country's population. After land privatization, predicted one liberal journalist, "a great number of new families, taking their produce, arts, and knowledge everywhere, will improve the towns morally and materially." New settlements were founded in the coffee districts and given names such as California and Berlín, signaling their orientation toward the wider world.[64] And to these new places came more and more migrants who had left the United States and Europe in search of a better life, who cast their economic exile as adventure, and who, unaccustomed to the

80

steaming heat of their new country, took to
dressing in "loose suits of white duck."[65]

steaming heat of their new country, took to dressing in "loose suits of white duck."

4.
EEL

James Hill disembarked at Acajutla, a knob of land formed thousands of years earlier by hot magma flowing downhill from the Santa Ana Volcano into the Pacific. The volcano had not given Acajutla a harbor, so ships dropped anchor offshore beyond the break, and disembarking passengers climbed into a metal cage that was lowered from the deck to a launch bobbing in the swells. When the launch reached the pier, the operation was reversed, the passengers climbing into a cage that was hoisted onto the dock by steam-powered crane.[1]

Stepping out of the cage, arrivals in Acajutla found themselves in a town that was nothing more than a "forwarding point" to the interior. The air was as thick as the steam of a Russian bath, and the streets were often deserted except for "almost naked Indians." James Hill took a train inland toward the town of Sonsonate, seventeen miles away and directly under the peak of the great volcano

Izalco. The train ran uphill from the coast, through swamps and dense groves of balsam, harvested for its resin and used in perfumes, smelling of vanilla, citrus, and cloves. In the early going the pleasures of the flora were usually offset by the effect of the thick air and low coastal fog, which trapped the choking exhaust of the locomotive near the ground. Then all at once the terrain opened up, and "the overgrown forests were succeeded by meadows supporting grazing cattle" and dotted with small houses.[2]

Sonsonate itself was a town out of a storybook. Stepping off the train there, under Izalco's vent, was like "standing at the base of a great smoking chimney." A clear stream bubbled over smooth rocks beside brown adobe houses that were topped by red tile roofs and shaded by palms and cacao trees. The streets were free of the beggars common in larger cities, and the residents were quietly prosperous. English was "very generally understood," and "women were more careful of their appearance" and perhaps worldlier than elsewhere in the region.[3] Hill rented a room in the center of town.[4]

For months he did what he had signed up to do, picking up shipments of textiles from the port and riding them around by railroad and mule to sell in Sonsonate and surrounding towns. It was a highly political and often unrewarding job. In 1889 there were at least fifty firms selling textiles in El Salvador, with British, French, German, American, and other merchant houses all competing for the same business.[5] Complicating the work further was the fact that Latin American buyers were known to have a taste for the world's finest things even when they could not afford to pay the world's highest prices. As a result, European manufacturers "sought constantly to improve one element of quality, that of finish, whilst at the same time avoiding parallel improvements in other elements, notably in fineness."[6] For the salesman on the ground, selling middling quality to people who wanted the best required tact above all. One British commercial agent in Latin America recalled the strict protocol: "In those days you did not go bald-headed for orders. You talked about things in general, about crops, about politics, above all, about your client's family and your own. Finally, after days, sometimes weeks, you got your order. . . . No bargaining. Just mutual confidence."[7] Most important, you spoke Spanish: a salesman who failed to learn the language of the people whose business he sought was a diplomatic incident waiting to happen.[8]

There were more ways to get in trouble in export-boom Central America than it was possible to know, for the laws of the region were somewhat flexible and enforced selectively. One story circulating about El Salvador caught the ear of the British traveler J. W. Boddam Whetham in 1877, for it illustrated the porous line between opportunities and perils.

A young foreigner of good standing saw a woman enter his warehouse and steal a roll of cotton; he followed her and took it away. Next day he was arrested, and accused of having stolen a diamond necklace from this woman (many of these people have old jewelry), and five or six witnesses swore that they had seen him take it. He indignantly refused to plead, and after some months — he had of course obtained bail — the President, who was a friend of his, came and informed him that he had been found guilty, and would be sentenced to five years in the chain gang; why did he not follow the custom of the country (which he had been long enough in to know), and contradict these witnesses? As he steadily refused to employ false witnesses on his side, the President at last said that the only way of settling it would be to make him an officer, thereby necessitating a new trial. He was consequently made a colonel, and nothing more was heard of the transaction.[9]

Whether as a result of the strain of insecurity, the stress of selling, the unpredictable hazards, or just simple homesickness, most of the young foreigners who got jobs as salesmen in Latin America did not keep them for long. Instead, "as soon as [they] had made some money and acquired useful experience," they turned around and went home "to England to do business from the comparative comfort of a warehouse in Liverpool or Manchester."[10] Yet those who were able to adapt to life in Central America found something more than an opportunity there. "By young men of self-denying and sober habits, possessing a capital of from $5,000 and a tolerable knowledge of the Spanish language, success either in commerce, agriculture or mining, may be confidently counted upon," wrote the British minister to Central America in 1896, "but they must avoid all interference in local politics. In these as in all other countries, the foreigner whose character and mode of life command respect will very seldom, if ever, suffer molestation at the hands of the authorities."[11] Of course, the converse was also true.

The ordeal of Charles Sawyer was the subject of much gossip in El Salvador in 1889, the year James Hill arrived. Sawyer was the artistic sort of fortune seeker: a dreamer, a wanderer, a "loose fish," as John Moffat, British consul in El Salvador, put it. Born in London on July 5, 1864, Sawyer sailed to Nicaragua in 1886 to work on the railroad, another of Victorian England's great export industries. When Sawyer finished in Nicaragua, he went to Honduras, where he found work in a silver mine owned by a New York consortium. There Sawyer ran afoul of his bosses when he refused to sign the company's employment contract. In retaliation, the mine's paymaster held back Sawyer's wages, and before long he found himself in Guatemala with less than a dollar in his pocket.

Sawyer got himself to the British consulate, explained his predicament, and secured a few months' work in the diplomatic service, which concluded when he won a contract to open a theater company in El Salvador. Yet in the process of relocating to San Salvador in January 1889, Sawyer was arrested for forging two bank drafts. He denied the charges and explained that he was only trying to buy furniture and hire "artistes" for his company.

After a night passed in a Salvadoran jail, Sawyer had a visit from the British consul, Moffat. Sawyer was then taken before a judge, interrogated in Spanish, a language he did not understand, and returned to jail indefinitely. For the first few weeks, members of the British colony in El Salvador checked up on Sawyer and brought him food. In contrast, Consul Moffat ignored Sawyer's many polite and elegantly penned requests for help.

Other prisoners in the jail worked to pay

for their board, such as it was. Being something of an artist, Sawyer thought he might earn some money by selling his drawings. He sent one to Moffat, on the assumption that the consul might like to buy it. Moffat was then moved to respond. He sent Sawyer a lawyer, a couple of dollars in Salvadoran currency, and a note: "No more."

As January turned to June, still Sawyer had no trial, no way to support himself, and no real friends in the country who could help. He was too embarrassed to ask his family in England for aid. Instead he wrote to Lord Salisbury, the British prime minister and foreign secretary. "I do not pretend to be a saint," Sawyer wrote, "far from it, I have always led a rather fast life and am sorry to say have a sort of passion for gambling, but even this and much more would not justify the treatment I have received here." At the same time, he wrote to the government of El Salvador. "When I was at school," Sawyer recalled, "I was taught that San Salvador was a civilized country. I am beginning to think now that my teachers were masters of sarcasm." When these appeals did not change his prospects, Sawyer played his last card, invoking the only status he had. He wrote to a compatriot in El Salvador on September 3, 1889, the same day James Hill sailed from Southampton: "I ask you as I am asking every Englishman whose name I am acquainted with here to use your interest on my behalf, and if concerted action were taken, little or no trouble would be incurred in obtaining me my liberty."

But what is lonelier than bad luck in a boomtown? "I have absolutely no friends here," Sawyer confided in another letter to Lord Salisbury ten days later, "although some of the English residents have helped me considerably; but at the same time others have added insult to injury by laughing at my misfortune and making remarks, afterward conveyed to me by various persons, such as ought not to proceed from the mouth of an Englishman, let alone a so-called gentleman."[12] And on that note of indignation, Charles Sawyer was lost to history.

Such risks were the price of opportunity. Virtually every time James Hill met a ship at the port of Acajutla, he would have seen coffee going out. Traveling to the coast and back, he rode a railway that had opened in 1882 to move coffee to port from Sonsonate, and which was in the process of being extended around the Santa Ana Volcano.[13] The new line would decrease the cost of shipping coffee to the coast for export. The country's new banks would make it cheaper to borrow money to buy land and develop plantations. Hill would not have failed to see it.

Yet there were also reasons for caution. El

Salvador was relatively late to coffee. By the 1880s Brazil already controlled more than half the world market, and coffee was also well established in European colonial possessions in South and Southeast Asia. In addition, the Berlin Conference of 1884–1885 divided up Africa into European export-processing zones that promised more colonial coffee production. Moreover, the nearby republics of Guatemala, Nicaragua, and Colombia had also gone in strongly for coffee during the Latin American export boom, joining established planters and exporters in countries including Costa Rica and Mexico.

But then, just around the time of James Hill's arrival in Central America, two events disrupted business in the world's greatest coffee-producing regions, and heightened the opportunity in El Salvador.

The first came on May 13, 1888 — Hill's seventeenth birthday, and the year he left Manchester for London — when the Golden Law abolished slavery in Brazil. Approved by the Brazilian legislature and signed by Princess Imperial Isabel while her father, the emperor, was in Europe, the law overturned the basis of the Brazilian economy. "The whole complex of . . . producing coffee" in Brazil had "meant ownership and direction of slaves" — but now the hundreds of thousands of people most responsible for producing the world's annual coffee crop could no longer be forcibly compelled to do so.[14]

This was a development Brazilian coffee planters had long dreaded, and for which they had tried to prepare. For decades Brazilian emancipation had seemed less a possibility than an eventuality, due in part to a campaign for global abolition that had begun in London at the end of the eighteenth century.[15] Abolitionist pressure on Brazil increased especially after 1850, when Britain began a naval blockade that all but forced the Brazilian government to outlaw the slave trade. The end of the trade in turn created immediate problems for the Brazilian slaveholders, owing to the astonishing rate at which they killed the people they enslaved. From a high of perhaps two and a half million in 1850, the enslaved population in Brazil declined to five hundred thousand by 1888.[16] At the same time, the enslaved people who survived were increasingly coming to "articulate questions of the legitimacy of their bondage," as historian Warren Dean put it.[17] Large-scale rebellion seemed increasingly likely, and this fear informed the passage of the "Law of the Free Womb" in 1871. The manumission of all children born to enslaved women made Brazilian slavery impossible to sustain. Within a generation, banks stopped accepting the enslaved as collateral for loans.[18]

The fate of their slave society inevitable,

Brazilian planters began to explore other sources of labor. The most obvious was immigration from Europe, and plans were made to pay the passage of laborers. Yet even with such inducements, the success of recruitment plans was hardly assured. Forty years earlier, in 1847, a group of 432 Germans, comprising sixty-four families, had been recruited to Brazilian coffee plantations under a similar program. On arrival they became indentured servants, indebted to the owner of the plantation where they worked for the reimbursement of their costs. The experiment initially seemed a success, but faltered when the new recruits organized against perceived breaches of their labor contracts, appealing to and winning the support of the German consulate — a pathway of redress that had never been open to enslaved Africans.[19]

The problems of the Brazilian coffee planters showed up as hope in the world's other coffee districts. The example of Haiti, where coffee had collapsed after the abolition of slavery and the overthrow of the French colonial government at the turn of the nineteenth century, was not so remote. The rise of coffee in wider Latin America — not only in El Salvador but in neighboring and nearby countries too, Nicaragua, Honduras, Colombia, and Guatemala, where the liberal government instituted a forced draft of Indian labor in 1877 — marked a contrapuntal rhythm to the fall of slavery in Brazil.[20] And for four or five years after abolition, this hope must have seemed well founded, as coffee production in the state of Rio declined by 50 percent.[21]

At the same time, running parallel to the upheaval of Brazilian emancipation was a different sort of crisis in the world's second coffee-producing center. In the early 1880s, spotty orange patches began to appear on the leaves of coffee trees across Asia, the result of a damaging fungus. In Ceylon, then a leading coffee producer, the blight gutted the industry, and production fell by more than 85 percent between 1881 and 1900.[22] In Java, which had supplied about 13 percent of the world's annual coffee crop since the 1830s, production fell by more than half in the same period.[23] The coincidence of emancipation in Brazil and the coffee blight in Asia created space in the world coffee market for other Latin American republics. In the five years before 1890, world coffee production fell substantially for the only time between 1850 and 1941, and in the same period average world coffee prices climbed 50 percent.[24] It was an open door for anyone who could make other people work coffee by any means other than slavery in any place other than Asia.

After long months selling textiles in Sonsonate, James Hill went looking for something more rewarding. He set out on horseback, riding forty miles east to San Salvador, following the road into ravines so narrow that it was customary to shout a warning before starting through.[25] From San Salvador, taking his time, traveling by mule, horse, train, and boat, Hill made a long loop through export-boom Central America, scouting for a place to make his living. He followed the Salvadoran coastline south until he ran out of land at the Gulf of Fonseca. There he boarded a ferry that took him toward the great volcano of Cosigüina and the port of Potosí, Nicaragua. From Nicaragua, then bustling with the promise of an American canal project that would later be abandoned, Hill crossed the border into Honduras near a mining town called El Paraíso, but he found it rather dismal and rode on, up the middle of the Central American isthmus into Guatemala. In 1892, after some time in Guatemala City — then the largest capital in the region, home to about 70,000 people — Hill turned south again, back toward El Salvador. He thought that the country's small size would be good for business.[26]

Hill crossed the border near Ahuachapán, a hot-springs town under the western slope of the Santa Ana Volcano. He looped around the base of the volcano over roads lined with dense coffee groves and "thronged with Indians carrying implements of cultivation" and dressed in "picturesque . . . costumes," all the way to the town of Santa Ana.[27]

If San Salvador was El Salvador's Manhattan, and Sonsonate was Albany, a transportation hub, then Santa Ana, the *New York Times* explained in 1889, was Buffalo, a town built for commerce in natural resources. Trade spilled out from the wide central plaza into all the surrounding neighborhoods. To serve the many new arrivals who had come to town to do business in coffee, even prominent residents turned their front rooms into shops "presided over by the lady of the house," and few considered themselves "too genteel to weigh out a pound of sugar or coffee" or to take in some sewing. By night these little stores became "resorts of the gallants." European and American men would stop in to "purchase a few trifles, and while waiting for the change to hold bits of conversations with the fair daughters" of the storekeepers. In this manner were "many flirtations and piquant affairs of gallantry . . . conducted across the counter with all the daintiness to be looked for in the most fashionable circles of the New and Old World, while rows of shelves of brown sugar, coffee, bananas, pottery, matches, and Indian clothes of picturesque patterns form a background not unbecoming to the dark-eyed, graceful recipients of this devotion."[28]

Just as often, commerce was in the foreground of romance. By day "the gallants" worked. Some were engineers managing the extension of the railroad to Santa Ana, which by then also had its own bank, the Banco Occidental, founded by Jonas and David Bloom, of San Francisco, and run by their nephew Benjamin. Benjamin's father, a German immigrant to California, had been one of the founders of Healdsburg, while his uncles had started as importers and exporters in San Francisco, over time doing more and more business in coffee. In 1889, the year after Brazilian emancipation, the Blooms opened the Banco Occidental in Santa Ana with a government concession as a bank of issue and started printing money.

Other migrants worked as brokers, channeling proceeds and profits from El Salvador's coffee boom toward their home countries. Alberto Deneke was a lawyer educated in Berlin who had come to Santa Ana in 1892 to work for the Blooms at the Banco Occidental. Deneke didn't last at the bank, but he stayed on in Santa Ana and used credit from German merchant houses to broker coffee deals. Deneke had his share of success, but then he engaged himself to a Santa Ana lady who had no property of her own, and word began to go around that he wasn't especially smart.[29]

Still other newcomers set up in adjacent industries. The Goldtree brothers were dry-goods dealers in San Luis Obispo, California, who moved their business to El Salvador in 1888.[30] Twenty-year-old Rafael Meza Ayau and his mother arrived in Santa Ana from Guatemala in 1886 to open a hotel. As Rafael helped his mother at the hotel, he also maneuvered himself into the employ of General Tomás Regalado. Regalado had acquired two large coffee mills in Santa Ana, which Meza Ayau helped to run, gaining in the process "a lot of influence over the General." Because he was important to the General, Meza Ayau became an important man himself, and gained the trust of creditors. Once his name and credit were solidly established, he borrowed money from the Banco Occidental and opened a brewery, which he called La Constancia.[31]

In Santa Ana, James Hill started much where he had left off, opening a tailor's shop dealing in fabrics imported from Europe. He was determined to make a success of the venture, for soon after arriving he had also begun to call at the house of the Bernal family. The family's late patriarch, Dionisio, had claimed a Spanish line stretching back to the conquistadors. Upon his death, the family coffee plantations had passed to his widow, Damiana, and they became a kind of dowry for the Bernal daughters, including twenty-year-old María Dolores, Lola for short, who was the reason for Hill's visits.[32]

Rafael Meza Ayau had also noticed Lola Bernal, and he was then in the process of making a good name for himself with the local elite. James Hill, in contrast, had a rather bad name, though that was not entirely his fault. Spoken Spanish erases the letter *h* into a faint smudge and stretches the *i*. As a result, pronounced in Spanish, the name Hill comes out sounding like "Eel." The problem for James Hill was that the name seemed to fit.

When people spoke of the man they called Eel, they did not always speak well of him. When the tailor's shop Hill opened in Santa Ana burned down, rumors circulated that he had collected a generous insurance settlement. He earned a reputation around town, and even beyond, of being "very slippery and tricky in business." Those who dealt with Hill knew instinctively to be careful.[33] In a town full of men who had come from far away to seek fortune in the coffee boom, there was plenty of evidence that promises and loyalties were only as good as business conditions.

In April of 1894, General Tomás Regalado led a group of forty-four Santa Ana coffee planters in a campaign to overthrow the president, a rival general in the Salvadoran Army named Carlos Ezeta. Four years earlier Ezeta had risen to power in the same way, by overthrowing the president, Francisco

Menéndez, who also happened to be his best friend. Menéndez, who put in place some of the liberal reforms that carried through land privatization, had offended his friend by placing an export tax on coffee, then representing between two-thirds and three-quarters of El Salvador's exports, to pay for the construction of a national palace and the extension of the railroad to Santa Ana. Yet after making himself president, Ezeta, instead of repealing the tax, increased it — to build roads, run telegraph cables, supply the military with $2 million worth of arms, and, primarily, to fill his own pockets — or so it seemed to the coffee planters and merchants who paid the tax. Then Ezeta raised the export duty again, and by 1893, when the tax reached more than two dollars for every 100 pounds of coffee exported, Santa Ana planters became unwilling to allow Carlos Ezeta to hand the presidency off to his brother Antonio, the vice president, as had been planned.[34]

General Regalado and his followers moved against the Ezetas in a surprise attack, raiding the vice president's residence and army barracks in Santa Ana at two in the morning on April 29, 1894.[35] After Antonio Ezeta fled in his nightshirt, the barracks fell without much resistance. The planters seized thousands of Remington rifles and cartridges, and from their stronghold in Santa Ana they forced President Carlos Ezeta out of the national palace in San Salvador. In place of the presumptive successor Antonio Ezeta, who escaped to the coast and boarded a ship bound for San Francisco, the planters installed a figurehead whose first action was to repeal the export tax on coffee.[36] In tribute to the planters' coup, Santa Ana became known in El Salvador as the Heroic City.

The same year, twenty-three-year-old James Hill asked Lola Bernal for her hand, and she became Lola Bernal de Hill in an elaborate wedding on Saturday, November 3, at the beginning of the coffee harvest. Six months later, after the harvest season was over, Rafael Meza Ayau married Lola's cousin.[37] By then Hill had begun his new life in coffee, and all the omens were good — he had made a promising marriage in a place favored by geology, politics, and foreign investors. And yet, for reasons well beyond his control, his timing could hardly have been worse.

5.

THE HILLS BROTHERS

As cotton was to Manchester and coffee was to Santa Ana, so were rocks to Rockland, Maine. All day long in Rockland, men cut and lifted pale slabs of the calcified remains of sea creatures out of the earth, broke the slabs into pieces of limestone, fired the limestone to burn the calcium carbonate down into calcium oxide — lime — packed it into wooden casks, and loaded it into one of the ships crowding Rockland Harbor in Penobscot Bay. In the second half of the nineteenth century, Rockland was one of the world's largest lime ports, producing more than a million casks in a good year.[1] In the form of lime, Rockland became mortar for brick buildings, plaster for walls and ceilings, and fertilizer for farms and plantations around the world.

Austin and Reuben Hills grew up in Rockland. Their father, Austin Hills, like James Hill's father, James, was in the transportation business, building the ships that carried lime around the world. In 1863, when he was forty, Austin Hills Sr. left his wife and sons at home, boarded a ship, and transported himself to California.

The California gold fields must have held a certain appeal to a man who lived next to a limestone quarry, but Austin Hills did not find gold there. Instead, as he had in Rockland, he worked where the hole in the ground met the sea, building ships. A decade later, in 1873, his sons followed him to California.[2]

Austin Jr. was twenty-two and Reuben was seventeen when they arrived in San Francisco. They started a grocery business — a market stall with eggs, butter, and cheese — and used the profits to buy a coffee roaster to compete with J. A. Folger, whose Pioneer Steam Coffee and Spice Mills had about a twenty-five-year head start. The Hills brothers called their new venture Hills Bros. Arabian Coffee & Spice Mills. Like most other American coffee businesses of the day, it was based on lies. The lies were built into the very name, and they were useful because they helped to fit an appealing version of coffee's history with an appealing version of American history.

Even before independence, coffee shaped the United States and its relationship to the wider world. "Tea must be universally renounced," John Adams wrote his wife, Abigail, in 1774. The year before, the Boston Tea Party had demonstrated what American colonists thought of taxation without representation, but the prospect of revolution raised more complex questions. Adams imagined building political independence out of economic self-sufficiency, which left no place for coffee, either. "I hope the females will leave off their attachment to coffee," he wrote to Abigail a little more than a year after the Declaration of Independence. "We must bring ourselves to live upon the produce of our own country. What would I give for some of your cyder?"[3]

Yet after the Revolutionary War, Adams's inward-looking vision lost out to a different model of independence. Faced with the practical problems of nation building, the new United States established strategic commercial alliances with the French, the Dutch, and even, haltingly, the British, all large colonial producers of coffee in the Caribbean.[4] The coffee commerce with France was especially important. "It will be a strong link of connection," wrote Thomas Jefferson, "with the only nation on earth on whom we can solidly rely for assistance till we stand on our own legs."[5]

Freed from British trade restrictions, American consumption of coffee, much of it coming from French colonial possessions, including Saint-Domingue, increased sub-

103

stantially in the last quarter of the eighteenth century, reaching 1.4 pounds per person in 1799 — seven times what it had been in 1772, the year before the Boston Tea Party.[6] In the upper reaches of American society, especially in coastal cities, where coffeehouse culture mirrored Europe's, coffee drinking became notably common, perhaps even more so than in France itself. "Our supper was rather scanty, but our breakfast the next morning was better," wrote a French traveler to Virginia in 1787. "We are perfectly reconciled to this American custom of drinking coffee."[7] Yet outside the elite, coffee was still too expensive to be an "American custom." In the rural interior of the new republic, hot beverages were more often teas brewed from whatever could be gathered locally, including chicory and nuts.[8] Otherwise it was beer and cider, morning, noon, and night.[9]

Then the map of the world changed. As historian Steven Topik has pointed out, to highlight the roles of revolution, independence, and freedom in the history of U.S. coffee drinking is to overlook the much greater importance of slavery.[10] In deference to Napoleon, the U.S. cut commercial ties with Haiti after the triumph of the revolution that won freedom for those enslaved on the island's coffee and sugar plantations and that culminated in the creation of the second nation-state in the Western Hemisphere —

costing France its richest colony in the process. Increased commerce with Brazil, where the rise of coffee meant importing more and more slaves, many of whom were supplied by American slave traders, made up the difference and then some.[11]

Alongside slavery, the other great pillar of coffee consumption in the United States, where coffee would become a mass product for the first time in its long history, was imperialism. The imperial aspirations of the young United States pushed the borders of the country across the continent and beyond. Unable to compete with richer and more powerful European empires for access to overseas markets and resources in Asia and Africa, the U.S. found a geographical advantage in the Western Hemisphere. Not long after Latin American nations gained independence from Spain and Portugal in the 1820s, the U.S. became the first world power to import coffee duty-free. The free trade in coffee in turn became a strategic linchpin of President James Monroe's 1823 vision of the Americas as a separate sphere free from European interference and colonization. U.S. imports of coffee doubled every decade between 1800 and 1850, and gained even greater economic and strategic significance in the second half of the century. As the export boom took off across Latin America, the U.S. purchased more and more influence through coffee.[12]

The transformation of the United States from British colony to expansionist empire profoundly changed the material conditions of American life. The first rations of George Washington's Continental Army included no coffee — instead the troops drank cider or spruce beer. In contrast, during the Civil War, the average Union soldier consumed about thirty-six pounds of coffee beans each year, enough for perhaps five cups a day.[13] The word "coffee" appears in Union diaries more often than "rifle" or "bullets."[14] After the Civil War, American coffee consumption continued to increase, while prices, thanks to increased production in Latin America, sank lower. Coffee was no longer merely for the coastal elite. It had become a drink for the exhausted: soldiers, pioneers, miners, immigrants, workers in early factories, and anyone with a keen sense of the stakes of remaining alert. Yet this democratization of coffee drinking in the United States depended on "the rise of scores of slave baronies in Brazil" — and vice versa.[15]

When the Hills brothers established their "Arabian Coffee & Spice Mills" in San Francisco in 1873, "Mocha" and "Java" were place names that had been turned into brand names (and sometimes combined as "jamoca"), distancing coffee from its origins in slavery. They were the names most redolent of a version of coffee history — exotic, romantic, and hazy — that lined up with the idea of the U.S. as an "empire for liberty." At the time, this sort of coffee history was especially easy to package and sell, though actual coffee from Java and Mocha was not — and that was the purpose of the lies.

During the gold rush, San Francisco grocers had been known for selling coffee that was already ground and wrapped up in "fancy packages" — ostensibly for easy transport to the mines, but also to conceal the contents.[16] Inside the elaborate packaging was usually a mix of ground coffee and cheaper adulterants, especially chicory and grains. As the city grew and became wealthier and more cosmopolitan, more and more coffee roasters and retailers began to distance themselves from this practice by selling coffee in the whole bean. Coffee in the whole bean was at least clearly coffee, though that was usually as far as certainty extended.

By the late nineteenth century, grocery stores in San Francisco revolved around the "magic coffee bin." From the stock of beans stored in the bin, "the fortunate owner could produce, at the bidding of the buyer, and without hitch, coffee of any known variety." Coffees from Mocha and Java were extremely scarce in the San Francisco import trade, but coffees sold under those names were very common in the San Francisco retail trade. "Mocha" sold out of the magic coffee bin might have been, "in the earlier stages of its being . . . any growth of peaberries," rounded beans from coffee cherries with a single, whole seed inside, rather than a seed split into halves.[17] Coffee planters in any region of the world interested in selling their crop as "Mocha" could encourage peaberry formation by stunting the vertical growth of their trees, lopping off the tops every year.[18] What came out of the bin as "Java" was often "made of any class of large bean, possibly grown by the very antipodes of the Javanese."[19] The magic of the bin made it possible for "every corner grocery" to have "a liberal supply of 'Java' and 'Mocha,' " as the *San Francisco Chronicle* reported in 1886, even if the customs receipts, reflecting imports, told a different story from that of the grocer's receipts.[20]

When the Hills brothers opened their "Arabian" coffee mill, most of the coffee coming into San Francisco was from Latin America.[21] In those years Latin America had no reputation as a source of quality coffee.[22] Yet when the Hills brothers advertised on the front of the coffee bin in their store near the Embarcadero that their "Arabian Coffee" was "The Best in the World," they could be fairly confident that they would get away with it. As the *Chronicle* pointed out, "The thousands

108

of people who will only drink Java coffee and wish to purchase it as cheaply as that from other countries are considerately duped by the dealers, who know that not one coffee drinker in a hundred can tell the difference between Java, Costa Rica, Salvador, or East Indian brands."[23]

This consumer suggestibility was exceptionally valuable to San Francisco coffee merchants. Geography had given them a special advantage in the coffee districts of Central America, which clustered along the chain of volcanoes that traced the Pacific coast, making San Francisco the "logical market."[24] El Salvador in particular was "almost at the door" of North America, and in the years before the Panama Canal it was comparatively inaccessible from European ports.[25] The problem was that the best conditions for growing coffee in Central America were found between 3,000 and 6,000 feet of elevation, and the coffee beans grown at such altitudes tended to be small, dense, and gnarled — notably different from the round peaberry passed off as Mocha and the large-bean coffees sold as Java.

Yet coffee was the commodity that San Francisco merchants had to buy if they wanted to win control of the Central American trade from British and European merchants, which the sustained growth of the city seemed to demand. By the 1870s the largest California gold veins had been emptied, and agriculture had replaced mining as the growth sector.[26] State-size swaths of the Central Valley were coming under wheat cultivation; by the 1880s, wheat production in California "was easily the most mechanized agriculture in the nation, if not the world." The forty million bushels produced there in a year fed a market that stretched from China to Britain, and all the way up and down the Pacific coast of the American continent.[27] In addition to coffee, spices and chocolate came into San Francisco in exchange for wheat. And though their British and European competitors were generally more experienced and better established in these trades, San Francisco importers were hopeful that they were "slowly but surely obtaining the whole of the trade in Central American coffee grown on the Pacific Coast," which would make it much easier to sell California wheat there.[28]

Among the dreamers of the wheaten dream were James Otis Jr. and Hall McAllister. Otis was the son of a former mayor of San Francisco and descended from a Massachusetts family celebrated for its role in the American Revolution. Hall McAllister was the son of a powerful San Francisco politician and the nephew of the original keeper of New York's social register. In 1892, Otis and McAllister founded a shipping firm in San Francisco that they called by their two names turned into one, Otis McAllister. They chartered two steam liners and made a plan to exploit the lazy extortions of the entrenched monopolist, the Pacific Mail Steamship Company. Then they promptly lost a nearly ruinous rate war with the Pacific Mail, which is how Otis McAllister got into the flour trade, milling California wheat and exporting it to Latin America, where it was in demand among the growing population of people who were used to eating European-style bread rather than corn tortillas.

Because they were in flour, Otis and McAllister started dealing in coffee, too, on commission. That was one of the easiest ways to get paid for flour exports, in part because many of the people in Central America who preferred to eat bread made of wheat flour were coffee planters and exporters. Soon Otis McAllister was among the leading brokers of coffee in San Francisco, competing with other American houses, such as the New York–based mining and shipping concern W. R. Grace, as well as established European merchants. Otis McAllister took consignments from Central American coffee planters and exporters and sold to San Francisco coffee roasters such as J. A. Folger's Pioneer Steam Coffee Mill and Austin and Reuben Hills' Arabian Coffee Mill, crediting the money from the sales — less 3 percent for their broker's cut — back to the coffee planters and exporters in Central America. Along the way, Otis McAllister also acquired their own coffee mill in Costa Rica, called El Brazil.[29]

With coffee leading the way in the Central American export boom, optimism for the continued growth of the Pacific coast trade was high in San Francisco. And it was in light of the potential riches available from trading one commodity crop produced on the Pacific coast of the Americas for another, a commerce seemingly foretold by the very shape of the earth, that the *San Francisco Chronicle* was pleased to hear, in 1894, of the "brilliant campaign" Salvadoran coffee planters had carried off against the Ezeta brothers in Santa Ana. "Commercial and agricultural enterprises" in El Salvador had "been paralyzed for two years" by the "grievous imposts" that the "tyrannical and barbarously cruel" Ezetas had placed on coffee exports and on imported articles, too. San Franciscans were even willing to accept as a refugee in their city the former Salvadoran vice president Antonio Ezeta, who had fled up the coast on a steamer after the Santa Ana planters ran him out of town, now that the prospects for business were looking up again.[30]

6.
THE SIGN OF APOLLO

In Santa Ana in 1894 the gallants had their "resorts" and their flirtations, but a coffee town didn't offer a married couple much in the way of social life after the sun went down around six o'clock, as it did all year round. So, after dinner, the planter class went to bed early.

After their marriage, James Hill and Lola Bernal began to re-create certain aspects of the life Hill had left behind in Manchester. In 1897 they had a daughter, named Alicia, after Hill's mother, Alice. Two years later Lola gave birth to another daughter, María — her mother's second name. In 1900 they had a son, named Jaime. "Jaime" is the way of saying James in Spanish that translates itself, for it looks most like the English version. But James in Spanish is also commonly rendered as "Santiago" — Saint Iago, Ya'kov, Jacob, James, the patron saint of Spain — which Jaime's father would have known, for "Santiago Hill" was the name written in the books of El Salvador's banks next to the sums James had borrowed.[1]

James Hill was borrowing money because at the same time he was starting a family, he was also developing coffee plantations. Exactly what it took to create a coffee plantation was a question of significant international interest in the years around Brazilian emancipation. "The constant and rapid increase in the consumption of coffee" in the United States especially — nearly doubling in the two decades after the end of the U.S. Civil War — had inflated expectations for the continued growth of the trade. And still some observers of the market thought that "consumption has not increased . . . as much as it should, in view of the increase in population and the prosperous condition of the United States." The "should" advertised a business opportunity. For though it was true that "coffee culture is being pushed in Mexico, Central America, and the United States of Colombia," the "new plantations have not yet reached a point where they are able to push exports abreast of Brazil, and until that time is reached high prices must rule."[2] Would-be coffee planters around the world were betting on it.

When James Hill went in for coffee on the Santa Ana Volcano, he read everything he could get his hands on about coffee planting in Central America and Brazil and everywhere else.[3] And if certain books from his childhood had predisposed Hill to make an adventure of life in Central America, there were other books to help him make it profitable.

Some of these books grew out of the Victorian fad for memoirs of self-invention: stories of the property-less poor boy or the luckless second son, who, lacking prospects at home, seeks his birthright in the wider world. Such young men staffed the remote frontiers of the British Empire, turning what had been forest and jungle into plantations. Once they had remade themselves as Planters — usually capital P — they wrote the stories of their lives and adventures to the specifications of the boys' fiction of the time, only — in contrast to *Treasure Island* — holding back no point of useful detail. Hence John Shortt's 1864 *A Handbook to Coffee Planting in Southern India;* Alex Brown's *The Coffee Planter's Manual,* which went through two editions, in 1872 and 1880; Arnold H. White's *Coffee Culture in Ceylon: Manuring of Estates,* honored with a prize by the Ceylon Planters' Association on its publication in 1875; and George Bidie's 1869 *Report on the Ravages of the Borer in Coffee Estates,* which ravages, Bidie made clear in his subtitle, did not preclude the *Further Development of the*

115

Productive Resources of the Coffee Districts in Southern India.

Standing out from this list of titles on "the planter's bookshelf" was Robert Henry Elliot's two-volume *The Experiences of a Planter in the Jungles of Mysore (with Illustrations and a Map).* In the estimation of a fellow planter-writer, Elliot had "thrown a glamour over the industry in the eyes of many an outward-bound 'griffin.' "[4] That was the common nickname for fortune-seeking travelers to British India, after the mythological creature with the body of a lion and the head and wings of an eagle.

Elliot had gone to India in 1855, his nineteenth year, with a "trifling capital" and "information of what is hungered after by younger sons, namely, a spot where a trifling capital can, with industry and enterprise, be turned into a comfortable livelihood." He learned the local language, acquired land through a government policy designed to promote coffee cultivation, which also provided for a tax exemption until such a time as the land yielded marketable coffee, and made friends with older planters whose "example and practice as to plantation management were consequently of the greatest value."[5] Yet the plot Elliot had acquired was twelve miles distant from these other planters, and his life in India, among the people

116

whose settlement his parcel abutted, and whom he hired to work his land, was anxious and solitary.

One afternoon, when he was sitting by himself in his tent seeking relief from the hottest part of the day, Elliot got word that a number of men from this settlement had taken up arms in opposition to his clearing of the forest adjoining their land. His repose interrupted, Elliot emerged from his tent armed "not with my gun and rifle, but with pen, ink, and paper." It was a clever choice of arms, for it was loaded with all the force of the government. "My people . . . had desisted from clearing until they had my orders to proceed," Elliot recounted. "My opponents, who were merely armed with knives similar to those used in clearing underwood, were in the minority, and I could easily have disposed of them had I wished to do so. But I caused my clerk to explain to them that, if the leader would sign a paper declaring they forcibly prevented my clearing the jungle, I would draw off my party. They assented, and my clerk drew up a brief statement to that effect, which they were imprudent enough to sign." Elliot then sent the statement to the local magistrate to prove that his rights as land grantee had been impeded. A few days later, the magistrate "came down with a strong force of police . . . investigated the case, adjudged that I was in the right, and ordered

117

some of the forces to the cut in his presence." Then the coup de grâce: Elliot begged the magistrate that his neighbors be pardoned rather than punished. The result, as he told it, was that "some of my opponents entered my service shortly afterwards, and one of them rose from the position of labourer, and is now the most valued and trustworthy overseer on my property."[6]

After he settled in El Salvador, James Hill studied the law of his adopted country — studied it so thoroughly that those who knew what he knew judged him the equal of native lawyers, so thoroughly that he sometimes was called to serve as a consultant to his "brother planters" on complex legal points.[7] Knowledge of the law was invaluable, certainly, for law was the architecture of Hill's opportunity. The law had created new parcels of land available to be transformed into plantations. The law had created a class of people who had no access to land of their own and so were compelled to sell their labor in order to eat. The law had created the police and the rules they enforced. But the law, no matter how favorably written, thoroughly studied, and efficiently enforced, was not enough, for the law did not itself make people work on coffee plantations in ways that produced coffee. This was the greatest task of any self-described planter: to figure out how make other people do the planting and everything else.

"It is a stern fact," warned the veteran planter Edwin Lester Arnold, "unfortunately impossible to ignore, that to grow Coffee we must employ labour, and to a large extent." Arnold's "handbook" on coffee cultivation, published in 1886, the year after European empires carved up Africa into colonies at the Berlin Conference, was written to help those who decided to make a go of coffee in such "new districts."[8] On this point there was virtually universal agreement: wherever there was the possibility of planting coffee, the mastery of labor was "the chief obstacle."[9]

The problem of labor was more complex than "la falta de brazos": literally the lack of arms, meaning a shortage of workers, endemic across the coffee regions of Latin America.[10] Even in densely populated areas such as El Salvador, the challenge was more complicated than merely finding people to work. "He who makes up his mind to create his own coffee estate," warned a *New York Times* correspondent in Central America in 1888, "must also be prepared to endure from four to six years of the hardest work. In clearing he must chop wood, cut away underbrush, and weed his land. He must be ready to work from sunrise to sundown. Neither the damp cold of the morning, the heat of noon, nor the heavy afternoon rains should

119

deter him from his work. It is true that he may hire native labor to assist him, but that labor cannot be depended upon should he turn his back upon it."[11] It was a question not only of finding people to work, but also of making them do it, and correctly. In Central America, the name given to this problem was "the mozo."

By definition the mozo was a male "Indian laborer." What made him a laborer by definition was his relation to land: he had none — in many cases, it had been taken from him because of his Indianness. Having no land of his own, the mozo had to work to eat, and so to live. In the eyes of planters, it was the mozo's native lot to be "a laborer for life" — an expression that summed up at once the terms of the deal he struck on the plantations every day, and his fate. In this double bind, "having no ambition," unwilling to "work more than is necessary for his own comfort," the best outcome the mozo could aim for, the *New York Times* concluded in 1888, was "the decent treatment of a good master" — a suggestive way of saying "employer" in the year of Brazilian abolition — plus "a slap-jack made of ground corn and water . . . and all the whisky he can get."[12]

To planters, the mozo was both an indispensable and an impossible character. The owners of plantations gave themselves and their occupation a name — planter — that conjured a reassuring fantasy of photosynthesis, as if producing coffee were as simple as dropping a seed in the ground. Yet in fact the planter depended on the mozo in the same way that the mozo depended on work: for his very existence. Just as the mozo needed to work to survive, so did the planter need the mozo if he was to continue to live as a planter.

The core difficulty of this dependence for the planter was precisely the mozo's essential simplicity — the fact that he required so little, "even less than a Chinaman," and seemed content with it. This simplicity complicated the mozo's relation to the planter and his work plans. Because he could "find enough work to keep him alive almost anywhere," the mozo moved incessantly from plantation to plantation, one week here, two weeks there, and gone again. Because he had so little to lose or gain, the mozo was "a 'devil-may-care' fellow" who would "laugh and talk instead of attending strictly to" the work in front of him, spend his wages getting drunk and gambling, take his losses out on his family, and make up the difference by stealing and lying about it.[13] With their plans and investments in the balance, planters could only conclude that the mozo's problems were inborn, a matter of race. The definite article in the very name of "the mozo" made it clear: the average case was also the extreme case. There was only one type of mozo, and he needed mastery.

While once planters had judged the racial character and quality of their workers by physical traits, beginning with skin color and extending to everything else they could get their hands on, by the end of the nineteenth century those superficial metrics no longer seemed satisfactory. Increasingly planters were looking for more "modern" solutions to labor problems inside the bodies of the people who worked for them. Robert Henry Elliot had lived through the change in the jungles of Mysore. "Hitherto it has been thought sufficient to weigh and measure people, and take casts of the head," he observed, "and this, of course, is very well as far as it goes; but, to complete our information, I am persuaded that an analysis of the blood is absolutely necessary." Elliot suspected that the deficit of "active virtues" he noted in his "Bengalee" employees could be explained at least in part by "a deficiency of red blood corpuscles," and he looked forward to the day when a truly penetrating science of labor could test that hypothesis and identify a solution.[14] Yet until such analysis was possible, it was down to the planter to make the workers work.

James Hill sought a loan from a British bank, the London Bank of Central America, which operated a branch in El Salvador.[15] Balancing his reputation for slipperiness, Hill had a number of credits in his favor. He had married into a family with years of experience in coffee in Santa Ana, and his wife, Lola, had inherited three established plantations, no small consideration in getting a young man from Manchester started in a new endeavor. Hill also had his own record of commercial experience in El Salvador, which certainly would have been known to the bank, one of only five operating in the country in 1894. And if the bankers had therefore known something of Hill's checkered reputation, they could also have known that he was at the same time considered "one of the hardest workers and most energetic men" in Santa Ana.[16]

Moreover, and perhaps most important, in the early 1890s coffee seemed a good bet, and coffee was the bank's business, not only in El Salvador but in neighboring countries, too, including Nicaragua.[17] In 1892, the year James Hill made up his mind to settle in El Salvador, world coffee prices rose to a historic high of seventeen cents a pound. In 1894, the year Hill got married and began to build his own coffee business, prices were still holding well above the ten-year average. The London Bank of Central America loaned Hill a "considerable amount of money," as much as $25,000, and the debt was secured by a consignment of his first crop, some years away.[18]

■ ■ ■

In the beginning there was much work to do and little hope of reward — "four to six years of the hardest work," as the *New York Times* had put it, before the coffee trees would begin to produce a mature harvest. Even the hardest-working, most energetic planter could not do it all on his own. In most cases, the land of the plantation ground had to be cleared to make way for coffee. While the clearing of the land was under way, the first coffee plants were to be raised in seedbeds, sited to receive the rays of the sun in the morning and shade at midday and in the afternoon, and filled with soil "of the same quality as the proposed plantation" that had been "deeply stirred" and thoroughly cleaned. In these beds, every two and a half inches or so, were to be planted seeds "perfectly sound and regular in shape and size," and covered with three-quarters of an inch of vegetable humus and sprinkled gently with water. After a year of light sprinkling and diligent tending and vigilant guarding against weeds, when the coffee seedlings had reached twelve to sixteen inches high, they were ready to be moved to the plantation proper.

The uprooting of the seedlings was best done when "the ground is moist from recent rains," to allow a ball of dirt to be easily taken up with the roots of the plant. During the transplanting, the seedlings were to be protected from direct sun, and if, on the plantation itself, shade trees were not already in place, a leafy branch was to be stuck in the ground next to each seedling. By the time James Hill began work in Santa Ana, it was standard for Salvadoran planters to cultivate coffee under shade rather than in full sun, which was the usual practice in Brazil. Full sun produced higher yields from each tree, but the heat sucked all the water out of the soil and rapidly exhausted the land, an especially dear resource in El Salvador.[19] With six to eight feet allotted between trees, 500 per acre was a standard. It was common, too, to trim off the top bud once the tree reached five or six feet high — untended coffee trees could reach twenty feet tall — to concentrate the tree's growth in an area that would be accessible to future harvest workers. Then it was a matter of waiting.

If everything had been done well, after four or five years of cultivation, the first harvest would announce itself in the blooming of the coffee tree's "beautiful, 'tube-rose-like' white flower," glowing "against the dark, lustrous green of the leaf." Soon afterward the petals would drop off and give way to the green berry, warming first to "a delicate pink, changing by degrees to a dark cherry red, when it is ripe and ready to be gathered."

125

And only then could a hopeful planter pause to "complacently contemplate" the years of work that had been invested in the plantation, and that seemed about to pay off.[20]

As he waited for white flowers and red cherries to arrive on his plantations, James Hill also began to build his coffee mill in the valley below. He chose a site about a mile outside Santa Ana, close to one of the plantations that his wife had inherited, called San Lorenzo, and he named the mill Las Tres Puertas.

Hill believed in signs. The names of things mattered to him. He named his children after himself, his wife, his parents, and his in-laws. Later, he named plantations for what he hoped they would become. And so he gave his mill, Las Tres Puertas, a name that linked his new life on the Santa Ana Volcano with his old life in Manchester. The key to understanding the significance of this name is the symbol that marks the mill even today. All large coffee mills had identifying symbols, distinguishing marks that were stamped on rough fiber coffee sacks to serve as a seal and a brand. Some planters simply used their initials, while others used shapes and glyphs.

The mark of Las Tres Puertas was two things in one, the first of which opens up to reveal the second. It was, in the first place, a hexagon with every other side swung in to meet in the middle as if on hinges: the three doors. Once open in this way, the three-doored hexagon became something else: a triskelion, from the Greek for "three-legged," a three-spoked spiral resembling a capital Y spun a quarter-turn around its focus.

Ancient cultures in Europe and Asia alike deployed versions of the symbol, including some variations — such as those that adorn the flag of Sicily and the coat of arms of the Isle of Man — whose spokes are human legs or arms. The triskelion adopted for Las Tres Puertas more closely resembles plainer variations sometimes mistaken for three-armed swastikas, similar to those stamped on the backs of coins under the imperial rule of Hill's hero Alexander the Great. In the time of Alexander, the triskelion was a symbol of the sun, and of the cult of the Greek god whom, more two thousand years later, Victorians would honor above all others: Apollo, sun god, god of health and life, who also gave his name to one of the streets in Collyhurst where James Hill lived as a boy.[21]

For the Victorians, Apollo symbolized something more than the sum of these historic and mythic meanings. He was also the figurehead of the profound shift in understanding of the universe that followed from the discovery of energy and the formulation of the laws of thermodynamics in the middle of the nineteenth century. Even after the publication of Charles Darwin's *On the Origin of Species* in 1859, the thermodynamic idea of energy was prominently celebrated as the most important discovery of a century of unprecedented scientific innovation.[22] Like Darwin's theory of evolution, energy transformed fundamental notions of how the world worked, sparking a revolution in scientific, economic, and social thought that had immediate and far-reaching practical applications. This idea of energy shaped virtually every aspect of the coffee empire James Hill built on the Santa Ana Volcano, as well as the wider political and commercial context, yet it originated far away, in two different places almost simultaneously: Java and Manchester.

7.
A GOD ON THE MAKE

Growing up in the quiet country town of Heilbronn, Germany, where he was born in 1814, Robert Mayer was the sort of boy who detested school and loved magic. An indifferent and impatient student, he spent hours studying the windmills near his house, dreaming of building a perpetual motion machine. Even after Mayer began to train as a physician at the renowned university in Tübingen, his attention remained fixed on larger questions. When he treated patients, he was not merely treating patients. He was also trying to figure out how the human body worked, how it processed the world into itself.

After he earned his medical degree, Mayer spurned the domestic physician's life. Instead he traveled to Amsterdam, where, over the strong objections of his parents, he signed on as a ship's doctor — which is how he found himself, at age twenty-five, in the middle of February 1840, setting out in the brittle light of wintry Holland aboard the *Java*, heading for same.[1]

By 1840 the Dutch were on the way to building an island colony whose name would become synonymous with the commodity it produced. Java had been an important center of coffee production for the European market as early as the first half of the eighteenth century, but it was only after the introduction of state-mandated cultivation around 1830 that coffee took over the island. Under what was known euphemistically as "the cultivation system," the "labor by which coffee is planted in Java and its produce collected" was extracted from the Javanese people by coercion. Each family of Javanese was required to cultivate a certain number of trees: five hundred trees in some districts, a thousand in others.[2] Coffee was not the only crop so controlled — the mandate extended to sugar, indigo, and tobacco as well — but it was the most important. The island's annual coffee crop quadrupled between 1820 and 1840, eventually exceeding 130 million pounds, and the Dutch colonial administration bought the produce at a price fixed well below the open-market rate. Given the emphasis on quantity, the Java coffee produced under the cultivation system was often inferior, but the profits were first quality.[3]

After a voyage of one hundred days aboard the *Java,* Robert Mayer and his charges

130

reached the city of Batavia, now Jakarta. In Batavia, much of the twenty-eight-man crew was stricken with what Mayer identified as an "acute affection of the lungs." He did what any doctor would have done in his place and cut the sick open for "copious" bloodlettings. As the blood drained out of their veins, he noticed that its color was much brighter than he had been trained to expect. It appeared too red to be venous blood, though he was certain it was. Mayer spent what would have been his shore leave aboard the *Java,* working "zealously and unremittingly" through the puzzle of the red blood.[4]

Not long after he returned to Amsterdam in 1841, Mayer thought he had the answer. He wrote up a paper and mailed it off to a German scientific journal. "It is the task of natural science to explain both the organic and the inorganic worlds in terms of their causes and effects," began his essay, which never received a reply.[5] Mayer would spend the rest of his days working to clarify and extend his thinking about the relations between causes and effects — about what the redness of the blood revealed about the human body, the world, and the relationship between the two.

Soon Mayer would come to see blood in a new way, as a "slowly burning fluid," the "oil in the flame of life." Building on the insights of German chemist Justus von Liebig, who mapped out the field now called organic chemistry, and the French physician and philosopher Antoine Lavoisier, who argued, against centuries of canonical philosophy, that the phenomenon called "life" was a chemical process rather than a matter of the spirit, Mayer concluded that his patients' muscles were burning less fuel in the heat of tropical Java than they would have in chilly Amsterdam. Because less of the fuel in the blood was burned up, it returned from the limbs and extremities less oxidized, and therefore redder. Hotter weather, less muscular work, less fuel burned, lighter blood; colder weather, more muscular work, more fuel burned, darker blood. The increased heat of the tropics, Mayer reasoned, had decreased the need of the muscles to consume fuel in the work of living; heat and muscular work must be substitutes, he concluded, different forms of the same thing.[6]

In 1842, Mayer tried again to write up his ideas, and the resulting paper was accepted for publication in a journal overseen by the chemist Liebig. "What are we to understand by *forces,*" Mayer began, still driving toward big concepts of cause and effect, "and how are these related to one another?"[7] He had begun to see not only that different forms of force, heat and muscular work, for example, could be transformed into one another, but moreover that "there exists only a *single* force," which was converted from one form to another and conserved across the conversion.[8] "It is my assertion," Mayer wrote to a friend in the same year, 1842, "that motion, heat, light, electricity and various chemical reactions are all one and the same object under differently appearing forms."[9] Keeping with the terminology of his time and place, Mayer called this single object *"Kraft,"* German for "force."[10] Within a decade it was called "energy."[11]

"Energy" had previously been a quality of persons and personality, adjacent to "vitality" and "will," and of course the word continued to be used that way, as in "Anglo-Saxon energy," or as in James Hill's reputation as "the most energetic man" in Santa Ana. But in the middle of the nineteenth century, "energy" also came to be the overarching name for the forces, once called "imponderables," that Robert Mayer saw to be connected. Motion, heat, light, electricity, chemical compounds (the fuel of the blood, the sugars in plants) — all were increasingly seen as different forms of the same thing, energy. Within a quarter century, Mayer's hypothesis that a unitary force governed the workings of the individual human body and the natural world alike would be "accepted by the leading scientific minds of all nations with remarkable unanimity."[12] And more than merely accepted, it would be celebrated as "the foundation and capstone of all science."[13]

To his profound disappointment, Robert Mayer had little to do with the ascent of the idea of energy. In Manchester, an amateur scientist by the name of James Joule was asking the same questions about the connections and relations among different forms of force, but he was going about it in a very different way.

The son of a brewer, Joule had grown up in Salford, not far from where the Engels family built Victoria Mill. Just as Mayer discovered his puzzle in the core business of the Dutch Empire, the clamor of Manchester's mills drove Joule's experimentation. In a sense, both men targeted commercial inefficiencies: while Mayer probed the physiology of the human body at work in a tropical climate, Joule set out to build a more reliable engine, an electric motor driven by magnets. While Joule succeeded in improving on past versions of electromagnetic engines, he could not approach the power of steam engines. The problem, he determined, was leakage in the transmission of electrical current from the battery to the mechanism.[14] His efforts to figure out where and how current was being lost led Joule to the question of the relation between heat and motion, a problem that had concerned engineers in Europe's industrial capitals for some time.[15]

It was entirely in keeping with the nature of Victorian science that Joule treated his honeymoon in Switzerland as a research trip. Looking for universal truths in natural phenomena, he tried to measure the difference in the temperature of the water at the top and the bottom of a waterfall. To the groom's great disappointment, the falls were too misty for him to get close enough to measure. At home in his laboratory, Joule agitated water with paddles and measured minute temperature changes. He published his conclusions in 1843: "The grand agents of nature are, by the Creator's fiat, *indestructible . . .* wherever mechanic force is expended, an exact equivalent of heat is *always* obtained."[16] In this "exact equivalent," Joule established by experiment what Mayer had theorized: the convertibility of seemingly distinct forces, implying the existence of a single, unitary force.

Joule's work in turn became an important source for an 1847 paper by German physician Hermann von Helmholtz, who generalized experimental findings into a rule. Helmholtz self-published the paper, titled "On the Conservation of Force," after it was rejected from the leading scientific journal of the day for being too abstract. It is now generally considered to be the earliest statement of the first law of thermodynamics: Energy is neither created nor destroyed, merely converted from one form to another. The pioneering British scientist of electromagnetism Michael Faraday judged the conservation of energy "the highest law in physical science which our faculties permit us to perceive." Philosopher Herbert Spencer called it "the sole truth which transcends experience by underlying it."[17] It seemed clear to many of the leading thinkers of the age that energy was the deepest level at which human beings could hope to understand how the world works.

In the decades around the turn of the nineteenth century, the great Romantic poets and artists had been entranced by the idea of an "underlying unity of nature," an interconnected and interdependent universe.[18] "All objects are as windows, through which the philosophic eye looks into Infinitude itself," Thomas Carlyle wrote in 1831, framing the Romantic vision.[19] The discovery of energy put this expansive idea of connection on solid empirical ground, and over the second half of the nineteenth century the Victorians put it to great practical use. By 1870, the idea of energy — the idea that all forces were manifestations of a unitary force that was neither created nor destroyed, that was finite but everywhere all the time, and that could be quantified and harnessed through thermodynamic science — had become the basis of a new theory of everything. This theory had great appeal, consequence, and value, and its implications would reach into and transform every part of the world. It was so appealing, consequential, and valuable because above all it was a theory of how to get work done.

Victorians glorified work as a "supreme virtue," even the meaning of life.[20] It made good sense to this work-obsessed people that the law of energy conservation demonstrated, "in a mathematically rigorous way, that you cannot get something for nothing."[21] This strict logic of cause and effect implied an initial cause, an original force, without specifically identifying it. According to the reigning Newtonian laws of motion, the universe was made up of categorically distinct forces, or causes, among them gravity, magnetism, and the animating vital force of life. Yet once all forces — "the movements of the planets, the forces of nature, the mechanical work of machines, and the work of the body" — were shown to be manifestations of a single underlying force, energy, the old categorical distinctions broke down.[22] "Energy" was defined as the ability to do work, and "work" in turn gained the technical meaning of the energy required to move a given mass a given distance. A new concept of a radically connected universe took shape, based on the idea that all energy, and all work, was ultimately derived from the heat and light of the sun.[23]

Today the rule is "Follow the money," but the leading scientific minds of nineteenth-century Europe followed energy from the sun through the mills to the bank. "The clover sprouts and blossoms, and the scythe of the mower swings, by the operation of the same force," English physicist John Tyndall explained in 1862. "The sun digs the ore from our mines, he rolls the iron; he rivets the plates, he boils the water; he draws the train. He not only grows the cotton, but he spins the fibre and weaves the web. There is not a hammer raised, a wheel turned, or a shuttle thrown, that is not raised, and turned, and thrown by the sun." A popular magazine put the same idea more concisely in 1866: "All the labour done under the sun is really done by it."[24]

Recast as the prime mover, the original source of all work, the sun became the focus of a new belief system, "the gospel of energy."[25] As much as any tribe, the Victorians were sun worshippers. Their gospel was a form of what historian Anson Rabinbach has called "productivism" — an ideology that joined a view of "nature as a vast machine capable of producing mechanical work" to the "imperative to maximize production by consuming ever more power and deploying it ever more efficiently."[26] In this view, "the cosmos was essentially a system of production," like a cotton mill.[27] Productivism appealed to Victorians not only because it made Manchester and other ugly industrial capitals look like a natural order, but because it made nature itself look like a vast pool of energy just waiting to be tapped and harnessed to make and build things, to transform, change, and improve the world, to be turned into work and, through work, into money. The gospel of energy translated thermodynamic principles into a blueprint for productivity and profits that was equally applicable in Britain, in El Salvador, or wherever the sun's rays were — through photosynthesis, steam-powered manufacturing, or simple hard work — being turned into cash. Commodity production became missionary work.

The productivist gospel of energy was not only an evangelical denomination of capitalism but also an updated cult of Apollo. The new Apollo was a god not only of sun and life and health, but also a god of everything that had become directly associated with sun and life and health: light, agriculture, business, work, "energy and ambition" — he was a "god of enterprise," a "god on the make."[28]

At the same time, in considering the history of the idea of energy and its impact on the Santa Ana Volcano and the wider world, there is another aspect of Apollo's significance to take into account, an aspect that was neglected and even suppressed within the fervent gospel of energy. The Greeks had more complex, ambivalent relationships with their gods than did subsequent ages, and Apollo was no exception. Alexander the Great had famously credited Apollo with aiding certain conquests, but this conquering power had dark shadings. For the Greeks, Apollo held so much power over health and life because he was also the sender of plague.[29]

8.
THE MILL

Though he had grown up in a place where mills meant cotton, James Hill was not entirely unprepared to run a coffee mill in Santa Ana. When he opened Las Tres Puertas in 1896, milling coffee in El Salvador was in certain ways like milling cotton in Manchester, and selling Salvadoran coffee abroad was in certain ways like selling textiles in El Salvador. Both prized surface over substance.

In Spanish, a coffee mill is a *beneficio,* from the verb meaning to benefit, to improve, to increase the value of. Milling coffee, like milling cotton, creates value by transforming a rough agricultural product of limited usefulness into a convenient commodity form. A coffee mill does so not by combining, building up, and weaving together, but by paring away. It's a jeweler's process: the finished form of the commodity is carved out of the raw material. Coffee came into Las Tres Puertas as a ripe-red, freshly picked fruit — a coffee cherry. It left the mill as a dry bean —

141

"green coffee." The difference between the two forms was time and money. The ripe fruit was vulnerable to decay, but the dry bean could be shipped long distances to the markets where its value was greatest.

There were and are two cost-effective ways to get a coffee bean from a coffee cherry. The older, simpler, cheaper way is the "dry" method: leaving the fruit out in the sun to shrivel and dry, then running it through a rough grinder to scrape the flesh away from the seed. The "modern" way — most often considered the better way, because the coffee that results is more consistent — is a "wet" process: using water to "wash" the fruit away from the seed. Anyone can fashion a rudimentary dry mill, but wet mills, especially in the nineteenth century, could be prohibitively expensive to build and operate, requiring metal tanks and mechanical depulpers and dehullers, and sometimes dryers and polishers, usually manufactured in Europe, plus steam engines to run the machines, plus a river of fresh water on demand. By Hill's figures, turning 500 pounds of coffee cherries into 100 pounds of export-ready coffee beans required 200 gallons of water. When Las Tres Puertas was running at full capacity, it would use as many as 200,000 gallons per day.[1]

The workers receiving the freshly harvested coffee cherries sent down from the volcano each day dumped the lot directly into a receiving tank full of water. Lighter, underdeveloped cherries floated to the top and were skimmed off, while the heavy ripe cherries at the bottom were funneled into a pulping machine. The depulper, driven by a steam engine, mashed the cherries, splitting the skin and tearing away the outer flesh. From there the seed — still encased in a sticky mucilage called honey and, under that, a thin fibrous wrapping called parchment — sluiced on toward fermentation tanks. After a day or two of curing in the tanks, the honey sagged off and the two halves of the seed split apart — except in the case of peaberry, the roundish variety often passed off as "Mocha," which was one seed to one bean.

From the fermentation tanks, the seeds, now stripped to their thin parchment wrappers, were swept by a stream of water into a series of narrow canals, through which they were pushed by men wielding paddles and rakes toward the drying patios, the most impressive part of any large coffee mill. Drying patios are impressive in the manner of cornfields, quiet monuments to nature's power to make men wait. At Las Tres Puertas, the patios came to stretch out for acres, a great plain of earthen bricks laid edge-to-edge. On the patios, barefoot men and boys — chosen because they were light — used rakes to spread the washed seeds into pale furrows that were tilled continuously to expose the coffee to the sun and air.

After a week or more, when the seeds were fully dry, workers scooped them into sacks and hauled them to the hulling machines to remove the now-brittle parchment sheath. With the parchment shorn away, the seeds became coffee beans. From the hullers, the beans were carried to the cleaners, who were women.[2]

All over the world women have been disproportionately employed as final inspectors of commodities. The usual story is fast hands and fine fingers, but any photograph of women bent over a pile of coffee beans on the ground or a table, under the baleful surveillance of a male supervisor, tells in a glance the much more complicated story of the economic value of gender inequality.

Women were hired as cleaners — in Spanish, *limpiadoras,* the name of the job itself taking on the feminine gender — at Las Tres Puertas and in coffee mills around the world for two reasons. The first is that sorting through all the individual beans in a year's coffee crop to pick out the damaged and deformed ones, along with any rocks and twigs and other trash, was a job almost incomprehensibly minute and vast at once — Las Tres Puertas processed millions of pounds of coffee each year, and each pound consisted of roughly three thousand coffee beans. Hundreds and hundreds of women were employed in the task, and it was a source of significant cost savings that women's wages were generally lower than men's wages, on the assumption that men were physically stronger and could do more work.

The second reason that women were hired as cleaners is that the work of inspecting and sorting the coffee, though requiring little in the way of brute strength, was a crucially important stage of the milling process — perhaps the single most important stage. In many cases, cleanliness was the most direct determinant of coffee's market value, and the quality of the inspection was the most direct determinant of cleanliness. The inspection therefore bore the financial weight of the entire milling business — and when the mill owner was also a planter, as James Hill was, it bore the weight of the plantations, too. This weight was placed on women in part because traditional patriarchic conceptions of male and female roles propped up the power of the boss to direct the work.

The minute he knew there would be coffee coming in soon, as early in the harvest season as possible, Hill would tell all the men on his plantations to tell all the women they knew to come work in his mill as limpiadoras, for it was a generally accepted principle that the first miller to hire women as cleaners each year would be the miller who had the most women that season.[3] It followed that whoever had the most women working as cleaners had the best chance of producing the cleanest coffee, for that miller could be choosy about whom he employed and set strict standards for the work they did. In turn, whoever produced the cleanest coffee had the best chance of getting a top price for it from an American or European coffee importer.

That was the point of being strict with the limpiadoras: to meet the standards American and European importers used to evaluate the quality and establish the price of coffee. When Hill first opened Las Tres Puertas in 1896, these quality standards, enforced in coffee mills in Santa Ana and around the world, were set on Hanover Square, Pearl Street, New York, New York.

The New York Coffee Exchange opened at that address in 1882, two blocks up from Front Street, where importing firms clustered in what was then New York's "green coffee district." The Exchange was born from an 1880 price collapse, the result of a surprise bumper crop in Brazil, that was considered devastating even in a trade known for spectacular collapses.[4] The first president of the Exchange was among those who had been bankrupted, and he claimed that the new governing institution had "redeemed the coffee trade."[5] Redemption meant fashioning a

146

market that would not break so violently and often, one with a "high degree of liquidity."[6] The sound of the word expresses the intention: commerce flowing along smoothly, no bubbles, no floods, no plunges.

A market with perfect liquidity is one in which everything can be exchanged for anything else, supply of one sort matched with demand of another. To that end, the Coffee Exchange created a futures market, as had been previously established for wheat and cotton, that depended on codifying standard grades of coffee. Standardizing grades made it possible for importers not only to ensure that they got what they had been promised by exporters, but also to hedge against the possibility of surpluses and shortages, and the changes in price that resulted from such fluctuations, by locking in specific prices for specific grades ahead of time.

The grading was done by licensed inspectors. The job of these inspectors was to examine a pound of beans from a given lot of imported coffee and determine what was wrong with it. Against a fixed, hypothetical standard of perfect coffee — standard number one, which did not exist in actual commercial practice — graders began by subtracting points for trash in the sample: a typical 135-pound bag of coffee imported into the U.S. in the middle of the nineteenth century contained about five pounds of sticks, stones, and dirt.[7] Then inspectors looked for "defects" in the beans themselves — points off for malformations, irregularities, breaks — and gave the lot of coffee beans a number grade between two and eight, eights being barred from importation altogether. In the early years of the Exchange, these grading standards applied across three distinct scales: Brazilian coffee from Rio and other ports, where beans tended to be harshly flavored; Brazilian coffee solely from the port of Santos, where the beans tended to be comparatively mellow; and "other."

The emphasis on Brazilian coffee in the standardization of grading scales reflected the fact that the largest crops came from Brazil, and the largest crops could most easily crash the market, and so were the most important to hedge. In other words, the structure of the exchange was designed primarily to protect people who were trading coffee, not to serve the interests of those who were drinking it. In fact, the grading process in New York made no specific accounting of the positive qualities of coffee beans, only of their imperfections and defects.[8]

The pessimistic scrutiny New York's licensed graders brought to bear on coffee arriving into the United States was mirrored in the dour surveillance of supervisors and the bent attention of limpiadoras in coffee mills around the world. The standards of the New York Coffee Exchange presumed that the women who inspected and sorted the world's coffee had failed to do their job. The question that darkened the eyes of supervisors and bowed women's backs over piles of green coffee beans was just how badly they would fail, on a scale of impossible to unacceptable.

And why did New York standards hold such power? The New York Coffee Exchange was the first incorporated international coffee exchange, though not by a decisive margin. The world's second coffee exchange also opened in 1882, in Le Havre, France, the port that warehoused the greatest part of the world's coffee crop. London, Amsterdam, and Hamburg, all of which had much longer histories as capitals of coffee financing, trading, and shipping, also opened coffee exchanges of their own shortly after New York.[9] Yet ultimately New York was one thing the world's other coffee ports were not: the commercial capital of the world's leading coffee-drinking country. And here the question of why New York standards and prices applied so widely intersects the question of why Americans were drinking so much coffee.

"Give me your tired, your poor, your huddled masses," wrote New York poet Emma Lazarus in 1883, the year after the opening of the New York Coffee Exchange. If they weren't on the Statue of Liberty, these lines from her poem "The New Colossus" could have made a decent advertisement for a coffee shop.

Immediately after the Civil War, Americans were drinking, per capita, just under five pounds of coffee per year, or approximately enough for two cups of coffee every three days. By the turn of the twentieth century, Americans were drinking more than twice that much, about one and a half cups each day, per capita.[10] The history of U.S. expansion, imperialism, and trade policy in the nineteenth century helps to explain the increasing supply and decreasing price of coffee in the United States, and forms a key part of the story of *how* the United States became a coffee-drinking nation. The early United States took shape as a political and economic project around the coffee trade, as commercial interests used coffee to build the national economy and foreign-policy makers used it to stabilize and later increase the power of the United States in the world. Yet this geopolitical history of coffee does not really speak to *why* Americans drink it. That question is impossible to answer without some understanding of Americans themselves, a group whose composition was changing quickly.

The 1870 census counted about thirty-eight million people in the United States. In the next three decades, twelve million more would arrive. While earlier "waves" of mass immigration had come largely from Britain, Ireland, and northern Europe, many of the Catholic and Jewish immigrants who made up the "flood" of the late nineteenth century came from central, eastern, and southern Europe. Even the rural and agricultural districts of these regions had strong coffee-drinking cultures, which had spread around the Mediterranean basin and north through contacts with the Ottoman Empire. When European emigrants transplanted themselves to American cities, coffeehouses were among the institutions they founded to maintain ties to their hometowns and compatriots.[11]

Yet if coffee was a form of continuity between immigrants' old homes and new, it was also a difference. None of the European origin countries was as close to Latin America as the United States; none did as much business with Latin America; none had an economy so tied up with the world's leading coffee-growing region. When European immigrants entered the United States in the late nineteenth century, they also entered a new relationship to Latin America. And when they found themselves tasked with new types of repetitive, strenuous, and poorly paid work that was increasingly governed by machines, artificial light, and the factory clock rather than the earth, the sun, and the seasons, they also found themselves in a place with more

151

and cheaper coffee.

As Danish immigrant Jacob Riis hauled his camera around the Lower East Side in the 1880s, investigating life among New York's recent arrivals, he observed the "Sweaters of Jewtown" on Ludlow Street spending the scant food money they earned sewing knee pants at home on bread, milk, meat, butter, coffee, potatoes, and pickles. He saw the boy bootblacks who inhabited the crowded dormitories of the Newsboys' Lodging House on Duane Street spending six cents on a bunk for the night and six cents on bread and coffee for breakfast. He noticed men and boys of all ages crowded around one-cent coffee stalls on the street. He met one young and pretty Broadway seamstress, whose case he took to be representative of many more, who, without a spare cent, took a cup of coffee at breakfast, no lunch, and her one meal of the day for dinner. He heard of a charity shop run by a well-known manufacturer giving out rolls and coffee for free.[12] Riis found that coffee was something even the poorest Americans could afford.

It was both the changing composition of the population and the changing place of the United States in the world that made coffee, for the first time in its global history, a mass beverage. By the turn of the twentieth century Latin America was the unchallenged global center of coffee production, and the United

152

States was unquestionably "the world's greatest coffee market."[13] Americans were drinking about ten pounds of coffee per person per year, considerably more than the population of any rival industrial empire — almost twice what Germans were drinking, more than double the French, quintuple the Austrians, ten times more than Italians, and more still than the British.[14]

In Santa Ana the hope for coffee had never been greater. In 1892, the year James Hill decided to settle in El Salvador, world coffee prices had reached a historic high of seventeen cents a pound. They were only slightly lower in 1894, the year Hill got married, and still holding well above the ten-year average. By the time Las Tres Puertas opened in 1896, world coffee prices had been stable at fifteen cents a pound or higher for more than a decade. Hill's new mill was one of perhaps twenty coffee mills around Santa Ana, but there was more than enough coffee growing on the Santa Ana Volcano to keep them all working: five hundred coffee producers in the city of Santa Ana alone, and many hundreds more in towns nearby.[15]

But then, just as Hill opened the gate of his mill to his first crop, three foundational conditions that had supported the hope for coffee in El Salvador began to collapse, one right after the other. And just at the moment

when James Hill might reasonably have
expected to cash in the guarantees that
Central America seemed to offer to those
who followed its rules, he had to worry about
simply hanging on.

9.
BAD LUCK

The first crisis was a price collapse.

It originated, ironically, in the same conditions that had helped to lift the price initially — for the same circumstances that increased demand for coffee in the United States also increased the supply of coffee in Brazil.

Nearly a million Italians, fleeing rural poverty in Southern Italy especially, arrived in Brazil between the passage of the Golden Law in 1888 and the turn of the twentieth century, more than arrived in the United States during the same period. The "overwhelming majority" of these new arrivals in Brazil went to work on the coffee plantations, replacing the enslaved workers who had been freed by royal decree.[1]

With the influx of new coffee workers, Brazil's coffee exports began to recover from the dip that had followed emancipation. By 1896, eight years after abolition, Brazilian coffee exports had stabilized at a level that surpassed even the largest crops ever produced with enslaved labor. This increased Brazilian production, added to that of the new coffee districts that had come online in Central America and around the world, was more than the international coffee market could absorb. The price of coffee fell from an average of almost sixteen cents a pound in 1895 to less than eight cents a pound in 1897, the first full crop year at Las Tres Puertas, and the year of the birth of James Hill's daughter Alicia.[2]

As prices fell, Hill watched the possibility of profits, once virtually guaranteed, turn by fractions of cents into certain losses. The first harvest he shipped out of Las Tres Puertas fell $30,000 short of covering his costs and debts, including the $25,000 he had borrowed, and to save his business Hill increased the mortgage on his mill and plantations by $50,000. Then, as coffee prices continued to fall, bottoming out near five cents a pound by 1902, a third of what they had been seven years earlier, Hill lost that money, too, making a total debt of more than $100,000.[3] Whatever he initially believed about the prospects for success in Central America, Hill soon came to understand that the coffee business was no "goldmine." Or perhaps, he would reflect, it was just his "bad luck."[4]

It is easy to see why Hill might have blamed bad luck for the coincidence of the price collapse and the opening of Las Tres Puertas, but in truth his problem was much bigger than that.

The second crisis threatened to shrink the world market for coffee, and it originated in the largest, nearest, most "natural" market for Salvadoran coffee in particular — the United States.

The Spanish-American War began in the spring of 1898 with the sinking of the *Maine* in Havana Harbor, and it ended that summer with a new global order. By the terms of the peace, the United States acquired the former Spanish colonies of Puerto Rico, the Philippines, and Guam, plus effective authority over Cuba — a settlement that created an uncertain new reality in the hemisphere. Spain, the oldest European empire in the Americas, holding on by a thread after the Latin American revolutions of the 1820s, was out at last. But the war had launched a "new empire," the United States, which also happened to be the first nation-state created through anticolonial revolution.

Since the earliest years of Latin American independence, the common revolutionary origins of the United States and the Latin American republics had inspired important appeals to hemispheric and Pan-American solidarity. "The principle of conquest shall not . . . be recognized as admissible under American public law," U.S. secretary of state

157

James G. Blaine had vowed in 1889 at the first congress of the International Union of American Republics, later the Pan American Union, later the Organization of American States.[5] The congress was timed to demonstrate that the United States was different from the European empires that had recently carved up Africa into colonies.

Yet a decade later, in the run-up to the inaugural Pan-American Exposition, which opened in Buffalo in May 1901, rhetoric of hemispheric unity was ringing hollow, and the fair itself was proof. Originally scheduled for 1899, it had been delayed in deference to the war that won its host new colonies and put its very premise into doubt. It was not merely the fact of U.S. overseas colonies that fit uncomfortably with the Pan-American ideal. Latin American skepticism was sharpened because the new U.S. colonies included some of the most productive coffee land on the planet. Cuba, the Philippines, and especially Puerto Rico had been important coffee producers for Spain, and their plantation economies flourished under imperial tariff protection. There was also coffee in Guam, Hawaii, and American Samoa. Through its defeat of Spain, the United States, the largest market for coffee in the world, and the world's only major coffee market without an import duty, had also become a colonial coffee producer. Ambitious American officials in the Philippines even had visions of the island of Mindanao supplying the world's coffee needs.[6] This gave coffee planters and exporters across Latin America new cause for worry. Would the U.S. protect its new colonial coffee industry behind tariff barriers and imperial preferences, as European empires had done, or would it continue to import coffee duty-free from the independent republics of Latin America, nine of which were then "largely dependent" on coffee exports?[7] Especially for those in Latin America who had invested heavily in coffee in the years around Brazilian emancipation, it was an urgent question.

In light of its economic and political importance in the hemisphere, coffee was a subject of "especial attention" at the Pan-American Exposition in Buffalo. The plan was to celebrate coffee in a way that outranked "any similar exhibit ever made." Coffee was featured in the galleries of the individual republics as well as in a third-of-a-mile-long display that ran down the center of the food hall, showing the steps from "blossom to cup." Expected to be of particular interest to the North American audience was the flowering and fruiting of the coffee tree — "for beauty it cannot be excelled even in the tropics. With its deep green shining leaves and pure white, fragrant, though transitory blossoms, together with the ripening fruit, it produces a picture peculiarly effective."[8] The "effectiveness" of the coffee exhibit was in depicting the hemisphere as a kind of seamless economic collaboration, business as nature, a theme that fit the fair as a whole. While Chicago had built a "White City" for the Columbian Exposition in 1893, Buffalo planned a "Rainbow City" for the Pan-American Expo: darker shades and poorer countries out at the edges, lighter shades and richer countries in the middle, and, in the very center, the "crowning centerpiece," a 375-foot incandescent "Electric Tower" powered by nearby Niagara Falls and topped with a white "Goddess of Light."[9]

Yet the symbols of natural unity scarcely concealed the tensions underneath the surface of the event, which broke through on President's Day at the fair, September 5, 1901. The day's program featured a speech by President William McKinley. McKinley had run for the presidency in 1896 as a war hero, and his campaign highlighted an unusual act of courage. During the Battle of Antietam, his Ohio regiment near exhaustion from fighting all day, the nineteen-year-old McKinley piloted a supply wagon past Confederate sentries to deliver vats of hot coffee, "the soldier's chiefest bodily consolation," to Union troops.[10] After the Spanish-American War, an analogy suggested itself. The man nicknamed "Coffee Bill" had done it again:

160

penetrated enemy lines to deliver coffee to his side, this time in the form of island colonies.

On a sunny Thursday in Buffalo, six months into a second term he had won easily, McKinley took the stage before a crowd of fifty thousand. He considered the speech he had prepared "the most important one of my life," for it aimed to address, and even resolve, the questions and tensions that had built up around the fair.[11] "Expositions are the timekeepers of progress," began McKinley, standing on a platform fringed by a wild topiary of flags and bunting, midriff thrust forward, right hand in his trouser pocket, pages in his left. "They record the world's advancement. They stimulate the energy, enterprise and intellect of the people and quicken human genius. They go into the home. They broaden and brighten the daily life of the people. They open mighty storehouses of information to the student. Every exposition, great or small, has helped to some onward step." The president was thinking of what difference the fair would make in history, and he had come to make some.

McKinley had long been a supporter of protective tariffs to support the growth of U.S. industries, and from one perspective the Spanish-American War was a promising continuation of that policy by other means, since the new colonies could serve as exclusive markets for U.S. exports and sources of U.S. imports, just as European empires enjoyed. Yet McKinley used the occasion of the fair to change his mind. Tariffs, he said, had nurtured U.S. industries so much that they had overgrown the domestic market, smothering it under surpluses that had led to a stock market crash and nationwide depression. "We must not repose in fancied security that we can forever sell everything and buy little or nothing," he argued. "We should take from our customers such of their products as we can use without harm to our industries. . . . God and man," the president concluded, "have linked the nations together. No nation can longer be indifferent to any other."[12] Still unanswered — and greatly complicated by the Spanish-American War and the new U.S. coffee-producing colonies — was the question of whose industries were whose.

While there was outsize hope for coffee in the Philippines, Puerto Rico was the crux of the matter. Coffee had thrived on the island under Spanish rule: plantations covered 200,000 acres and produced an annual crop of sixty-six million pounds. Planters formed an important element of the elite and middle classes, and employed much of the island's working class.[13] But while Puerto Rican coffee had sold for about fifteen cents a pound in Spain, identical lots now went begging in the U.S. market at eight cents a pound.[14] The loss of the Spanish market for Puerto Rican coffee had been exacerbated by an unusually destructive hurricane in 1899. Despairing at the prospect of rebuilding while also cutting their production costs — including wages — in half to compete in the open U.S. market, Puerto Rican planters appealed to their new government for help. "We form part of this great nation," Puerto Rican planter Antonio Mariani argued, "which amply protects its products, and her duty is to protect our coffee as a product that belongs to the United States to-day, and not to permit that part of her territory, protected as it is by the Constitution and its glorious flag, to remain in so dreadful a condition."[15] For Puerto Rican coffee planters raised under Spanish rule, empire meant protection.

Mariani had a point. European empires, Germany for example, used import taxes on coffee to raise government revenue and to encourage coffee cultivation and economic development in their own colonies, which, properly managed, also served as reliable markets for industrial and consumer products. Nor was the idea of tariff protection for coffee far-fetched in the wider context of U.S. colonial policy. Puerto Rican sugar and tobacco enjoyed protected access to the U.S. market, so why not coffee, too? The Foraker Act of 1900, outlining the terms on which

Puerto Rico would be governed by the United States, had provided limited tariff protection for the island's coffee planters, putting a tax on coffee imported into the island and thereby preserving the local market for local growers. And finally President McKinley himself had given signals that he looked favorably on Puerto Rican coffee.

On the evening of his Pan-American speech, McKinley and the First Lady would view the dramatic illumination of the fair's Goddess of Light.[16] The next morning he would travel by train to see Niagara Falls, whose tremendous energy had been harnessed and converted to electricity to light up the Rainbow City and the Electric Tower. Afterward, in the late afternoon, the president would return to the fair to meet the public. As he shook hands with the crowd gathered to welcome him back, McKinley would be shot twice in the stomach at close range and mortally wounded by an anarchist who had lost his factory job in the economic slump the president hoped to remedy through freer trade.[17] But before all that, having finished his speech, left the stage, and set off on a walking tour of the grounds, McKinley stopped at the Puerto Rican pavilion for a cup of coffee.[18]

It turned out to be an empty gesture. McKinley's about-face on tariffs heralded a new era in American economic policy, and coffee was the pivot for the change. Going forward, the U.S. economy would be based more and more on exports and trade, and as the leading product of Latin America — the principal commodity available for sale in exchange for American-made goods — coffee was too important to grow in the new colonies.[19] The protective tariffs necessary to appease the planters in Puerto Rico and indulge the ambitions of colonial officials in the Philippines would have weakened the position of the U.S. in the Western Hemisphere, its self-proclaimed domain, by compromising its ability to buy coffee.

Coffee remained on the U.S. duty-free list, and the message Puerto Rican coffee planters received from their new government was clear: as part of the United States, they were on their own economically. In effect, when coffee became a "domestic" American product through the acquisition of colonies in 1898, it also became the first American mass-consumer commodity to be outsourced abroad as a matter of political and economic strategy. This was welcome news in Central America, but it was a disaster in Puerto Rico, where coffee cherries rotted on the trees, and the collapse of the industry caused "widespread suffering" and hunger "in every village and town."[20]

At the end of the Pan-American Exposition,

just before the fairground was to be closed up for the Buffalo winter, Frederic W. Taylor, the fair's director of concessions and superintendent of food and horticulture, honored standout products with gold, silver, and bronze medals. No Puerto Rican coffee medaled — not even an honorable mention — but the coffee produced by General Tomás Regalado of El Salvador won a gold, and the peaberry produced by James Hill of Santa Ana won a silver.[21]

For a man with a growing family and a growing debt, the news that his coffee — and specifically a variety, peaberry, often marketed as and mistaken for highly valued Mocha — was prized in the United States must have been some relief, even vindication, coming as it did on the heels of the price collapse and the uncertainty in the market. Yet even as Hill's coffee was awarded a silver medal for its quality, and even as worries about the U.S. market lifted, a "revolution" in coffee values was under way in the United States that upended the most basic standards by which coffee was judged and priced.

This revolution was also, in a sense, a result of the Spanish-American War, and at first it might have appeared to be a third, compounding crisis. It took hold just when Hill could have reasonably concluded that he had a silver medal to prove that he knew good coffee, and it meant, in the short run, that the standards by which his coffee had done so well would no longer apply. But instead, far from a crisis, this revolution in values would prove to be a rich opportunity for Salvadoran coffee planters, and especially for James Hill.

10.
THE TASTER

After the Spanish-American War, San Francisco grocers Austin and Reuben Hills were shipping tons of butter preserved in brine to American soldiers who were still fighting in the Philippines to disabuse Filipinos of the idea that Spain's ouster meant independence. The trip to the Philippines did not improve the freshness of butter packed in brine, so the Hills brothers began packing it in vacuum-sealed tin cans. Vacuum packing had been developed in the last quarter of the nineteenth century in Chicago, "Hog Butcher for the World," as Carl Sandburg famously described it, a city in which it was especially clear that there was money to be made by stopping time so food could move to distant markets without spoiling.

Once they started vacuum-packing butter, the Hills brothers began to think about doing the same with coffee, which was similar to butter in one significant way. "There is no item which enters into the supply of our tables, with which I am acquainted, unless it be butter, which is so easily injured in flavor as coffee," wrote New York merchant Francis Beatty Thurber in 1881.[1] The problem in both cases was fat. A coffee bean is about 12 percent fat — the source of the shimmer on roasted beans and the tiny oil slicks that sometimes appear on the surface of a cup of coffee as it cools. In unroasted green coffee, the solid fat is locked inside the structure of the plant cellulose. Roasting coffee transforms the fat into oil and releases it to the surface of the beans. This oil is responsible for much of coffee's aroma and flavor, but once exposed to the air, it begins to spoil in about a week, and grinding speeds up the decay.[2]

Before vacuum packing, the scope of a business like the Hills brothers' Arabian Coffee and Spice Mills was limited by the half-life of roasted coffee's freshness. The farther they shipped their coffee from San Francisco, the higher the likelihood that it would get stale before it was sold. As a result, many nineteenth-century grocers roasted coffee themselves and sold it in bulk, scooping beans from the bin or barrel in an amount the customer would use in a week. The other grocery options at the time were packaged brands of coffee, and the most important of these were based on proprietary solutions to the problem of fat spoilage. Brooklyn-based Arbuckles' Coffee became the first national brand in the last quarter of the nineteenth century by hermetically sealing each roasted bean inside a glaze made of sugar and egg whites. Packed for travel, Arbuckles' was "the coffee that won the West."[3] Boston's Chase & Sanborn packaged their "Seal Brand Java & Mocha" in a screw-top can that was stamped with a Latin motto: *Ne cede malis,* yield not to evil.

When Austin and Reuben Hills began using their new butter-packing machine to preserve coffee inside vacuum-sealed tin cans in San Francisco in 1900, they were hopeful that they had solved the problem of freshness, yet they were not at all sure how good their solution was. One side of their first vacuum cans was golden, and adorned with text promising that the coffee would stay fresh for twenty years; the other side was bright red, and it claimed that the coffee would stay fresh for "a lifetime." These were not simply throwaway lines. On the contrary, what the can looked like and said was exceptionally important, because the can made the coffee itself invisible, which made it impossible, by the reigning standards of quality, to say if the coffee was any good.

Once the graders at the New York Coffee Exchange had counted all the imperfections, a coffee's quality, as distinct from its grade, was a question of appearance and origin. A direct relation between the two criteria was assumed: coffee beans from a particular place looked a particular way. This is how large-beaned coffees from anywhere in the world could pass as Java, and how peaberry coffees of any type could pass as Mocha. The coffees that looked the best were judged to be the highest quality, and the best-looking coffees were those that showed most "handsomely in the hand," with the largest, brightest, cleanest beans.

Everyone in the coffee trade knew that handsomeness of the beans had nothing to do with the drink they made — that "a bright, large-beaned, handsome looking sample will sometimes turn out to be woody and comparatively flavorless." And everyone knew that "it is impossible to judge accurately of the quality and strength of coffee without roasting and making an infusion with boiling water . . . and yet, strange as it may seem, it is not customary, even with the largest dealers." The standard of handsomeness survived because it was a useful standard, and it was useful precisely for its superficiality.

Evaluating coffee by its appearance saved importers time and money. It was a quick way to judge the worth of coffee in a sack moving across a dock along with thousands of similar sacks. Only occasionally did importers take the time to roast up samples to see how the beans looked in the form in which they would reach most consumers.[4] More significant, handsomeness was useful because importers had no control over what happened to their coffee between the time it left a mill like Las Tres Puertas and the time it reached its destination port. Sacks of coffee beans might be carried from a mill to port on the backs of sweating mules; once on a ship, they might spend the whole trip sitting in the hold in a pool of bilgewater, or piled up next to other ripening cargoes, absorbing "strong foreign aromas and flavors from odoriferous substances."[5] Green coffee from Latin America especially was often shipped alongside green hides, another important Western Hemisphere product that had long been imported into the U.S. duty-free. When the essence of the animal skins seeped into coffee, the beans became "hidey," a term that came into more general use as a synonym for "sour."[6] If an importer was being exceptionally careful, he might smell a handful of newly arrived coffee to determine if it was hidey, but that was the exception, for even hidey coffee usually looked good enough to roast and sell.[7] Handsomeness could disguise the deepest flaws.

But the most important thing about handsomeness as a quality standard was that it turned the most common coffee beans into the best. The most common coffee was Brazilian, and most Brazilian coffee was grown under direct sun and on relatively low, flat ground: conditions that generally produced large, full, smooth, and consistent beans. On the other hand, Brazilian beans had a reputation for second-rate flavor — "Rio" was even turned into an adjective, "Rio-y," that signaled a musty, "off" taste. To avoid these associations, Brazilian coffee was often sold as something other than Brazilian coffee. While as much as three-quarters of the coffee consumed in the United States was the product of Brazil, very few coffees were labeled Brazilian. Conversely, many Brazilian coffees were labeled as other coffees. "Every plantation in [Brazil] produces the Java and Mocha of the markets of the United States," wrote one nineteenth-century observer of the coffee trade. "It is only an affair of sieves of differently sized meshes to classify the products of Brazilian plantations into the falsely named kinds, in order to demand a higher price from the buyer."[8]

While "Mocha" was distinctively round, like peaberry, "Java" was characteristically bigger and brighter, distinguished by a sheen that developed during long sea passages in steamy cargo holds. To produce "Java" in the absence of the genuine article, dyes and chemicals, including "very dangerous powders or mixtures," were used "to color the beans, the practice being resorted to in order to meet the prejudices of consumers in certain sections." In 1879 the U.S. Department of Agriculture made an investigation of adulterants and dyes in coffee and found lead chromate, barium sulfate, and burnt bones.[9] The dyes could be crude in part because many coffee deals were conducted on the basis of samples of green coffee "presented in sealed glass jars," so the beans never even made it as far as the hand.[10]

Under the standard of handsomeness, there was little reason for coffee millers and exporters in places other than Java and Mocha not to try to improve the appearance of their beans. For those who could get away with it, the rewards were great. In 1901, for example, the year James Hill won a medal at the Pan-American Exposition in Buffalo for his peaberry (the kind most often passed off as Mocha), "Mocha and Java" was retailing in San Francisco for thirty-five cents; Costa Rican coffee for twenty-five cents; and Salvadoran coffee wasn't advertised at all.[11] James Hill would not have sold his coffee to an importer as Mocha or Java — but, with his prizewinning peaberry, he could have sold an importer the opportunity to sell it that way in San Francisco.

Judged on the basis of its appearance, James Hill's peaberry was good coffee. After the Pan-American Exposition in Buffalo, he had the medal to prove it. But producing good coffee, producing the best coffee, was not just a question of medals, prizes, ribbons, and awards. It was not just a question of pride. Hill owed more than $100,000 to the Banco Salvadoreño, which had taken over the accounts of the London Bank of Central America. He was paying off the debt in coffee, at the rate of 1,000 bags a year, and with prices at historically low levels, it was a much bigger debt than it had been when he first borrowed the money.[12] In these circumstances, the quality of his coffee was a question of his personal success or failure — and not only his. It seemed to those who saw him at work at Las Tres Puertas during these years that James Hill was doing absolutely everything he could to get ahead for his family's sake — including some unusual things.[13]

The first unusual thing was that, in trying to make his coffee the best, Hill was humbling himself, doing something that most planters would not lower themselves to do.

Planters were a notoriously proud group, often holding forth as if they were distinguished professors of coffee. Hill, in contrast, put himself in the position of a student. He wanted to make his coffee the best, so he asked people who knew how to do it. Again the British Empire was his classroom, and its far-flung planters were his tutors. He struck up correspondences with planters and millers in the leading coffee countries in Latin

America — not only in neighboring countries with comparable conditions, but also in Brazil, renowned for its high-volume production, and in Costa Rica, renowned for its quality.

Hill's correspondent in Brazil was the manager of the Dumont estate, owned by a British syndicate and probably the largest coffee plantation in the world at the time, encompassing five million trees on more than thirteen thousand acres, all "kept like a garden," according to a *Los Angeles Times* reporter who visited in 1899. Except that this was a garden with forty miles of railroad track, on which ran a Delaware-made locomotive pulling freight cars loaded with coffee. More than five thousand people, almost all Italians, lived in twenty-three separate settlements on the plantation, which also had its own sawmill, drugstore, and bakery. The *Times* reporter had watched as the drying beans were raked on the patio by barefoot men who sweated heavily while they worked, and then taken to be sorted in a "vast room filled with Italian girls of all ages, from 10 to 20 and upward," many of whom, he saw, were "quite pretty. They have the large eyes and the bronze rosy faces of Neapolitan peasants. They have gay handkerchiefs tied about their heads, and as you enter their great dark eyes look at you." The reporter noticed that limpiadoras too were all barefoot, digging their

176

"pink toes" into the coffee sacks as they worked.[14]

Hill also exchanged letters with the manager of a mill in Costa Rica, home of perhaps the largest British interests in Central America and a well-established coffee industry. The first studies on coffee in Costa Rica had been published in 1840, the same year that commercial coffee cultivation had begun in El Salvador, and the country was renowned for its technically sophisticated coffee mills.[15]

At Las Tres Puertas, Hill had adopted a hybrid method of milling his coffee that was often used in Costa Rica, employing dry tanks in his "wet" mill for fermenting the fresh coffee cherries after they had been pulped. The process was more or less the same as in fermentation tanks filled with water — after a couple of days, the honey sagged off, and water channels carried the coffee to the drying patios — but the period of dry fermentation seemed to impart a deeper, more distinct flavor to the finished coffee bean.

Through these correspondents, Hill was linked into other conversations. In particular, he talked to the brokers and importers who roamed the Salvadoran coffee districts looking for coffee to buy and opportunities to sell products in return: flour, fertilizers, machinery, luxury goods. These roving buyers were in the business of judging quality. And if talking to these men about what they considered good coffee and how to produce it seems the obvious thing to do, the fact that Hill was eager to do it was something of a surprise to the buyers themselves — a pleasant, promising surprise.

Around 1900, the most influential — the largest and probably the richest — group of these traveling coffee buyers was German. Germans had settled Central America thickly in the middle of the nineteenth century, marrying into many prominent local families, learning the coffee business intimately, and funneling much of the Central American crop toward the German consumer market via German brokers and shippers — and, just as important, selling German products to Central American planters. In competition with the Germans were a growing number of buyers who worked for firms based in the United States, and in San Francisco in particular, where importers and exporters were hopeful of increasing their standing in the region.[16]

Among these traveling coffee buyers was James Vinter, an Englishman who, on behalf of the San Francisco flour exporters and coffee importers Otis McAllister, rode a pack mule on a slow circuit of the hot and rainy districts of Central America — San José, Costa Rica; Matagalpa, Nicaragua; Comayagua, Honduras; Santa Ana, El Salvador; Retalhuleu, Guatemala; and up through Mexico

— taking the measure of places and people and judging what could be gotten from and sold to each.[17]

In the years before he went out on the road, Vinter had worked in a coffee mill in Costa Rica. When Vinter came through Santa Ana — which was often, for he considered El Salvador the best place to do business in Central America, "even better than Costa Rica," and he thought that Santa Ana in particular had the potential to produce the best coffee he had ever seen — James Hill would invite his fellow Englishman up to Las Tres Puertas to compare notes. Vinter would take some documents out of his case and talk of his experience in Costa Rica, and Hill would bring out some data of his own he had collected from Costa Rican mills, plus figures from his own mill for comparison.[18]

There was something in it for both men. Vinter was so impressed by what he saw at Las Tres Puertas, including the dry fermentation method, that he wanted to make other coffee mills in El Salvador more like Hill's, and he told his employers in San Francisco to send out a letter instructing other millers on how to prepare their coffee as Hill did. For his part, Hill asked Vinter to ask his bosses to inspect his coffee and provide their "candid opinion" about what he could do "to improve it for the San Francisco market." In Vinter's long experience in Central America, this eagerness to learn was not only rare, but it also marked Hill as a promising bet. It was the "Dr. Know All's," Vinter had seen, who always got into the most trouble. And when, in 1904, Vinter made a list of the best coffee producers in Santa Ana — the best place for coffee in all of Central America — he put James Hill's name at the top.[19]

Yet as impressed as he was by the coffee coming out of Las Tres Puertas, Vinter could not ignore the shadow of a different feeling about its owner. He could not shake his suspicion that James Hill was something more than just the eager student, and he worried that by dealing with Hill he and his bosses might find themselves on the losing end of a longer game. On his travels around Central America, Vinter had met many people with opinions to offer on the subject of James Hill, and none were good. In Santa Ana, moreover, Vinter had seen how everyone who dealt with Hill did so cautiously. Everyone, that is, except the bankers, who seemed, for some reason, to be doing the opposite.

The second unusual thing Hill was doing to "get ahead for his family's sake" was very different from the humility he displayed in his efforts to learn. At a time when everyone else was wary of depressed prices, Hill was acting boldly, borrowing more and more money and jumping out ahead of the market.

180

When the Santa Ana coffee crop was late in 1905, buying and selling was lagging, too. Most years the market began to pick up in the late fall, but in early January 1906, Vinter reported to Otis McAllister in San Francisco that "hardly any transactions" had taken place. In fact, he said, James Hill "was the only man buying coffee of all descriptions this year in Santa Ana." While every other mill was rather quiet, Las Tres Puertas was "open day and night," and Hill had just secured a new credit of $100,000 to spend on coffee — this on top of his existing debt.[20] Vinter could not figure out Hill's game — why he seemed so confident, and why the banks were supporting him so liberally.

Then, the next month, a group of planters in São Paulo, Brazil, adopted a new approach to the depressed market that had taken hold a decade earlier, after the influx of Italian immigrant labor pushed Brazilian crops to new levels. The São Paulo planters began to hold their coffee off the market, reducing supply as a way to increase the price. To do so, they borrowed money from a group of international financiers, in effect buying their own coffee, with an eye toward selling it once the price rose. Perhaps the largest estate in São Paulo, where the new scheme had originated, was the Dumont estate — managed, of course, by James Hill's correspondent.

As word of the São Paulo plan got out, the

181

coffee buyers roaming Central America began to fear that prices were about to shoot up. Because James Hill was the only one who had been buying all through what had been a bad season, as if he had known that a price increase was coming, he soon found himself in a very strong position.

Hill's corner on the supply in Santa Ana was matched by extraordinary demand from around the world. In addition to San Francisco, he was selling in Copenhagen, in Winnipeg, in Toronto, in Australia, in New Zealand, and especially in France.[21] Thanks "to his superior method of preparation," Hill had no shortage of offers for his brand El Pinal — "the pine grove," named for a peak above his mill — which had an especially "nice appearance," James Vinter acknowledged in a letter to San Francisco. So strong was the demand for Hill's coffee that Vinter knew that it would be difficult to get any for Otis McAllister, despite the relationship he had cultivated with Hill, and despite certain assurances Hill had previously made, which was, Vinter complained to his bosses, "exactly his nature when it suits him."[22]

But just at that moment, Vinter believed he saw through Hill at last. "I have been giving my very stricktest attention," Vinter wrote to San Francisco, more formally than usual, "to the colour of Hill's coffee, and now I am prepared to prove to you," he went on, "and will do so when next in San Francisco, that the PINAL mark is artificially coloured, although . . . you cannot detect it by rubbing it [with] your handkerchief, or even by moistening it." The sophistication of the fakery only increased Vinter's satisfaction with himself. "It is very cleverly done indeed and I think I have found the process, and I will try it . . . when I come to Frisco."[23] Even in cheating, Vinter ranked Hill the best.

Yet no sooner had he posted these allegations than Vinter received, in quick succession, four letters from his bosses expressing their eagerness to secure some of Hill's El Pinal. "As you seemed anxious," Vinter replied, "I thought it the best policy to cable you the lowest price you could obtain same at, owing to the good demand Hill has for it in France today."[24] Vinter had missed his chance — the dyeing allegations did not come up again. And even if they were true, they no longer mattered, at least in San Francisco.

Once they started vacuum-packing coffee in tin cans at the turn of the twentieth century, it was much easier for Hills Bros. to get Java and Mocha. They no longer had any need for magic coffee bins or colored powders or even peaberry. Instead, they could simply write the words on the can. The phrase "Java and Mocha" appeared five times on their first

183

cans: twice in large, bold print on the sides meant for display, and three times in smaller explanatory text: "We guarantee this to be the very best grade of Java and Mocha packed in the United States." This guarantee was hardly as straightforward as it sounded, not only because the coffee inside was almost certainly not Java and Mocha — not exclusively, anyway — but also because the Hills brothers were developing their own definition of "best."

Dealers of butter, milk, and eggs would have been particularly sensitive to the limitations of judging coffee quality by handsomeness. Anyone who has cracked a rotten egg or glugged sour milk knows that appearance is not the most reliable indicator of freshness. It was in keeping with their experience as grocers that the Hills brothers began, at the end of the nineteenth century, to judge coffee by its invisible qualities. Working backward from coffee drinking, they began to evaluate coffee beans in terms of the coffee they made: its aroma, its flavor, its properties "in the cup." The Hills brothers were among the first coffee importers and roasters in the country to value coffee this way, but the new standard of quality caught on quickly.[25] Especially in San Francisco, it made good business sense.

Before there was a canal cut across the Central American isthmus, San Francisco importers and roasters struggled to compete with New York, New Orleans, and European ports for a share of the Atlantic trade. They enjoyed privileged access to coffees from the Pacific coast of Latin America, but these coffees did not show well by the standard of handsomeness in the hand. Grown at comparatively high altitudes, on steep slopes, and under shade, Central American beans especially tended to be small, gnarled, and irregular compared with Brazilian beans, and less consistent, too, since individual lots from plantations and mills were smaller than what the vast Dumont estate, for example, could produce in a year.

Disadvantaged under the standard of handsomeness, San Francisco roasters invented a new standard. This new standard was derived from a new method of analysis and expressed in a new language of quality. The new method was the cup test, which took appearance as the starting point rather than the last word. First a visual evaluation of the green bean, and then a visual evaluation of the roasted bean, and, finally, the real test: brewing, smelling, tasting.

Conducted in the high laboratory style characteristic of corporate attempts to objectify sensuous experience, these procedures came to be rigidly structured. The coffees under consideration were roasted, ground, and portioned into cups arranged around the edge of a circular table. A standard volume of water, heated to just below the boiling point, was added to each cup, and the mixture was left to steep for a fixed period of time. When the brew was ready, the expert tester went to work.

His instrument was a spoon: he dipped it into a cup, pushed the grounds to the side, brought the liquid to his lips, and sipped, "holding each sip in his mouth only long enough to get the full strength of the flavor. He spits out the coffee into a brass cuspidor which is designed for the purpose. The expert never swallows the liquor." Then the expert began to judge: "if the drink has body and is smooth, rich, acidy, or mellow; if it is winy, neutral, harsh, or Rioy; if it is musty, groundy, woody, or grassy; or if it is rank, hidey (sour), muddy, or bitter."[26] With cup testing, judging the worth of coffee was no longer a matter of examining its appearance and counting its imperfections. It was now a matter of deriving adjectives from nouns to describe the experience of drinking a cup. There were no fixed numerical standards, just a flexible new vocabulary.

From its origins in San Francisco, cup testing spread east to become the universal standard for evaluating coffee in the United States in the first quarter of the twentieth century. Its spread was helped along by the increasing power of coffee roasters, more of

186

which grew into important consumer brands once they solved the problem of freshness and expanded their markets geographically. There were clear benefits to the rise of cup testing in the United States. As the desirable qualities once strictly associated with Mocha and Java were discovered closer to home, the map of coffee quality was redrawn. "When the roasters began to examine coffees for their taste, values were of course revolutionized," increasing the commercial stakes of the coffee trade with Latin America. This was especially true of coffees from Central America, where San Francisco merchants had the strongest economic interests. "High-grown coffees, that had theretofore been penalized for the small size of the bean," such as those grown on the Santa Ana Volcano, "soon brought a premium, and have ever since been in great demand."[27]

The findings of cup tests underwrote a new categorical distinction in the coffee market: "Brazils" versus "milds." At first "mild" coffee simply meant coffee from anywhere other than Brazil, which had a reputation for producing coffees that were "quite the reverse of mild."[28] But over time, as it was necessary to define the category for the purposes of trading contracts, "mild coffee" was formalized and capitalized, "Mild coffee," and took on a more specific meaning: coffees that were definitively "sweet in the cup."[29] These coffees were known for having "more body, more acidity, and a much finer aroma" than Brazils, as well as more "distinctive individual characteristics," being produced under more diverse conditions than Brazilian coffees.[30] Brazilian coffees came to be considered "price" coffees, while mild coffees were increasingly known for "quality."[31]

The definition of mild coffees as quality coffees that were "sweet in the cup" went hand in hand with the rise of the vacuum-sealed coffee can, the justification for which, after all, was the preservation of flavor. Especially because canned coffee was more expensive than bulk beans, one San Francisco coffee trader reasoned, "a highly advertised vacuum-packed coffee must have a distinctive flavor to assure permanent favor with the public," and a distinctive coffee, in turn, had to have a large component of mild coffee. He predicted: "Larger volumes of vacuum-packed coffee . . . will mean increasing importations of mild coffee to the United States."[32] Mild coffees made up the "flavor" component of the characteristic blends used by national brands. Brazils were used as filler.

Yet even as quality "mild" coffees from Latin America, including those produced on the Santa Ana Volcano, gained in value in the coffee trade of the United States, they failed to gain in public renown. Part of the reason for this, ironically, was the U.S. law that aimed to end mislabeling — the 1906 Pure Food and Drug Act.

The immediate purpose of the act was to protect consumers in the United States against manufacturers who promised one thing and delivered another — not only foreign substances passed off as pork or beef but all products that were "adulterated or misbranded or poisonous or deleterious." This emphasis shaped the act's directives largely in the negative: it prohibited lying — for example, labeling Salvadoran coffee as Mocha — but it did not strictly mandate truthfulness: it did not require that Salvadoran coffee be sold as Salvadoran coffee.

After the passage of the Pure Food and Drug Act, Hills Bros. could no longer sell their vacuum-packed coffee as "the highest grade of Java and Mocha," but they did not have to say precisely what it was. Instead, they rebranded their top-of-the-line vacuum-packed product as "Highest-Grade Vacuum-Packed." Several years later, they changed the name again, this time to what everyone already called it, "Red Can Brand."[33] As the brand became the can, the can became the coffee. And though they no longer claimed to be selling genuine Java and Mocha, Hills Bros. kept the trademarked image they had created for their first vacuum cans, a figure of an Arab in a flowing *thawb,* drinking deeply from a coffee cup. This was "the

189

taster," and a statue of him still stands in the courtyard of what used to be the Hills Bros. factory on the Embarcadero, and is now the San Francisco campus of the Wharton School of the University of Pennsylvania.

What the Pure Food and Drug Act did not outlaw was the coloring of coffee. On the contrary, it specifically allowed for the use of "harmless colorants." Yet with Java and Mocha now largely off the table, and a new standard of quality based on "sweetness in the cup," the color and size of the beans were no longer so important. Unlike size or color, "sweetness in the cup" came from sugars developed in the coffee cherries as they ripened, and from the care taken in the mills. It came from specific types of work done in the process of cultivating, harvesting, and milling coffee, under particular conditions, in certain parts of the world — for example, Hill's dry fermentation process. And in this way, as it became the new standard on the Pacific coast and then across the U.S., the vacuum-sealed coffee can at once preserved and highlighted distinctive conditions of production in Central America, but also made those conditions and those places disappear within a blend and behind a brand name.

From this invisible place, James Hill turned his plantations, his mill, and his family to focus more directly on California. The rise of the vacuum-sealed coffee can had heightened the incentive to improve his coffee for the San Francisco market, and he sent his children to study there.

11.
SPECIAL WORK

It was a rainy Monday, September 10, 1917, when thirteen-year-old Federico Hill, James Hill's youngest son, steamed into San Francisco Bay aboard the Pacific Mail's aging single-stack SS *City of Para*. Federico — or, as the hastily completed Emergency Certificate of British Nationality secured two days before his departure had it, "Frederick Alexander Hill," British subject born in El Salvador — was traveling comfortably in first class, with five hundred dollars in his pocket. On the other hand, he was alone, he could not speak, read, or write in English, and he expected to be away from home for seven years.

Federico had boarded the *Para* at the Salvadoran port of Acajutla two weeks earlier. In San Francisco he expected to find a friendly party waiting for him on the dock: Miss Mary L. Lockey, principal of the Castilleja School in Palo Alto, California; her students, Federico's sisters, Alicia and María

Hill; and Edward Polhemus, of the Hamberger-Polhemus Company, coffee importers, his father's agent in town. James Hill had written to Edward Polhemus ahead of his son's ship, though not much ahead, asking him to meet and look after the boy. Polhemus was already managing the administrative details of the California educations of Federico's four older siblings — brothers Jaime and Eduardo, sisters Alicia and María — and he knew what to do.

Polhemus promptly wrote to the Commissioner of Immigration on Angel Island in San Francisco Bay, expressing his willingness to assume responsibility for the son of "Mr. J. Hill, a wealthy English coffee planter in Salvador." He promised that Federico would be placed in school as his father intended, certified that his firm was willing to pay bonds in any amount prescribed by law, and requested that immigration inspectors "pass the boy through" as speedily as possible.

To help pass Federico through, James Hill had sent his son with a certificate of good health made out by the family doctor in Santa Ana and notarized by a lawyer, and also offered his own testimony: "His parents are both strong & healthy people and he has lived most of his time out of doors, amongst the coffee plantations." Nevertheless, because Federico was under sixteen and unaccompanied, U.S. immigration inspectors flagged him for examination and further inquiry. As soon as he disembarked from the *City of Para,* Federico boarded a ferry that took him back out into San Francisco Bay, to the U.S. Immigration Station on Angel Island. He spent his first night in the United States in a bunk in the men's detention barracks, awaiting a hearing before the Board of Special Inquiry.

When the board met the following day, Edward Polhemus was there, as he had promised. Called as a witness, Polhemus explained that he handled virtually all of James Hill's business in San Francisco, and he made the board understand that it was business he did not take lightly: "We are only too happy," Polhemus said, "to do whatever he asks of us." For his part, Federico Hill gave no indication that his trip, not to mention the prospect of staying seven years in a country to which he had never traveled and whose language he did not speak, troubled him in the least. On the contrary, the boy who appeared before the three-member Board of Special Inquiry was "a clean-cut youth, apparently very refined." Through an interpreter, Federico gave good account of himself, where he had come from, and where he was going. For five years, Federico said, he had been studying in El Salvador. But there were "no colleges there to continue my studies," so he had come to San Francisco "to complete my education." His father, he explained, had paid his passage.

"In what business is your father engaged?" asked the Board of Special Inquiry.

Federico answered definitively: "Bookkeeper."

"In what concern?"

"He is a bookkeeper and coffee merchant and planter in Santa Ana."

In light of his refinement, his appearance, and his bearing, in light of the fact that his father was a man of affairs, and in light of the fact that the witness Edward Polhemus was a man of standing in the community, the Board of Special Inquiry did not hesitate to let young Federico Hill into the United States "outright."[1] So began his education in America.

There was no doubt that El Salvador was "very much behind in education," as Mauricio Meardi put it. Meardi was an Italian immigrant who dominated commercial agriculture in eastern El Salvador, and one of the richest men in the country, but in September 1917 he was babysitting — escorting two of his grandchildren, ten and twelve, from El Salvador to San Francisco to place them in school. The three of them had arrived in San Francisco on the *Para* with Federico Hill. When his grandchildren had their hearing before the Board of Special Inquiry, Meardi admitted that he didn't know where he was going to enroll them. He had "not sufficiently studied the matter," primarily because he thought that children should be sent to Europe to be educated. And indeed his grandchildren would be, he said, once the war was over. In the interim, he planned to "find something suitable" in or near San Francisco, and until he did, the children would stay with him in the Hotel Richelieu on Van Ness.[2]

If James Hill agreed with Mauricio Meardi that education was very much behind in El Salvador, behind to the degree that there was no suitable place where his children could be educated after primary school, he disagreed on the relative merits of a European education. In 1912 he had accompanied his older boys, Jaime and Eduardo, to San Francisco to get them started in school there, and since then they had studied at a number of boarding schools around the Bay.[3]

The five hundred dollars Federico brought to San Francisco was half of the first year's tuition at the Manzanita Hall School for Boys, founded in 1891 by an acolyte of Stanford president David Starr Jordan to funnel students to the university.[4] Manzanita also had the advantage of being in Palo Alto, near the Castilleja School for Girls, where Federico's sisters were enrolled. Federico's eldest brother Jaime had attended two other schools in the area: the Mount Tamalpais

Military Academy in San Rafael — by 1912 the only school in the West that still offered cavalry and artillery training — and the Montezuma Mountain School for Boys, founded in 1911 by Ernest A. Rogers in the farmhouse of a plum orchard in the Santa Cruz Mountains outside Los Gatos.[5] Rogers's first job was at the Mount Tamalpais Military Academy, but he left because he had a different idea for how to "develop men from boy stuff," as the Montezuma motto put it. The development of Montezuma men was based on a strict regimen of health and discipline (no coffee or any other stimulants were permitted, and regular chores were required), active self-governance (students made the rules and enforced them), and a course of education in ethics designed to prepare the sons of the elite to lead.[6] Many students went on from Mount Tam, Manzanita, and Montezuma to Stanford, but the Hill boys were on a different trajectory. As Federico had testified, they had come to California to learn how to be coffee merchants and planters in Santa Ana. And in certain ways their father was right — San Francisco was the best place to learn that.

By the time Federico became Frederick in the summer of 1917, what happened in San Francisco mattered very much in El Salvador's coffee districts. The city's influence derived from a Pacific coast coffee trade that was, as Edward Polhemus testified before the Board of Special Inquiry, eager to have James Hill's business and everyone else's, too. The development of San Francisco into the mercantile capital of the western United States, combined with the advantages that the city's coffee roasters had discovered in cup testing and vacuum packing, had increased the stakes of winning control of the Central American coffee crop away from the European empires, especially Germany, that had been working to consolidate their own commercial power in the Americas.

For years, San Francisco merchants had lamented the strong position that Germans had achieved in Central America by marrying the locals. For jealous American coffee dealers, the "sentimental" tendency of the Latin Americans to favor family in business gave German firms a decided advantage in buying coffee and, just as important, selling exports. Before the turn of the century, San Francisco had established itself as the best U.S. market for Central American coffee, yet it took a comparatively small slice of the region's annual harvest: 200,000 bags a year or so from a crop sometimes ten times that size.[7] And even that portion began to look increasingly tenuous after 1899, when the Hamburg-based Kosmos Line began steam service to the Pacific coast of the United States.

The first Kosmos steamer, the *Tanis,* sailed into San Francisco Bay on December 14, 1899, three months after departing Hamburg. It was "a splendid carrier" capable of making "fourteen knots on a very economical coal consumption." San Francisco papers reported that the captain, a German by the name of Schultz, was known in the Spanish-speaking ports he plied as "El Simpático Capitán." Packed on board was two thousand tons of cargo valued at three-quarters of a million dollars, which the *Tanis* had picked up at ports all the way up and down the Pacific coast of the American continent, discharging German-made goods as she went. Alongside the *Tanis,* the Kosmos line was putting into Pacific service the *Volumnia, Hathor, Octavia,* and *Luxor.*[8] For San Francisco merchants and shippers, the omens were not good.

With its geographical advantage in Central America now under threat, the Pacific Mail Steamship Company responded to the encroachment of the Kosmos Line in exactly the same way as it had responded to James Otis and Hall McAllister — with a rate war. Coffee was what Central American exporters had to send: the only product available in quantities substantial enough to make a difference in shipping revenues. Eventually the Pacific Mail even offered to transport coffee

199

"not only without charge, but to pay the shipper a premium for the privilege of carrying his freight."[9] By degrees, the preferential shipping rates toward San Francisco pulled the Central American coffee trade not only away from Germany, but from New Orleans and New York, too.

The shift was locked in after 1914, when Atlantic shipping lanes were cut off by naval blockades and European banking was frozen by war. San Francisco merchants took full advantage. More and more import-export houses sent representatives to ride the Central American circuit, getting to know each individual plantation and planter, assessing from observation and conversation who would be a reliable client and who would produce good coffee.

The delicate cup qualities that determined the value of Central American coffees in San Francisco were known to "vary from plantation to plantation" so widely that "on adjoining plantations there is from three to five cents a pound difference in quality, from the standpoint of cup merit." From the standpoint of cup merit, it was not enough to get coffee from a particular region of the world, or from a particular country, or even from a particular region within that country. Cup quality came from the individual plantation, from the practices of the individual planter. San Francisco buyers traveling in Central

America not only attempted to judge a planter's credibility and creditworthiness, as J. H. Vinter had done for Otis McAllister a decade earlier, but also to predict the cup qualities of the coffee from the condition of each plantation and each coffee mill.

During the war years, San Francisco merchants, operating in a commercial vacuum, collected their own "intimate knowledge" of every plantation and mill in Central America. Those planters whose plantations and mills suited the eyes of San Francisco brokers and importers found ready credit and eager buyers.[10] By the end of the world war, San Francisco merchants had taken control of the Central American coffee trade. They were buying on an outright-purchase basis five times more coffee than they had a decade earlier, a million bags a year, 12 percent of U.S. imports, and rising.[11]

The Hill boys were in California to learn how to make themselves, their plantations, their mill, and their coffee appeal to San Francisco coffee importers and roasters. After graduation from Montezuma, Jaime Hill, James Hill's eldest son, went not to Stanford but to the University of California's agricultural school at Davis, located in the orchard land outside Sacramento. Along with his studies at Davis, Hill undertook "special work" at the University of California, Berkeley, in the

201

spring of 1920 "to fit him for helping manage his coffee plantations in El Salvador."[12]

What was there to learn of coffee plantations in Berkeley? Coffee, actually, had been one of the first items on the agenda of Dr. Eugene Woldemar Hilgard when he was hired to establish agricultural science at the University of California in 1874, at the height of the wheat boom. The serious and stubborn Hilgard was a good choice for the position. He had trained in leading laboratories in Germany, including Bunsen's, and had worked on the frontiers of commercial agriculture at universities in Michigan and, during the Civil War, Mississippi, where he helped Lee's army source salt and nitrates. Before his career was over, Hilgard would be celebrated as "the American father of soil science."[13]

Yet not long after arriving in California, Hilgard found himself with bad news to deliver. A shrub that many suspected to be coffee had been discovered high on the steep and rocky slopes of the Sierra Nevada and brought to the lab in Berkeley for a thorough workup. It fell to Hilgard to reveal that the shrub was not coffee but California buckthorn, very similar to coffee in some ways — bearing bright red berries almost identical to those that cluster on the branches of a coffee tree — but endowed with none of the properties that made coffee commercially valuable. The unhappy implication: coffee was not native to California.

Yet that hardly discouraged Californians from trying to grow it. At the same time many Latin American republics were moving into coffee production in the second half of the nineteenth century, Californians harbored their own hopes for coffee. Inspired by and jealous of schemes to establish coffee plantations across the post-emancipation cotton South in Florida, Louisiana, and Texas, Californians sent eager letters to the Department of Agriculture requesting seeds. So Hilgard got a new assignment: make coffee grow in California.

He began some experiments in 1877, using seeds purchased from a Philadelphia merchant with interests in Liberia, and making early trials around the university. The following year, he added plantings grown from Guatemalan and Costa Rican seeds. Hilgard offered Guatemalan seeds for trials in Southern California, too, and some hopeful planters reported success in germinating seeds acquired from the Kona district of Hawaii. By 1879, these experiments appeared so promising that the California State Agriculture Society deemed local coffee production inevitable.

Yet the trees never flourished. By the mid-1880s, it was clear to Hilgard that coffee trees could not endure the frosts that iced even the most promising growing areas. The failure of six coffee trees that had seemed to thrive in Riverside for four years was especially disappointing. When the last of these died in 1888, the year of the abolition of slavery in Brazil, Hilgard again wrote the eulogy for coffee agriculture in California — and again he was premature.[14] There would be no coffee crop in California, at least not until the temperature rose, but, as the Hill boys would learn, there were valuable lessons for coffee planters growing everywhere on the trees.

The wheat boom that followed the gold rush transformed California's landscape, and so did the subsequent wheat bust. By the 1880s, the state's grain fields had become so highly mechanized that production outpaced global demand. The resulting fall in prices encouraged landowners to shift their resources to new crops: sugar beets, vegetables, and especially tree and vine fruits. With the arrival of the refrigerator car in 1888, the orchards and groves of the great valleys, San Joaquin, Salinas, Sacramento, Santa Clara, and others, became California's new gold mines, producing oranges, lemons, plums, pears, grapes, apples, figs, dates, apricots, olives, and more. Orchard crops accounted for only 4 percent of the value of California's agricultural produce in 1879. Fifty years later, they were 80 percent.[15] As California became the world capital of fruit orchards, it also became an important center of pomology, the science of growing fruit. On the University Farm at Davis, out in the orchard land around Sacramento, and later at Berkeley, Jaime Hill was learning coffee by analogy: orchards to plantations, one type of stone fruit to another.

The studies of the Hill boys in California tracked their father's mind across the Santa Ana Volcano, echoing his hopes and worries, asking his questions in their voices. During his studies at Berkeley, Jaime Hill recorded in his notebook a three-part dialogue among his father, his professors, and himself. Perhaps the most complex conversation, and the most important question Jaime Hill tried to answer during his time at the University of California, stemmed from one of his father's own experiments in coffee agronomy.

The experiment had begun one afternoon in 1910 or so, two years before he sent his older sons to California, when James Hill was invited to lunch at the plantation of a German friend, Federico Bockler, just outside Santa Ana, near the small town of Chalchuapa. Bockler was married to a daughter of a well-known politician, and through this connection a former president of Guatemala had given him some coffee seedlings different from what was most common in El Salvador, a strain of Arabica known as *común,* or *typica.* The foreign seedlings were a cultivar of

Arabica called Borbón, or Bourbon, after the island (now Réunion) off the coast of Madagascar where the French had introduced coffee by fiat two centuries earlier. Bourbon coffee, which had been brought to Guatemala by Jesuit priests, was also grown in Brazil. Historically its market value derived in part from the fact that its seeds did a passable imitation of Mocha, and in part from the fact that it gave unusually high yields. Bockler had planted a corner of his plantation with Bourbon, and he told Hill that he expected to get two or three times as much coffee from those trees as from the standard Arabica.

Intrigued, Hill arranged to buy that year's Bourbon harvest from Bockler to mill in Las Tres Puertas, with the idea of also planting some of the seeds he extracted from the harvested cherries on his own plantations. Of course any planter would have been eager to triple his crop, but the math in this case was not so simple. It was not a question of straight multiplication. There was also subtraction to do. Bourbon produced higher yields, certainly, than the variety of Arabica most common on El Salvador's plantations, yet it was also considered to be of lower quality, perhaps as a result of its association with Brazil, a significant factor especially in a country whose coffee was valued in terms of its difference from Brazilian coffee. In fact, after Hill processed the harvest he bought from Bockler, he sent some of the milled Bourbon coffee to his agent in Trieste, some to his agent in Bremen, some to his agent in Hamburg, and some to San Francisco. From Europe James Hill heard good things — that the Bourbon coffee, when roasted, gave exactly the color Europeans liked. But from San Francisco — where coffee's appearance was less and less important, in light of cup tests and vacuum packing — the response was not favorable. San Francisco importers told Hill he was going to ruin the country's reputation for quality if he started producing Bourbon.[16]

There was a calculation to be made, and a risky one. On the hand, if the higher yields proved high enough, they could make up for the lower quality. If Hill could increase the quantity by three times without decreasing the quality by two-thirds, he would still come out ahead. He planted Bourbon on four plantations, including one where the soil seemed exhausted and the crops had been unimpressive.

When word of the Bourbon plantings got out around Santa Ana, the local response echoed the thinking in San Francisco. Planting coffee trees known for producing lower-quality beans on the Santa Ana Volcano threatened the reputation of the entire region. The banks that had lent Hill money were so troubled by the project that they sent a hast-

207

ily organized board of review, two bankers and a fellow coffee planter, to see if he had lost his mind.

Yet when the first crops came in, the results were better than Hill had hoped they would be, and each tree produced about four times what he had gotten out of standard Arabica trees.[17] And Hill discovered another property of Bourbon that also had to be factored into the business calculation. Bourbon trees proved to be hardier than typical Salvadoran Arabica, thriving in climates where other varietals struggled: high altitudes where the temperature was colder than ideal, as well as low altitudes previously thought too hot for coffee.[18]

The hardiness of Bourbon trees opened up more and more of El Salvador's land to coffee. Hill began to buy old, unprofitable, unproductive plantations and convert them to Bourbon. On this new land, the new trees produced larger crops. Raising trees known for quantity in a district known for quality, Hill was, in a sense, Brazilianizing Salvadoran coffee — mass-producing mild coffee. As other planters followed suit, coffee climbed farther up and reached farther down the slopes of the volcano and the foothills all around, and Bourbon coffee became the foremost cultivar in El Salvador — so much so that within decades it came to be called *"nacional."*[19]

Planting Bourbon coffee also took Hill away from his original focus on producing the best coffee by any means necessary. How to be the best was no longer the question. The new question was arguably more complicated, from a pomological point of view. For despite its quantifiable benefits, there was another, perhaps unanticipated, disadvantage to Bourbon. In the days when coffee was sold in bulk and judged by its appearance, the small size of the Bourbon coffee bean, the basis of its resemblance to Mocha, had been an asset. But when the rise of cup testing and vacuum packing made appearance less important, the small size of the Bourbon bean became a liability. While it was true that Bourbon trees produced more cherries than did other types of trees, their smaller seeds also meant that more Bourbon cherries were needed to produce the same amount of coffee — for coffee that entered international commerce was measured by weight, not by the number of beans in a lot. With typical Salvadoran Arabica, five hundred pounds of cherries produced one hundred pounds of export-ready green coffee. Yet it took six hundred pounds of Bourbon cherries to produce the same hundred pounds of beans. So the new question, which Jaime Hill put to his professors at the University of California, was how to increase the size of each Bourbon seed until 500 pounds of ripe Bourbon cherries produced the same 100 pounds of export-ready coffee beans as standard Arabica.[20]

In California, Jaime Hill tried to break down the problem. Drawing on his training in pomology, he assumed that each chemical component of the soil corresponded to an attribute of the coffee tree growing in it: potash to the development of the fruit, nitrogen to the development of the leaves, phosphoric acid to the development of the roots, and lime to the development of the trunk and branches. But he could identify no chemical that specifically contributed to the size of the seed. The problem hit precisely on the way in which coffee was unlike California's orchard crops. The seed in the middle of a plum was a pit to be thrown away, and fruit growers had no interest in increasing the size of the waste. With coffee the opposite was true: the seed was the coffee bean, the only part worth anything. Working with his professors, Jaime concluded that the only way to increase the size of the seed — the tree in miniature — was to give the tree more of everything it needed to make itself grow, and the only way to give the tree more of everything it needed was to make the soil richer and more conductive, to increase what the tree's roots were taking in — water, chemical fertilizers, and ambient nutrients.[21]

At this point, Jaime Hill, though he was

210

three thousand miles from Santa Ana, ran into the same problem that his father ran into on his plantations: the problem of holes. Twice a year, the soil of the plantations needed to be turned over, which meant digging holes of twenty-seven cubic inches that would be stuffed with weeds and bean vines and other green fertilizers. With three hundred holes per acre, more than 7 percent of the land area of each plantation would be dug up in the process. Sitting at his desk in Northern California, Jaime thought his father might manage to increase the size of the Bourbon coffee bean if he was able to increase the size of each of these holes and get more of everything coffee trees needed into the soil. But Jaime worried that the change would be impractical, if not impossible, to carry through in Santa Ana because, as his father had told him so many times, it would be hard to find people to do the work, and harder still to make them do it right.

It is familiar now to talk of factory farms. The term captures the overwhelming scale and scope of modern agricultural operations, the targeted microbiological interventions into and genetic modifications of plant and animal natures, and the mechanization and automation of farming's basic labor processes in the name of high yields and low costs all year round. Without diminishing the conse-

211

quences of the industrialization of nonhuman nature, it is worth pointing out that the description of farms as factories originally referred to what it was like to work on them.

During the worst years of the Great Depression, two decades before the start of his career as editor of *The Nation,* Carey McWilliams worked as a labor lawyer in Los Angeles. The cases that came across his desk made him wonder why the California landscapes that looked so placid produced such bitter conflict between employers and employees. McWilliams began to "spend long hours in the library" and "make forays into the San Joaquin Valley to see . . . just what went on in the fields and in the labor camps." There, beneath the surface of that "quiet word," agriculture, he found a clamorous "large-scale, intensive, diversified, mechanized" race to the bottom. In his 1939 book *Factories in the Field,* McWilliams described how, beginning around 1870, after the California gold rush had slowed down, a new class of "industrial agriculturalists" took over California's land and economy. They made water flow backward, conjured gardens from wastelands, and in the process became as rich as sheikhs. The source of their extraordinary power and wealth was a "miserable . . . intimidated . . . starving, destitute" army of migrant laborers, the latest group of new arrivals always pitted against the previous. Chasing grueling work and barely adequate food and shelter across the state's wide valleys, this "agricultural proletariat" made up "a more motley crew" than any ever "assembled in this country by a great industry." The story of the shift from farm to the "farm factory," as McWilliams put it, was the story of "the exploitation of farm labor."[22]

Yet farm labor was a subject scarcely addressed at the University of California's agricultural extension. The vast majority of the courses offered while Jaime Hill was enrolled there focused on plants and land rather than people. None of the new or ongoing research projects registered by the university in 1920–1921 dealt with labor. And labor was the focus of only one of the fifty-plus circulars and pamphlets available free from the University's Agricultural Experiment Station.[23] Nevertheless, the fact was plain to all orchard men — just as it was clear to every coffee planter — that without labor, and without the effective control and management of labor, there was no farm and no farming.

The absence of labor from the agricultural curriculum at Davis can be explained in part by the fact that there was already a well-established school of thought governing the management of farm workers in California. It involved, as Carey McWilliams discovered, the pitting of social groups, defined by race

213

and ethnicity, against each other. "White Laborers" — the Irish, Norwegians, Danes, Germans, Poles, and Austrians — against "Italian and Portuguese Laborers," against "Negro Laborers," against "Mexican Laborers," against "Indian Laborers," against "Japanese Laborers," against "Hindu Laborers," against "Chinese Laborers," against whatever new groups arrived to seek less difficult lives in California.

Yet one professor at the University of California, Richard L. Adams, did see room for refinement within this framework, and he took up the question of farm labor in his scholarship.[24] A popular teacher at at the agricultural extension in Davis and in Berkeley, Adams recognized that on the question of labor "hinges the success or failure" of the farm. His definitive treatment of the subject was published in 1921, while Jaime Hill was in residence at the university, puzzling over the problem of the small Bourbon bean and wondering how to put his academic insight into practice on the Santa Ana Volcano.

Professor Adams was from Dorchester, Massachusetts. After graduating from Boston University in 1905, he moved to California at twenty-three to sell insecticide, and subsequently he was hired as a manager for two of the state's largest factory farmers: Spreckels Sugar Company, and Miller and Lux. The first was a beet-sugaring enterprise in the

214

Salinas Valley run by the German immigrant Claus Spreckels, who controlled a good share of sugar cultivation and refining in both California and Hawaii. Miller and Lux were also German immigrants. Their San Francisco–based cattle-raising/butchering/ meatpacking operation was the only agricultural concern to rank among the country's two hundred largest industrial enterprises in 1900, and its workforce was rigidly structured along racial and ethnic lines.[25]

Adams's academic approach to the question of labor was based on his experience in the field. His work for two vertically integrated operations had pointed his thinking in a direction that diverged from the traditional California model of racial and ethnic competition. Instead, he ascribed to the state's diverse social groups distinct traits. "Negro Laborers" took "readily to handling horses and mules" but were "notorious prevaricators"; "Mexican Laborers" were "peaceful, somewhat childish, rather lazy, unambitious, fairly faithful" but "not particularly adept at milking"; Japanese were "good hand workers" but "not mechanically inclined"; and so on. Adams believed that such differences among the races suited them to different tasks, even within the same operation and on the same farm, and his book included capsule guides to "handling" the different types: courtesy for Mexicans, bathtubs for Japanese, patience for Negroes.[26]

On the one hand, Adams's racial hierarchy of characteristics and capabilities was of limited use in El Salvador, even for a planter such as James Hill, whose operation combined plantations and mill. Compared with California, there was little racial and ethnic diversity on Salvadoran plantations. Managers were sometimes foreigners, as were many planters themselves, but otherwise imported labor was rare. To make up the bulk of the everyday labor force on the plantations there was only the mozo, the "Indian laborer" described by a San Francisco coffee importer in words that could have come from Adams: "Native Indians, very frugal in their habits and requiring little for their maintenance, but also limited in their working capacity."[27] The miserly body of the mozo, needing little, giving less: for the Hill boys, this was the problem hanging over all their California studies in coffee, just as it was for their father in Santa Ana. Yet even in the absence of significant racial and ethnic diversity, there were other important social divisions in El Salvador's coffee districts that could be exploited in the fashion Professor Adams prescribed. Over time James Hill developed novel strategies for doing so that would set him apart from his fellow planters on the volcano.

216

■ ■ ■

Military school to agricultural school, orchards to plantations, boys to planters: there
was never a thought that James Hill's sons
would be anything else. When the Board of
Special Inquiry on Angel Island asked young
Federico Hill in the late summer of 1917
what he planned to do after his schooling in
California was complete, the thirteen-year-
old had answered confidently: "I will return
again to Santa Ana."[28] He had a boy's belief
in his father's power to make a place for him
in the world.

217

12.

THE HISTORY OF HOLES

On March 28, 1920, a quiet Sunday at the beginning of a new crop year, his three boys away at school in California, James Hill was sitting in his office thinking in numbers. The numbers on the sheet of paper in front of him stood for people. On paper, everyone did the work Hill ordered when and as he ordered it. The unwavering reliability of these imaginary working people was what made it possible for Hill to think in numbers in the first place, as if his office were a counting house and he were a bookkeeper after all.

The problem on Hill's desk was an addition problem. He was buying more land on the Santa Ana Volcano, more than 150 acres of it. The new acreage bordered two of his existing plantations, one of which he had acquired in 1912, the other in 1914. Together the three plantations would form a contiguous expanse of more than 500 acres, and the deed was to be drawn up later that afternoon. The new property was already planted in coffee, but the planting was not up to Hill's standards, so he was doing it over, planting Bourbon and planting as much as he could. In anticipation of the transfer of ownership, Hill was planning the work ahead. In one year's time, starting in the spring of 1921, he wanted to plant 42,000 coffee trees.

Hill got to that number, 42,000, this way. When the land in question was last surveyed, in 1905, it had been assessed at 168 acres. Its owner, soon to become its former owner, said that the parcel was larger than that, but Hill trusted the surveyor over a man who had lost control of his land. The land was not ideal for coffee: Because it was relatively low, only about 2,000 feet above sea level, it was hot. Because it was hot, the sun baked much of the moisture out of the top layer of soil, leaving it dry and sandy. To account for the heat and the dry soil, Hill put extra space between the trees. Planting wide, Hill planned on roughly 250 trees per acre. In all, 42,000.

From that number, it was a matter of simple arithmetic to derive the numbers that would govern the work to be completed in the year leading up to the 42,000 plantings. To begin, each tree needed to go in a hole, and each hole had to be dug. Hill wanted the holes dug before the rains came, so the freshly opened earth could absorb the water, and the rainy season usually began around the end of May. So, as of late March, James

219

Hill had roughly two months, or fifty working days, to dig 42,000 holes. Digging 42,000 holes in fifty working days meant completing over 800 holes each day. That was half the job.

The other half was planting the seeds that would become the year-old seedlings that were to be planted in the holes. This part of the job was as delicate as digging was rude. To yield 42,000 healthy trees, Hill planned to sow 80,000 seeds in nurseries constructed and cultivated with special care.

The final task required was marking the boundary of the new plantation, but in Hill's view this was only a formality, because the most important way that he would mark the property as his was through the digging and the planting and the cultivation.[1] Only by managing the new land correctly would he truly make the plantation his own. And it was with this goal in mind that, while all the other work was ongoing, Hill hired a separate crew to begin building a kitchen in the new plantation.

Like the San Francisco merchants roving the Salvadoran coffee districts in greater numbers, Hill viewed plantations as living expressions of the owner's mastery and, in turn, of the quality of his coffee. Poorly managed plantations looked to Hill's eyes like plantations with no owner at all, evoking the wasteful disorder of common land. When a section of one of his own plantations fell into neglect, he worried that it would be a discredit to his name, for all the neighboring farms were cleaner.[2] This was more than a simple point of pride — the appearance and condition of plantations affected a planter's standing with brokers and bankers. So until he had put his stamp on the disorderly plantation he was about to acquire, Hill would continue to call it by the name of the man from whom he had bought it, the man who had lost it, the German lawyer of dubious intelligence who had married a Santa Ana lady with no property: Deneke.

Alberto Deneke was hardly the only Santa Ana planter who lost land in the years around the Great War. Once the planters in São Paulo began to hold their crops off the market in 1906, coffee prices partially recovered from the crisis that had taken hold ten years earlier. Yet the Brazilian price-control system, sometimes called "valorization," also had a secondary and somewhat counterproductive consequence, which was, in effect, to subsidize an increase in coffee production across the rest of Latin America. The improvements in the world market price the Brazilian planters achieved again made coffee a viable export crop, and the coffee they held off the market was replaced by new plantings elsewhere. By 1914, Salvadoran production, for example, had increased by 25 percent over the average for the previous decade.[3] The result of this subsidized expansion of supply was that when European markets were cut off by war in 1914, prices fell again, and even harder than before, so that by the time the U.S. entered the war in 1917, coffee prices in New York were lower than they had been in a century, accounting for inflation.[4] With prices so low, many planters struggled to pay their mortgages. In turn, mortgage holders lost money but acquired the foreclosed plantations, leading to the concentration of land in fewer and fewer hands. For example, James Hill's neighbors, the Guirolas, owned a majority share in the Banco Salvadoreño — the bank to which Hill himself had once owed more than $100,000, and to which he still, in 1920, owed about $25,000. Before the war, in 1914, the Guirolas had also owned three coffee plantations. Fifteen years later, they had twenty.[5]

As much as he felt the pressure of his own debts, missing even the birthday celebrations of his youngest daughter, Julia, in favor of work, Hill had come through the wartime economic volatility better than most of his neighbors. Perhaps he had not done as well as the Guirolas, but none of the plantations that were now theirs had been his. He had not lost — on the contrary, he had expanded his holdings from five to eleven plantations between 1912 and 1919, through the bottom of the wartime downturn.[6] Planting Bourbon trees gave Hill something of an advantage, allowing him to transform low-lying tracts where the climate was less than ideal for Arabica into productive coffee land — as he had done on the two plantations that bordered Deneke, one bought in 1912, the other in 1914. Given the timing of Hill's expansion, it is probable that his acquisitions mapped the failures of smaller planters whose reserves were stretched to the breaking point by the war.

The war accelerated a trend that was disadvantageous for small planters. The consolidation of land in fewer hands was increasingly built into the structure of the coffee trade in Santa Ana. The San Francisco importers who took over the financing of more and more of the Salvadoran crop during the war years favored and valued sweetness in the cup, and they rewarded it with high prices. Sweetness in the cup derived from the sugars that developed in each coffee cherry as it ripened. And ripeness, far from a mere stage of fruit development, was a function of labor: particularly the labor of picking the coffee cherries during the limited window when ripeness was at its peak, and the labor of milling the coffee cherries into coffee beans. The planters and millers who were most likely to produce coffees that were sweet in the cup were those who could afford to pay for the labor it took to harvest and process ripeness into its commodity form. This is what the San Francisco merchants trolling the Santa Ana Volcano were looking for: the signs of a sweet crop coming, the markers of wealth, diligence, and industry — order on the landscape and in the mills.

As a result, El Salvador's small coffee growers, those without impressive plantations and mills, often went begging for the advances that helped planters get from harvest to harvest. When these small growers needed to raise cash, they were forced instead to borrow what they could from their richer neighbors, who were known to "lend at exorbitant rates on short terms," and always with an eye toward acquiring more land.[7] A usurious loan, combined with an unforeseen drop in the world market price for coffee, or an unexpectedly small harvest, could be disastrous. For small coffee farmers, the looming threat of the loss of land was written in the flourishing of the large plantation next door, which in Alberto Deneke's case had been James Hill's plantation Santa Rosa.

On Monday, March 29, at the ceremonial hour of eight a.m. — work usually began at six — Hill went with two of his best men to take title of Deneke's plantation. Hill had summoned these two men specifically because he believed that they could translate what he had written on paper onto the land. He had sent them the numbers the day before, and by showing up they signaled their agreement with his plan: 800 holes a day, just to start.

One of the men there on Monday morning was Hill's second-in-command, the administrator of his plantations, Elias de Leon. By March 1920, de Leon was in his eighth year working for Hill and his third as administrator. The job gave him broad authority over everything that happened on the plantations, but de Leon was finding the top a treacherous place to be.

The year before, a man named Wohlers had come to Santa Ana. The word about Wohlers was that he knew coffee, so at a time when Hill was adding plantations, he hired Wohlers as a kind of efficiency expert. Wohlers's brief was to roam the plantations, overseeing, checking, correcting, and reporting back, and Hill expected a lot from him.

Elias de Leon, on the other hand, thought Wohlers was a fool. In particular, he thought Wohlers was ruining the detail work that expansion required. Wohlers, as it happened, held the same view of de Leon, and because the two could not agree on the question of who was a fool, they did not get along, as anyone who worked with them could see — or read, for they used the memo books of the plantations, in which they should have been recording their progress on the work of expansion, to trade insults. Eventually de Leon was proven right, but vindication was not quite so sweet as it might have been. Hill scolded his administrator harshly — didn't he know that, instead of calling names, he just should have provided the evidence necessary to make his case?

Elias de Leon had worked for James Hill for at least eight years. Surely eight years was enough time to learn that Hill had one standard by which he judged things: product less costs, output minus input, tallied in pounds of coffee harvested, sacks exported, prices earned, and profits gained. Surely eight years was long enough to know that these measures would eventually say what needed to be said about Wohlers, saving de Leon a trip to the office at Las Tres Puertas to tell his boss that he had been fooled.[8] It had been a deliberate calculation, for de Leon did not keep quiet about everyone he believed to be a fool. Certainly he had not been shy about speaking up when it came to Pedro Bolaños — the third man in the party that went to take possession of Deneke — and this had not seemed to dim Hill's opinion of Bolaños at all.

In March 1920, Pedro Bolaños appeared as a star among moons. Bolaños managed Hill's plantation Santa Rosa, which bordered Deneke on one side, and lived there with his wife. That was one reason why Hill had chosen Bolaños to lead the work in Deneke, but it was not the only reason. Bolaños was not Hill's longest-serving employee — that was Eduviges Medina, who had been put in charge of another important expansion project on a plantation called La Reserva. But recently Pedro Bolaños had been looking more and more like the best.

The most Hill hoped for from the rest his of managers was that they did what he asked: that they reflected his orders onto the people under their charge and, through them, onto the plantations. But Pedro Bolaños was different — he was active, he took the initiative, he was thoughtful, careful, and precise. Hill had even suggested to Elias de Leon that the work of Pedro Bolaños might serve as a kind of model for everyone else. The year-old coffee seedlings growing in the nurseries of Santa Rosa were impressively leafy and green, which was exactly what Hill wanted to see in all the nurseries.

Pedro Bolaños also stood out for his eye — how much he saw, the interest he took in everything, the meticulous records he made and reports he sent. Sitting behind his desk and reading the daily work reports that Bolaños sent in from Santa Rosa, Hill could see without leaving his chair what had been done and what remained to do, readily translating one day's reports into the next day's orders. In all these ways, Pedro Bolaños shone — he and his brother Enecón both did.

Hill believed in family trees. When he found a manager he liked — a man who could read and write, who was honest and willing to learn — he wanted to know if the man had brothers he could employ as well.[9] So Hill put Enecón Bolaños in charge of a plantation called Ayutepeque, and he put Pedro Bolaños in charge of two plantations at once, adding to his existing duties in Santa Rosa responsibility for the transformation of Deneke from a discredit to its former owner's name into a testament to Hill's mastery written in trees and soil and holes.

A coffee plantation is made of holes: holes for applying fertilizers, holes to help the rain sink in, holes for planting shade trees, holes for planting coffee seedlings. Nothing could be more fundamental and more troublesome to a planter, an occupation whose very name presupposes the existence of holes. The problem is that holes, with notable exceptions, do not open themselves.

On the one hand, this quality of holes was useful for a planter. Because holes do not lie, the work of digging them supervised itself, and it was it was easy to see what had been done and what was left to do. On the other hand, holes were problematic for a planter for this very same reason, which put the person tasked with digging into a blunt relation to a job that must have been one of the very first that human beings learned to hate. When there were a lot of holes to be dug, it was often the case that there were not many people around looking for work — Hill suspected that they made themselves scarce because they didn't want the job. This was Pedro Bolaños's first problem in Deneke.

Bolaños had been assigned to make 42,000 holes in two months, more than 800 holes per day. But the sheer number of holes Bolaños needed to dig was not the only challenge he faced. As big as the job already was, Hill wanted to make it bigger — and to do so in such a way that none of the people actually doing the work itself would notice. While the standard size for a planting hole was one *vara,* thirty-three inches, in every direction, Hill asked Bolaños if it would be possible to do exactly what Jaime Hill was studying in California, and make each of the holes bigger than normal — one cubic yard, thirty-six inches rather than thirty-three — without telling the diggers themselves about the change. Hill thought a strong, active man could dig twenty-four such holes in a day, while a worker of ordinary strength could manage sixteen. With a mix of strong workers and ordinary workers — below-average workers didn't figure into the calculation, because if Bolaños was doing his job, he wouldn't hire any — it would take forty men, digging an average of twenty holes each, about two holes an hour, to open 800 holes in a day.

And yet, for some reason, almost as soon as work began in Deneke and Pedro Bolaños's exacting reports began coming into the office at Las Tres Puertas, the numbers were off. Bolaños did not even have half the men he needed to do the job. One day, he put sixteen men to work digging holes in Deneke, fewer than half of the forty diggers Hill expected. More to the point, altogether these sixteen men had dug 256 holes, less than a third of the daily total Hill wanted to see. That was one problem with writing precise reports: Pedro Bolaños made his own inadequate progress on the holes vividly clear. Without leaving his chair, Hill could see that the numbers did not add up to what he had planned. He did the math, typed up a bulletin, and sent the bad news back to Bolaños. At the pace he had been working, it was going to take seven months to make 40,000 holes. Hill wanted it done in two, and he assumed that, because Pedro Bolaños was a man of good sense, he would know where and how to look for the men needed to do it.

When Hill had work that supervised itself, like digging holes, he assigned it by the task.

The task system — the most common form of labor management on El Salvador's plantations, just as it was in many of the workshops of Victorian England — was a piecework system: the completion of a given task earned a given wage. The great historian of the English working class E. P. Thompson wrote that the value of the task system for employers and employees alike was in making work comprehensible at a human scale.[10] For James Hill and the people he employed, this human scale was a ratio of work to food.

Wages on Hill's plantations had two parts: money and ration. The ration earned in the completion of one task was usually made up of two thick corn tortillas plus whatever quantity of beans could be balanced on top of each. In addition, Hill served coffee, likely brewed from beans not good enough to sell abroad. These provisions cost him very little. In the process of opening 42,000 holes in Deneke, Hill expected to pay out more than six hundred dollars in monetary wages, but he calculated the cost of the rations at less than half that amount.[11] Yet though rations cost less in monetary terms, they were in certain ways more valuable to Hill and the people who worked for him.

In the first place, food gave the task system its daily structure. The baseline assumption was that working people should be able to do two meals' worth of work in the course of a single working day. If the size of the task was properly calculated, it should also be possible for people working at an exceptional level to complete three tasks and earn three meals in the course of a single day's work. By the same token, if the size of the task was small enough that working people could complete four or more tasks in a day, earning four or more rations, that was a waste of resources, and the task was adjusted accordingly.

The value of the ration, over and above its cost, was especially evident in its use as an incentive. When there was urgent work to be done, Hill used food rather than money to attract people to do it, offering an extra half-ration, one tortilla and beans for the completion of each task. The extra rations were always given as breakfast, which was a double incentive, for only workers who arrived at the plantations before 6:00 a.m. qualified for breakfast — serving stopped and work started at 6:00 sharp, the first full hour of daylight all year round. And if people were showing a lot of interest in the breakfast tortilla, that is, if they seemed especially hungry, managers were to give out the extra tortilla only between 5:30 and 5:45, to ensure that workers were ready to start work at 6:00 promptly. Stragglers would go without, even if there was food left over.[12]

The possibility of using a small breakfast to compel people to show up for work on time underscores the significance of the ration in the plantation districts. After communal landholding was abolished in El Salvador, and as more and more private land fell into the hands of large coffee planters, more and more Salvadorans lost the means of feeding themselves. In order to eat, they were compelled to work for someone else, selling labor to buy food. This common truth of life under capitalism was sharpened around Santa Ana by the fact that cash wages earned on coffee plantations had limited value for buying food.

By the 1920s, the Santa Ana Volcano was an agricultural world increasingly dominated by large plantations. Small villages, presumably including a market or store, dotted the foothills around the volcano, but the large commercial centers of Santa Ana and Sonsonate were miles away from most plantations, and the terrain was rough. The largest commercial enterprises outside the towns were the plantations themselves. In these monopoly conditions, planters tightened their hold over life on the volcano by paying monetary wages with tokens known as *fichas*. Some planters repurposed worthless foreign money, while others custom-ordered metal tabs from California or Germany that were stamped with the mark of the plantation, the initials of the planter, an image, or a simple number — anything to mark them as a proprietary form of currency valid only in the store of the plantation where they had been issued. James Hill gave out at least two denominations of fichas, one made of copper and the other brass, the latter punched through with holes.[13] With planters running stores as sovereign extensions of their plantations, the rations earned as part of the daily wage certainly made up a significant part, and probably in many cases the largest part, of the diets of the people who worked coffee.

One additional point will highlight the extent to which coffee workers relied on plantation rations for sustenance. This is the fact that Sunday was, in Hill's view, the best time to go out looking for the additional men needed for digging holes in Deneke. Except during the harvest season, Sunday was a day off from work — a day when people would be out and about, and, just as important, a day without rations. Perhaps even better than Sunday, in this regard, was Monday morning, a full thirty-six hours after the last meal on the plantations had been served. It was on hungry Sundays and Mondays that people who needed to work to eat entered Hill's plantations and became his employees.

To get the digging done in Deneke, Hill wanted Pedro Bolaños to reach the empty stomachs of forty strong and hardworking men, who would show up at the plantation before 6:00 a.m. wrapped in dusty layers of rough calico against the predawn chill to eat

234

their steaming breakfast tortillas before the sun rose on another workday. Of course, such men were not the only ones who woke up hungry, and digging was not the only job that needed doing.

Whatever James Hill managed to learn about El Salvador and Salvadorans before he arrived from England, there were still certain things about the place and people that surprised him. One of these was the women.

At the height of cotton manufacturing in Manchester, women made up more than half the workforce of the city's mills, and sometimes as much as two-thirds.[14] El Salvador was different. While many women worked in the coffee mills as limpiadoras, that specialized job lasted only as long as the harvest season, roughly November to February. The rest of the year, Hill had been surprised to learn, women didn't work. Instead, as he explained to American journalist Arthur Ruhl in 1927, they did "nothing — just take care of their babies, cook for their husbands, and potter round their places." A father many times over, Hill certainly understood that this household labor was not "nothing." Yet women's domestic work "round their places" was not contributing directly to his plantations, and in this he saw a missed opportunity. So, he told Ruhl, he "kept urging them to work." And soon he had "plenty" of women

235

doing just that on his plantations.[15]

"Kept urging them to work": the phrase paints a strange picture. Hill claimed to be not only one of the first planters on the volcano to get the women to work on his plantations, but also one of the first planters to deviate from the task system and put people to work by the day. There is no reason to doubt these claims. Both women working and people working by the day were reported to be the exception rather than the rule in El Salvador — to the frustration of many planters — before Hill arrived.[16] More to the point, the two claims are complementary, fitting together into one system of labor management. Getting women to work on the plantations went hand in hand with assigning work by the day.

Just as Hill wanted strong men for digging in Deneke, so did he also have jobs he thought best for women. For example, once the holes were opened in Deneke, they had to be stuffed full of green fertilizers — weeds and leaves and other vegetation, cut in the morning and packed in the afternoon — and capped with dirt, so the whole mix could decay over time into a rich planting soil. The fertilizing of the holes was a job for women, who were assumed to be physically weaker than men. For this reason, their labor carried a lower price, and they generally earned about half the wages men did. Only rarely, in cases of particular urgency, did Hill pit men and women against each other by making them compete for the same jobs, giving a job to men that would usually have been done by women or vice versa. Getting women to work saved money on all the jobs Hill judged to be well suited for women. The savings were especially significant because the most important of these jobs were assigned by the day rather than by the task.

For example, the other half of the job of remaking Deneke was raising and tending to the coffee seedlings in a nursery for a year, and then transporting and replanting the seedlings in the rich soil that had been moldering in the holes. The fragile sprouts and seedlings could easily be harmed by sloppy or rushed work. Assigning this job by the day, Hill removed the incentive to work quickly that was built into the task system. He replaced the food-based governance of the task system with an on-the-job supervisor, one per twenty-five women, who was always a man, just as the supervisors who watched over the limpiadoras inspecting and sorting coffee in the mill were always men. Reserving such delicate jobs for women working by the day made up for the cost of the supervision, and also gave the male supervisor a kind of power that he would not have enjoyed if he had been supervising men doing the same work.

237

Women's comparatively low wages made them exceptionally valuable employees. Just as Hill wanted to have as many limpiadoras as possible for inspecting and sorting beans before shipment, so did he want to ensure that there were women available to work other important jobs when they were needed. When he knew there were jobs for women coming up, he would sometimes give them rations — and three meals a day, rather than two — even before there was actual work to do, just to make sure he had, as he said, "plenty."

Still, there were things about the women who worked on his plantations that Hill could not make sense of. His tailor's eye had noticed that women often wore brightly printed cotton dresses to the plantations, and spent part of their earnings on imitation silk stockings that they wore under their dresses as they worked. Because the women worked barefoot, their stockings snagged and tore on branches and brush. Hill had seen their bare feet and legs peeking out of the holes in the ripped stockings, and he worried that if his female employees were so comfortable ruining their stockings in that way, perhaps they were becoming a little too prosperous.[17]

Once the women had "done nothing" — cared for their babies, cooked for their husbands, and puttered around their places. As more and more women came to Hill's

plantations, they began to do, by his definition, something, and where there once had
been puttering, cooking, and care, there was
now work and coffee. But what then of the
houses, the husbands, and the babies?

For someone who had grown up in Manchester, probably the world capital of child
labor in the middle of the nineteenth century,
James Hill had a low opinion of children's
work. He had seen that they weren't strong
or clever enough to do things well. On one
trip to check on the fertilizing of holes in
Deneke, he saw a girl of eight struggling to
lift her hoe, and another with two hoes on
her shoulder walking around aimlessly looking for a place to use them.[18] It wasn't only
that such "work" wasn't worth paying for,
but also that sloppiness damaged the trees.
This was especially true during the harvest,
when Hill prohibited the hiring of children
under fourteen. The one role he did reserve
for children, especially the children of his best
and most loyal employees, was the job of
messenger, delivering memos from Las Tres
Puertas to managers of distant plantations.
Children who had grown up amid the plantations, whose parents had worked there for
years, knew the terrain instinctively. And
there was another reason that children made
good messengers — they were largely dependent on their parents for food and shelter. If

the young messengers Hill employed failed to deliver, at least he would know where to find them.

Children were good employees because they were traceable, but older people were good employees because they were invisible. Hill had no interest in employing the sick, the weak, the infirm, or the elderly in any capacity that required real work. But the difficulty older, sick, and weakened people had in finding work on the plantations did make them useful for something, because they could be bought for a low price. Hill employed old people as spies: old men as spies in the plantations, older women as spies among the limpiadoras in the mill. When these spies gave him a bit of valuable information, he rewarded them with a few coins.[19]

There were, however, limits on James Hill's power to attract people to his plantations, and to make them work as he directed for the wages and rations he offered. Each of the many hundreds of plantations around the Santa Ana Volcano was equally governed by the calendar and the seasons, meaning that their requirements for labor were overlapping if not identical. Hill's neighbors had the same work to get done at more or less the same time, and the resulting competition for working people drove up labor costs and limited the planter's power to make people work as ordered, since there was always other work to be found nearby.

There were ways around the problem of neighborly competition, but even these were not fail-safe. During the summer of 1921, when Hill was planning to plant 2,000 trees a day in Deneke, a dip in coffee prices put a premium on economy. Taking the initiative, Hill wrote to neighboring planters, including his banker Ángel Guirola, with the idea of organizing a cartel to push through a reduction in wages. The planters agreed that one task for diggers should be fixed at twelve holes of one cubic vara, raising the expected day's work to twenty-four holes, well beyond the sixteen holes Hill thought a man of average strength could do in a day. And they agreed that women working by the day should earn about one and a half Salvadoran *reales,* or about fifteen cents, for a full day's work.[20]

If it worked at all, the cartel didn't last long, for at that time cooperation among planters was the exception rather than the rule.[21] It was much more common for Hill to be constantly tweaking the wages he was paying, adjusting the ratio of work to food, offering the breakfast tortilla when there was urgent work to be done, taking it away when there was not, refining the relation between what the people who worked for him needed and what they could be compelled to do in order to get it. Depending on which jobs needed

241

doing, women got breakfast sometimes, men got breakfast at other times, and at exceptional times, when Hill needed as much labor as he could get from everywhere he could get it, he offered a half ration to children who came to the plantations with their parents, in the hope that he could turn the children's dependence on their parents into their parents' obedience to him.

It was an impersonal, calculating approach to managing the people who worked for him — and one Hill shared with the most technically sophisticated employers and governments in the world.

242

13.

THE GLASS CAGE

Early one morning in March 1896, amid the stuffed bison, fossilized dinosaur tracks, and Egyptian mummy on display in the Orange Judd Museum of Natural History on the Middletown, Connecticut, campus of Wesleyan University, a young Dartmouth graduate named A. W. Smith stepped into what newspapermen in attendance described as a "glass cage." The cage — in fact a copper chamber housed in a box of zinc and wood, with a single glass observation window — was seven feet long, four feet wide, and six and half feet high. Smith had been granted time off from his job as an assistant in the Wesleyan electricity laboratory, and he was planning to stay inside for ten days.[1]

When the door closed behind him, A. W. Smith became the focus of intense round-the-clock observation. During the day a rotating cast of five men in lab coats peered in at him through the window. They watched him exercise with weights. They watched him

243

sit at a table and perform what the newspapers called "severe mental work" — studying German-language books on physics. They watched him "vegetate." And they watched him consume a strict diet fed to him through a special portal. At 7:30 in the morning, Smith's minders served him breakfast: Oatmeal, 21 grams. Milk, 150 grams. Sugar, 20 grams. Bread, 75 grams, butter, 20 grams. Baked beans, 120 grams. Lunch at noon: 125 grams of hamburger; 120 grams of mashed potatoes; 75 grams of bread; 25 grams of butter; 125 grams of apples. At 6:30, a light supper: 250 grams of Boston brown bread and 500 grams of milk. Plus all the water he wished. Every night, a team of three new observers watched Smith unfold his cot and go to sleep. The air temperature inside the chamber was recorded every few minutes. Everything going into and coming out of Smith's body was accounted for. It was noteworthy, for example, that on Tuesday, March 24, Smith did not eat all of his butter.[2]

The "glass cage" had been designed by Wesleyan professor W. O. Atwater. Atwater earned his doctorate in chemistry at Yale in 1869. After postdoctoral work in Germany, he began teaching at Wesleyan in 1873. When Wesleyan organized the first state-funded agricultural experiment station in the United States in 1875, Atwater became its director.

Twelve years later, he was appointed director of the national office of experiment stations in the Department of Agriculture. From this position Atwater would shape American agriculture around his own specialty, the science of human nutrition, and particularly around the thing he was studying in the basement of Orange Judd Hall: the calorie.[3]

Derived from the old notion of "caloric" — the invisible fluid once thought to carry heat from one object to another — the calorie was a unit of measure first used in France early in the nineteenth century as an index of the efficiency of steam engines.[4] The discovery of energy conservation in the 1840s made it clear that the calorie could have many other useful applications. As Hermann von Helmholtz, author of the first law of thermodynamics, put it in 1854: "[In] the last century . . . [we] did not know how to establish a connection between the nutriment consumed and the work generated. Since, however, we have learned to discern in the steam-engine this origin of mechanical force, we must inquire whether something similar does not hold good with regard to men." The issue was philosophical as well as physiological: Were human beings exceptional creatures, or did they operate on the same principles as machines? Helmholtz suspected the latter, but he also thought that the experiments that would prove it were so complex as to be impossible.[5]

Four decades later, that had changed. Nutrition and dietary science had become well established in Europe, and especially in Germany, where research focused on the diets of working families. In contrast, Atwater's experiments won little attention in the United States until 1885, when he met Edward Atkinson. Atkinson was a Boston industrialist who had also funded the radical abolitionist John Brown and was himself an active opponent of slavery, which he viewed as economically inefficient.[6] Atkinson saw in the science of nutrition the possibility of improving labor relations without increasing wages — by, in effect, reverse-engineering wages from dietary requirements and food prices.[7] With Atkinson's patronage, Atwater made multiple trips to Germany to observe the latest studies in nutritional science. In 1894, with $10,000 from the Department of Agriculture, Atwater began to build what was called a respiration calorimeter at Wesleyan on the model of those he had seen in Munich, only bigger and better ventilated, so his research subjects could stay inside longer, and the experiments could be extended to more aspects of human life: working, studying, resting, eating, and sleeping.[8]

By all indications, A. W. Smith was quite comfortable in Atwater's calorimeter, hermetically isolated from the world. The temperature was set to his liking, and he had chosen the menu himself. While his original plan was to stay inside ten days, in the end Smith made it to twelve and a half, a new record. When the door opened at 3:00 p.m. on Saturday, April 4, and Smith stepped out, he had lost two pounds, and he was feeling rather well.[9]

Smith's record-setting stay in the calorimeter would be one of almost five hundred such experiments Atwater performed at Wesleyan over a decade.[10] Though he was a dedicated foe of overindulgence on moral grounds, Atwater's experiments were not intended to put upper limits on the human diet, or to establish a particular standard of health or beauty. Instead he was interested in "what quantity of work and heat can be gotten out of common foods when fed to the human engine."[11] The calorimeter was a device for testing the application of the thermodynamic law of energy conservation to the human body. "The chief object," as the *Chicago Tribune* explained, was "to be able to determine the balance of income and outgo of the body," and to express that balance "in terms of matter and of energy."[12] The result was the quantification of the relationship between food and work, human needs and capabilities: life reduced to numbers — calories.

Clarifying the relation between work and

food promised to make visible the internal mechanism of the human body, and in turn to suggest an answer to an old question that had acquired new relevance in the United States: What makes people work?

Three decades earlier, at the end of 1864, New York publisher D. Appleton brought out a primer on the conservation of energy. The volume collected papers previously published in Europe — where the idea had been elevated to a new "gospel of energy" — in order to bring Americans up-to-date on what the editor, Edward L. Youmans, touted as "the most important discovery of the present century" and "the highest law of *all* science."[13]

Youmans, who would go on to found the magazine *Popular Science* in 1872, was a friend of the abolitionist editor Horace Greeley.[14] He had grown up in modest circumstances, in part on a farm in upstate New York and in part among Quakers in Manhattan, but as a young man he had traveled in scientific circles in Europe. His travels led him to believe that Americans needed to know more than they did about energy, which he had come to see as a way of thinking about the world with revolutionary implications for business, politics, and society alike. In collecting the most important work on the subject into a single volume, Youmans wanted to perform a "useful service to the public."[15]

As Youmans saw it, the United States had fallen badly behind the theoretical and experimental work on thermodynamics ongoing in Europe. Nevertheless, he hoped Americans might still lead the way when it came to putting the science to practical use, thanks to one of the standout "peculiarities of American character."[16] Though "widely reproached for being over-practical," the United States had "produced just that kind of working ability that was suited to translate this profound question from the barren to the fruitful field of inquiry."[17]

Youmans had a specific idea of energy's potential fruitfulness, and this shaped his collection. Notably, he included three papers by Robert Mayer and none by James Joule. In one way, this was a surprising choice, for Joule's work had clear practical aims: he wanted to build a better engine. By contrast, Mayer's approach, as many of his critics had pointed out, ran toward the metaphysical. Yet while Joule's work focused on engines, Mayer focused on the human body. Thinking as he was of the United States, Edward Youmans saw the inner workings of the body, the place where Mayer's speculations had begun in Java, as the most promising, and potentially "fruitful," frontier of thermodynamic science.

The paper Youmans chose to close his anthology pointed in the direction he hoped

Americans would take the idea of energy. The author was William Carpenter, a British zoologist and physician, and the title was "On the Correlation of the Physical and Vital Forces." The philosophers had been wrong, Carpenter wrote: vital force — "life" in all of its forms and expressions — was not a manifestation of an intangible "spirit," but a phenomenon that could be understood in thermodynamic terms, as if the body itself were "a Cotton Factory in full action." A cotton factory, Carpenter explained, was an interconnected system of diverse operations that all originated from a single source: the energy derived from the sun, stored in coal, released in a steam engine, "the mainspring of our mechanical power; the *vis viva* [living force] of our whole microcosm." Likewise, while the operations of the human body appeared diverse and various, in fact they originated from the very same single source as the cacophonous workings of a mill: the sun's energy, stored in food.[18] Tracing energy from the sun through plants and into the human body in the form of food, Carpenter, citing Mayer, depicted man as merely another "instrument" for the conversion of energy into work.[19] Writing the year after the Emancipation Proclamation, Youmans was captivated by the comparison of the human being to a cotton factory — a very complicated, but ultimately predictable, thing.[20]

In 1864 the question was anything but academic. Youmans was thinking about governance. Extrapolating from one body to many, he argued that the same principles applied to society, recasting thermodynamic law as civil law. What made this logical leap possible was an underlying universal truth, one shared by every individual as well as every collectivity. Just as the need for and availability of food governed an individual's potential for work, so did the food supply govern a society's productivity and survival. That was plain enough to see, but the challenge was striking the right balance. Without food, a society, like a human body, could do nothing, but too much was also harmful. Youmans argued that in the individual body "excessive action of the digestive system exhausts the muscular and cerebral systems," and the same held true in society at large. "More and more," he wrote, "we are perceiving that the condition of humanity and the progress of civilization are direct resultants of the forces by which men are controlled." The most direct forces by which men were controlled — more effective even than legislation, especially when considering "the producing, distributing, and commercial activities of the community" — were food and eating.[21]

It was an idea finely tuned to its historical moment. Mapped onto the individual and social body through food, the idea of energy reduced the human being to the status of a work-producing instrument precisely as chattel slavery — rooted in the legal classification of persons as things — was outlawed in the United States and on the decline around the world.[22] Put another way, energy provided the age of emancipation with a new way to think about persons as things and how to work them. Crucially, energy was a concept of what makes people work that was derived not from a premise of inequality, such as the racial logic of American slavery, but rather from a premise of universal human equality: everyone needs to eat.

In a sense, German philosopher Friedrich Nietzsche was Edward Youmans's nightmare. Youmans translated the ideas of Robert Mayer and others into a principle of governance he believed would advance the progress of prosperity and civilization. Nietzsche also embraced Mayer's "vision of the totality of life and energy as a great cosmic harmony," but he took the idea in a different direction.[23]

Nietzsche's 1872 study of Greek drama, *The Birth of Tragedy,* described two modes of being: the Apollonian, characterized by reason, clarity, and discipline, and the Dionysian, sensuous and wild. After he read Mayer's essays in 1881, Nietzsche saw these concepts in a new light. He reimagined the Dionysian world as "a monster of energy, without beginning, without end; an immovable, brazen enormity of energy, which does not grow bigger or smaller, which does not expend itself but only transforms itself, a household without expenses or losses, but likewise without increase or income . . . eternally self-creative . . . eternally self-destructive."[24] This image of Dionysus was more than a sharp contrast to the productivist "gospel of energy" that venerated Apollo. At the time, the specter of energy "without income" was a kind of apocalyptic vision.

The productivist view had equated business with goodness. According to the gospel of energy, the extraction, concentration, and application of the energy latent in nature to profitable ends was "the eminently moral supreme purpose to be achieved."[25] The many evangelists of this gospel, including Edward Youmans, were powerfully motivated by the fear that time — and energy — was running out. The second law of thermodynamics, formulated by German mathematician Rudolf Clausius and British engineer William Thomson (later Lord Kelvin) around 1850, and based largely on the prior work of French army engineer Sadi Carnot, stated that the available energy in any system decreases over time. This decline toward unproductivity was given the name "entropy," which, as an index of opportunities lost and resources wasted, became one of the defining anxieties of the age.[26]

Since its coinage in the middle of the nineteenth century, "entropy" has evolved into a common synonym for disorder and chaos, but originally it was a chilling prophecy of the end of the world, one anticipated by Robert Mayer, among others.[27] In a self-published 1848 essay titled "Celestial Dynamics" (reprinted in 1865 by Edward Youmans), Mayer wrote: "Every incandescent and luminous body diminishes in temperature and luminosity in the same degree as it radiates light and heat, and at last, provided its loss not be repaired from some other source of these agencies, becomes cold and non-luminous."[28] In the short run, entropy meant opportunity lost. In the long run, it meant the "heat death" of the sun, a prediction that became a Victorian fixation.[29] "Heat is par excellence the communist of our universe," wrote the Scottish physicist Balfour Stewart and the English astronomer Norman Lockyer in a popular 1868 essay, "and it will no doubt bring the present system to an end."[30] The second law of thermodynamics cast the passage of time as a zero-sum game: energy versus entropy. Life was an opportunity for productivity, but time was wasting. Until the lights went out, what was required, productivists believed, was "a great delicacy of organization" that would put the greatest portion of the dying sun's energy to good use.

254

■ ■ ■

W. O. Atwater's calorimeter at Wesleyan was a tool for refining the delicacy of the productivist order by specifying the relation of inputs and outputs, food and work. It gave readings in units of energy, calories, that needed no conversion: 50 calories of food provided energy for 50 calories of work. Measuring work in terms of food and food in terms of work helped achieve the proper balance between need and capability that Edward Youmans had envisioned: supplying the individual body enough food to power productive activity, but not so much as to take away from power of the brain and muscles. "The physiological chemistry of to-day looks upon the body as a sort of machine," W. O. Atwater wrote. "The body creates nothing for itself, either of material or energy; all must come to it from without. . . . Like the steam-engine, it simply uses the material supplied to it. Its chemical compounds and its energy are the compounds and the energy of the food transformed." Tally up the "daily income and expenditure of the body" in terms of energy through "a kind of chemical book-keeping," and all aspects of human life could be managed through a form of cost accounting.[31]

There is a reason this sounds like a business plan. Business had been Atwater's first laboratory. Before he built his calorimeter, he had begun his work in the field, studying the diet and the labor output of bricklayers in Massachusetts and Connecticut. This was an industry in which it was comparatively easy to calculate the total work done, the energy expended to move a given weight a given distance, because the weight of the bricks was a constant. The laboratory calorimeter improved on this method by pushing past a general theory of the relation of food and work toward a detailed index, cross-referencing types of food with types of work.

Over hundreds of studies involving more than 10,000 subjects, specific foods were evaluated alongside specific tasks.[32] By 1910, it was possible to determine "the amount of energy furnished to the human system by a pound of beefsteak, an egg, or vegetable soup . . . to an absolute figure."[33] The first foods to be evaluated in this way were "foods that just now are of special interest for the purpose of avoiding the use of meats in the diet of laborers: lard, olive oil, beef suet, butter, peanut butter, cottonseed productions" — cheap, efficient fat and protein substitutes.[34] By the same token, one of the earliest variations on the laboratory calorimeter was a modified version of it specifically designed so that a "subject may carry on his daily work while the energy used in the operation is recorded."[35] There was also in development a version of the calorimeter that was big enough to hold a family of four.[36] Just as Edward Atkinson had hoped, these experiments ultimately made it possible to figure out how to accomplish a certain amount of work for the least amount of money.

From business, the calorie was called into the service of government. The energy consumption and expenditure of workers and households were questions with far-reaching domestic as well as geopolitical implications. Not only was the calorie potentially useful in Progressive-era campaigns to calculate — and adjust — the cost of living, but from the outset it was Atwater's patriotic hope that counting calories could help the United States achieve a stable and prosperous place in a world marked by increasing population and inter-imperial competition for resources. To that end, through his position at the U.S. Department of Agriculture, Atwater shaped American farming around the priority of cost-efficient calories.[37]

In the hands of business and government, the calorimeter was more than a scientific instrument for experiment and investigation. Instead, by rendering all forms of bodily activity, and even inactivity, in calories, units of energy that clarified the "possibilities of any person for mental and physical labor," the calorimeter helped to bring into being a world that was more like a calorimeter itself, a world in which it was impossible to avoid working.[38] Seen through the calorie, as through the window of the calorimeter, work was the human body's most basic function.

Writing just after the turn of the twentieth century, historian Henry Adams suspected that the ascendant idea of energy had opened a new era in human history. Adams's own encounter with thermodynamics had changed his view of how the world worked, how history happened. As he studied the records of past societies with energy in mind, Adams had begun to see "lines of force" where he had once seen "lines of will."[39] This was a profound shift for a man who, as a longtime Harvard history professor and the great-grandson and grandson of presidents, had tended to view historical periods through the lives of their leaders. In a letter to a friend in 1902, Adams considered what this would mean for society at large in the new century: "We have created and established a new philosophy and a new religion, which I think will endure," he predicted, "the religion of energy with very big E, and of man with a very small m."[40] Energy was the great prize, and life itself had been devalued.

14.

THE HUNGER PLANTATION

Among the well-fed in El Salvador, the importance of hunger to coffee production was axiomatic. In 1885, when the U.S. State Department was surveying business opportunities in Central America, diplomat Maurice Duke assured prospective planters that there was a well-established solution to the problem of how to make people work. When a worker on the coffee plantations lagged behind the required pace, explained Duke, a planter himself, "the man's food is withheld, and this quickly puts activity into his unwilling limbs."[1] The will, planters knew, was connected mechanically to the stomach, and under this guiding principle they forced food and work into a rude equivalence. Their equation turned the human body inside out: hunger gave energy for work, satiety produced idleness. People would work to eat, not eat to work.

Most often hunger is understood to be a consequence of economic crisis or catastrophe — a famine, for example. In fact hunger is the bedrock foundation of all capitalist economies, though in some the bottom is far enough away that it usually remains invisible. The standard account of the relationship between hunger and work under capitalism focuses on land privatization. In principle, after common resources have been transformed into private property, the only way to eat is to sell labor in the market in exchange for a wage, and then spend that wage buying food. By this account, capitalism operates through a kind of economic deism: land privatization starts a clock on hunger that ticks away each working day.

In practice it was not so simple. Every day of James Hill's life as a planter was complicated by the fact that hunger was not the inevitable consequence of land privatization. On the contrary, energy overspilled property lines. Even after the abolition of communal lands, the possibility of eating without working survived in the fruit growing on trees that shaded the coffee and also flourished in out-of-the-way corners of plantations, cashews, guavas, papayas, *jocotes,* figs, dragon fruits, avocados, mangoes, plantains, tomatoes; in the beans planted as ground cover all around the coffee trees to prevent erosion and return nitrogen to the soil; and in the animals that fed on the chemically enhanced richness of the coffee ecosystem.

Stealing food from the plantations was a crime as old as the plantations themselves. Early on in the age of coffee in El Salvador, working people learned to look for a plantation "well stocked with fruit trees," and they helped themselves liberally. James Hill told journalist Arthur Ruhl in 1927 that the practice of eating fruit from a plantation's trees was so widespread that if a planter had good fruit trees on his property, he might as well just cut a hole in his fence, or hungry working people were sure to do it for him. Hill took this as evidence that the people who worked for him had no concept of private property, looking on the fruits that grew alongside coffee as "gifts as common as the sun or the rain." Yet this conclusion is contradicted by the fact that the working people often ate the fruit they stole off the trees while it was still green and unripe, leaving planters to marvel at the heartiness of native digestion.[2] Clearly, working people knew the value of taking what fruit they could get — neatly packaged hits of sugar and water during hot, hungry workdays — before it was ready for market.

A coffee plantation was a regime under threat every time the sun shone. Veins of nourishment ran through the coffee monoculture, and wherever there was food, however scant, there was freedom, however fleeting, from work. Land privatization was a necessary condition for creating the hunger that drove people onto the plantations and into the coffee mills to work, but it was not a sufficient condition. What was needed to harness the will of the Salvadoran people to the production of coffee, beyond land privatization, was the plantation production of hunger itself.

Some planters cultivated hunger through the most direct means available to them — violence and the fear it bred. More accurately, some planters used the most direct means available to them that also kept them out of harm's way, delegating violent discipline to their plantation managers and overseers. There is a good reason why the diplomat and planter Maurice Duke used the passive voice when describing how a flagging worker's "food is withheld," as he put it. While planters kept their distance, their lieutenants enforced their property lines through "the constant application" of beatings, stabbings, machete slashings, and threats of the same.[3]

Brutal punishments gave the threats a sharp edge. A workingman was caught stealing two bunches of plantains from a Santa Ana plantation. When he resisted arrest, he was shot and killed. Another Santa Ana planter kept a grove of orange trees on his plantation, probably to produce a small crop for local markets. When his overseer caught a group of workers picking oranges instead of coffee, he shot one of them in the head.[4] An overseer on another nearby plantation was said to have beaten a ten-year-old to death for picking and eating a mango.[5]

From one perspective, these killings over food merely took the principle of private property to its logical conclusion. Dividing masters from mozos, planters from workers, rich from poor, the fed from the hungry, property lines marked a border of life and death. The grid of lots and deeds established after land privatization underlay both El Salvador's coffee economy and a "culture of violence" that would soak Salvadoran society through. With so many competing coffee plantations on the volcano, this violence had costs for its perpetrators, too, driving working people to other plantations and hardening into thick antagonism that crowded in on everyday business — and which sometimes came back on bosses as retaliation from workers, who had machetes of their own. The risk was not merely hypothetical. When the administrator of one Santa Ana plantation withheld a laborer's food as a punishment for unsatisfactory work in 1910, the hungry man took out his knife and struck back.[6] Planters' fears were well founded, if also self-induced.

James Hill, for one, took a different approach. He explained to Arthur Ruhl in 1927 that he was known to be "*delicado,* because he treated his trees and his work-people more thoughtfully than was the custom in the neighborhood."[7] There is good reason to believe the claim. In contrast to those planters who used physical force and acute injury to enforce their property lines, Hill wanted to make his plantations known as good places to work, the better to attract the workers he needed when he needed them. He discouraged direct physical violence as a strategy of labor management on his plantations, and he specifically sought to hire managers who would not be rough with the people under their charge.[8]

Yet there is also evidence to suggest that if indeed Hill was known as "delicado" on the Santa Ana Volcano in the late 1920s, it was because he had changed.

While much of the everyday violence of coffee production has been lost to history, the case of Florentino Díaz survives. It survives in part because it was unusual: the case of a punishment so terrible that it stood out even from the record of brutality that is the history of coffee in El Salvador.

Díaz was a Spaniard. In 1910, he had recently arrived in El Salvador and was working as an overseer on one of James Hill's plantations. During that year's harvest, Díaz caught a young laborer by the name of Miguel Hernández in the act of stealing a sack of coffee. Díaz then ordered three men who worked alongside Hernández to hang him. As a larger group of workers looked on, the three tied a rope around Hernández's neck and strung him up.

Díaz and the three workmen who had done the hanging were arrested and charged with murder. Díaz's plight, chronicled in the local papers, attracted the sympathy of the Spanish community in El Salvador, and he was able to secure a defense lawyer. During the trial, the lawyer called to the stand several doctors who testified that Hernández had died not from hanging but from fright, or from some sort of physiological attack, while he was being hanged. This theory of the case fit Díaz's defense strategy. He contended that he had not been trying to kill the man, merely teach him a lesson. When Díaz demonstrated his remorse by collapsing in court, suffering an attack of his own, he was removed to the hospital, where he lay "near death" as the trial went on. In the end, he had nothing to fear. Díaz was acquitted, while the workers who carried out his orders were found guilty.[9]

Perhaps James Hill changed as a result of the Díaz case. Or perhaps Hill changed because it became easier over time for him to be more delicate. After 1912, El Salvador created a National Guard modeled on Spain's famed

Guardia Civil and far more numerous than previous national police forces. More than four hundred officers, who were required to have at least a year of military experience plus a year of specialized training, were posted to large plantations throughout the coffee districts. There they became a "constant presence," taking much of the direct burden of enforcement and discipline off overseers, managers, and planters. Hill and other planters often requested that pairs of National Guardsmen be posted on their properties full-time during the harvest.[10]

Or perhaps Hill changed because he began to pursue a different means of preventing thefts and enforcing his property lines. This new approach was, in a sense, "more thoughtful" than direct violence, and more delicate. It was a sort of "rationalization" of El Salvador's coffee industry in that it shifted the mechanism of domination out of the realm of direct physical violence and into the realm of ideas. The method of work discipline Hill developed and instituted on his plantations goes to the center of the triskelion that came to mark Las Tres Puertas. Under the sign of Apollo, Hill engineered a system of labor management that mirrored the productivist gospel of energy, joining together hunger, food, and work into a highly efficient coffee factory. To maintain the monopoly of basic human needs that drove people to work coffee, he shaped the ecology of his plantations to route the sun's energy toward coffee production, feeding his trees and starving his workers, producing coffee and hunger in corresponding amounts. This was the means by which Hill made people into "work-people," as he called them, and the means by which he made them "his."

A family story — good enough to be legend, but true — will clarify what was novel about Hill's approach to the plantation production of hunger. His late father-in-law, the man who had established the coffee plantations Lola inherited, who claimed Spanish heritage through the conquistadors, was named Dionisio. And in a sense his plantations had fit Nietzsche's idea of a wild and unruly "monster of energy," for he cultivated groves of jocote — the small, native, sweet-tart plumlike tree fruit — alongside his coffee, creating a source of food that would have been as tempting to people who worked there as it was difficult to police.[11]

Not Dionisio's son-in-law. Hill may have told Arthur Ruhl that "his work-people" had "little concept of private property," eating the fruits they found growing on the plantations as if they were "gifts as common as the sun and rain," but he was hardly willing to concede the sun and the rain as common property.

When Hill saw a dragon fruit tree on his land, he ordered it cut down. When he saw tomato plants and blackberry bushes growing in an unruly tangle, he ordered them ripped up. When he saw a great old wild fig, a revered tree in Central America, its wide crown providing a shade often used as an extension of interior domestic space, he told Elias de Leon to turn it into boards.[12] Instead of fruit trees, Hill planted *madre de cacao* to shade his coffee. Native to Central America, madre de cacao subsequently spread around the world for use as shade on plantations. It was suited to the purpose because it grew quickly to heights of thirty feet or more, well above the coffee trees; it helped to return nitrogen to the soil; its leaves made excellent green fertilizer for filling holes; and while its seedpods could be fed to cattle, oxen, and other ruminants, they were inedible, even toxic, to humans. Hill was known for having the best shade trees in the region.[13]

Covering the ground below the coffee trees were beans. Bean plants, like madre de cacao trees, returned nitrogen to the soil, sent down roots that held the soil to the steep sides of the volcano, and provided another layer of shade that helped to keep moisture in the ground. But beans were not simply beans. Different varieties were suited to different uses on a plantation. Near new trees, Hill planted cowpea, or black-eyed pea, especially good for enriching the soil. In steeply sloped areas, he planted cowpea or jackbean, whose deep roots prevented runoff and erosion.

These varieties of beans, in addition to making excellent compost material to bury in fertilizer holes, were also important food crops. In consideration of this, Hill ordered Elias de Leon to harvest and collect the pods as soon as they were ripe. Once the beans were harvested, they were to be buried in fertilizer holes immediately, lest they become food for people rather than trees — and Hill had seen people trying to carry off the cuttings.[14] He had seen chickens pecking at the cowpea too near the coffee nurseries, so he reminded his managers that keeping chickens was a violation of long-standing rules, and any chickens that did happen to live in the plantations belonged in the pot of the planter rather than that of the people.[15]

In certain high-traffic areas, Hill planted a third type of beans. Velvet bean was native to Asia. Traveling the reverse path of madre de cacao, it had been introduced to Central America in the early twentieth century on the Atlantic coast banana plantations of the United Fruit Company. It was ideal for planting around the coffee nurseries, in the public spaces, and along the borders of plantations, all the public roads and fences, because it grew fast and tall and thick, forming a living fence whose fine, fuzzy coating was exceptionally itchy to touch. And most important, it was largely inedible. Unless prepared carefully, boiled and reboiled just so, velvet bean caused whoever ate it vomiting and cramping intestinal pain at best, and acute toxic psychosis at worst.[16] Chickens couldn't eat it, either. Planting velvet bean where public roads intersected his private property, and all along his property lines, Hill marked out the boundaries of his hunger plantations. By policing the trees, the plants, and the domestic animals, Hill extended his property lines to the part of the sun that shone on Santa Ana.

And as for wild animals, the monkeys, armadillos, and anteaters once considered last-resort "starvation food" in El Salvador — as well as the big cats, coyotes, and foxes that might have preyed on the chickens and been preyed on themselves — these were largely "exterminated" with the rise of coffee in the first half of the twentieth century.[17] The expansion of coffee production in El Salvador was also the contraction of the country's plant and animal life, and, in turn, its culture and its stomach. The transformation of the volcanic highlands into a coffee monoculture flattened the diet of El Salvador's working people into a featureless plain of tortillas and beans.

But still — why fight a war on a wild-growing

270

bounty so diverse and plentiful that it required constant vigilance to suppress, only to serve as rations the same two foods three times a day, six days a week? If the point was to draw people to work on the plantations, to win their obedience by treating them thoughtfully, why not vary the rations by serving some of the foods already growing on the volcano? Why, considering the work and resources required to root out and choke off these abundant sources of wild food — why tortillas and beans, meal after meal after meal?

When Spanish conquistadors reached the land that became El Salvador in 1524, it was not the economic backwater it would be when they left. On the contrary, the region — then divided into two main provinces, Cuscatlán and Izalco — was populated by more than a hundred thousand people and comparatively wealthy. This was not good news for the Pipil Indians, who, along with smaller indigenous groups, had made it so, because with wealth came attention from the Spanish Empire, and with attention came exploitation.

The Pipil had moved south from what is now Mexico perhaps a thousand years ago, establishing thriving settlements in the fertile basins between the volcanic peaks, including impressive cacao plantations. They used cacao as money — a medium of exchange and a currency of tax and tribute payments — and they also traded it, probably in return for cotton and obsidian, with other indigenous societies as far away as Mexico.[18] The conquistadors built their colonial economy on the foundations of indigenous wealth already in place. After the conquest, as the Spanish took control of cash crops by force and as disease became epidemic in the hot coastal lowlands, many Indians sought refuge in the highlands, where the steep shoulders of the volcanoes were cultivated extensively with corn.[19]

Cacao was money, but corn was life. Corn was domesticated from wild grass beginning around nine thousand years ago in what is now southern Mexico. When it was paired with the beans growing abundant and wild in the region — and domesticated around the same time — the two plants made a complete, life-sustaining protein.[20] Yet corn was elevated even over beans when, around three thousand years ago, Mesoamericans began to treat it in an alkaline solution of lime and water before cooking. This process, called nixtamalization, helps to soften the kernel and separate the germ from the hull, making it easier to grind into paste and form into dough. Treated corn is also easier to digest and more nutritious, with its niacin, calcium, and amino acids made accessible.[21] It also cooks faster, and it was most often shaped into tortillas for griddling on the earthen *comales* characteristic of the region's kitchens.

With the spread of nixtamalization, corn became the basis for the ancient Olmec society that shaped subsequent indigenous cultures, including the Maya and Aztec civilizations, both of which were influential in the region that became El Salvador.[22] As recorded in the Popol Vuh, the sacred Maya text, the fox, the coyote, the parrot, and the crow brought corn in tribute to the gods who were then in the process of creating the world. The goddess Xmucane ground the corn into paste and molded it into human flesh.[23] Similarly, in the Aztec Nahuatl language the word for human flesh, *tonacayo,* can be used for corn as well, and the number one, *ce,* is derived from another word for corn, *cintli.*[24]

The Spanish named the Indians' corn rounds *tortillas,* little cakes. In Central America, the Pipil made a variation on the familiar thin Mexican tortilla: a dense disc of the approximate dimensions of a breakfast pancake. Rather than wrapped around beans, it was usually torn into pieces, which were used as scoops. In addition to corn and beans, the Pipil cultivated squashes and pumpkins, tomatoes, chiles, peanuts, avocados, along with some root crops, and they tended the native fruit trees that grew around their settlements.

273

The central role of corn and beans in the diet of Mesoamerican Indians was not a matter of ease and convenience.[25] On the contrary, corn does not reproduce in the wild, growing only where it is planted and tended. Worse, because either corn or beans alone are insufficient to sustain human life, the interdependence of these crops doubled the vulnerability of people who relied on them.

On the other hand, corn and beans do share characteristic properties that made them the basis for thriving and complex civilizations across millennia. The edible part of each can be easily dried and stored over long periods of time. Once dried, the individual grains are small and uniform, and therefore easy to measure and pack in standardized containers and quantities, and likewise to divide when necessary. As a result, they can also be easily transported and shipped from place to place. Moreover, both are difficult crops to grow in secret, thriving in sun and sending stalks up out of the earth that announce the extent and timing of the expected crop to passing tax collectors. In other words, corn and beans are ideal government food, readily subject to centralized political administration. In the indigenous empires of Mesoamerica they were often collected as taxes and tribute, an abundant supply of food being an exceptionally important form of wealth and power in an agrarian society.[26] And as in the ancient

274

empires of the Americas, so in later empires of coffee.

As he rooted out wild foods on the volcano, James Hill increased his control over the corn and beans he served as rations by building kitchens on his plantations. Some planters around Santa Ana permitted working people to cook for themselves in their houses, but for Hill a central kitchen was a key to a well-run plantation. When Hill acquired Deneke, he began not only by digging holes and constructing nurseries for the coffee trees, but also by building a new kitchen, a crucial part of his plan for turning the land into a flourishing plantation.[27] The plantation kitchens functioned as the engine rooms of the coffee factory Hill built on the Santa Ana Volcano, and like any engine room they were fitted with precision gauges that measured and recorded the operation of the whole thrumming thing.

The kitchens themselves were spartan: a shelter with a heat source and a channel in the ground to carry away the solution of lime and water used to break down corn into flour for tortillas. The only equipment necessary was a comal for cooking tortillas and a pot for beans. Tortillas were formed by hand, patted out in palms whose size and shape they took on, and beans could be stirred with anything, as long it was clean, for the last thing Hill wanted to come out of his kitchens were rations that weakened the people whose labor he bought with them.[28]

As simple as they were, these kitchens registered everything that happened on Hill's plantations. If the kitchen was well run, the amount of food prepared and served matched the amount of work performed on the plantation. Because corn and beans were so uniform and easy to portion, it was simple to keep track of these amounts. When the figures recorded in the bulletins didn't match up, Hill went to the kitchen in question, or told his overseer Elias de Leon to go, to check on how much food the cooks were making. Because he knew that the people who worked for him would be hungry — that they would eat the rations he served — Hill could track them through the kitchen where their food was prepared. He could count the supplies, count the rations, count the work-people, count the work completed, and make sure the numbers added up to productive order.

Hill was able to track how many rations his cooks were making because he bought food on international markets when prices were favorable and sent it to his plantations through a centralized distribution system. Shipments of corn and beans were picked up from the railway station, stored at Las Tres Puertas, and carted to the plantations on the basis of expected need.[29] Once on the plantations, food was stored in locked iron bins in the granary and dosed with carbon disulfide, a toxic insecticide.[30] The guardians of granaries, and of the kitchens themselves, were the cooks, who were always women.

Kitchens and the cooks who worked them occupied a crucial place in the Apollonian order of productivity Hill engineered on the volcano, not only because they indexed the relation of food to work, but also because, as centers of sustenance among hungry people, they were centers of social life. As centers of social life, kitchens were also centers of information and portals into the world of the plantations. When Hill wanted to find someone or something on one of his plantations, he went to the kitchen first.[31] He assumed that he and his deputies would be able to get important information from the kitchens most effectively when the cooks were female and alone, the physical strength of the male managers — propped up again by the cultural power of gender — facilitating whatever interrogation was needed. He rewarded loyalty by keeping cooks on the payroll year-round, even if there was no other work to do on the plantations.

Along with centralized distribution and preparation of food itself, Hill tried to control the ingredients of food production, not all of which could be easily locked up in iron bins around the clock. For instance, cooks used

277

lime to treat the corn that would be ground into dough for tortillas, but lime was also an important agricultural supply. Spread over the ground, turned over with the dirt during digging and cultivation, lime sweetened the soil that the roots of coffee trees turned acidic. To short-circuit the possibility of unauthorized cooking and eating, Hill tried to manage the transit of lime through his plantations strictly, yet some managers, missing the point, just left it on the ground where anyone could take it. This was especially problematic in Deneke, which had no round-the-clock resident manager, since Pedro Bolaños lived with his wife next door in Santa Rosa. So James Hill came up with a different way to guard his supply of lime from would-be home cooks. He told Elias de Leon to shape the pile of lime into a chain of small white volcanoes, and then sprinkle each one with a layer of dark dirt. The smooth shape of the cones, along with the stark contrast in colors between the lime and the soil, would act as an alarm system, deterring theft. It was a planter's fantasy world in miniature: a chain of volcanoes from which it was impossible to steal.[32]

15.
LOVE IN THE TIME OF COFFEE

If he could have, James Hill surely would have hired teams of men to hammer together sheets of copper and zinc within a wood frame large enough to enclose the entire Santa Ana Volcano, and he would have hired more teams of men to stand outside the box dressed in lab coats, recording the energy consumption and expenditure of the people working within, watching them closely as they worked, feeding them no more than the stipulated rations at precisely the appointed times. Yet in the absence of a volcano-size calorimeter, and beyond the simple counting of rations served and tasks completed, Hill developed certain methods and techniques that allowed him to measure work to exacting standards and ensure that his orders were being carried out.

First Hill examined the work itself, measuring the muscular effort of the body by the mark it left on the earth. Jobs assigned by the task, such as digging holes, were easy to evaluate in this way, but more delicate jobs, including those assigned by the day, were harder to judge, and for such jobs there were more refined standards. When a "work-man" was hoeing by the day, Hill explained to Arthur Ruhl, he wanted to see him working in a way that turned over about eighteen inches of soil. To demonstrate, Hill stuck the point of his "stout walking-stick" sharply into the softened earth so the stick stood straight up. Anything less was "merely scratching and not really cultivating," and the scratchers would hear about it.[1]

As he watched people work, Hill also measured their respiration. If he heard people talking while they worked — or worse, if he heard them laughing and joking — he knew they weren't working hard because they weren't breathing hard, and he put them on piecework, to make them prove that they had earned their rations.

Finally, there was a third standard, even subtler, which integrated Hill's knowledge of the work itself, the atmospheric conditions on the Santa Ana Volcano, and human respiration and metabolism. When "work-people" were working as they should, Hill expected them to begin to get hot within half an hour. If he saw any "work-man" with his jacket still on after half an hour of labor, he put the man on piecework. Hill knew the man could have been working harder, for he had measured in terms of sweat.[2] Yet even when he was able to monitor working people in these ways, work was much harder for Hill to keep track of than rations. This was one of the crucial differences between even the best-kept plantations and laboratory calorimeters. Plantation workers were generally not as eager as A. W. Smith to follow the rules. Moreover, they far outnumbered the observers, who were anything but detached and objective themselves, and not always trustworthy.

One day in the middle of his postwar expansion, James Hill was out surveying the work in progress when he saw on the horizon the leafy crown of an avocado tree towering over a row of year-old coffee seedlings. Hill was dismayed to see the old tree, but not surprised. He had seen the same thing in other places, big old trees whose branches were jeweled so lavishly with ripening fruit that they threatened to snap and crush the coffee below. Elsewhere he had seen blackberry bushes and tomato plants growing thickly along the ground, sucking up fertilizers meant for the coffee trees. This was hardly the intricate Apollonian order of coffee production he had envisioned. Where Hill saw edible plants on his plantations, he saw waste, disorder, loss — he saw his land and resources and labor becoming something

281

other than coffee.[3] He had ordered all the fruit trees taken down, but there they were still, in defiance of his orders, and he thought he knew just what the problem was: bribes, passed from working people to managers, to protect certain out-of-the-way fruit trees, so there was food.[4]

The Apollonian engineering of the Santa Ana Volcano into a coffee factory required more than cutting down fruit trees and seeding the ground with poisonous plants. Some rules were only as good as their enforcement, and these rules therefore required policing the ways people related to one another, imposing new, businesslike priorities on much older forms of community, solidarity, and intimacy.

Before land privatization and the rise of coffee, access to food and resources in El Salvador derived from belonging: to specific Indian communities, to villages, townships, and municipalities, to families. To belong was to eat. The transformation of communal lands into private lands and coffee plantations did not at once sever these old social ties and eradicate deep customs of sharing, but it did make many of them illegal.

With the rise of coffee in El Salvador, both resources and people became concentrated on the plantations, so it was to the plantations that people went in need. When they needed work, they went to where their relatives and friends worked. When they needed water, they walked long distances to get it from people they knew had water access in the kitchens of plantations. When they needed a place to sleep indoors, they asked family and friends who lived on the plantations if they could make space in their small quarters. As coffee plantations took over more land and employed more people, more and more of the basic needs and private desires of people in rural El Salvador — even those who lived outside the plantation system — became subject to the planters' rules and laws.

Yet so too were the planters' rules and laws subject, in certain ways, to the needs and desires of the people who worked for them.

The numbers coming in from Deneke on Pedro Bolaños's bulletins suggested that something was amiss. Bolaños claimed that the women workers were fertilizing thirty holes a day, 20 percent more than the twenty-five holes Hill expected of them. Bolaños had meant to highlight an accomplishment, but his boss read it as a problem — the figures, Hill suspected, were too good to be true, so he stood up from his desk and went to find out for himself.

When he got to Deneke, Hill discovered that while Pedro Bolaños was employing a good number of women to fertilize holes, he had also hired some girls under ten years old.

The idea was that, by working, the girls could earn their own rations rather than have to share their parents'. Sharing food was one of the most important ways adults protected children, not only their own but also the children of their relatives and friends. Children the cooks knew always ate well. Children the managers and their wives knew always ate well. James Hill, who managed his own children's lives with an eye toward the thriving of the family business, knew that the people who worked for him favored and protected children in this way, and he thought this form of love was beyond his ability to legislate, so he tried to get some benefit out of it, often employing the children of cooks and managers as messengers.

Yet it was not only a matter of a task here and a ration there. While Hill was in Deneke, checking on the work he had assigned to Pedro Bolaños, he ran into a young woman who had set down her hoe and walked away from the area where a group of women was preparing holes for coffee seedlings. When Hill stopped her, she said she was following the orders of her supervisor, but Hill heard a lie in that story. He knew that the supervisor in question, working under Pedro Bolaños, was just a boy himself, and probably too young for the job of managing young women. He still wore his hair in a boy's cut, straight down in his face. Hill assumed that the young woman must be special to him or to someone else, and something in her manner told him that she knew it.[5]

The love of parents for children was one thing, but romantic love was out of place on the plantations, for it threw off the mechanism linking hunger, work, and food. After his trip to Deneke, Hill began to suspect that Pedro Bolaños was being tricked by people who were in love.[6]

The ties that bound working people to one another on the volcano grew not only from necessity and love. There were also ties of pleasure. People who worked together met on their own terms outside work. They met to play cards, they met to drink together, they met to rest and to talk. The problem with these activities and meetings, from a planter's perspective, was that they forged relationships that carried over into working hours and made the job of managers more difficult by building loyalties among working people themselves and between managers and the people Hill expected them to manage.

There was a large foreign element to the managerial class on Salvadoran plantations: for example, the disgraced German agricultural expert Wohlers and the Spanish overseer Florentino Díaz. In theory, one of the benefits of employing foreign managers was emotional distance, differences of place of birth, language, and culture — and in many cases physical traits, too — marking out an empathetic rift that would permit, for instance, one man to hang another.

Just the same, there were certainly more Salvadorans than foreigners in supervisory roles on Hill's plantations, and on a day-to-day basis the divide between managers and workers was porous. So Hill took measures to instill and increase this useful emotional distance. Just as he sought managers who avoided violence as a disciplinary strategy, Hill also tried to hire managers from distant regions, in the hope of avoiding preexisting social bonds. When this wasn't possible, Hill tried to teach his managers indifference, instructing them to cut themselves off from socializing with workers, lest they begin feeling too friendly to be in charge.[7]

Because his managers were men, Hill was especially worried about their socializing with women. Women who hung around the plantations were known as *arrimadas* — freeloaders, scroungers, dead weight. Hill found a pack of them loitering around one of his kitchens: the cook grinding corn, the manager's wife, plus two women who were known to go from plantation to plantation asking for favors. Women who roamed between plantations were always under suspicion of trading sex for special treatment, and were always seen as trouble when they arrived.

To whatever extent they were shaped by priorities other than coffee, the personal and family lives of Hill's managers weakened the mechanism of hunger, work, and coffee by which Hill's commands, written down in Las Tres Puertas, became work performed on the plantations. One manager brought his mother to live with him on one of Hill's plantations, and once installed there she started scolding people and asking to be served as if the plantation were her own. Another manager had insisted on employing two of his sisters-in-law, plus their families, in favored kitchen jobs. Hill found women living on another of his plantations while they worked on someone else's, and he figured out that these women paid rent to the plantation's manager, who had set himself up in business as the landlord of a building he didn't own.

Hill knew that his power over sex was limited. He took for granted that his managers had opportunities to trade food and favors for sex — such was the prerogative of men who controlled access to essential resources among poor and hungry people. He could only threaten to fire those who allowed themselves to be corrupted — and hope that this threat would make a seal around his plantations to keep out all of those who didn't contribute to their productivity, and keep in everyone and everything that did.[8]

The difficulty Hill had in getting his managers to follow such rules — the frustration he felt when he had to repeat orders again and again, the anger that rose up in him when he had to reiterate over and over what to him was common sense — suggests something of the complicated position Hill's managers were in, how hard it was for them to balance their privileged status on the plantations against their roles as husbands, sons, lovers, friends, and compatriots, and, perhaps, how reluctant they were to allow their boss to treat their people as if they were "his work-people."

The question was whether Pedro Bolaños was being fooled by the people who worked under him, or whether he was doing the fooling himself — neither was good, but the latter was worse.

When it first appeared that Bolaños had gone off course with Deneke, Hill was willing to give him the benefit of the doubt. Even he could hardly keep track of all the jobs Bolaños had to do, which is why he brought in a separate crew of carpenters to build the new kitchen in Deneke. And when Hill started to see things he didn't like in Pedro Bolaños's bulletins, at first he tried to spin them optimistically, on the basis of the man's past record of good work.[9]

But soon Hill's patience wore through. In the busy years of acquisition and expansion that followed the Great War, Pedro Bolaños had risen to preside over more land than any other of Hill's managers, almost 350 acres, and the largest number of working people — at certain times up to a third of the people working on all Hill's plantations. Though Bolaños had the training and judgment to know what needed to be done to remake Deneke, and though he had the intelligence to calculate the right way to do it, somewhere in that vast expanse of land, among the hundreds of people at work there, he took a wrong turn. He found the people he needed to fill Deneke with holes, but then he lost his way.

One day Hill went to Deneke to check on work there, but couldn't find Pedro Bolaños anywhere. He went to ask Bolaños's wife, who said he was with women fertilizing holes. The women fertilizing holes said he was with the women in the nursery. When Hill went to the nursery he didn't see him. So Hill stopped where he was and whistled three times and waited. For fifteen minutes he waited, cringing whenever the women working around him stepped on a seedling. Then he went to the place where people were planting coffee and waited some more. Then he went to search three smaller plantations he owned nearby, but no one told him anything about Pedro Bolaños.[10]

To be unaccounted for was to be under suspicion. When he began to monitor Pedro Bolaños's work more closely, Hill concluded that it was in this aspect of the job that he came up short: presence. On one visit to the plantations under Bolaños's management, Hill came upon some stacks of firewood on the side of the road. From a distance they looked like good stacks, but when he looked closer, he discovered that they had been arranged into a metaphor for Bolaños's career: they were hollow in the middle. Pedro Bolaños could attract people to work, but he could not make them do so properly, and Hill came to believe that those two things were related — that the reason Bolaños always got plenty of people to work for him was that he let them get away with doing less than they were supposed to, and then covered for them.[11]

For Pedro's brother Enecón Bolaños the problem was different. Enecón, who had taken over management of Hill's plantation Ayutepeque, was just slow. He could not keep to the schedule, and worse, he no longer seemed to care.[12] Under Enecón's watch, the plantation was developing so slowly that it seemed to be moving backward in time.[13] As snags and problems became the rule rather than the exception, Hill suggested changing its name from Ayutepeque to "The Delay."[14]

Sometimes Hill named his plantations for their problems, and sometimes for what he hoped they could be. When he was finally ready to rename Deneke, Hill chose a name that was at once testament and wish: "San Isidro," the patron saint of farm workers. That's what the plantation needed — either workers who were good, or a miracle.

Then there were times when Hill's lessons did take.

While the Bolaños brothers were falling in their boss's esteem, Hill's oldest employee, Eduviges Medina, was demonstrating how and why he had stuck around for so long. Medina was supposed to be overseeing the spreading of lime that preceded the cultivation of the soil and the digging of holes in La Reserva, another plantation where expansion was under way. The spreading of lime had always been a job for women, paying about ten cents a day. But the caustic compound, which neutralized the acids in the soil, burned and peeled the skin of the women's palms as they dug their hands into the sacks of lime they carried. The lime they cast over the ground burned and peeled the skin on the bottom of their feet as they walked. The women did not want to be burned anymore, at least not for so little money, so they asked for fifteen cents a day.

Hill didn't want to hear about peeling hands and feet, didn't want to hear about fifteen cents. If the women burned themselves it was because they hadn't slaked the lime with enough water. And if water was scarce now, the whole job should have been done earlier in the year, when there was plenty of water, when the work could have been done cheaply, without the complaints and difficulty now arising.

Eduviges Medina was always getting into disputes with his workers over pay, for which Hill had often scolded him, but this time he had a good idea. When the women refused to work for the customary wage, and the lime sat unspread in chalky heaps where anyone who passed by could steal it and turn it into food, Medina came up with a solution, cost-effective but time-sensitive. The veteran manager turned to a reserve army of labor not in great demand on Hill's plantations but well suited for light tasks. He hired children to spread the lime at the wage their mothers had refused.

Perhaps James Hill wanted his plantations to operate like calorimeters: isolation chambers that contained only people who worked for him and earned their food, monitored and administered day and night by authorities who stood at a remove from the small world they oversaw. But ultimately plantations were not like calorimeters at all. Hill's "work-people" were doing things that a body inside a calorimeter could not do, things not possible for the isolated subject who looked out at the world through the window of his glass cage and saw only the people who had put him in there. They were making sure their children ate. They were sharing water with neighbors. They were giving their families jobs and places in their homes. They gave themselves to one another for love and sex, they allowed themselves to belong to one another in ways that refuted the fantasy of mastery Hill expressed every time he talked about "his work-people." They were doing things that left no doubt of the differences between human beings and steam engines. They were refusing to work. They were taking one another into account. They were deciding how to live. And increasingly their ethics of taking one another into account was becoming a politics.

16.
THE TRUTH ABOUT COFFEE

William H. Ukers, not much over thirty, started working on his book in 1905, traveling and gathering material for a year. After he returned home to New York, he scoured nearby libraries and museums. Wherever he couldn't go himself, he sent auxiliaries, appointing research assistants to mine collections in Europe, especially in London and Amsterdam. After seven years of research, Ukers began to organize the material he had collected, even as it continued to come in. Six years later, he began writing. As he wrote, new questions came up that he spent months trying to answer. After four years of writing, Ukers, now almost fifty, tracked down his last fugitive fact in the spring of 1922. In June, *All About Coffee* went to the printer.

The book was published by the Tea and Coffee Trade Journal Company, which also published a monthly bulletin, one of two trade papers for the coffee industry. The other was *The Spice Mill,* founded by New York coffee roaster Jabez Burns in 1878. Ukers had started his career as a reporter at *The Spice Mill*, and he was promoted to editor in 1902. He left in 1904 to take over the *Tea and Coffee Trade Journal*, which, in contrast to *The Spice Mill*'s emphasis on the grocery business, focused more on international trade.[1] Every month, as he worked on his coffee book, Ukers was also writing, editing, and publishing a magazine on the same subject.

Trade journals aside, coffee had not been the subject of literary output equal to its importance in American life. In his foreword Ukers noted that *All About Coffee* was the first serious work on the topic published in the United States in more than four decades: the first since Francis Beatty Thurber's *From Plantation to Cup* in 1881, and, before that, Robert Hewitt Jr.'s 1872 *Coffee: Its History, Cultivation, and Uses*. Ukers was being generous. In fact his book had no precedent. It spanned nearly 800 large-format, two-column pages of small type, plus 17 color illustrations, 500 black-and-white illustrations, 100 portraits, and 30 maps, charts, and diagrams. Among the features Ukers was most proud of were the "Coffee Chronology," marking 492 dates of historical importance; the "Complete Reference Table of the Principal Kinds of Coffee Grown in the World"; and the "Coffee Bibliography," encompassing 1,380 references, the last section of the book before the index, itself 28 three-column pages.

William H. Ukers knew everything there was to know about coffee, but there were also some things about coffee — some of the most important things — that seemed unknowable. In the middle of his book were two chapters under the byline of Charles W. Trigg. Ukers had commissioned Trigg to write about "The Chemistry of the Coffee Bean" and "The Pharmacology of the Coffee Drink." The complexity and difficulty of these subjects, and their stakes, demanded the authority of a specialist.

Trigg was a chemical engineer by training. By trade he was probably the country's leading authority on instant coffee. Soluble coffee manufactured on the model of Japanese soluble tea had made its public debut at the Buffalo Pan-American Exposition in 1901, and the first widely available retail product was known by the fairly menacing brand name Red E. Among its backers were executives from railroads, sugar refining, and the Singer sewing machine company, a consortium of interests that illustrates the role coffee drinking had come to occupy in the American economy. Trigg had done his academic research at the Mellon Institute, in Pittsburgh. When *All About Coffee* was published in 1922, he held the position of chief chemist at King Coffee Products in Detroit, where he was working on two products with clear value in America's industrial cities: an instant brew called "Minute Coffee," and a line of coffee-based soft drinks called "Coffee Pep."[2]

The industrial orientation of Trigg's work came through in the chapters he contributed to *All About Coffee*. "When the vast extent of the coffee business is considered," he wrote, "together with the intimate connection which coffee has with the daily life of the average human, the relatively small amount of accurate knowledge which we possess regarding the chemical constituents and the physiological action of coffee is productive of amazement."[3] He did not use "amazement" in a positive sense. "It is possible to select statements from literature to the effect either that coffee is an 'elixir of life,' or even a poison. . . . This is a deplorable state of affairs," Trigg went on, "not calculated to promote the dissemination of accurate knowledge among the consuming public."[4] The implication was that it was calculated to promote something else.

Arguably the loudest anti-coffee voice in the country was C. W. Post, cereal mogul, moralist, recovered neurasthenic. Neurasthenia was a common diagnosis in late-nineteenth-century America, a condition indicated by symptomatic exhaustion that left its sufferers weakened to the point of bed rest. Post's case had gotten bad in 1890, when he was in his mid-thirties and down on his luck. In search of a cure, he went to John Harvey Kellogg's sanitarium in Battle Creek, Michigan. Kellogg was a dedicated opponent of coffee, which he identified, along with tea, as "a grave menace to the health of the American people." The larger fear behind the American epidemic of neurasthenia was that the nation itself was getting weaker. Kellogg considered coffee an addiction that was sucking Americans' vitality right out of them, leading to premature old age. For breakfast Kellogg's sanitarium served his own patented cereal blends and what he called Caramel Coffee, made from bread crusts, bran, and molasses.

For most neurasthenics, sanitariums were places for soaking up the healing properties of the sun. In addition to this, Post took Kellogg's ideas. By 1892, Post was well enough to open a sanitarium of his own in Battle Creek, which he called La Vita Inn. To provision it, he began to make his own strengthening foods, including, in 1895, his own coffee substitute, which he called Postum. Soon he began selling the mix to grocers, toting a portable stove from store to store and brewing up a pot at each stop. The recipe called for twenty minutes of brewing, plenty of time for a pitch. "When well brewed," Post claimed, "Postum has the seal brown color of coffee and a flavor very like the milder brands of Java." Even more important were his health claims. "It makes red blood," Post promised as he raised start-up funds to bring Postum to the mass market.

To promote his blend of roasted grains and molasses, Post, like Kellogg before him, cast coffee as a poison. Advertisements warned coffee drinkers of "coffee heart," "coffee neuralgia," "brain fag," blindness, ulcers, disintegration of brain tissues, indigestion, reduced work time, low energy, poverty, obscurity, and paralysis. By 1902, Post — a habitual coffee drinker himself — had made a million dollars. After Post's daughter, Marjorie, married in lavish style in 1905, William H. Ukers wrote a scathing editorial in the *Tea and Coffee Trade Journal* bemoaning the "gullibility of the American public," who had after all paid for the wedding.[5]

"Tell the truth about coffee" — that was the assignment William H. Ukers gave Charles Trigg, and it meant putting Post in his place with science.[6] "The ingestion of coffee infusion is always followed by evidences of stimulation," Trigg wrote in *All About Coffee*. "It acts upon the nervous system . . . increasing mental activity and quickening the power of perception, thus making the thoughts more precise and clear, and intellectual work easier without any evident subsequent depression.

The muscles are caused to contract more vigorously, increasing their working power without there being any secondary reaction leading to a diminished capacity for work." Having noted these benefits, Trigg proceeded down a list of the charges against coffee, refuting every one: insomnia, enervation, gout, addiction.[7] There were, he acknowledged, certain people who had tricked themselves into believing that coffee was bad for them, including the 1 to 3 percent of Americans who were "very nervous" — neurasthenic, like C. W. Post. "So," Trigg concluded, reasonably, "if one is personally satisfied that he belongs to the abnormal minority, and has not been argued by fallacious reasoning into his belief that coffee injures him, he should either reduce his consumption of coffee or let it alone."[8]

Still, there was one ambiguity at the heart of coffee science that Trigg could not resolve. In refuting Post, he cited multiple laboratory experiments that had concluded that coffee drinking led to an "increased capacity for work." Yet while the effect was clear, the cause remained obscure: the existing experiments had not definitively established why coffee drinking increased working capacity. As much as he would have liked to clarify the "deplorable" contradictions that had been put forth about the "effects of coffee drinking on the human system," Trigg could not explain the precise nature of the relationship between coffee, the human body, energy, and work.[9] Though he deferred to Trigg on most scientific questions, William H. Ukers had in the course of his exhaustive research come up with an explanation that seemed right to him. Coffee, Ukers wrote in his foreword, was "a corollary of human energy and human efficiency." It was "the most grateful lubricant known to the human machine."[10]

Today caffeine is extraordinary because it is so mundane. Used daily by the great majority of Americans — perhaps 80 percent — it is "by any measure, the world's most popular drug . . . the only addictive psychoactive substance that has overcome resistance and disapproval around the world to the extent that it is freely available almost everywhere, unregulated, sold without license, offered over the counter in tablet and capsule form, and even added to beverages intended for children."[11] Yet two centuries ago, at the moment of its discovery, caffeine was anything but mundane. Instead it was a window on nature's sublime intricacy.

Toward the end of his life, Johann Wolfgang von Goethe, the most celebrated intellect in Napoleon's Europe, could see in his mind the invisible connections that bound the world together. He rejected Descartes's separation of the mind and the body. He rejected Newton's idea that the universe could be chopped into free-standing parts, each of which could be analyzed in isolation from the others. Instead Goethe sought evidence of the wholeness he envisioned, some concrete example of "how the various parts work together."[12] He told a friend in conversation: "In nature we never see anything isolated, but everything in connection with something else which is before it, beside it, under it, and over it."[13] His thinking pointed in the direction science was going. German physician Hermann von Helmholtz, who described the conservation of energy in 1847, credited Goethe with anticipating the idea.[14]

In 1819, the seventy-year-old Goethe, once an avid coffee drinker, gave to a younger acquaintance whom he thought "quite promising" — a physician named Friedlieb Runge — a box of coffee beans from the port of Mocha and a challenge to figure out what was inside them, how they worked, what they did, what invisible connections they had to the wider world. At the time there was little clarity about the cause and nature of coffee's effects on the human body: it had confounded centuries of medical thought based on the humoral system, and modern medicine was barely in its infancy — Louis Pasteur, for example, was not even born.

Runge was up to Goethe's challenge. After

a few months of work, he isolated an alkaloid, a plant base, which he called *Kaffeine* — a compound of the German for "coffee" plus the suffix "ine," from the Latin for "of the nature of."[15] For some time, the terms of this discovery were strictly enforced. When an analogous alkaloid was isolated from tea leaves in 1827, it was called "theine," even after it was shown to be chemically identical to caffeine, which is now thought to have evolved in plants as an insecticide against certain harmful creatures and a stimulant to certain helpful ones.[16] Runge would go on to a successful career in commercial chemistry, among the milestones of which was his pioneering work in synthesizing blue dye from coal tar, permitting textile manufacturers to color their cloth with the by-products of its fabrication, and forcing indigo producers around the world — including El Salvador — to turn to other cash crops.[17]

The chemical analysis of coffee cast new light on the question of its effects. Coffee was found to contain three "active principles," or "causes." In addition to caffeine, there was caffeone, its essential oil, the source of its aroma and flavor, and caffeic acid, its essential acid, which also contributed to the flavor. These findings established a fixed definition of coffee that had important implications for the food business, increasingly concerned with substitutes and purity. Individually, wrote one coffee merchant, "each of these elements possesses virtues or powers of its own, and plays a part in the general effect produced by coffee"; together, these three "active" components gave coffee its "individuality" as an item of commerce.[18] Whatever didn't have them wasn't coffee.

Yet even as the definition of "coffee" took shape around these three "active principles," their action and effects in the human body remained a matter of speculation and disagreement. What exactly did caffeine do, and how? "Coffee acts on the diaphragm and the solar plexus, where it spreads to the brain via immeasurable emanations that escape all analysis," Honoré de Balzac wrote in 1839. "However, we can presume it is the fluids of the nervous system that conduct the electricity which this substance releases, and which it either finds or stimulates in our bodies."[19] For many years, the science remained at once definitive and ambiguous. More than a century after Runge's discovery, one investigator counted more than seven hundred scientific articles on coffee — by "chemists, physiologists, psychologists, dietitians, physicians and food inspectors, in fact from every type of scientist who has anything at all to do with the preparation, analysis or effect of foods and articles of diet."[20] Two hundred thirty-two of these, fully a third, focused on the question of coffee's effects on the body. Their findings, as Charles W. Trigg lamented, were often wildly at odds with each other.

Even in W. O. Atwater's calorimeter, where the operation of the human body was measured with unprecedented precision, coffee's effects were obscure. Though German studies of workers' diets had previously tried to account for coffee's contributions to labor power, Atwater set coffee and tea apart from other foods, delinking caffeine's effects in the body from the small number of calories — derived from the fat, or essential oil — in a cup of coffee. In studies of the food necessary "to live a day of the life of an ordinary man, say a mechanic or day-laborer, doing a fair amount of manual work," Atwater acknowledged that many subjects were drinking coffee regularly, but he left it out of his final energy accounting in an effort to "simplify the calculation."[21] "Tea and coffee," he wrote, "are not foods in the sense in which we use the word" — "material which, when taken into the body, serves to either form tissue or yield energy, or both."[22] He knew coffee was doing something to the body, and to respiration and metabolism specifically — "it has an invigorating effect, and may at times aid digestion" — but he could not make sense of these effects in terms of calories, so it seemed dubious. "Perhaps most of us would be better off if we did not drink tea or coffee," Atwater concluded, and kept to the principle in his laboratory.[23] While A. W. Smith was in the calorimeter, laboring over German treatises on physics to understand the laws his body could not help following, he had only water and milk to drink.

Atwater's reservations about coffee were shared by the other pioneering Gilded Age inspector of the human body at work, Frederick Winslow Taylor. In the decades around the turn of the twentieth century, factory mechanization, artificial lighting, and standardized clock time made the physiological limits of the human body at work look like the last great obstacle to unbounded industrial productivity, and an urgent problem to be solved. In famous time and motion studies begun in the 1880s, Taylor analyzed workers' movements to engineer the most efficient way of performing a given job, in the interest of reducing fatigue, maximizing output each workday, and paring the costs of production down to a hard minimum. In his personal habits and his trademark system of "scientific management" alike, Taylor emphasized consistency, steadiness, and sobriety as the keys to maximizing the productive use of "one's forces." As a result, he avoided stimulants and intoxicants of all kinds, including alcohol, tobacco, and coffee, for fear that they would throw off basic physiological functioning and lead to inefficiency.[24]

Its reputation clouded by conflicting opinions and claims, coffee did not fit neatly into Atwater's and Taylor's mechanistic concepts of the human body. So the two people most responsible for the scientific study of work and quantification of labor in the United States joined Kellogg and Post, the two people most responsible for breakfast, in disapproval of coffee.

Coffee's vexed relation to health, energy, and work was a problem Brazilian planters believed they could solve. In March 1918, war ongoing in Europe, Africa, and Asia, the planters put up a million dollars, with another $150,000 coming from American coffee roasters, to establish the Joint Coffee Trade Publicity Committee in New York.[25] The coffee committee's brief was to boost demand for coffee, and in turn prices, by promoting what employers in Restoration England, sweatshop workers on the Lower East Side, executives of the Singer sewing machine company, Charles Trigg, William H. Ukers, and Balzac, among many others, already knew instinctively to be true, even if proof remained elusive: coffee was a boon to work.

The coffee committee spent most of its seed money at the Philadelphia advertising agency N. W. Ayer, which ran ads in *Good Housekeeping*, the *Saturday Evening Post*, and other magazines that together reached an audience of more than thirteen million people each month.[26] The ads spotlighted Brazil's "chief service to mankind," and especially to the "active, virile" United States. "As a nation we require food that sustains body and brain at high efficiency," and for that purpose there was coffee: "the favorite beverage of millions of healthful, energetic Americans . . . helps men and women to endure exposure and withstand hard work."[27] Other ads were testimonials of coffee's contributions to everyday vitality for "the grocer," "the mechanic," and "the executive," the last of whom testified that, since he started drinking a cup of coffee toward the end of the day, he was able to do "more work now from four to five than I used to do all afternoon."[28]

In addition to the magazine ads, the coffee committee published its own literature: a newsletter that went out to 27,000 people across the coffee trade in the United States every month; and six pamphlets, a million and half copies of which were sent to American schools and homes between 1919 and 1925. One of these pamphlets, titled *Coffee as an Aid to Factory Efficiency,* told the story of a transformation at the W. S. Tyler Company in Cleveland.

In 1918, the year after its founder and namesake died, the W. S. Tyler Company began an experiment. The firm repurposed a room in its Superior Avenue metalworks as a Coffee Kitchen, supplying "its employees coffee, and the best coffee it can buy, topped off by genuine cream, also the best quality available in Cleveland, not at cost, but absolutely free," during the noon lunch hour. Tyler wasn't the first factory to give out coffee to its employees, but still the advantages of the service were "not appreciated as they should be." Free coffee was hardly a giveaway or "welfare," the company's assistant treasurer, E. P. Disbro, explained.[29] On the contrary, he said, any "plant which has not followed these principles is not working up to its full capacity." (In the late nineteenth century, following the widespread acceptance of the idea that work of all kinds required energy derived from the sun, it had become customary to refer to factories as plants.[30])

At the Tyler factory, Disbro had run the numbers. He knew what the coffee cost the company: about $200 in start-up funds, most of which went toward three 35-gallon percolators, plus daily expenses of about twenty dollars. The $20 covered twenty-two pounds of coffee, six gallons of cream, plus "the wages of the woman who makes and serves the coffee." That was enough coffee for the five hundred men who wanted it — each of whom had put down a quarter for a pint-size white enamelware mug, which they could return at the end of their tenure at Tyler to recoup the quarter. The mug held "the equivalent of two large breakfast cups," meaning that Tyler was serving about 1,000 cups of coffee every lunchtime, at a per-cup cost of about two pennies. This "high average" cost was due to the fact that "the company buys the very best coffee it can get and serves it with a liberal allowance of pure cream." Yet despite the high cost of giving away free coffee, Disbro insisted, the coffee service was considered "one of the plant's contributions to the efficiency of its force, and it pays."

Free coffee paid in a way that was difficult even for Disbro, the corporate treasurer, to quantify. He had not been able to figure out "in dollars and cents what rate they are getting on their investment." Nor did he believe that serving coffee had led to a direct increase in gross output. Instead, coffee had paid in "maintaining a standard of perfection in the product," helping the company to avoid the problem of the declining "mental and physical powers of the workman" over the course of the working day. Among other metal products, Tyler made wire screens through which wood pulp was extruded to make paper. "A wearied, devitalized workman who lets a flaw slip by him interferes not only with the reputation and the integrity of the W. S. Tyler Company but with the paper manufacturer who buys the imperfect product, and with everyone who comes into contact with the results of the imperfection."

The Tyler plant served coffee because executives had concluded that "it stimulates the digestive organs to keep a man 'fit' throughout the day," holding "the standard set by the early morning hours more nearly stable" through the afternoon. It was an intricate calculation, a delicate engineering of human mental and physical capacity across time, against fatigue, and with coffee.

The quality of the coffee was also a variable. "You'll never keep up the standard of production on cheap or adulterated coffee," Disbro warned plant managers thinking of following Tyler's example. "Just as a question of mechanics, I can't overestimate the necessity of maintaining quality in the coffee served. To my notion, it is just as foolish to supply the men with a poor coffee as it would be to buy a poor grade of oil for a very delicate machine."[31]

The ambiguities that characterized even the strongest endorsements of coffee as an "aid to factory efficiency" shaped the third component of the Joint Coffee Trade Publicity Committee's work. In addition to its advertisements and publications, the coffee committee also gave about $40,000 to Samuel C. Prescott, a prominent member of the biology department at MIT. Then as now, research at MIT was tightly entangled with business interests, and Prescott, who would later be

311

promoted to dean of science, had a good track record on big accounts. In 1914 he had set up the United Fruit Company's first banana research laboratory in Costa Rica.[32]

For the coffee job, Prescott outfitted a "Coffee Research Laboratory" in Cambridge. His brief had two parts. First, he was "to add so far as possible to our knowledge of the chemistry and physiological action of this beverage, which has assumed a world-wide importance." Second, he was to "inform the housekeeper, the restaurant manager or any one who has to do with the serving of this beverage how best to prepare this medium so that it should be most acceptable in aroma and flavor."[33] Research into this second question mostly entailed making coffee every day and serving it to the lab staff and their friends on campus. After three years of this, Prescott developed a publicity-friendly recipe for an MIT-approved "perfect" cup: coffee freshly ground, water a few degrees below boiling, and a glass vessel for brewing.[34]

Fortunately for the coffee committee, Prescott's findings on the "physiological action" of coffee were bolder. He reviewed hundreds of articles and came away with "the conviction that no group of investigators has undertaken the work from a sufficiently broad viewpoint."[35] As a result, anyone with a bad opinion of coffee could find articles "dealing with the ill effects of Coffee" on the human body, while anyone looking for an endorsement could read that coffee was one of the world's "most valuable beverages": "a prompt diffusible stimulant . . . [that] supports . . . the appropriate powers of the system, whips up the flagging energies, enhances the endurance" — though it was "in no sense a food."[36] Prescott's accomplishment was to broaden the "viewpoint" on coffee until what had been negatives — especially coffee's dubious relation to food, calories, and energy — began to look like positives.

Central to Prescott's insight was the work of H. L. Hollingworth, a professor at Columbia Teachers College, who in 1911 had led the way in remaking the scientific method in the service of American business. The business was Coca-Cola, which had been sued by Harvey Washington Wiley, head of the U.S. Department of Agriculture's Bureau of Chemistry and the chief author of the Pure Food and Drug Act. Wiley had no problem with coffee — in fact he promoted it as "America's National Beverage" — but he thought parents would be outraged if they knew that their children were consuming caffeine when they drank a bottle of Coca-Cola. In 1909, at Wiley's behest, government agents stopped a truck carrying forty barrels and twenty kegs of Coca-Cola syrup from the factory in Atlanta to a bottling plant in Chattanooga. Two years later *United States v. Forty*

313

Barrels and Twenty Kegs of Coca-Cola went to court. Under the Pure Food and Drug Act, Coca-Cola was charged with selling a beverage that was not only mislabeled, containing neither "coca" nor "kola," but also injurious to health, thanks to the added caffeine.[37]

To make its case, the government called "religious fundamentalists who argued that the use of Coca-Cola led to . . . sexual indiscretions by coeds and induced boys to masturbatory wakefulness."[38] For its defense, Coca-Cola commissioned a scientific study of caffeine. H. L. Hollingworth's doctoral advisor at Columbia, psychologist James McKeen Cattell, declined the commission, but Hollingworth needed the money — and anyway, he later wrote, he "had as yet no sanctity to preserve."[39]

The hypothesis was clear. Earlier tests, including those surveyed by Charles Trigg in *All About Coffee,* had found a clear quickening of nerve activity beginning fifteen to twenty-five minutes after coffee drinking. On the basis of those findings, all previous studies had reached the conclusion that "caffeine stimulates the capacity for muscular work." But the sample sizes had been small; the experimental conditions had not been tightly controlled; and, most important, explanations for the observed stimulant effect remained speculative.[40] Aiming for empirical rigor, Hollingworth rented a six-room apartment in

Manhattan, selected sixteen subjects, ten men and six women, mostly graduate students and university wives; asked them to give up all other stimulating drinks, including beer, and maintain a regular eating and sleeping schedule for the forty-day testing period; and then began running them through cognitive and motor tests. The cognitive tests approximated office work: color naming, naming of opposites, adding, editing, and response time. The motor tests approximated an assembly line: holding a metal rod steady in a hole without touching the sides, tapping the metal rod against a metal plate four hundred times as quickly as possible, and inserting the metal rod into one of three holes one hundred times as quickly as possible, which was to be done with the left hand, the right being tired from all the tapping. At the same time, one of the subjects was put through a different experimental course, one reflecting the division of labor in American workplaces. Her task was to type a copy of the Victorian art critic John Ruskin's *Sesame and Lilies,* on the unique abilities and duties of men and women.

Being "well aware," even painfully aware, of the "tendency to discredit the results of investigations financed by commercial firms," Hollingworth made his studies double-blind: both the subjects of the investigation and the investigators themselves were in the dark about whether a given subject was in the drug group or the control group. For a week none of the subjects was dosed. The next week they were all dosed with evaporated milk powder. Then the caffeine dosing began.

At the end of the forty days of experiments, the trial in Chattanooga was well under way, but Hollingworth swooped in from New York with good news. Caffeine had improved the performance of the subjects in each of the motor tests, and the improvements were evident quickly after consumption. In the cognitive tests, the positive effects were slower to show up, but they lasted longer. The only thing Hollingworth still couldn't say was why. "That the increased capacity for work is produced [by caffeine] is clearly demonstrated," he concluded in his write-up: "the drug effect" was genuine. "But whether this increased capacity comes from a new supply of energy introduced or rendered available by the drug action, or whether energy already available comes to be employed more effectively, or whether the inhibition of secondary afferent impulses is eliminated, or whether fatigue sensations are weakened and the individual's standard of performance thereby raised, no one seems to know."[41]

In the end, Hollingworth's testimony didn't make a difference in the trial. The federal judge in the case decided that because caffeine was part of the original Coca-Cola recipe, it wasn't an additive. On the contrary, it was "essential" to the nature of the beverage: "de-caffeinized, so to speak, the product would lack one of the essential elements and fail to produce upon the consumer . . . the most characteristic effect which is obtained from its use."[42] The suit was dismissed. Yet Hollingworth's findings did have important implications for the coffee industry.

Working for the Brazilian-American coffee committee, Samuel Prescott seized on Hollingworth's proof of caffeine's "drug effect" as the key to understanding coffee's "physiological action." Coffee was not a food, Prescott argued — it was better than that, providing some of the positive effects of food without certain negatives. That was the benefit of caffeine: "one of the most useful stimulants known because of the immediate action which is obtained with relatively small quantities and the fact that its reasonable use is not followed by narcotic or depressive effects." Put another way, the value of coffee was precisely that it was not subject to the processes and timescales of digestion and metabolism, the conversion of food to work via the body, that W. O. Atwater had measured with the calorie. Instead, coffee's stimulant effects bypassed the usual metabolic processes to immediately become available to the body. It was a form of instant energy — a work drug.

Coffee, Prescott concluded, "increases the

power to do muscular work by more vigorous contraction, increases power of mental effort and therefore quickens the perceptions and enhances the power to do sustained intellectual work."[43] In celebrating coffee for adding working power to the muscles and mind without taking any away, Prescott was suggesting that coffee provided energy for physical and intellectual work that did not come from the prior conversion of any other source or form of energy. The implication was that the human body on coffee was no longer subject to the laws of thermodynamics — the laws of energy and work, consumption and expenditure — that governed the rest of the universe.

In addition to his novel interpretation of the scientific literature on coffee, Prescott did conduct one new experiment for the joint coffee committee. First his team at MIT isolated caffeine from coffee, dried it into crystals, and dissolved the crystals in water to make a supersaturated solution. Then the scientists stuck rubber catheters down the esophagi of thirty rabbits and poured the caffeine solution into their stomachs until the rabbits died. Prescott calculated that the fatal rabbit dose of caffeine was equivalent to 150 to 200 cups of ordinary coffee for a 154-pound person.

To be certain that the solution of pure caffeine hadn't skewed the results, Prescott's team repeated the experiment with freshly brewed coffee, a good-quality medium-roast Brazilian. When they found that rabbit stomachs were too small for the coffee to accumulate in amounts that would add up to a lethal dose of caffeine, the researchers concentrated the coffee and tried again. Still the rabbits did not die as reliably as those fed pure caffeine. The beverage form of coffee, Prescott concluded, seemed to be protecting coffee drinkers from any negative effects of caffeine.

For the Brazilian-American coffee committee, trying to jump-start a sluggish postwar coffee market, the payoff of Prescott's research came in the advertising campaign that followed in 1923: "Read What This Famous Scientist Says About Coffee." "The Facts About Coffee." "Coffee Gives Comfort and Inspiration." "The Proof at Last!" "Coffee Is a Safe and Desirable Beverage." A full report was sent to doctors across the country.[44]

As it turned out, it was easy to encourage Americans to explore the upper reaches of the safe range of coffee consumption. Coffee-drinking contests that tested the thresholds of "the human machine" emerged as the newest trend in "athletic exercise" in the years after the war. In 1926, Gus Comstock, a barbershop porter from Fergus Falls, Minnesota, established a record that seemed unlikely to be broken when he drank sixty-two cups in ten hours. But then H. A. Streety, of Amarillo, Texas, gulped down seventy-one cups in nine hours, spurring Comstock to try again.

At seven o'clock in the morning on January 11, 1927, Comstock sat down in the lobby of the Kaddatz Hotel in Fergus Falls and took his first sip. Within an hour, he had drained eighteen cups. Around noon, a doctor checked him over and pronounced him healthy, except for a slight increase in body temperature. Two hours later, after seven hours of coffee drinking, Comstock finished his eighty-fifth cup as the crowd gathered in the lobby cheered him on. "His gulps were labored," reported the *New York Times,* but he felt like a hero.[45]

17.
THE AMERICAN CURE

Despite increased coffee drinking in the United States after the world war, prices did not climb as high as many in El Salvador hoped. By 1921, the chronic slump that had begun around the turn of the twentieth century was entering its third decade. It had not only cost small-scale farmers and careless planters such as Alberto Deneke their plantations, and challenged even successful planters like James Hill to economize, but also nearly bankrupted the Salvadoran government, which derived much of its revenue from export taxes on coffee. Increasing the tax was tantamount to inviting a coup, as the fate of the Ezeta brothers proved, so instead the government cut its spending. Payments to British and American firms that had built railroads and other infrastructure were suspended. Salaries of government officials went unpaid. With bills overdue both at home and abroad, the fall of the Salvadoran government seemed not far off, and that was an

321

outcome the U.S. State Department hoped to avoid.[1]

During and immediately after the Great War, American bankers, like San Francisco coffee importers, had made inroads in Latin American countries formerly dominated by British and European banks, including El Salvador.[2] The State Department encouraged the new business enthusiastically, with an eye toward consolidating U.S. power in the hemisphere against the possibility of a resurgence of European imperialism after the war. There was also concern that the spirit of the Mexican Revolution — which had begun in 1910 as a rebellion against a profiteering dictatorship and led in 1917 to a new constitution much less friendly to foreign business — would spread throughout the region. After the 1917 October Revolution in Russia, the name given to this threat was Bolshevism. In this context, it was good news in Washington when in 1921 the Salvadoran government asked one of its creditors, Minor C. Keith, a founder of the United Fruit Company and the head of the International Railways of Central America, to arrange an eight-figure bank loan that would cover the country's existing debt and fund some new rail construction and economic development, too.

The plan was not so well received on Wall Street. New York bankers had a front-row seat to years of market turbulence at the coffee exchange in Lower Manhattan, and they justifiably viewed the Central American coffee business as a dubious bet. Facing skepticism from bankers, Keith turned to the State Department for help in pitching the loan as an investment opportunity. He sold Washington on a quick exchange of notes with the Salvadoran government — no congressional approval required — that empowered the secretary of state to appoint a customs inspector to monitor El Salvador's foreign trade (while skimming a percentage of the customs revenue off the top, to pay down the loan), and stipulated that any disputes between lenders and the Salvadoran government would be arbitrated by the chief justice of the U.S. Supreme Court. His plans for a Salvadoran loan now secured by the authority of two branches of the U.S. government, Keith took his proposal back to Wall Street.[3]

There was already a template for this type of arrangement. The contract with El Salvador was one of a handful of "controlled loans" for Latin American governments that the U.S. State Department backed after the war. With the federal government acting as a guarantor, American banks fronted money to bolster Latin American governments favorable to the U.S. In return, Latin Americans were compelled to accept conditions and contingencies — including the supervision of their economies by State Department-appointed advisors and, in many cases, far-reaching economic reforms. The unstated implication was that defaulting on the loan payments would open the door for U.S. military intervention.[4] The State Department denied this, but the American troops already deployed in Haiti, the Dominican Republic, Nicaragua, Cuba, and Puerto Rico constituted a de facto statement of policy.

The architect of these "controlled loans," marrying the wealth of Wall Street with the power and authority of Washington, was Edwin Kemmerer, a Princeton University economist known as "the money doctor." Kemmerer had worked in the Philippines in 1903, Mexico in 1917, and Guatemala in 1919 before making his reputation in Latin America in the twenties, treating "sick nations" with "the American cure," as the New York Times put it in 1928.[5] He and his students and allies in government and banking alike helped to arrange loans for five Latin American nations, including El Salvador, in the 1920s.[6] All packaged cash with obligatory economic oversight and reforms.

"The money doctor" was an apt nickname. Kemmerer's approach to treating "sick nations" aligned with experiments in physiology and nutrition that he had seen in action when he was in college, at Wesleyan. He had arrived on the Connecticut campus in the fall of 1895, just as W. O. Atwater was beginning trials with the calorimeter. On Saturday, March 28, 1896, near the end of his freshman year, Kemmerer visited Atwater's lab to witness A. W. Smith's record-setting stint in the calorimeter, and spoke with Smith using the telephone system Atwater had rigged up.[7]

The same day, Kemmerer attended a lecture on campus given by the postmaster general of the United States, William L. Wilson, on the subject of "Politics as a Duty." Wilson had risen to national prominence as a Democratic congressman from West Virginia, and like many southern Democrats he was a dedicated free trader. In 1894, with the U.S. economy in the grip of a serious depression, Wilson sponsored a controversial tariff bill that lowered duties on imports to spur foreign trade and U.S. exports, while making up for the expected loss in government revenue with the first peacetime income tax. The rate was 2 percent on earnings over $4,000, which affected only the richest tenth of the population but was enough to make the bill anathema to elites, whose narrow self-interest Wilson came to resent. "The economic and financial questions call for as much heroism as was displayed by our forefathers on the battlefield," Wilson said at Wesleyan. "Our present system of finance is patchwork . . . College men, educated men, and business men must come to the front. They can not stand idly by."[8] All year,

Kemmerer had been a diligent if uninspired student. Perfunctory diary entries recorded without enthusiasm the hours he put in at his desk. Yet he was moved by Wilson's "excellent" speech, and the following day he called on the postmaster general at W. O. Atwater's house in Middletown.[9]

Over the course of his career as an economist, Kemmerer would answer Wilson's call to duty by developing the logic of Atwater's calorimeter into a system of international financial governance. The "American cure" he prescribed for Latin American governments was based on a three-part formula of debt, discipline, and exports: an injection of borrowed cash paired with top-down reforms that ranged from monetary and commercial policy to penal codes, all directed toward the goal of increasing export production.[10] The idea was that an infusion of money into a national economy could be efficiently routed, through good government and administration, toward the most efficient and productive sectors. The conditions Kemmerer and his advisors wrote into the loan contracts invariably included the appointment of a customs inspector, usually one of Kemmerer's American acolytes, who stood in the same relation to the country he inspected as the lab-coated monitors of the calorimeter to the subjects inside.[11] Early in his career, Kemmerer had even pushed to develop a single unit of currency for the Western Hemisphere — a sort of financial calorie — to clarify the relation between a nation's economic input and output and bolster hemispheric commerce.[12]

It was strict calorimeter thinking. Putting more in, and making sure it was used properly, made it possible to get more out. Yet this symmetry was not merely a coincidence of Kemmerer's experiences at Wesleyan. After his freshman year, he began to take classes in economics, a new discipline rooted in ideas that would have encouraged a student with interests in finance and politics to see the calorimeter as a perfect world.

For much of its history, economics belonged to a larger area of inquiry called moral philosophy.[13] Moral philosophy was rooted in ethics rather than equations and laws. It asked questions about how resources should be used and distributed within a given society, and worked toward answers that took particularities of custom, place, and culture into account. Something of this heritage survives in the fact that prices are often called "values," and things "goods."

After roughly 1870, the contextual and ethical aspects of the field largely fell away as economics was redefined as an exact science, objectivity making special considerations unnecessary. The hinge of this transformation

327

was the newly formulated idea of energy and the associated laws of thermodynamics.[14] English economist Alfred Marshall, one of the founders of the discipline, summed up the new economic science as "a study of mankind in the ordinary business of life." The phrase has often been taken to mean that life is like business — that the basic principle is to use resources to create wealth and "satisfy . . . desire."[15] But it is arguably more revealing to read it the other way around. Economics became an "objective" science, based on a set of universal laws, when economists began to study business as if it were life — as if it operated on the same principles as the human body.

Scientific economists took their conception of the body from thermodynamics. "Life seems to be nothing but a special form of energy which is manifested in heat and electricity and mechanical force," wrote William Stanley Jevons in 1874. A professor of logic and moral philosophy at the University of Manchester, Jevons was a pioneering figure in mathematical economics who is perhaps more popularly known for his theory that sunspots determined the business cycle. "The time may come, it almost seems, when the tender mechanism of the brain will be traced out," Jevons wrote. "Must not the same inexorable reign of law which is apparent in the motions of brute matter be extended to the subtle feelings of the human heart? . . . If so, our boasted free will becomes a delusion, moral responsibility a fiction, spirit a mere name for the more curious manifestations of material energy." Jevons himself looked skeptically at the reduction of all "the mysteries of existence" to forms of energy in the name of science, in part because he could see where it was headed. In the "coming religion" of materialism, the human will was cast as an effective "nonentity."[16] In the new scientific economics, the "ordinary business of life" was a mechanized industry.

Borrowing the thermodynamic view of the body as an energy-based mechanism allowed scientific economists to write new laws of human behavior. This had been something of a sticking point in the past, and with reason. People break and defy all sorts of laws all the time, and earlier economic thinking had hedged against the possibility of such "irrationality," rebellion, contingency, and accident. Yet the science of energy had identified thermodynamic laws that the human body could not help following, and in the last decades of the nineteenth century these were translated into the founding principles of what is now called neoclassical economics.[17] First among these was the absolute inevitability of work.

It has often been said that neoclassical economics has no core theory of production

— that it is not concerned with explaining how employers individually and collectively organize their businesses and interests to make their employees work. In one sense there was no need for the scientific economists to ask what makes people work, for the new, thermodynamic conception of human life had already provided an answer: People made themselves work. The mechanics of the body left them no choice. To live was to work and to eat. The one implied the other. To generalize the principle, the need to eat was recast as the desire to consume — to maximize marginal utility. The analogy was explicit: utility was to economic science as energy was to physics — the all-pervasive force, the medium of every action, the cause of all effects, the thing everyone needed, the unbreakable law.[18] In the world of neoclassical economic thought, the human being was reduced to a mechanism, driven to produce by the need to consume.

Real life was not so simple. Just as James Hill — like employers the world over — worked hard to produce the hunger that obligated his employees to work, it was the job of economists who found employment in government to make policy that enforced the laws of their discipline on the ground. In the same way that the calorimeter made work appear to be a natural function of the human body, Edwin Kemmerer's "controlled loans" presumed exports to be the natural product of a healthy economy. All that was required to make it so was control itself: the elimination, at the level of the nation-state, of the world outside the box, the eradication of alternatives, the foreclosure of the possibility of unproductive eating, being, doing — ways of living that were not directly convertible into cash on the world market. And that was the job of the inspectors and the reforms that came along with the money.

Once the Salvadoran loan acquired the seal of the U.S. government, American bankers began to look favorably on Minor Keith's proposal. In 1922, the Chatham Phoenix National Bank & Trust of New York put up $6 million, financed by bonds yielding a rich 8 percent. Secured as it was by customs revenue, including an export tax on coffee, the deal vested the bank, its bondholders, and its guarantor — the U.S. government — in the success of James Hill and his fellow planters. It also yielded big profits for Minor Keith, profits so generous that the State Department thought them practically "unconscionable." But Edwin Kemmerer said the terms were fair, so they stood.[19] On the other side of the table, in addition to the cash, El Salvador got a new American customs inspector, a new American chief of agriculture, and a new American commissioner for its elite

331

police unit, the National Guard.

At first the Salvadoran elite balked at the idea of an American customs inspector. Local bankers, especially Benjamin Bloom of Santa Ana's Banco Occidental, had traditionally been in charge of arranging financing for the government — also known as "debauching the governments of this country," as an American diplomat in El Salvador put it — and they resented the competition.[20] But the Salvadoran national assembly approved the loan deal because there were bills due, and the money could be used to build highways and railroads that would open up land that had previously been inaccessible to coffee production.[21]

William W. Renwick was chosen as the customs inspector for El Salvador by the Chatham Phoenix National Bank, and his appointment was approved by the U.S. State Department. Renwick's new job put him in a position not unlike a "High Commissioner following an occupation," reporting on the everyday operations of the Salvadoran economy to the bank and the Department of State.[22] Much of the revenue he collected came from the export tax on coffee, two cents a pound, or about two dollars a bag.

It turned out to be not as burdensome to host Renwick as many Salvadorans expected. He was hardly the "ill-dressed and depressing foreigner who looks as if he might be get-

332

ting a tenth of the salary your little country is compelled to pay him had he stayed at home" — a type Latin Americans were learning to loathe. On the contrary, Renwick was a "slim, cheery, wide-awake" young American, "a go-ahead human being trying to contribute something."[23] He lived modestly. His bearing was professional and free of condescension. He hired Salvadorans for his staff and trained them well.[24] Most afternoons he could be found at the country club, out in a quiet corner of the golf course practicing his drives, which were already impressive. He and his wife made friends with Salvadorans and expatriates alike. He had enough freedom and flexibility to travel with Edwin Kemmerer to Chile, where he served as a consulting expert in customs collection for a comprehensive economic reform that Kemmerer was undertaking there.[25] Renwick also volunteered his time, free of charge, as an economic consultant to the Salvadoran government, and his work was so good that the Salvadorans kept giving him more of it.[26]

The capable W. W. Renwick was not the only American hired by the government of El Salvador after the loan. In September 1923, Frederic W. Taylor, a California-based agricultural consultant, moved into an office in the national palace in San Salvador and began working to strengthen the country's export economy from the ground up.

When the job offer had reached Taylor at home in the Los Angeles spring, he immediately saw it as a natural capstone to his career. He had grown up in Iowa working in his family's nursery. As a young man he had held an ascending series of positions in commercial agriculture, eventually rising to be the superintendent of horticulture, forestry, and food exhibits, as well as director of concessions, at the 1901 Pan-American Exposition in Buffalo, in which capacity he had awarded a silver medal to James Hill's peaberry coffee. Buffalo went so well that Taylor was hired as Chief of the Departments of Agriculture and Horticulture for the Louisiana Purchase Exposition of 1904, the St. Louis World's Fair.

Working for the fairs launched Taylor's career into an international orbit. In 1911, he was appointed director of agriculture for the Philippines, where Edwin Kemmerer had also worked as a young man. When Taylor arrived in the Philippines, he immediately identified a key agricultural and social problem. Rice was the linchpin staple crop, but while the islands were well adapted for growing it, in fact they imported great quantities. With "whole provinces . . . engaged in growing other than food crops," Filipinos were entirely dependent on the market for sustenance. The resulting situation was potentially volatile and unfavorable for American rule, the terms of which were still being worked out after the Spanish-American and Philippine-American Wars. Taylor's solution was a program to increase the rice crop by 25 percent. While taking pressure off the food supply, he also worked to increase the production of the principal export commodities: Manila hemp, coconuts, and sugar.

After his tour in the Philippines, Taylor picked up contract work as a private agricultural consultant for American firms with tropical interests. In 1920 he made a trip to El Salvador to look over some land for a New York rubber concern, staying long enough to make an impression on the Salvadoran elite. With the American loan about to be finalized in the spring of 1923, Taylor's Salvadoran contacts got in touch and explained that one of the conditions of the loan was agricultural reform.[27] They asked Taylor to set up an office in the national palace and begin work to put El Salvador's agriculture on a "scientific" basis — which meant reshaping the country's landscape in a way that would help to repay the loan, even if coffee prices remained depressed, or worse.[28]

Taylor replied enthusiastically, though he knew practically nothing about coffee, by far El Salvador's most important crop, accounting for 80 percent of the country's exports in 1921, and rising.[29] He had awarded medals to James Hill and others in Buffalo on the basis of the appearance of the beans rather than knowledge of coffee cultivation, which had not been part of his professional experience. Despite the history and potential of coffee in the Philippines, it had never been a U.S. priority there.

Nevertheless, Taylor believed his work in the Philippines, where he had "greatly increased the general efficiency," had prepared him well for El Salvador. He asked for a salary of ten thousand dollars a year, plus expenses — below his normal rate, in consideration of the fact, he explained, that he "should very much like to do this particular work, for I see just how it can be done, and the enormous value it would be to your country, which I much like."[30] He sailed from Los Angeles in August.

Taylor's first days in El Salvador were reassuringly familiar. He was especially pleased with his new office on the second floor of the national palace, with "a private retiring room adjoining, telephone on desk, and everything as fine as could be asked for," he wrote to his family soon after arrival.[31] After settling in, Taylor began to look around the country. He found coffee and the second crop, sugar, in fairly good shape. But everything else, including corn, beans, rice, horses, cattle, and hogs, lagged far behind, which was not a surprise:

"That is no doubt because the coffee and sugar growing is in the hands of the large land owners, who can afford to spend the money necessary to produce good crops, while the other crops are for the most part grown by [small farmers], who use no intelligent selection of seed, and have no modern implements with which to prepare their land, or cultivate their crops, and who have no good male animals to use in breeding."[32] Part of the problem was lack of scientific training, even among the elite. Taylor advertised openings for staff in the United States, seeking graduates of the University of California in particular.[33]

After about a year in-country, Taylor reported to the editor of an agricultural journal in the United States that he was "finding the work extremely interesting. It is in many respects very similar to what I was doing in the Philippines," he explained, though the "crops are somewhat different."[34] The crops were different in part because the Salvadoran government had little interest in increasing food production, as Taylor had done in the Philippines. Instead the government wanted to increase export production, the source of the customs revenue that would keep the country out of default on its loan. In particular, the Salvadoran government wanted to establish secondary export crops that would pay the bills if something happened to coffee

337

— as when the coffee leaf rust reached the Philippines, once an important producer, at the end of the nineteenth century. Taylor's job was purpose-building El Salvador's agricultural economy around the need for exports and customs revenue.[35] The diversification of second-tier export crops made monoculture rational.

Taylor oversaw the transformation of those parts of the Salvadoran countryside not planted in coffee into a laboratory of export commodity production. He arranged for the importation of pineapple and coconut seeds from Hawaii, brought some cattle in from California, and secured "from the great sugar-producing countries, seed of the best and most profitable varieties," and he carried on a correspondence with Harvey Firestone about the possibility of establishing a rubber plantation like the Firestone operation in Chiapas, Mexico. Jute was out, given the fact that it was produced so cheaply in India, but the production of henequen, another versatile tropical fiber, was increased substantially, and Taylor thought "the Manila hemp, of the Philippine Islands, offers a promising field for experiment."[36] In effect, Taylor turned rural El Salvador into an economic microcosm of the Pacific Rim.

Yet all of these new crops were minor compared with the key part of Taylor's plan for remaking El Salvador's export economy

338

on "a scientific basis" — cotton. Taylor had shipped down from California 200 tons of Acala cotton seed, the variety that thrived in the state's Imperial Valley, enough to plant 20,000 acres, most of which would be low-lying coastal land too hot for coffee.[37] He helped the Santa Ana–based Banco Occidental — the largest coffee investor in the country, run by Benjamin Bloom — learn the cotton-financing business, and he helped landowners learn cotton planting.[38] In his first year on the job, Taylor received applications and issued permits for the planting of cotton on almost 50,000 acres, and he scrambled to get more seed.[39] "At least a dozen of the biggest land owners of the republic have been in to talk with me about cotton," he reported home. "The people here are wild about cotton."[40]

Not all of the early plantings turned out, but nevertheless cotton was by far the most consequential of Taylor's contributions to Salvadoran agriculture. As the cultivation of Bourbon coffee spread down the volcano and into lower altitudes and higher temperatures, cotton reached inland and uphill from the low coastal plains. The progress of the two crops toward each other squeezed out food production, in particular corn, El Salvador's most important staple crop.[41] During Taylor's time in El Salvador, between 1922 and 1926, the price of corn doubled, the price of beans more than doubled, and the price of rice tripled. The country began to import more and more food.[42]

Despite Taylor's hard work — he often felt as if he alone were doing the work of an entire staff — and the substantial changes he worked on the landscape, he did not fit in in El Salvador as well as W. W. Renwick did. Landowners complained that Taylor had not systematized and circulated a set of instructions for cotton cultivation. Coffee planters complained that he had diverted the resources of the Ministry of Agriculture away from coffee — as was clear from the fact that the Ministry had not published a study that James Hill had made of coffee in Brazil during his last trip there.[43] Taylor's candidacy for membership at the Casino Salvadoreño, the country's leading social club, was blackballed.[44] When he attended a society wedding with a thousand other guests, he found it a "harrowing" affair and left early.[45]

Being shut out of the social circuit was one thing, and Taylor mostly laughed it off. Yet he also found himself the target of protests and demonstrations that were not so easily dismissed. "There is a very bitter feeling against the United States," he wrote to his family just after the New Year, 1927. "Sunday, there was a gathering, in front of the palace, of sympathizers with the movement to object to the action of the States, and, while it was

340

mostly made up of young men, of about high school age, there were a lot of them, probably a couple of thousand, and they made a good deal of noise, and waved banners attacking the Yanquis."[46] Taylor knew there was increasing anti-American sentiment across Central America and the Caribbean basin, and he knew that the loan in particular was a flashpoint in El Salvador, but he didn't quite understand the source of the trouble. "We are here because they asked us to come," he wrote, "to do things they wanted done and had never been able to carry out themselves."[47]

Most of all, Taylor was homesick. His wife, Marion, had stayed behind in Los Angeles with their children, and he had begun planning her first visit to El Salvador two months before she was scheduled to arrive.[48] When the chance arose to take a job with a rubber company that would allow him to go home in the spring of 1927, before his contract was up, Taylor grabbed it. From San Salvador he cabled his wife with his itinerary: "Sailing Colombia eleventh hallelujah."[49]

The departure of Frederic W. Taylor did nothing to quell the anti-American protests gaining intensity in El Salvador. The resentment was much deeper than that. Taylor's letters home had given voice to a question at the center of heated debates about American

341

foreign relations in the 1920s. Was the active role the United States was taking in the affairs of foreign nations, and especially in Latin America, improving or eroding the place of the U.S. in the world? Was the United States — which had long been at pains to set itself apart from the European tradition of conquest and colonization in the Americas — imperialistic?

It was a strange question, considering that the U.S. had acquired a handful of colonies in the Western Hemisphere and the Pacific almost two decades earlier, after the Spanish-American War. Yet at its core the question was less about colonies and more about how the United States related to the parts of the world it did not formally rule, especially Latin America, the strategic foundation of American international power and wealth. More and more, the "Yanquis" had their hands in everything. Total U.S. investments in Latin America more than tripled between 1914 and 1930, from $1.5 billion to more than $5 billion.[50] The U.S. military occupation of Nicaragua — in force since before the world war — was perhaps the clearest instance of the problem, though hardly the only one. In addition to Nicaragua, U.S. Marines had occupied Haiti more than once. The economy of the Dominican Republic was under U.S. control after a loan default and customs receivership. American corporations, especially the United Fruit Company, had transformed the nations lining the western shore of the Caribbean into "banana republics." And now there was the loan program.

In addition to Taylor's agricultural reforms, the Salvadoran loan funded infrastructure improvements, including paving city streets and building roads to move exports more efficiently to the coast, and upgrading police forces. In 1923, the year the loan deal was finalized, the United States had convened a Conference on Central American Affairs in Washington, pressing the participants into signing a treaty that would deny recognition to any government that took power by force, and proposing the enhancement of military police in each country — both ways of buttressing friendly regimes. As part of the package, El Salvador, along with Nicaragua, signed up to have its National Guard trained by the U.S. military.[51] The following year, 1924, the Salvadoran government, with money to spend, moved to expand the ranks of the National Guard, offering financial incentives for veteran guardsmen who wanted to extend their terms, and offering bounties for "heroic acts" committed in the line of duty.[52] These were not programs all Salvadorans prioritized equally.

Between 1923 and 1931, "the money doctor" Edwin Kemmerer also oversaw loans to and economic reforms in Colombia, Ecuador,

Bolivia, Chile, Peru, Mexico, and Guatemala.[53] To Samuel Guy Inman, a missionary and historian with extensive experience in Latin America, Kemmerer's "controlled loans" — even factoring in the generous returns — were not worth the price in popular discontent. In an article titled "Imperialistic America," published in *The Atlantic Monthly* in July 1924, Inman opposed "dollar diplomacy" on both moral and strategic grounds. "Out of the twenty Latin-American republics," Inman wrote, "eleven of them now have their financial policies directed by North Americans. . . . Four . . . of these Southern countries have their economic and fiscal life closely tied to the United States through large loans and concessions, giving special advantages to American capitalists." He predicted that the resulting "resentment and enmity" would lead to the diminishment of the place of the U.S. in the world, its own decline and fall. "The continuation of this 'dollar diplomacy' means the destruction of our nation just as surely as it meant the destruction of Egypt and Rome and Spain and Germany," Inman prophesied, "and all the other nations who came to measure their greatness by their material possessions rather than by their passion for justice."[54]

Inman's dire forecast prompted angry responses from entrenched interests. Nationalist leaders of Latin American countries pridefully contested his assumption of U.S. predominance. The director of the Pan-American Union, dedicated to promoting hemispheric cooperation, insisted that inter-American relations had never been stronger. F. J. Lisman, a German-American banker who had a stake in the Salvadoran loan, wrote two critical letters to *The Atlantic,* with copies to the Department of State, taking particular exception to Inman's dim view of U.S. financial advisors.[55]

Perhaps the most comprehensive rebuttal to "Imperialistic America" came from the U.S. Department of State itself, in the form of a dissent from the desk of Sumner Welles. Welles had worked both in the State Department and on Wall Street, but he was hardly an imperialist bully. On the contrary, he had temporarily quit the State Department in 1922 over concerns that the U.S. military was becoming an adjunct of U.S. business interests. Welles shared many of Inman's concerns, even as he questioned his central assumption. "Is America Imperialistic?" asked the title of Welles's reply to Inman, published in *The Atlantic* in September 1924. Against Inman's image of a rapacious America, Welles argued that the "dollar diplomacy" of the United States had been welcomed by "the vast majority of responsible Latin Americans who were engaged in constructive and productive pursuits." Countering Inman's premonitions of the decline of U.S. power abroad, Welles insisted that the follow-on effects of increased commercial activity would be positive. "It is almost axiomatic," he concluded brightly, "that development of commercial relations between countries brings about a better understanding and a clearer perception of their mutual advantages and common needs."[56]

Even as Welles wrote, changes in the coffee market were putting that theory to the test.

18.
THE COFFEE QUESTION

From a banker's perspective, the loan Minor Keith arranged for El Salvador was brilliantly timed. When Keith had begun to put the deal together in 1921, the world price of coffee was about ten cents a pound, where it had been stuck for most of a quarter century. When the loan was finalized in 1923, coffee was above 13 cents a pound. In 1924, it topped 17 cents. In 1925, the average world price reached 22 cents per pound.[1] At those prices, American bondholders were all but guaranteed to cash in on their 8 percent returns. The chronic depression that had plagued the market since 1896, the year James Hill opened Las Tres Puertas, was over.

The improvement in prices was equally auspicious for Hill, who was producing more coffee than ever. As late as 1923, three years after he bought Deneke's land, put Pedro Bolaños in charge, and began to plant it with Bourbon, the plantation Hill renamed San Isidro had produced no harvest to sell. But in 1924, as prices began to rise, Hill got the first harvest, nearly 6,000 pounds of export-ready beans. The following year he got 10,000 pounds. In 1926, he got 17,000 pounds. From La Reserva, which had been under the charge of the veteran manager Eduviges Medina, Hill had gotten only 1,000 pounds of beans in 1920 — six years later, he got ten times that amount.[2] In 1926, Hill sold a large crop, more than three million pounds, for 25 cents a pound, and for the first time in three decades in coffee, he was able to pay down his debt to near zero. He was beginning to feel "somewhat free," and he knew that the credit was due to his "Brazilian friends."[3]

Hill was not referring to the million-dollar promotional campaign that the Brazilian-American Joint Coffee Trade Publicity Committee had under way in the United States. The dramatic upswing in price had not come from better scientific studies, more convincing advertisements, or increased coffee drinking at factories. Instead it was the result of the renewal of the price-control program São Paulo planters had begun back in 1906, when they borrowed more than $125 million from an international consortium of bankers and merchants to buy up their own coffee and hold it in warehouses in New York and Europe until the price rose. Back then, the Brazilians and their financiers had called this strategy "valorization." It worked perhaps

348

slightly too well, and in the United States it was decried as monopoly.

In 1911, the world price of coffee having doubled, Nebraska senator G. W. Norris called for a federal investigation, claiming this "coffee trust" was costing American coffee drinkers $35 million a year. A year later, the U.S. attorney general sued the syndicate of American, English, German, French, and Belgian bankers who had loaned the money to the São Paulo planters — the planters, and the Brazilian government itself, falling outside U.S. jurisdiction. In 1913, in the spirit of trust-busting, and believing that the executive branch was dragging its feet due to diplomatic considerations, Senator Norris pushed a bill into law authorizing the seizure of coffee whose price had been manipulated.[4] Busted in the United States, the coffee trust shifted operations to Brazil.

The outbreak of the world war in 1914 froze international financing and mostly precluded large-scale intervention in the market, but after the war, Brazilian planters shifted their approach and started again. In 1922, while the Brazilian-American joint committee was promoting coffee consumption in the U.S., the state of São Paulo established the Institute for the Permanent Defense of Coffee. Two years later, in 1924, the "coffee defense" plan was expanded throughout the country, in the form of eleven warehouses capable of storing three and half million bags, or about a half a billion pounds of coffee, beyond the reach of U.S. lawmakers.[5] By 1926, world coffee prices, again having doubled, attained levels untouched in a century.[6] For planters across Latin America, the Brazilian defense of coffee was an answered prayer — but in the eyes of the U.S. secretary of commerce, Herbert Hoover, it was a scourge.

In light of his response to the Great Depression, Herbert Hoover has been cast in American history textbooks as ineffectual in the face of crisis and callous in the face of suffering. In many ways that is a strange and ironic fate for a man who, before he entered the White House, was celebrated internationally as "the Great Humanitarian" — a title he earned, in large part, by fighting hunger around the world.

Hoover was a member of the inaugural class at Stanford University, where he studied geology. After graduating in 1895, he began a lucrative career as a mining engineer in the American West and across the Pacific in Australia and Asia. The complex work of mining — extracting once-inaccessible resources from the earth and making them available for society to use — set the template for his politics. Hoover brought to business and government alike a potent strain of the characteristic Progressive-era belief that the world could be improved through diligent planning and the application of professional expertise. "It is a great profession," he wrote of engineering in his memoirs. "There is the fascination of watching a figment of the imagination emerge through the aid of science to a plan on paper. Then it moves to realization in stone or metal or energy. Then it brings jobs and homes to men. Then it elevates the standard of living and adds to the comforts of life. That is the engineer's high privilege."[7]

Hoover entered public life with the outbreak of war in Europe in 1914. Appointed chairman of the Commission for Relief in Belgium, he worked to get a billion dollars of food and supplies to civilians caught behind a British blockade meant to demoralize Germany. "I did not myself believe in the food blockade," Hoover explained in his memoirs. "I did not believe that it was the effective weapon of which the Allies were so confident. I did not believe in starving women and children. And above all, I did not believe that stunted bodies and deformed minds in the next generation were secure foundations on which to rebuild civilization."[8] When the U.S. joined the fighting in 1917, Hoover was appointed head of the United States Food Administration, charged with balancing the nation's basic needs against war's urgent demands. After the peace, he served as head of the European Relief and Rehabilitation Administration, directing the distribution of food and other emergency supplies to areas of Central Europe devastated by almost five years of war.

Hoover continued to fight hunger even when it was no longer strictly his job. In 1921, he was appointed secretary of commerce by President Warren Harding. That summer, Hoover, a dedicated anti-Bolshevik, read a report of a famine sweeping Russia. He took the opportunity to show that capitalism could be compassionate, initiating a vast two-year relief campaign that fed as many as eleven million people a day and rescued millions from starvation.[9]

Hoover gave no quarter to capitalists who ignored larger questions of living standards and social good. In 1925, serving another term as secretary of commerce, this time under Calvin Coolidge, Hoover led a successful campaign against high rubber prices that had been artificially inflated by British imperial control of the world's supply.

Coffee was different from rubber in that coffee-producing countries were not part of globe-spanning empires that ruled distant colonies as monopolies, but sovereign nations with their own political constituencies and economic priorities to serve. Yet coffee was like rubber in that it was, as Hoover explained, another example of the "intrusion of governments into trading operations on a vast scale . . . a growing menace in international commerce and relations."[10] American coffee drinkers, Hoover said, wouldn't "sit still and take their punishment" just because they were citizens of a "nation who had none" — coffee, he meant.[11]

When his office was flooded by letters from U.S. coffee roasters protesting the Brazilian coffee "defense," Hoover took quick action. He sent deputies to Brazil to try to negotiate an end to the program. He sponsored congressional hearings. He made plans for a coffee boycott. And — as had he done to great effect in the case of rubber — he began to look into the possibilities for domestic coffee production in the island colonies gained in the Spanish-American War, whose coffee industries the U.S. had since "allowed to retrograde."[12]

Brazilian coffee defense gave new life to the idea of domestic American coffee production. In 1906, at the start of the first round of Brazilian valorization, Puerto Rican coffee growers had petitioned Congress for an import tax that would give a boost to coffee produced in Puerto Rico, the Philippines, and Hawaii. Similar tariff protections for Puerto Rican sugar had quadrupled the island's production, and coffee growers wanted the chance to show that they could do equally well with the same treatment: even "a small duty of 5 cents a pound" would make a difference.[13]

Two decades later, with Brazilian coffee defense in full effect and prices soaring, that possibility began to look more appealing, even sensible. Early in 1926, William H. Ukers wrote to Herbert Hoover to review the possibilities for coffee production "under the American flag" — the colonies of Puerto Rico, Hawaii, the Virgin Islands, and the Philippines — and also in other places under American occupation, including Haiti and Cuba.[14] Ukers himself had traveled to the Philippines while researching *All About Coffee* and was told by American agricultural officials there that "the island of Mindanao alone had enough land" to supply the whole world with coffee.[15] That was an unpleasant prospect in Latin America, where Hoover became "the dread" of coffee planters.[16]

Hoover was eager to fight Brazilian valorization not only because he opposed greed, monopoly, and political interference in the market on moral grounds. Rubber and coffee were also alike in that they vividly illustrated the dependence of American life on tropical sources of raw materials located far outside the borders of the United States. Rubber was the choke point where the great American automobile industry met the world market. And coffee, beyond its "contributions to factory efficiency," had become the crucial junction where another key sector of the U.S. economy drew from the wider world. In the years since the start of the world war, the American grocery business had been completely reorganized around coffee.

In the first American grocery stores, shopping meant having a conversation. The typical store was a single room of about 500 square feet, usually owned by the grocer himself and knit into its neighborhood by shared language, culture, tradition, and tastes. Combining what had been diverse trades in produce, dry goods, and meat and dairy, these stores appeared in the second half of the nineteenth century in cities that had outgrown their central markets. With the assistance of one or two clerks, the grocer helped customers from behind a counter, listening, advising, selecting, portioning, weighing, wrapping, tallying, packing, and making change.[17]

Neighborhood grocers served a relatively small number of customers — some fraction of the people who lived within walking distance — so they depended on steady profits from the items they sold most frequently, especially coffee. For these small grocers, selling coffee profitably meant retail prices padded with substantial margins above wholesale prices, which were necessary to pay the costs of doing business — the costs of waiting on customers in the store, making home deliveries, carrying sales on credit, and so on. Most grocers padded their margins by pushing bulk coffee, which was cheaper at wholesale than packaged coffee and could be blended and diluted to meet almost any preference and price level. These high margins weren't a problem for neighborhood grocers before World War I, because they generally didn't compete against each other on price.[18]

That changed during the war, when increases in food prices made small independent grocers especially vulnerable to competition from new, centrally managed, vertically integrated chains of hundreds or thousands of stores. In many cases, the chain stores set up shop in small grocers' coffee margins, cutting off their business at the pressure point of price, and no chain more so than the immense coffee business known as Great Atlantic & Pacific Tea Company — the A&P.

Even in 1863, when it was one tea shop among many in Lower Manhattan, the A&P called itself "great."[19] Historian Richard Tedlow has described why tea was a good business "for an ambitious grocer to concentrate on" at the time. The great distance between tea plantations and American stores, and the many businesses traditionally involved in the process of getting the product from one to the other, meant that retail tea prices were usually high. A&P found an advantage through vertical integration, bringing the functions of tea importer, roaster, wholesaler, and retailer together under one roof, and often beating other grocers' tea prices by a third.

Success in tea subsidized the growth of its stores. A&P had 200 outlets at the turn of the twentieth century and 650 by 1914. These early stores were similar to independent neighborhood grocery stores. They were based on customer service: taking orders, packing them up, financing purchases with credit, making home deliveries. But after 1914, A&P developed a new type of store, called Economy Stores, that were designed to hold prices down against wartime inflation, and the company began to grow at an even faster rate: from 650 stores in 1914, to 1,500 stores in 1915, to 3,250 in 1916, 9,300 in 1923, and nearly 16,000 by 1930.[20]

As A&P expanded, tea fell by the wayside, but coffee took off. Coffee was good business for the same reasons tea had been — because it was traditionally a high-margin product. And coffee was even better business than tea because over the second half of the nineteenth century it had become a much more popular drink. In 1908, A&P opened its own coffee-roasting plant in Jersey City. A decade later, after the turn to Economy Stores, A&P

357

incorporated an international branch, the American Coffee Corporation, with offices in Santos, Brazil, and began importing millions of pounds of coffee a year for its roasting plant. By 1921, A&P was selling more than forty million pounds of coffee a year at retail, and it had become the largest coffee business — the largest importer, roaster, and retailer — in the world.

Coffee was instrumental in A&P's expansion. Economy Stores undercut small grocers in part by taking their coffee trade. A&P engineered the layout and design of Economy Stores to produce low costs and low prices. They were "small, low-rent" spaces "with modest fixures."[21] Economy Stores restocked twice a week, turning over the merchandise at least four times as often as independent grocers. To speed up the regular inventory and stock work, A&P standardized the layout and shelf position of the items. The stores accepted cash only, no credit, and made no deliveries. Rigidly structured in these ways, an Economy Store could be operated by minimal staff, usually one manager and one stock boy. Customers served themselves.

These economical spaces also shaped the food A&P sold. As the stores got smaller, so did packages, requiring shoppers to buy more often.[22] Economy Stores also nudged customers toward the items that earned the highest margins. This was an old principle of successful retailing, but A&P accomplished it in a new way. What independent grocers had done by the power of friendly persuasion, self-service Economy Stores did by limiting choice. Economy Stores sold A&P's own three brands of coffee exclusively: Eight O'Clock was the cheapest and most popular brand, probably the best-selling coffee in the world; Red Circle was a mid-priced brand; Bokar was the top of the line, its name signaling origins in the growing regions around Bogotá and Cartagena, Colombia. There was no magic coffee bin, no shelf stocked with an array of choices, no specifying precisely how much of what kind. Instead there was a small display tightly packed with bags of A&P coffee. By 1930, to supply its nearly 16,000 stores, A&P was importing more than 100 million pounds of green coffee beans a year through New York and New Orleans, and roasting, grinding, and packing it in seven plants around the country.[23] No one sold more coffee than A&P, and no one sold it cheaper.

Other chain grocers, including Safeway, Kroger, and National Tea, also popped up in the decade between the end of World War I and the onset of the Great Depression. A few moved into importing, roasting, and packing their own brands of coffee, as Safeway did after the investment bank Merrill Lynch took control of the company in 1926.[24] As a result, small neighborhood grocery stores had lost about half of their coffee business by 1929, when the average independent grocer sold coffee to only 41 percent of his customers.[25] With the price of coffee rising through the mid- and late twenties, even shoppers who remained loyal to neighborhood stores took their coffee business to the chains, where they could expect to save ten cents on the dollar.

A&P and the other chain stores, relying heavily on Brazilian coffee to make up their low-price brands, strongly opposed the Brazilian coffee defense plan. Berent Friele, the president of A&P's coffee importing and roasting business, did everything he could to convince Herbert Hoover that U.S. citizens should not be paying $200 million each year in "coffee tax" to Brazil — the net cost of the price-control program.[26] But as little as A&P executives liked the Brazilian coffee defense, which raised the cost of their raw materials, it served them well, for they could move coffee into stores at costs and prices lower than anyone else's. No one knew this as well as independent grocers and smaller coffee roasters, who had argued again and again that A&P was a monopolist itself.[27] Yet their arguments had little impact because A&P, unlike Brazil, was the kind of monopolist that used its market power to try to drive prices down for American shoppers — exactly the kind of monopolist of which Secretary of Commerce

Herbert Hoover heartily approved.[28]

For every letter Hoover's office received asking the secretary of commerce to do something to fight the high coffee prices brought on by Brazilian coffee defense, another arrived asking him to stop fighting.

This second type of letter came most often from coffee importers, who as a group had much at stake. Of course A&P was an importer, too — in fact the largest importer of coffee in the country — but a different kind of importer. A&P imported coffee for its own account, selling only to consumers, as grocers did. In matters international, A&P gave voice to the discount grocer's perspective — that lower prices on the plantations made for lower prices in the stores. On the other hand, most coffee importers bought from planters and millers like James Hill and sold to roasters like Hills Bros., taking a percentage of the sale, so any improvement in the world price went partially into their pockets. Yet if this clear financial interest provided one strong motivation for the reams of letters American coffee importers mailed to the office of the secretary of commerce, those who wrote made a compelling case that there was something else, something bigger, at stake too.

Importers based on the Pacific coast were especially vocal. They did a large part of their business with Central America, and they saw the question of coffee prices from a unique perspective.

If all coffee tasted the same, A&P would have been unbeatable. But A&P had based its coffee business in Brazil. The huge Brazilian crops of inexpensive and relatively low-quality coffee produced on comparatively flat, low terrain, under full sun and generally looser work orders than were usual in Central America, were the foundation of the A&P business model. This left an opening in the retail market for high-quality mild coffees, known for "sweetness in the cup," in which Central America and Colombia specialized. Prices for Central American coffee had been pushed up alongside Brazilian prices as a result of the coffee defense — this was precisely why James Hill was so grateful to his "Brazilian friends." Yet these high prices were not necessarily at odds with the interests of the roasters and importers who dealt in high-quality mild coffee from Central America.

On the contrary, the San Francisco–based Hills Bros., for example, had responded to the rise of chain grocers and A&P Economy Stores by pricing their coffee high to signal its distinctive quality. In 1912, Hills Bros. had offered twenty-three varieties of coffee for sale, ranging in per-pound price from 18 cents for "Royal" to 33 cents for "Fancy East Indian Timingo." Each type could be processed into four different grinds — medium, fine, pulverized, or whole bean — and packaged in containers ranging from one-pound vacuum cans to 150-pound steel drums. All told, Hills Bros. customers had around a thousand choices, a coffee for every price and quantity.[29] In addition to coffee, Hills Bros. sold tea and spices, imports that had traditionally gone together with coffee.

Under pressure from the economy chains, Hills Bros. streamlined their business. In 1914 they discontinued blends of coffee that included chicory or cereals and began to "specialize in the sale of sound, sweet drinking coffees."[30] Two years later, they closed the spice and extract departments, and then shuttered the tea department in the spring of 1923.[31] Then they discontinued their low-priced blends of coffee, and then their line of bulk coffees, until the entirety of their business was high-grade, vacuum-packed "Red Can," as it had become known.[32] In 1926, Hills Bros. opened a new roasting and packing plant that had been "designed and constructed for the sole purpose of producing a high-grade roasted coffee packed in vacuum cans."[33] Hills Bros. was the anti-A&P, a coffee business focused on high quality rather than low price.

As Hills Bros. and other San Francisco roasters, including Folgers, made quality their core business, these brands became increasingly associated with places defined by their difference from Brazil. "This Time Try Coffee from Central America," proposed one Folgers ad published during the height of price increases caused by the Brazilian coffee-defense plan. "Over 70 per cent of all the coffee entering the United States regardless of brand names comes from one common region — giving it the same common taste. *Nature herself makes Folger's coffee different.* For it is grown in another region altogether — in the high volcanic districts" of Central America.[34]

Brazil was price, Central America was quality. For advertising purposes, the difference was "nature herself." But when it came time for dealers in Central American coffee to make their case for higher prices to Hoover, they told a much more complex story. Importers especially took it upon themselves to educate Hoover and American coffee drinkers alike about this other region, "the high volcanic districts" of Central America. Detailing working and living conditions on coffee plantations, they proposed not only that Hoover should stop trying to force down prices that the Brazilians had lifted — they also claimed that if Hoover the renowned humanitarian could only see what was happening in Central America, if the good-hearted and well-meaning coffee drinkers of the United States could only see what life was like there, they would have to admit that coffee prices, after doubling and more, were still strikingly, unjustly, and even dangerously low.

What would it take to get American coffee drinkers — and their representatives in government — to think beyond the cash register, to figure prices and value in a frame wider than the family budget, according to a set of considerations and calculations that was international, even global, instead of narrowly domestic?

First importers of "quality" coffee tried to differentiate Central American planters from their monopolistic Brazilian counterparts. San Francisco merchant J. H. Polhemus — brother and partner of Edward Polhemus, who had looked after James Hill's children in San Francisco — wrote to Herbert Hoover in 1925 to explain that, "going back over the coffee business with Central America and Mexico for the past 75 years, the planter has as a rule been a very struggling fellow."

In contrast to the popular idea of a Brazilian robber baron, Polhemus sketched a figure in the image of James Hill. Central American "planters as a rule were the overflow of overcrowded European countries," he explained, "who naturally had no money to start with, or they would not have left the comfortable life in their own home countries to go to the tropics, cut down jungles, work with Indians, take chances in unhealthy climate such as they found . . . of having their years of work lost through volcanic eruptions or commercial failures through revolutions cutting off their credit and their possibility of exporting or through poor crops or poor prices." The life of the planter, as Polhemus described it, was a life made of problems: "labor problems, agricultural problems, transportation problems, health problems, family problems, political problems," plus all the personal difficulty that came with starting over in a "cutthroat" business in a new part of the world.

Yet planters' problems were not the crux of the issue. Invoking the recent Mexican Revolution and the Bolshevik Revolution in Russia, Polhemus noted that the upswing in coffee prices had come just in time, "as labor insists upon sharing in prosperity." And this was not, he observed, such a bad thing: if the "souls that are doing the work on coffee plantations at less than what labor is paid in this country" made more money, they could buy more American products.[35] The economies of the United States and Latin America were so closely tied together that prosperity in the former depended on prosperity in the latter. High coffee prices were good business for coffee drinkers, too.

Polhemus's letter sparked a debate in Herbert Hoover's office, for it went to the heart of what the American press called "the coffee question": What did cheap coffee cost, and for whom?[36] At what point did grim living and working conditions on Latin American plantations intrude on life in the United States? Or, turned around, what was a "good" price, or even the "right" price for coffee — one that would allow workers on coffee plantations to live well, and to buy American goods? It was hardly a new point — a century earlier, British abolitionists had imagined that emancipation would turn the enslaved into better consumers of British goods — but it was still compelling, in light not only of the Mexican and Bolshevik Revolutions, but also the increasing anti-Yankee sentiment in Central America.

While Hoover and his staff looked into the matter, other importers appealed directly to the American public. Here too there was reason to think that a lesson was in order. On the one hand, Sumner Welles had been right that the increasing economic interests of the United States in Central America had sparked curiosity about the "other" American republics. As the products of the "jungle" filled "every grocery store," Central America especially became an object of an American fascination both romantic and strategic.[37] A new crop of impressionistic travelogues captured the spirit of adventure and dominion in their titles: *Gypsying Through Central America; Rainbow Countries of Central America; The Southland of North America.*

The last was the work of George Palmer Putnam, grandson and namesake of the founder of the New York publisher G. P. Putnam's Sons. Putnam traveled to Central America with his new bride, Crayola crayon heiress Dorothy Binney, in 1912. Their honeymoon coincided with the final stages of construction on the Panama Canal, cinching the region up toward the United States all the more tightly. "So far as the United States is concerned," Putnam wrote, "the Canal practically means the rediscovery of Central America." Like those of the original conquistadors, Putnam's discoveries conformed to the image of what he had come looking for. The account he sketched up, a "souvenir of a delightful tropical trip," was dedicated to his wife and published by the family office in 1913, a year before the canal opened.[38]

To Putnam, Central America was a fixer-upper: "a little-known land of glowing possibilities, unique problems, and grave responsibilities."[39] The possibilities, problems, and responsibilities were all equally the property of the United States: the golden glow of the first cast an urgent light on the second, suffusing his and similar travelogues with a deeply patronizing conception of the third.

368

This point of view made it hard for Putnam to penetrate to the core of life in Central America, even when he got close to the action. He saw everything in terms of home.

Arriving in El Salvador in January, in the middle of the coffee harvest, Putnam went to look around a coffee plantation and mill owned by the Dueñas family, who, a generation later, would be joined with the Hill family by marriage. On the plantation, women and children employed to inspect and sort the freshly milled coffee beans were paid "about fifteen cents a day," Putnam reported. "In addition to this munificent wage, every worker is entitled to two meals a day, one at noon and the other in the evening. The luxury of a breakfast is omitted," he wrote.

The two meals the Indians do get consist of two *tortillas* a man per meal, with as many black beans, or *frijoles,* piled on top as the recipient can contrive to balance. As the tortillas are about five inches in diameter the reader with a trend for mathematical calculation can readily figure out how many rusty-looking beans constitute the allotment.

The meals are prepared by old women. A dark hole of a room, ventilated only by the door and a single window that opens into the courtyard, serves as kitchen. Along one side, on a sort of counter of stone, are four or five charcoal fires, giving much the ap-

369

pearance of a blacksmith forge. Over the
fires are crude gridirons. And here the *tortillas,* distant and solider cousins to our
Yankee hot cakes, flourish. Nor do the eaters fail to enjoy the tough and unsalted
dough; the care with which the earthenware
crocks containing the uncooked cornmeal
batter are guarded would seem to hint that
there are enthusiasts who would even
tackle that!

Of course, the beans figure heavily in this
culinary department and great steaming
pots over the smaller fires are watched
hungrily by all eyes. *"Tortillas* and *frijoles!"*
Faith, what epicure would ask for more! . . .
The applicants for meals file in and are allotted their share of the plunder, a strict tab
being kept upon them, so that it is quite
impossible for "repeaters" to operate successfully. As they go out balancing their
meal in one hand, with the other they grab
up huge handfuls of salt to sprinkle over the
beans. The amount of salt used is phenom-
enal. With a saucerful of beans it is safe to
say that the average native will use a heaping tablespoon of salt, if he is fortunate
enough to get so much.[40]

Viewing Central America in terms of the
United States, Putnam missed the difference
between appetite and need, between a taste
for raw masa and hunger, between wanting a

370

second helping and not having enough food, between salt the seasoning and salt the mineral craved by dehydrated and malnourished people working in the hot sun on plantations where water supplies were closely rationed and the diet was, to understate the case, monotonous. Overall, Putnam found El Salvador a "positive delight as a place to visit."[41]

Coffee importers, who had fortunes tied up with the coffee question, tried to teach Americans how to think about life on Central American plantations. E. A. Kahl, who traded coffee for W. R. Grace and served as vice president of San Francisco's Green Coffee Association, argued that Americans should be paying even more than they had been under Brazilian defense, which had barely lifted the market above the "starvation prices" that had long ruled. "Were coffee produced at anywhere near our normal day wage, roasted coffee would cost us probably $1.50 a pound," Kahl told the Housewives' League of San Francisco in 1925, when the retail price was around one-third that. "I am of the opinion that, retarded as the coffee-producing countries are," Kahl informed the Housewives, "they cannot possibly much longer continue to resist the spirit of the times, which is for a decent day wage."[42]

Kahl drew stark contrasts between the lives

of coffee drinkers and the lives of coffee workers. "Those of us who have traveled extensively in producing countries have vividly in our minds the fact that in many sections the laborer and his family does not go much beyond a garment made out of a flour bag nor much beyond sustenance consisting of corn and bananas," he wrote. "We believe that properly enlightened . . . the coffee buying public would not want to have cheap coffee, solely at the expense of nearly slave labor in the producing countries, and there can be no doubt but that we can have what we used to consider cheap coffees only on that basis."[43]

The coffee question took on greater urgency in the beginning of May 1926, when Nicaragua, which had been under American occupation for a decade and a half, broke into civil war. The insurgent faction was led by Augusto César Sandino, who declared war on the "country-selling" conservative president installed by the United States, and by proxy on the U.S. itself. The "fate of the laborers in producing countries" hung on the coffee question, E. A. Kahl and his fellow importers pointed out, and tied up with the fate of the coffee workers were both the position of the U.S. in the wider world and the material comforts of everyday American life.[44] More and more, it seemed as if coffee drinkers could either accept higher coffee prices or risk paying a higher price still.

The next year, 1927, New York publisher Alfred A. Knopf brought out a new edition of a classic novel about coffee. The book had been little read in the United States to that point, but Knopf was expecting that would change, for the story had acquired new relevance. First published in 1860 in Amsterdam, and often celebrated as the greatest Dutch novel, *Max Havelaar* documented "the abuses" that characterized colonial Java under the cultivation system — the requirement that each Javanese household produce a fixed amount of coffee or other export commodity. The title character, Max Havelaar, is cast in the role of the last honest Dutchman in Java. He was a proxy for the author, a civil servant born Eduard Douwes Dekker, who published under the pen name "Multatuli," Latin for "I have suffered much." Dekker had gone to Java in 1838, at age eighteen, and he served nearly two decades in colonial administration there before an unceremonious dismissal. His book, an exposé disguised as a novel, was intended as revenge.

Dekker had in mind *Uncle Tom's Cabin* set on a coffee plantation. But while Harriet Beecher Stowe's 1852 indictment of American slavery was a classic example of the power of showing rather than telling, sentiment over screed, Dekker was at pains to explain what just was wrong in Java. Local "chiefs," doing the bidding of colonial administrators, had sold out their constituents to the Dutch imperial government. While the chiefs and bureaucrats grew fat, the common Javanese went hungry. "Only a few years ago, whole districts died of starvation," Dekker wrote. "Mothers offered their children for sale to obtain food. Mothers ate their children."[45]

Didacticism was not the only difference between the books. While Stowe had written for the end of slavery, Dekker wrote to preserve Dutch rule. He assumed that his novel would cause the government to change the terms by which it governed Java, or risk the loss of the colony to uprising.[46]

For the new edition, Knopf commissioned D. H. Lawrence to write an introduction that placed the book in its historical moment: the age of high European imperialism. The alarm Dekker had raised rang well beyond the Netherlands, Lawrence wrote, echoing even down to the present. On this point Dekker had the advantage over Stowe: while the abolition of slavery had made *Uncle Tom's Cabin* a "back number," the persistence of imperialism kept *Max Havelaar* current. Its author's seething hate — for corrupt colonial bureaucrats, for merchants who traded in the products of misery, for consuming classes who gorged on others' hunger — kept the book fresh. *Max Havelaar* was "a pill," Lawrence admitted, but a necessary one, for the "social constipation" was "as bad as ever."[47]

Reviewing the new edition for the *New York Times,* columnist Simeon Strunsky agreed that the timing was apt. "It is not merely that the Dutch Government was confronted only the other day with native unrest in Java," Strunsky wrote, referring to a 1926 communist insurrection in the western part of the island. "The general problem of white rule over the lower breeds is in essence what Dekker found it to be seventy years ago." Projected onto Central America, the Knopf edition of *Max Havelaar* could be read as an object lesson in imperial governance, especially because Dekker had succeeded. His book set off an outcry, the cultivation system was ended in 1870, and Java remained a Dutch possession. Yet Strunsky, a Russian-born critic of the Bolshevik Revolution, wasn't entirely convinced by the analogy: "To speak of white 'imperialism' and 'exploitation,' " he wrote, "is to fall into a soap-box rhetoric. . . . The problem is more complicated than that."[48]

The complicated problems that made agricultural consultant Frederic W. Taylor so happy to flee El Salvador, that were up for debate in Herbert Hoover's office, that E. A. Kahl tried to explain to the Housewives' League —

375

these were the same complicated problems that inspired Arthur Ruhl to go to Central America. "Much is said about revolutions in Central America," Ruhl wrote in 1928. "But the real and tragic revolution in these pastoral countries, for which nobody is to blame and which no amount of good-will on either side can stop, is the industrial revolution which came to most of the rest of the Western world a century or so ago."[49]

By the time Ruhl visited Las Tres Puertas, James Hill was recognized as something of an authority on these subjects. Amid the broader debate over the coffee question in the United States, William H. Ukers had increased the coverage of conditions on Central American plantations in the *Tea and Coffee Trade Journal.* He began to publish regular dispatches from Hill as "Staff Correspondence," some signed, some under the pen name "PLANTER," and some anonymous.

In April 1927, Hill's report was downbeat. The year's crop had been small, and the harvest season had been the shortest of his three decades in coffee. The trees had given less than half of what he had gotten the previous year, and the omens for the coming crop were not good, either: "The prophets" had forecast 1927 to be one of the driest years on record. Given that coffee "requires from 100 inches of rain up," Hill explained, "dry years are just the opposite to what we pray for."

Just as troubling were new labor problems. "What we cannot get down is the workmen's wages," Hill complained, "and the moment we try they go elsewhere," many finding work on road-building projects funded by El Salvador's American loan. There were also signs that working people were starting to look for more than just better pay. "The whole of Central America seems to be coming under Socialist ideas," Hill wrote. He hoped for an additional increase in coffee prices to help snuff it out, but he worried that the opposite was more likely.

Already apparent were "all the signs of an impending crisis," Hill continued. "Motor cars are being offered at greatly reduced prices, though some of them are only a year old and not much used. Prices for land are declining and houses are being offered for sale by people who find that with the reduced prices for their coffee and the meager crop just passed they cannot keep up with their families' expectations." Still, planters had learned from experience how to survive hard times. "People here," Hill explained, "when anything of the kind threatens, close their town houses and go to live on the plantations, where they eat things grown on the land and wear old clothes. They stay away until things clear up. There are no fixed bases which oblige people to maintain any position, and when there is no money people don't spend any; so the hard times pass without any visible effects remaining."[50]

When he arrived in Santa Ana, Arthur Ruhl wanted to know more about labor unrest. As they walked around Las Tres Puertas, Hill told him that he was hearing more and more objections from "his work-people." "They all used to do more work for less pay than they do nowadays," Hill complained. "They could do twice as much as they do, if they wanted to, but they're born lazy, and once they've got enough to eat, don't care. By cutting down their work, they've really increased their wages. . . . And you have a hard time nowadays getting men to work barefooted on the drying floors — they complain the stone floor's too hot and that the coffee beans hurt their feet!"

A decade earlier, Ruhl had been in Russia during the first stage of the revolution that overthrew the autocratic tsarist government, and he published a book about it in May 1917. Six months later, the Bolsheviks rose up and took power, and Ruhl raised the subject with Hill. "Bolshevism? Oh, yes," Hill answered. "It's drifting in. The work-people hold meetings on Sundays and get very excited. They say: 'We dig the holes for the trees! We clean off the weeds! We prune the trees! We pick the coffee! Who earns the coffee, then? . . . *We* do!' " There seems to have been a small misunderstanding on this point

— what Ruhl heard as "earns" was most likely "owns" pronounced with a Manchester accent. Hill knew "his work-people" were increasingly thinking of themselves as land-owners. "Why, they've even picked out parcels that please them most," he continued, "because they like the climate or think that the trees are in better condition and will produce more. Yes," Hill concluded, "there'll be trouble one of these days."[51]

Arthur Ruhl's book, called *The Central Americans,* was published in 1928. Its frontispiece, facing the title page, was a photograph of a smoking volcano.

In May of the same year, James Hill traveled to New York, on the way to Paris for the summer with his wife, Lola, and their daughters, and he stopped in to chat with William H. Ukers at the offices of the *Tea and Coffee Trade Journal.* Hill was in good spirits, for many of his predictions from the year before had not come true, and Ukers quoted from their conversation in an article headlined "Salvador Conditions Good." With Brazilian coffee defense continuing, European buyers in particular were paying high prices for Salvadoran coffee. Hill thought the strong market would hold up for "another year at least," and he hoped that the "roasting community will find stable values suitable, and arrange their prices . . . in a way which will leave room for all to make a decent living."[52]

By that time, presidential candidate Herbert Hoover was thinking more or less along the same lines. He had dropped his fight against high coffee prices, for he had come to understand that "a collapse in coffee prices would cause the most harm to Brazil's competitors," including the mild coffee countries of Central America.[53]

19.
THE PARADISE OF EATING

People who knew Miguel Mármol said that he had shown up in the world to cause trouble. It had begun even before he was born on July 4, 1905, near Lake Ilopango, outside San Salvador, when the earliest evidence of his existence got his unwed mother, Santos, kicked out of her house. Then Miguel Mármol turned out to be an ugly kid, and Santos's disgrace was doubled.[1]

When Santos told her son about his childhood, she told him that they survived because people shared food with them. On especially hungry mornings Santos would light a small fire under her oven and kneel before it and pray. Eventually, sure enough, a neighbor would call over, "Santos, I've got some dough left over, wouldn't you like it to make some tortillas with?" When she couldn't get food any other way, they stole fruit from nearby farms, fished, and picked through the garbage. Looking back, Miguel Mármol concluded that his hungry childhood had been good for him — that all the hardship was the reason "why we poor people have such tough hides." But as a boy he dreamed of a different life. Watching birds glide by high overhead, he imagined flying to Mexico, the edge of his known world.[2]

In 1916, when he was eleven, Miguel Mármol went to work on the lake as a fisherman. First he fished with a group of men who used poison and dynamite and paid him "two or three fish after working all night long." Then he fished with his silent, drunk, cruel stepfather, whom his mother had married because they were hungry. After two years of fishing, Miguel Mármol "had quit being a kid for good." He went to work as a houseboy in the barracks of the National Guard, and then he enlisted himself and was given a rifle and fifty bullets. Before long he began to think that his fellow guardsmen were extortionists and torturers, and he could not stop wondering "if it was right to continue supporting myself in the Guard." His mother didn't want him to work on the plantations, and he couldn't afford to study to be a teacher, so he apprenticed himself to a man who taught him how to make shoes and how to see the world.[3]

In the shoe factory, Mármol and his boss, Felipe Angulo, read the newspapers together. The Salvadoran press in 1919 was "filled with propaganda against a revolution that had happened in a far off country," but the old shoemaker told him not to believe everything he read, and that what was happening in Russia was not as distant from El Salvador as it seemed, which was precisely the reason for all the agitation in the papers. Working for Felipe Angulo, "all the big prejudices" Miguel Mármol had carried with him from early childhood, his "basic conception of the world and things, suffered devastating blows." He began to think that "the most beautiful capacity of man is the capacity to struggle . . . for the freedom and happiness of everyone." And at the same time he began to think that the people running El Salvador, the ruling line of planters created by the overthrow of the Ezeta brothers in 1894, were running the country "as though it was a plantation," which was something worth struggling against.[4]

In the years immediately after the Great War, Mármol went to work against the coffee planters' government as a political organizer. When that work ended in electoral disappointment, he began to study at the People's University in San Salvador, a free school founded in 1924 — the year after the American loan — by a coalition of labor unions. In courses on economics, law, and political science, Mármol learned to see the United States as El Salvador's first mortgage holder and "the principal enemy of our people." As he studied, he also came to see Augusto

César Sandino, the leader of the war against the American occupation in Nicaragua, as "the human embodiment" of what was possible in El Salvador.[5] The labor unions behind the People's University thought they could learn from Sandino. In 1928 they elected representatives to embed with him in Nicaragua. One of the representatives was a quiet, serious, dark-skinned thirty-five-year-old whom Mármol had met at the People's University, Agustín Farabundo Martí, whom everyone called "El Negro."

Martí's complexion disguised his family wealth.[6] His father, though born poor, had amassed two farms comprising nearly five square miles of land in the coastal highlands. Yet as a young man Martí rejected the landlord's life and began to fight against capitalism and imperialism, and for the cause of the working poor.

At the time he was chosen to embed with Sandino in Nicaragua, Martí was hanging around the People's University after leaving, through some combination of choice and expulsion, El Salvador's national university, where he had studied law. The end of Martí's career as a law student in good standing came in February 1920, when he was arrested as part of a group planning a demonstration against the Guatemalan dictatorship across the border. The group included sons of the Salvadoran elite, and all involved were called before Salvadoran president Jorge Meléndez for a lecture. After President Meléndez dismissed the scions with a warning, he condemned the leader of the group, the son of no one special, to an island prison. Martí then asked the president whether the fact that they were all guilty of the same offense did not mean that they should all receive the same punishment. As an answer, Meléndez sent Martí out of El Salvador and into exile — and like that Martí was done with the law.

In exile Martí studied by working. He worked in factories, he worked construction, he worked on farms in Guatemala. After he made an unauthorized return to El Salvador in 1925, Martí began to work with the group of labor unions that created the People's University. Three years later, the group sent him to embed with Sandino in Nicaragua.

On his roundabout trip to meet Sandino, Martí traveled to New York. There he linked up with the All-America Anti-Imperialist League, which had its offices on Union Square. The group was leading the protests against the U.S. occupation of Nicaragua, which also meant supporting Sandino, whose half brother, Sócrates, was a carpenter in Brooklyn. From New York, Martí picked his way south through Cuba, Jamaica, Belize, Guatemala, Honduras, and finally to Nicaragua, where he caught up with Sandino on June 22, 1928. By then Sandino's campaign was losing ground, but Martí felt triumphant. He wrote a friend: "Our war against the invaders of Central America is now formally launched. In Nicaragua the liberating struggle of the Americas has begun and it is to be hoped that the joint action of all the oppressed lands of the continent will sweep away the last vestiges of Yankee imperialism."[7] He was thinking well beyond Nicaragua.

Martí's boldness helped him become one of Sandino's most trusted lieutenants. In 1929, Augusto César Sandino and his new personal secretary, Agustín Farabundo Martí, traveled from Nicaragua through El Salvador and Guatemala and up into Mexico to secure the support and supplies they needed to regroup. But in Mexico they had a falling-out, for Sandino's ultimate purpose there was different from Martí's. Focused on Nicaraguan problems, Sandino distanced himself from international communism. He wanted national liberation, not social revolution. Martí tried to convince him of the synergy of the projects, but on this question, late in 1929, they split.

When Martí returned to El Salvador in May 1930, he carried with him both the prestige of the position he had held in Sandino's organization and the prestige that came from outflanking Sandino to the left. Martí transformed these credentials into a role as the leader of a nascent movement to upend

El Salvador's economics, politics, and society, subsuming into his own revolutionary vision the practical idealism of the group that had been hard at work in El Salvador during his absence. While Martí was away, this group, which included Miguel Mármol, had made three key advances. They had established the Communist Party of El Salvador in March 1930, because they thought the unions weren't doing enough. They had established a chapter of International Red Aid to do humanitarian work. And they had begun to push out of the capital into the coffee districts to the west, where the economic crisis of the world depression was making bad conditions worse.[8]

The world depression did what Herbert Hoover had not — cut the legs out from under the Brazilian defense of coffee. From 1929 to early 1933, the four years of Hoover's presidency, world coffee prices fell by more than 60 percent, from over twenty cents a pound to under ten, wiping out the gains of the previous decade. The decline in prices squeezed all levels of Salvadoran society, but not evenly. Foreign importers offered Salvadoran exporters and millers lower prices for their crops. Millers cut the advances they paid to coffee planters. Planters, who depended on these advances to pay workers, hired fewer people and paid them less. Working people, already accustomed to making do with less than they needed, went without.

In rural districts generally, unemployment may have been as high as 40 percent.[9] On the coffee plantations, it was probably even higher than that. Antonio Flores Torres owned a large plantation just outside Santa Ana. In the spring of 1927, Flores Torres employed an average of forty-five people a week digging holes for new trees, cleaning the weeds around existing trees, and preparing for the next crop. In the spring of 1931, he employed an average of nineteen people a week.[10] Those who kept working coffee did so on the barest of terms. Planters pushed down wages to match the fall in prices — often between 50 and 60 percent, and in some cases as much as 75 percent.[11]

For people who worked coffee, the solution to hard times was not so simple as the planters' backup plan James Hill had described — just closing up their town homes and going to the country, where they could wear old clothes and eat things grown on the land until the crisis passed. Eating things grown on the land was exactly what working people could no longer do.

The growth of El Salvador's coffee economy in the 1920s made the crisis of the thirties worse. It was the third market collapse in a half century.[12] This volatility had completed what land privatization had begun: the concentration of coffee land in the hands of the people who could afford to pay the most for it. "Until recently," the U.S. consul in El Salvador reported in 1929, "the plantations were practically all limited in size and yields were consequently small." But that had changed: "Large plantations have been formed by a few individuals and companies by buying small tracts from time to time and these employ large-scale production methods, modern transportation, improved housing for labor, efficient organization and accounting systems."[13] Salvadoran journalist Alberto Masferrer confirmed the outlines of the American report. "About forty-five years ago the land in this country was distributed among the majority of Salvadorans," he wrote in his newspaper *La Patria* in 1928, "but now it is falling into the hands of a few owners."[14] Those who lost their land often picked up stakes and set out in search of a place to squat: "on the fringes of private estates, on government land, along the roads and highways, and eventually even in the riverbeds that intersect the capital city of San Salvador."[15] Some of the displaced returned to the plantations annually to work the harvest and supplement the bare livelihoods they made elsewhere.

As land became concentrated in fewer and fewer hands, harvest workers were in greater and greater demand. One consequence of "large-scale production methods" and "efficient organization and accounting systems" was increased output: in the two decades before 1929, annual coffee exports had nearly doubled.[16] Over the same period, the total revenue from coffee had tripled.[17] But coffee had grown at the expense of everything else, transforming the countryside into a monoculture. Masferrer understood this aspect of the problem at a deeper level than did the U.S. consul, for he had seen what "efficient organization" really meant for the landscape and the people.

In the nineteenth century, the entire landscape of El Salvador had appeared to be "one mass of luxuriant orange and mango trees, bending beneath their load of fruit."[18] But Masferrer had watched coffee replace oranges, mangoes, bananas, yucca, and everything else. "There are no longer crises," he observed. "Instead, there are chronic illnesses and endemic hunger. . . . El Salvador no longer has wild fruits and vegetables that once everyone could harvest, nor even cultivated fruits that once were inexpensive. Today there are the coffee estates and they grow only coffee." The hardy Bourbon tree, so tolerant of heat and poor soil, was taking over new swaths of land. "The conquest of territory by the coffee industry is alarming," Masferrer wrote. "It has already occupied all the high ground and is now descending to the valleys, displacing maize, rice, and beans. It goes in the manner of the conquistador, spreading hunger and misery."[19]

Like Miguel Mármol and Farabundo Martí, Alberto Masferrer wanted to solve the problems of hunger and misery.[20] Masferrer was born in El Salvador in 1868. He lived with his mother until he was nine, but then she sent him to stay with his demanding father and his new stepmother, who in turn sent him away to boarding school in Guatemala. As soon as he could, Masferrer fled the school and spent his teens traveling around export-boom Central America, much as James Hill would do a few years later: first through Honduras and Nicaragua, then Guatemala and Costa Rica. But while Hill went looking for a business opportunity, Masferrer saw suffering everywhere. He came to believe that Central Americans lived in "semi-barbarism and tyranny" because they were isolated from each other, locked in their own struggles for subsistence, too focused on meeting their own basic needs to help one another or organize politically. He began a career as a journalist in order to show El Salvador to Salvadorans, so that they could see how to save themselves. "As long as justice is not the same for everyone," Masferrer wrote in 1928, "none of us is safe."[21]

Masferrer's idea of justice stemmed from his concept of the Salvadoran nation as a single living organism. Here his thinking drew on the European tradition of vitalism, a philosophy based on an idea that had fallen out of fashion after the discovery of energy and thermodynamics — the idea that life was a phenomenon distinct from all other phenomena, imbuing human enterprise with a special character. Vitalism's twentieth-century exponents, including the French philosopher Henri Bergson, would emphasize the special nature of "mind energy," or "spiritual energy," in opposition to those who, like W. O. Atwater, were eager to reduce cognition and imagination to just another mechanical process. For vitalists, "life," rather than energy, was the universe's least common denominator. "Time, heart, thought, muscles, and nerves, tendons and bones, blood and sweat, all are consumed by work," Masferrer wrote, "and a bit of the individual is transmuted into life in general."[22] Elevating "life" to special status was a way of appealing to human decency, of cultivating empathy and a sense of connection among individuals.

Decency and empathy were at the core of Masferrer's reformist politics, which took shape as a program he called "the vital minimum." The first two tenets of the program, designed in "recognition of the desperate conditions of the lives of Salvadorans," were "honest, healthy and justly-paid work," and "nutritious and wholesome food in sufficient quantities." Then came "ample housing that was clean, dry and well-aired," "potable water in sufficient quantities," "clean, well-fitting clothes of good construction," "sanitation and access to medical attention," "swift justice, easily and equally accessible . . . free and effective primary education . . . [and] sufficient rest and recreation." This was Masferrer's list of life's basic necessities, his prescription for making justice universal and saving his country.[23]

Masferrer rooted his vital minimum in observation and experience, but his concept of politics was less practical. The purpose of the state, he argued, was to provide for "the moral, cultural, and physical health of the nation." In turn, "adequate food, housing, and clothing" were simply "a nation's responsibilities to its people." Masferrer expected coffee planters and their government to listen to his ideas, see the country's situation in a new light, and give away part of what they had claimed as their own. "*Dar* [to give] is a divine word," he wrote in 1928, "one of those that encompasses the mystery of creation and its standards." He quoted the Theosophist Annie Besant: "The law of life is to give." He decried those who "have the souls of a checkbook and the conscience of an account ledger." In 1929, Masferrer formed a political party, the Vitalistas, with a platform of the vital minimum. The party came up with a symbol and painted it on their flags and banners. It was a sun, "radiating outward," plus the initials "V.P.T.," *vida para todos,* life for all.[24]

Salvadoran coffee planters responded to the crisis of the world depression by innovating new ways of taking, new strategies for claiming the sun and the rain as their own. Food crops that had not already been plowed under as Bourbon coffee spread down from the hills and cotton climbed up from the coastal plains were targeted for destruction. Miguel Mármol heard of landowners setting fire to fields planted in subsistence crops and stampeding cattle through corn, creating larger groups of desperate people looking for work because they were hungry.[25]

As conditions on El Salvador's plantations deteriorated, two strands of political opposition, one focusing on "Yankee imperialism" and the other focusing on labor exploitation, came together in new ways.[26] Mármol had been schooled in both. Putting his experiences together, he began to see through "the quiet hardness of life" in El Salvador. Beneath it he felt "a tremendous force that only awaited an outlet to become an active living protest against the injustice and misery," and increasingly Miguel Mármol made it his job to "crack the shell of tradition, fear, and suspicion" that kept working people isolated from each other.[27] He began organizing.

Because Mármol had been a fisherman, he started with fishermen. He knew what they needed: above all, access to the beaches that had been fenced off by landowners who wanted to claim ownership of the lakes and rivers, too. Working along the shore, he made connections with people on the surrounding plantations. When he went into the plantations, Mármol threw out his dress shirts and leather belt. He wore work shirts and started to hold up his pants with a hemp rope. Talking with people who worked coffee, Mármol and his fellow organizers spoke the language of the plantations, pushing for strikes for "bigger tortillas in the daily meals, more beans all year round, coffee with meals," better working conditions, better living conditions.[28] Mármol's success in reaching working people lifted him up through the ranks of the Salvadoran left.

In early June 1930, just days after Farabundo Martí returned to El Salvador after his split with Sandino, Mármol was elected to represent the Salvadoran Communist Party at the fifth Congress of the Red International of Labor Unions in Moscow. For a thousand reasons, he didn't want to go. He had never been out of the country, his mother was sick, he had organizing work to do, he had never seen the ocean, he was afraid that the ideas of a poor peasant wouldn't hold up to international scrutiny. Then a fellow organizer told him he was being an asshole, and Mármol found the courage.

He sailed on a German steamer "bigger than a building" and bound for Hamburg. In damp Hamburg, Mármol was smuggled into the hold of a Russian freighter that cruised into Leningrad surrounded by submarines. Postwar Leningrad, a focus of Stalin's five-year-plan for rapid industrialization, appeared poor, crummy, and muddy. It was a disheartening introduction to life under communism, but Mármol thought he saw something familiar in the way people lined the piers holding fishing poles that never kicked and bent. In the surrounding countryside, the forced relocation of peasant farmers in the name of agricultural collectivization had led to widespread imprisonment and famine. From Leningrad, Mármol took a train to Moscow.

For his speech, Mármol wanted to bring everyone gathered in Moscow back to El Salvador's coffee plantations. He wanted to show them his country's problems in vivid detail, and make them feel the possibilities he felt. He told delegates assembled from all over the world about what daily life was like on a plantation owned by the Guirola family,

James Hill's neighbors in Santa Ana. He spoke of working from dawn to dusk in rags for a wage of fifteen cents and a ration of tortillas and beans. The presentation "caused a deep impression" on the conference.[29]

For days afterward Mármol talked with representatives of other Latin American countries at the Congress. Together they sketched a path toward revolution in Latin America: "confiscation of lands stolen by the governments, confiscation of lands usurped by the [planters] and . . . redistribution among the peasants, nationalization of foreign companies . . . nationalization of the banks, stimulation of industrial development, etc." Their outline was based on the Leninist thesis that "a small yet popular communist party" with leadership over the masses "can start a revolution."[30] This became the foundation of a plan of action Mármol carried back to El Salvador.

But when he arrived home, Mármol found that two things had changed. The first was that the ranks of the Salvadoran left had doubled in size in a matter of months. New ground had been won in industry and agriculture. There was a new union at La Constancia brewery, owned by James Hill's friend and relative by marriage Rafael Meza Ayau, while in the countryside the union had grown to include as many as 80,000 agricultural workers.[31] And the second change was that

397

Farabundo Martí had become the leader of the Salvadoran branch of the humanitarian group International Red Aid, and from that position he was ruling with a renunciate's dark charisma over increasingly dark days.

As Salvadoran workers' groups grew in size and strength, they drew new attention. Coffee planters urged the national government to act against "outside agitators." The United States, on guard against Bolshevism in the hemisphere, also pushed Salvadoran officials to crack down.[32] In August 1930 the Salvadoran government banned rallies and the printing of Marxist propaganda, and the National Guard arrested six hundred agricultural workers who protested the ban. In October demonstrations against stores, individuals, or the authorities were also outlawed, and this new ban had the same effect as the first. Protest and repression were concentrated around the Santa Ana Volcano. In November the National Guard was called in to break up a demonstration in Santa Ana, and in December the guard killed eight protesters in the city. A coordinated series of raids swept up twelve hundred people, including Martí, who was arrested in Santa Ana on November 27.

Martí's jailers were masters of a world too small to encompass two sides of an issue. Their idea of politics was a perpetual purge.

They didn't want Martí in jail, in Santa Ana, in San Salvador, or anywhere in the country, so they asked him to leave. On December 19, after Martí had been in jail for three weeks, a government official brought a pen, ink, and a piece of paper into his cell and asked him to write a letter requesting a passport, no return visa. "My response," Martí later recalled, "was that he, his idea, and those writing things ought to get out of my cell."[33] The official left and Martí stayed.

The jailers came back in the middle of the night. They dragged Martí out of his cell, carted him to the coast, and loaded him onto the California-bound steamship *Venezuela,* whose captain had been paid to carry Martí a safe distance away. Locked below decks, Martí rode north as the ship sailed up the coast past Guatemala, Mexico, and all the way to the port of San Pedro, California, on the southwestern edge of Los Angeles. When he disembarked in San Pedro, Martí was welcomed by local leftists but detained for two weeks by immigration officials, who put him back aboard the *Venezuela,* headed south on its return trip. Martí remained locked up until the ship called at La Libertad, El Salvador, and the captain said he could go ashore. When he did, Martí was quickly swept up by the police. The new plan was to send him to Peru. On the way there, Martí decided that he would rather live as a fugitive than an exile. At the end of February 1931, Martí jumped ship in Nicaragua and sneaked back into his country.[34]

The political situation had shifted during the two months of Martí's exile. In January, Salvadorans had elected a new president, Arturo Araujo. Araujo was the son of a coffee-planting family, but not in the same way that past presidents had been. As a young man Araujo had studied engineering in England. For a time he worked in a factory in Liverpool, Manchester's port, where he lived in the house of a shop steward who was also an official of the British Labour Party. When Araujo returned to El Salvador to join the family coffee business, he ran his plantations not as steam-powered factories but as small welfare states. He spent thousands of dollars on housing, health care, and education for the people who worked for him.[35]

Arturo Araujo's ideas for social reform drew on Alberto Masferrer's. When Masferrer's Vitalista party declined to run a candidate in the presidential elections scheduled for January 1931, Araujo adopted the "vital minimum" as his own platform. Araujo chose a military man as his running mate, General Maximiliano Hernández Martínez, who shared Masferrer's Theosophist beliefs, and Masferrer supported Araujo in the election, vouching for his "generosity and heart." El

Salvador in 1931 was a place where the minimum would have been a welcome change, and Araujo won something of a surprise victory.[36]

After Araujo's election, there was window of possibility for reform — though a small one, for he had become president of a country with millions of dollars of debt and, after the collapse of the world coffee market, no way to pay it down. Virtually everyone in El Salvador was against the American loan. Students and workers on the left objected to the controlling conditions attached to it. Coffee planters and millers paid the export taxes that serviced the loan, and many of them — including Ángel Guirola, the man whose plantations Miguel Mármol had described in Moscow — advised Araujo that he should suspend payments. Bankers including Benjamin Bloom, head of the Banco Occidental, whose role as the government's banker had been usurped, agreed.

Almost alone the new president remained optimistic. "The fiscal situation," Araujo announced shortly after taking office, "is grave but fortunately there is no reason to despair. We rely on the living force of the country and we shall not require more than the application of energy in the form of sufficient cash in circulation, peace and order to attain in every sense normal productivity."[37] Araujo's nod to the "living force" of the country drew on Alberto Masferrer's vitalism. The president's equation of energy and cash in circulation, on the other hand, put him exactly in line with economic thinking in the United States, and the principles of economic science promoted by "the money doctor" Edwin Kemmerer and his colleagues.

There was at least one other person in power in El Salvador with a positive view of the economy: the customs inspector, W. W. Renwick. Late in 1930, Renwick reviewed the conditions prevailing in El Salvador with the loan in mind. While it was true that business in general was paralyzed, Renwick reported to New York, business in general was not the most important consideration. The key to the repayment of the loan was the exportation of coffee. The key to the exportation of coffee was the power of planters to make people work. And from that point of view, the "economic situation" was "excellent."[38]

What made it excellent was the low cost of production; what made the cost of production low, in turn, were conditions on the plantations. Renwick was well attuned to the implications of this sort of savings. His report also included recommendations to his employer, the Chatham Phoenix National Bank, El Salvador's principal creditor, for managing the country's finances going forward. His first recommendation was that part of the customs revenue should be "set aside to pay the armed forces of the country for the months of November and December and if possible create a reserve sufficient to take care of a part of January. This has been suggested to the President who assures me that it will be done." If the army was paid, "tranquility" might be maintained, labor costs might remain low, and the loan might just be repaid.[39]

Arturo Araujo had won the presidential election with strong support from the working poor, including agricultural workers mobilized by his vision of social harmony. So it came as a something of surprise to his supporters when, within weeks of his taking office at the beginning of March 1931, and within days of his emphasizing the importance of "peace and order" for productivity, Araujo too started using violence to achieve order, sending the National Guard to break up demonstrations and hold the coffee economy in place.[40] He even pushed through a law that gave the police and the army expanded power to put down public protests by force.[41] The repression undercut whatever hope there had been for reform and pushed the expanded Salvadoran left toward politics by other means.

After he jumped ship in Nicaragua and sneaked back into El Salvador, Farabundo

Martí returned to the volcanic highlands between San Salvador and Santa Ana, the heart of the coffee districts.[42] He was rumored to be at the center of clashes between the army and demonstrators on March 22 in Santa Ana. In early April he led a march on the national palace in San Salvador. On May 3, he was arrested and jailed again.[43]

Martí was "a born fighter who was never shaken," said his friend Miguel Mármol, "with an aggressiveness that would distress anyone, a spirit that came from his absolute identification with the cause of the humiliated."[44] In jail he began a hunger strike. For the first six days, the government hid Martí's hunger strike from the public, but then news of it ran in the papers. Hundreds of his supporters rallied to demand his release.[45]

President Araujo could see the martyrdom in progress, and he feared that he might end up crucified. "The Government is well aware of the situation," reported a top U.S. diplomat in El Salvador to Washington on May 12, a week into the hunger strike. "I am informed that the authorities consider that it would be a mistake to let Martí starve himself to death and they will take measures to prevent this. . . . Martí is a person who is intelligent and not unattractive to certain elements of the population of this country, and he aspires, doubtlessly, to a position similar to that occupied by Sandino."[46] A week later, the

American diplomat reported again. Because Martí was "persisting in his hunger strike . . . forced feeding, it is understood, is being resorted to."[47] The diplomatic use of the passive voice echoes the tortured logic of "forced feeding" as a technique of repressive governance in an economic system rooted in hunger.

On May 20, fifteen days into his hunger strike, Martí was transferred from prison to the hospital. On May 31, President Araujo ordered Martí's release, and this time Martí went voluntarily. After twenty-six days without food, he walked out of the hospital with assistance, and his supporters met him at the gate with a glass of orange juice. Martí posed for a photographer from the newspaper, and then the crowd lifted his diminished body and carried him away. When he regained his strength, Martí returned to the coffee districts, where his campaign to transform hunger into power resumed.[48]

There was a story going around El Salvador during the rise of coffee that was taken as truth by nearly everyone in the countryside. The story concerned a snake, a fat brown boa constrictor called the *masacuata,* that was very common in rural districts. The masacuata was said to be harmless to humans, with one exception. It was known to coil in the eaves of houses where mothers with nursing children lived, winding languidly around the roof poles until everyone was asleep. Then at night it would drop down and slither between mother and child, attaching itself to the breast. When a young child was thin and frail, everyone would say, "His mother must have suckled a masacuata." And so well did this story explain the appearance of children in the Salvadoran countryside that even the rich and college-educated, their own children safe from snakes, repeated it as fact.[49]

Born in the cities among students, tradesmen, and industrial workers, the Salvadoran revolutionary movement grew up in the coffee districts between San Salvador and Santa Ana. Here the landscape of coffee production favored the organizers. Thousands of years of heavy rains, running downhill over soft volcanic soil, had carved deep ravines into the hillsides. These ravines became gathering places. At night Miguel Mármol and Farabundo Martí and their fellow organizers met with working people in hidden hollows. The meetings were announced by a call on a conch shell and marked out by oil lamps and red flags strung up in the trees. Child guards were stationed around the perimeter and armed with small bells to ring on the approach of the police or the National Guard.[50]

Sometimes fewer than a hundred people gathered in the ravines, sometimes more than three or four hundred. They brought whatever food they could: "bundles of tortillas, coffee, and sometimes even mats to sleep on when necessary," Mármol recalled. When possible, the organizers slaughtered pigs or a calf to roast and share. Corn tamales were served. Because they had been starved, people spoke to each other in a language of food. "We can't go on just working for the tortillas!" became a rallying cry in the coffee districts, and "the response was always thunderous applause."[51]

It wasn't hard for Mármol and his fellow organizers to convince the people they met in the countryside, most of them coffee workers, that there was a problem. "There was no need for demagoguery," Mármol recalled, "no exaggeration, no special emphasis or fancy interpretations." Everywhere he went Mármol saw "horrible misery" and "widespread hunger lashing out in all directions."[52] Working people in El Salvador's coffee districts knew hunger as unmistakably as they knew their own bodies and the bodies of their children, and they were no longer willing to blame the masacuata. "These hungry little kids break your heart," said one organizer, an electrician, at a union meeting. "It's for them that we have to struggle."[53]

When Miguel Mármol and his fellow organizers traveled in the coffee districts around Santa Ana, they found more than "real

407

starvation and true despair."[54] They met people who were accustomed to taking one another's needs into account as a matter of daily survival. People who worked coffee lived by a communal ethic — sharing food, water, shelter; looking after children; watching each other's backs at work — that land privatization planters' rules had not broken. Organized communism projected this communal ethic from the plantations onto the political space marked out by El Salvador's borders.

Many working people could not read, so men who had worked as supervisors on coffee plantations, whose jobs required that they read and write, often served as intermediaries between the organizers and the workers.[55] The discussions began with hand-drawn maps and pictures that the organizers carried with them on their circuits of the countryside. These drawings explained how the world of the plantations worked, and how it might be changed, pictures of a problem and its solution. The maps put U.S. imperialism in the center of the frame: "Nacional City Bank," "Yunay Frute" (United Fruit), the "Internacional Rail-way." Their cartographic symbols included the American flag, the U.S. dollar, the Union Jack, heavy artillery, and warships. They showed "the displacement of British imperialism by U.S. imperialism" and the customs revenue being sucked out. They showed lines of power crossing the oceans:

telegraph cables that carried price quotations from the United States; the wakes of steamships carrying coffee to overseas markets, and of gunboats carrying soldiers and arms in the opposite direction.[56] Other drawings depicted the structure of Salvadoran society, capital and *capitalistas* on top, then the police and the National Guard, the president, the army, lawyers, the press — and finally, below, the world of the poor.

After the organizers described the meaning of the maps and drawings, the focus of the meetings often shifted to daily life in the coffee economy, and working people spoke of conditions on the plantations.[57] The structure of the discussion implied cause and effect.

The organizers also drew pictures of what was possible outside the lines of power. They drew the world they believed they could bring into being — "the dictatorship of the proletariat." At the top was food production, cornfields and livestock. Everything else followed from grain and meat. From the fields and the stockyards, resources moved through the general economic council, and then, immediately under the economic council, into the warehouses and stores. All other forms of power, industrial power, military power, electric power, derived from the power of the people to feed themselves. The image addressed both the insistent demands of hunger and the "overwhelming popular demand" for the redistribution of land, which James Hill had heard spoken of in meetings on his plantations as early as 1927.[58] The core argument of the popular communism that arose in El Salvador in opposition to the hunger-based system of plantation coffee production was that, if to be human was to be hungry, the goal of government should be provision not privation, satiety not starvation. The "dictatorship of the people" was El Salvador turned upside down, transformed into a paradise of food and eating.

20.
INSIDE THE RED CIRCLE

Working people were coming together in new ways to meet the crisis of the Depression, but it was not clear that their employers could do the same, and this worried everyone invested in Salvadoran coffee. "An atmosphere of helplessness prevails," reported a U.S. diplomat in San Salvador to Washington in January 1930. Especially troubling was "the defeatist attitude of business."[1]

The coffee planters, in fact, were trying. They had begun to wake up to the possibility that perhaps they had grown politically complacent, having enjoyed a virtual monopoly on national politics since purging the Ezeta brothers in 1894. At the end of 1929, following the example of California fruit growers, Salvadoran planters founded the Asociación Cafetalera de El Salvador, formally organizing their interests for the first time. James Hill played what his fellow planters considered a "very important" role in setting the agenda at the outset. On his own,

411

Hill had conducted detailed studies of nearby coffee countries, and he shared his conclusions with the group: El Salvador's export taxes on coffee were roughly twenty times as high as Colombia's; the cost of getting coffee to port was seven times as high as in Colombia; and the cost of shipping coffee from El Salvador was almost twice as high as from Colombia — and Colombia, as the leading producer of mild coffee, was El Salvador's primary competition.[2]

On the morning of December 18, 1929, the coffee planters' association gathered for a meeting at the Casino Salvadoreño, the country's most prestigious social club, to address these issues. They resolved that Hill would lead the creation of a group within the group: a "Society for the Defense of Coffee" modeled on what Brazil had done earlier in the decade, and funded by a new tax on each bag of coffee exported. Hill would use the money to direct studies of the problems facing the production, distribution, and consumption of Salvadoran coffee, both nationally and abroad — just as the Brazilians had funded coffee research and advertising in the United States — and to communicate the importance of the group's work to the Salvadoran president and political authorities.[3] Having organized and institutionalized their interests in these ways, coffee planters became an even more "powerful political force" in El

Salvador than they had been.[4]

Yet as the planters became more powerful politically, they bumped up against the limits of their authority. As they articulated more clearly what they wanted to do, they gained a sharper understanding of what they couldn't do. In April 1930 representatives of Central American coffee countries met in Guatemala City with the idea of organizing warehouses on the model of Brazil's, where coffee could be stored until prices recovered and it could be sold "under more favorable conditions." The mild-coffee congress also proposed advertising Central American coffee in the United States and Europe, and hiring experts who would analyze coffee plantations and mills according to the principles Frederick Winslow Taylor had applied in factories in the United States.[5] Yet this congress had no power to do anything more substantial than make recommendations, and no saving cartel took form.

There were obstacles at home, too. After customs inspector W. W. Renwick was informed of the creation of the Salvadoran coffee defense plan, he delivered some unwelcome news to James Hill and his fellow planters. Renwick informed them he was required by the terms of the loan agreement to collect 70 percent of the new tax, too, the one meant to fund the defense of coffee. Renwick, once admired, became a target. "Articles containing untruths and malicious statements" were published in the papers, and rumors against him were sent around elite circles, "part of a campaign to create unfriendly feeling" among exactly those people with whom Renwick had so successfully ingratiated himself.[6]

Still, Renwick had a job to do, and it was tied to coffee production and exportation, an increasingly tenuous proposition. Early in 1931, Renwick learned that El Salvador's police and armed forces had not been paid for a month. Alarmed, Renwick went over to the American legation to meet with the U.S. consul and an executive of the Anglo-South American Bank. The two bankers agreed to make a small loan of $75,000 to tide the government over. If fiscal and social discipline was demonstrated, a larger loan might be considered.[7]

Salvadoran banks that had once lent eagerly and profitably to the government were in no position to help. In the past the banks themselves had borrowed from larger European and U.S. institutions to fund their advances to planters and politicians alike, but by the middle of 1931 they were unable to draw a penny of additional credit.[8] Selling coffee abroad was virtually the only way to raise cash, but with prices sinking lower and lower it was not a good one.[9]

And then, on December 2, the president,

414

Arturo Araujo, who had been in power for eight months and one day, was overthrown.

The first suspect is always the vice president. In this case, Araujo's vice president, General Maximiliano Hernández Martínez, was also the minister of war — or he had been, until he was removed from the latter position in favor of Araujo's brother-in-law. Though there were a number of suspects beyond Martínez, who emerged from the coup to claim the presidency, and though the general denied any role in the plot that opened his path to office, his denials were not entirely convincing.

Not that there was much outcry against the coup within El Salvador. Before his ouster, Araujo had been on the way to running a budget deficit of $4 million. Basic government operations were unfunded. The police and the army were unpaid. Araujo had failed to restore the country's vitality, offering instead only more violence and repression, and the public had "become incensed by his failure." The year ahead promised no relief: the coffee crop was shaping up to be small.[10] The pressing question for Salvadorans — certainly more important than the question of whose hand had dealt the fatal blow to Araujo's disappointing presidency — was what General Martínez would do with the office he now occupied.

415

Because he had not known his father, General Maximiliano Hernández Martínez went, unconventionally, by his maternal surname. But this was perhaps the least unusual thing about General Martínez, who was also known as "El Brujo," the witch doctor.[11] Martínez was a military man and a Theosophist. He believed in telepathy, reincarnation, and the transmigration of souls. He peddled home remedies for toothaches, cancer, and heart disease. He strung up colored lights around the capital to ward off a smallpox epidemic. He went on the radio and said that in fact there were ten senses — procreation, urination, defecation, thirst, and hunger being the five that physiologists had missed. He advised his constituents that children should not wear shoes — as plants and animals did not wear shoes — so that they could absorb the earth's vibrations through the soles of their feet.

None of these eccentricities was politically disqualifying, even in the eyes of El Salvador's American creditors. From the vantage of Washington, the most important thing about Martínez was that he was not Araujo, who had mismanaged national finances. Yet the politics were complicated by the 1923 Pan-American treaty, designed to discourage revolution in the hemisphere, which now stood in the way of the U.S.'s granting official recognition to the Martínez government.[12] In line with the treaty, the State Department broke off diplomatic relations with El Salvador.[13]

Spurned internationally, Martínez looked for allies at home, and he found plenty. The military, the coffee planters, and certain factions on the left all saw Martínez as a potential vehicle of their interests, diverse as those interests were.[14] The army had not been paid in some time, but it seemed likely General Martínez, an army man himself, would rectify that. The coffee planters, accustomed to having a president who was one of their own, and suspected by Washington of involvement in the coup, were eager to win Martínez's loyalty for their side, and they lent the new administration badly needed cash.[15] On the left, meanwhile, there were two schools of thought, both optimistic, though for different reasons. Some leaders of the workers' groups were hopeful of bargaining with the new president, who was, after all, not a coffee planter. Farabundo Martí, on the other hand, thought that the conditions for communist organizing would be "even better" under Martínez, because his tyranny and misrule would make revolution more appealing.[16]

Miguel Mármol, Farabundo Martí, and their allies did not wait long to test Martínez. A week after the coup, on December 9, 1931, coffee workers around the Santa Ana Volcano set off an unprecedented series of strikes. It was the first coordinated wave of labor stoppages in the country's history, planned to coincide with the coffee harvest. For months organizers had moved from plantation to plantation spreading the word. They targeted the largest plantations, owned by the richest planters, with the idea that high-visibility actions would spark a nationwide general strike. Mármol found working people exceptionally open to their message, as if "the plantations and haciendas were already the people's."[17]

The strikes lasted for ten days and yielded new hope. Seeking a base of popular support, Martínez appeared willing to negotiate. He met with labor leaders in the capital, assuring them of his "great desire to gain from the bosses concessions that will improve the material lot of the workers." On another occasion he was overheard to say that "this bone has ants," meaning that the existing system was rotten through.[18] This was one source of hope.

At the same time, however, Martínez seemed equally eager to placate the coffee elite. Members of the coffee planters' association from Santa Ana pressed him to provide "greater and more efficient property guarantees against Bolsheviks and communists who have here become a serious threat against . . . productive activities," and planters began supporting the Salvadoran National Guard with donations of thousands of dollars a day.[19] When nine hundred workers on plantations owned by the Regalado family struck for access to water and an increase in wages, the Regalados asked Martínez to send troops, and he did, with orders to shoot. Yet when the guardsmen got to the plantation, they opened up a line of communication with the strikers. The National Guard, murderous under Araujo, now seemed to adopt a peacemaking role. This was another source of hope.

There was also some evidence that planters were softening their approach. Near San Salvador, on six plantations owned by the Dueñas family, twelve hundred harvest workers striking in coordination won a 50 percent increase in wages, from twenty to thirty cents per bag of picked coffee cherries. One coffee planter, after watching workers on a neighboring plantation strike for better food, wages, hours, and treatment of child workers, appealed to his fellow planters. "It is worth asking," he wrote in the Santa Ana newspaper, "what are the employers going to do? Are they going to ask the government to send the armed forces to shoot up the bands of unarmed indios? The boss who has that point of view would be stupid. The longer it takes to realize that violent measures cannot resolve the problem, the worse it will be for [the boss]." Other planters, lacking the money they needed to pay their own mortgage obligations, and reluctant to put up a fight to defend coffee crops that were nearly worthless, simply fled their plantations, and the people who had worked for them moved in and took over.[20]

On December 19, the U.S. State Department sent a special envoy to El Salvador to assess the country's unsteady political situation. The envoy was Jefferson Caffrey, U.S. ambassador to Colombia, who had previously served in El Salvador. His brief was to investigate the Martínez regime and review the possibilities for putting Salvadoran politics back on a constitutional — and therefore internationally legitimate — basis, preferably by persuading Martínez to give way to another general, one not so obviously implicated in the coup.[21] On December 22, Caffrey met with Martínez and told him that the United States would not recognize his regime under any circumstances. Martínez, by then emboldened by support from "the better elements" of Salvadoran society, who were also hopeful of a strong and stable government, was not thought to be especially intelligent. Yet he told Caffrey that the position of the United States was most unfortunate, for Article 52, paragraph 5, of the Salvadoran constitution prevented the vice president from resigning.[22]

Just before Christmas, a U.S. military attaché in Central America sent his own report from El Salvador back to Washington.

About the first thing one observes when he goes to San Salvador is the number of expensive automobiles on the streets. . . . There appears to be nothing between these high-priced cars and the ox cart with its bare-footed attendant. . . . Thirty or forty families own nearly everything in the country. They live in almost regal style with many attendants, send their children to Europe or the United States to be educated, and spend money lavishly. . . . I imagine the situation in El Salvador today is very much like France was before its revolution, Russia was before its revolution, and like Mexico was before its revolution. . . .

The authorities seem to realize that the situation is dangerous and are quite alert in their fight against communistic influences. One thing in their favor is that the people never go hungry. The poor can always get fruit and vegetables for nothing and they can steal wood and maybe a few chickens from the coffee fincas, so no matter how poor they are they never become desperate. Also, since they never had anything, they do not feel the want very acutely of things they have never had. . . . A socialistic or communistic revolution in El Salvador may be delayed for several years, ten or even twenty, but when it comes it will be a bloody one.[23]

The attaché, of course, was wrong on one important point. In many places in the coffee districts it was no longer the case that the poor could get fruits or vegetables or firewood or chickens simply by taking them, and there the loss of land was felt acutely.

In Santa Ana the year 1932 began with "the expectation of violence." Municipal elections had been scheduled for Sunday, January 3. Noting the upsurge in strikes, local officials requested detachments of troops, and police confiscated the voter registration rolls of the Salvadoran Communist Party. During the repression, party officials were hopeful. Their platform called for the prohibition of child labor, a six-hour day for workers under eighteen, a seven-hour day for women, an eight-hour day for men, food aid for the unemployed, and, for plantation workers specifically, the "right to food and lodging even when they are not given work." Strikes on plantations were halted so working people could vote. On the strength of their popular support, communist organizers thought they might win nearly 50 percent of the vote. On the day of the election, turnout at the polls was high, a good sign.[24]

Yet when the votes were counted, the first-ever communist candidates for office in El Salvador fared poorly. Reports from the polls, especially in the coffee districts, told of

422

blatant fraud.[25] Looking over the results, the top British diplomat in El Salvador, D. J. Rodgers, saw the outcome in a different light. The truly extraordinary thing, he thought, given the stakes of the election, was that the frauds had been so subtle, that "the authorities were so impartial that the 'communists' nearly won." A coffee planter himself, Rodgers was well aware that "the reds are gaining ground all the time," and for this he blamed his fellow planters.[26] Many had tried to force their way out of the economic crisis by saving on labor costs, extracting more work for less money — an "unwise course," Rodgers knew, though not as foolhardy as "the still unwiser expedient" many others had adopted: cutting "down on the food supplied to the laborers." Putting his experiences on the plantations and in politics together, Rodgers understood that hunger and electoral fraud had together generated a new kind of "discontent." They had provoked demands for a "fundamental change in the economic constitutions of the country." Santa Ana in particular had been threatened with "a general sack" and subsequently placed under heavy guard.[27] "It is in districts where the most unpopular planters have their estates," Rodgers observed, "that there is the most unrest."[28]

After the stolen vote, the "great enthusiasm" Miguel Mármol had observed during the elections, undercut by fraud, gave rise to "even more violence and more discontent." "Bitter strikes" followed, and the government responded with "a wave of criminal terror," as Mármol described it, centered on the Santa Ana Volcano.[29] On the north side of the volcano, the army confronted a group of four hundred strikers with deadly force, breaking the picket lines and hunting for three days those who fled cross-country, killing as many as sixty.[30]

With violence reaching new levels, Mármol proposed a meeting with the president, and Farabundo Martí backed him up. Martínez initially agreed to meet, but when the group arrived at the national palace on January 8, the president begged off with a toothache, sticking his head out a window to show off the handkerchief he had tied around his face, holding his mouth closed.[31] Rebuffed by Martínez, Mármol and Martí turned back to their base of support.

On January 10, Martí convened an emergency meeting in the capital to debate the possibility of revolution. Miguel Mármol was also pushing for an uprising, "given the ripeness of the revolutionary situation." Martí consulted a French translation of Marx's *Capital.* More and more, he feared that the people he aspired to lead would charge ahead toward revolution by themselves and be slaughtered.[32] It seemed a matter of "duty" and "honor" that the self-appointed leaders of the Salvadoran people lead their revolution.[33] The debate lasted through the night.

The politics of the Salvadoran left in the twenties and thirties has sometimes been dismissed, even by the most sympathetic historians, as a "reductionist Marxist-Leninist" strain of communism.[34] This dismissal underestimates the extent to which Farabundo Martí, Miguel Mármol, and the people they led found a remedy to fit their predicament. Just as James Hill brought parts of Manchester to the Santa Ana Volcano, so too did the people who opposed the dictatorship of coffee. Their politics had also been developed in part in Manchester, and had also been shaped by the idea of energy.

By the time Friedrich Engels left Manchester in 1844, he was no longer fixated simply on the lives of the working poor. Instead he wanted to understand the relationship between the poverty he witnessed in the city's slums and the wealth created in its factories. At the heart of the larger economic puzzle was the question of how his own family's wealth was connected to the "condition of the working class" he had described.[35]

On the way home to Germany, Engels stopped in Paris to visit an acquaintance, Karl Marx. The conversations they had there changed Engels's plans.[36] For the next four years, the two men lived and studied and wrote together in Paris and Brussels, making periodic research trips back to Manchester and publishing *The Communist Manifesto* in 1848. The following year, both coauthors chronically short on money, Engels returned full-time to his family's mill in Manchester to work as a bookkeeper. He regularly sent half of his substantial income, in addition to painstakingly detailed information about how factories actually operated, to Marx, who had settled in London and immersed himself in the question that interested both men, the connection between poverty and wealth.[37]

The question was compelling, and complicated, because it pointed to a hole in the logic of the market. At the moment when one thing — including money — changes hands for another in a free marketplace, the two things have nominally equal value: that is what makes it possible to trade them for each other. But given this exchange of equal values, where does profit — and the inequality that accumulates with profit — come from? What makes it possible, as Engels put it, to "constantly sell more dearly than one has bought" — to bring a thing to market that cost a certain amount to make, and leave with something of "equal value" that is also of greater value, pocketing the difference as profit? Profit came, Marx contended, not from simple cheating, extortion, or coercion, nor from the time elapsed between production and exchange, nor from any difference in taste or fashion from one market to another, but from the process of making the thing itself. Labor created value above its own price — and this "surplus value" was the basis of profit. Marx considered his work on surplus value to be his most significant contribution to economic analysis, he told Engels in 1867, the year of the publication of the first volume of *Capital,* and Engels agreed.[38]

Previous studies by leading political economists, including Adam Smith and David Ricardo, had noted the significance of the difference between the price of labor and its value. Yet they had focused on this discrepancy as the solution to the puzzle of profit. In contrast, Marx made it the beginning of a new inquiry.[39] Where did surplus value itself come from, and how was it produced? How did labor create value above its own cost? These questions shaped the investigations Marx undertook in London after 1850, and they frame the story he told in *Capital.*

While Engels came to his interest in economics via Manchester, Marx claimed that his own curiosity was sparked by a controversy that he had observed in Germany in 1842, where he was working as the editor of a newspaper. As the result of a new law, many peasants were being arrested for taking firewood from the forest — even wood that had fallen to the ground — and then imprisoned and forced to work without pay for the landowner. The law followed from the subdivision of large landed estates into smaller private plots for commercial agriculture, one stage in a longer process that eradicated what had been customary rights for the poor and led to the privatization of resources critical for survival: "not only fuel, but also forage, materials for houses, farm equipment, and food." The availability of these necessities in the forest had once permitted peasants to "reject those terms of work and exploitation that German capital was seeking to make available in the factory."[40] But as the enclosure of common resources within private plots of land progressed, peasants were increasingly compelled to work for a wage. Studying in London, Marx came to see the past privatization of land and natural resources as the original fund of surplus value: profit was its compounding interest.

The story Marx told in *Capital* tracked surplus value from the earth to the factory through the working bodies of laborers and into the pockets of capitalists. This helps to explain why Marx and Engels alike found the idea of energy and the rapidly developing field of thermodynamic science so promising. Both men "closely studied" the scientific works of Mayer, Joule, Helmholtz, Thomson, and Clausius, as well as popular works on the productivist "gospel of energy." Ahead of the publication of the first volume of *Capital*, Marx attended a series of lectures by English physicist John Tyndall, the leading promoter of Robert Mayer's work in Victorian England, who had claimed in 1862 that "there is not a hammer raised, a wheel turned, or a shuttle thrown, that is not raised, and turned, and thrown by the sun."[41] The discovery of energy had opened a tantalizing possibility: empirically tracing the origins of surplus value, long hidden underneath the market, by accounting for all economic inputs to production in the same terms, and using that analysis to build a more just economic system. For against the division of the world into rich and poor, Marx imagined a society organized around a different principle: "From each according to his abilities, to each according to his needs," he wrote in 1875. According to his vision of a just society, goods would be priced according to the labor they contained, so that "the same quantum of labor that [a worker] has given society in one form" — to be measured not only in time but also in the intensity of the work done — "he receives back in the other."[42]

Followers of Marx attempted to translate these principles into a practicable system of accounting. Around 1880, Ukrainian physicist Sergei Podolinsky proposed an "economic thermodynamics" — an analysis of value in terms of energy.[43] The proposal caught Marx's attention in 1882, and he wrote to Engels to see what he thought. Engels was intrigued, but deemed it implausible, for the calculations required were so intricate as to be impractical if not impossible. Podolinsky's work had not taken account, for example, of the light the sun provided to the laborer, or of the temperature of the air.[44] Instead he had treated the working body as if it were a simple machine, matching input with output. "The body is not a steam-engine, which only undergoes friction and wear and tear," Engels wrote. "Along with every muscular contraction or relaxation, chemical changes occur in the nerves and muscles, and these changes cannot be treated as parallel to those of coal in a steam-engine . . . their external results, yes, but not the processes themselves without considerable reservations."[45] These "reservations" marked the very tension — that human labor could be quantified and analyzed as if the body were indeed a steam engine, though it was most certainly not — that made communism so urgent.

Vladimir Lenin drew significantly on this scientific dimension of Engels's thinking. One of the founders of Russia's Bolshevik Party, Lenin himself spent a month in the British Library in 1908 studying the idea of energy

430

and the "crisis" it had caused in scientific thought. His research was prompted by the failed Russian Revolution of 1905. A mass mobilization of industrial workers and peasants had pushed the tsarist regime to the brink — but not over the edge. The outcome was the establishment of a legislature and prime minister under the tsar, but the possibility of greater change had been snuffed out by the army: "peasants in uniform . . . enforcing state order against rebellious workers, students, and fellow peasants."[46] The question before Lenin and his fellow Bolsheviks was why.

The inquiry developed into a bitter debate between Lenin and Alexander Bogdanov, a cofounder of the Bolsheviks. Bogdanov believed that the revolution had failed because the masses weren't sufficiently prepared to carry it through. In particular, they lacked the revolutionary consciousness that social transformation required. This diagnosis was based on Bogdanov's conception of society as an extension of the natural world, a notion he got in part from Darwin and mostly from thermodynamics. Bogdanov's readings in science taught him to view energy as the basis for all phenomena, natural and social alike. By this thermodynamic model, the transformation of a whole society required the work of a whole society. Ideology was a sort of "motive force," a form of energy available for doing the work of social change. All that was needed in Russia was more of it. Bogdanov's proposal was to build the revolutionary culture until the minds of the people were ready.[47]

Lenin thought this was "refuse" — a pretentious misreading of the science. He mocked the idea that "the external world . . . reflects a 'property' of our mind" — it was clear instead that "our thought . . . reflects the transformation of energy in the external world."[48] Revolution could not be thought into being, if only enough people would think it. Capitalists certainly did not wait for working people to decide they were ready to work more, filling them up with more food in the meantime — just the opposite. "The most widely discussed topic today in Europe, and to some extent in Russia, is the 'system' of the American engineer, Frederick Taylor . . . [which] Taylor himself has described . . . [as] 'scientific,' " Lenin wrote in *Pravda* in 1913. "What is this 'scientific system'? Its purpose is to squeeze out of the worker three times more labour. . . . They . . . mercilessly drain him of all his strength, and are three times faster in sucking out every drop of the wage slave's nervous and physical energy. . . . In capitalist society, progress in science and technology means progress in the art of sweating."[49] Revolution, Lenin predicted, would come when capitalism's opponents

432

took the same aggressive approach — when "a few professionals, as highly trained and experienced as the imperial security police, were allowed to organize it."[50]

When the leaders of the Salvadoran Communist Party realized that they would have to fight for power, they wrote to Moscow to ask for money and weapons.[51]

Preparations were also under way on the volcano. In Santa Ana on January 12, James Hill's eldest son, Jaime, was putting his American education to work. Now thirty-one, Jaime had returned from California a decade earlier, working by his father's side through the years of growth and prosperity in the 1920s. Since the onset of the Depression, he had also taken a leadership role in the coffee planters' association.[52] His father was sixty, and Jaime Hill was growing into the position that he expected by custom to inherit.

With that future now under threat, Jaime opened the catalog of the Winchester Repeating Arms Company, New Haven, Connecticut. He turned through pages of rifles and handguns until he got to ammunition. At some point in his schooling, Jaime had learned that bullets made of soft lead, and tipped with points that had been hollowed out into truncated cones, exploded against flesh like small molten bombs, resulting in the highest likelihood of tissue destruction,

433

bone fracture, blood loss, extrusion of the internal organs, shock, loss of consciousness, resignation, and death — what the American gun trade had begun to call "stopping power."

"Stopping power" was the solution to a problem that arose during the Philippine-American War. U.S. soldiers fighting in the Philippine archipelago to suppress the independence movements that led to Spain's ouster in 1898 had become concerned about the effectiveness of their service weapons. Battlefield reports said that the Muslim Moros who lived around the coffee island of Mindanao were distressingly unaffected by standard bullets. One man had charged a group of American soldiers from a hundred yards away, absorbing ten shots before falling a mere five yards from the gunmen, where he was finally killed by a shot to the head.[53]

In 1904, the army commissioned a study of the problem by ordnance officer John T. Thompson and Major Louis La Garde, a doctor in the medical corps. Thompson would soon retire from the army and go into business selling his namesake invention, the Thompson submachine gun, but La Garde was dedicated to the science of inflicting and treating gunshot injuries, and in 1914 he published the results of the study as a four-hundred-page book. "The stopping power of firearms is of vital importance on certain occasions," La Garde wrote. "At war with savage tribes or a fanatical enemy, a military man seeks to arm his soldiers with a rifle that delivers projectiles with telling effect. A fanatic like a Moro wielding a bolo in each hand who advances with leaps and bounds and who never knows when he is hit . . . must be hit with a projectile having a maximum amount of stopping power."

By shooting cows tied to posts in Chicago's stockyards, La Garde and his team determined that stopping power depended largely on the "sectional area of a bullet and the amount of energy which it delivers at the point of impact," and they identified significant differences in these performance criteria among different types of guns and bullets. Leading the way were "cup-pointed bullets" of soft lead — "man stopper[s]" that "might be issued to troops fighting savage tribes, and fanatics in the brush or jungle." Experiments had shown how the round "readily mushrooms upon striking cartilage and the joint ends of bones," increasing the possibility that the bullet would stay lodged in the body of the target, transforming "every particle of energy" it carried into a wound.[54]

Jaime Hill found what he was looking for on page 100 of the Winchester catalog. In red he drew a neat circle around a picture of a nine-millimeter soft-tip hollow-point bullet, which he knew would fit in his semiautomatic SIG Brevett Bergmann rifle.

■ ■ ■ ■

"The communist agitation among the plantation laborers is steadily increasing in seriousness," British consul D. J. Rodgers wrote the next day, January 13, 1932, to the foreign secretary in London. It was most serious in "the west of the republic, around Santa Ana, Ahuachapán, and Sonsonate," Rodgers reported. "There can be little doubt now that this is not a Labour movement aiming at an increase in wages and improvement in living conditions." The goal instead was "general division of lands and property and government by the proletariat." The plan for achieving it was "the slaughter of the landowners and the appropriation of their lands."

While Rodgers believed that "the troubles which have taken place have been mostly on estates where the labourers are known to have been badly treated," he had not heard of any strikes on any of the British-owned plantations — but this was hardly a comfort. On the contrary, the absence of strikes had led to "the apathy and selfishness of some planters who imagine that, because no troubles have taken place on their own estates, they do not therefore require to unite with other planters in carrying out combined measures." This attitude was troubling because there was, as far as Rodgers could see, "no energetic Government policy" with any chance of mustering any real support from the planter class, "who have difficulty in combining about anything and have lost money lent to previous Governments." On top of this, Rodgers reported, "the pay of the troops" was "some weeks in arrears."[55]

Farabundo Martí, Miguel Mármol, and the organizers set a date and time for the uprising: January 16 at midnight. Then they postponed for three days, in the hope of gaining the support of breakaway factions of the army fed up with working for no pay. Then they postponed again, three more days, to the twenty-second.

The delays opened up cracks in their ranks, and the plan leaked out. When the leaks got back to Mármol, he went to see Martí immediately, to warn him that the police knew where he was staying and knew what he was planning. As he listened to Mármol's warning, Martí smiled under his mustache, and he laughed and told his friend not to be afraid and sent him away with a package of homemade bombs.[56]

A final call to arms sounded on January 20, written by the organizers in the voice of the people they hoped to free: "We the workers, they call us thieves . . . and steal our wage, paying us a miserable wage and condemning us to live in filthy tenements or in stinking barracks, or working day and night in the fields under rain and sun. We are labeled thieves for demanding the wages that they owe us, a reduction in the workday, and a reduction in the rents that we pay to the rich who take almost all our harvest, stealing our work from us. . . . According to the wealthy, we do not have a right to anything, and we shouldn't open our mouths."[57]

"Grave danger of general rising of communists who intend to sack city," cabled British consul Rodgers to the Foreign Office in London on the same day, January 20.[58] The previous evening, he reported, a "large body of well armed Communists provided with dynamite bombs preparing to attack San Salvador were dispersed by government forces."[59]

By the following day the situation had become more perilous. "Communists have made detailed plans to blow up banks, take possession of railways and plantations, kill members of Government, Army officers and women, sack town and establish soviet republic," Rodgers wrote frantically to London. "In view of imminent danger to British bank, railway, Canadian electrical company, and other British life and property, I suggest consultation with U.S. Government with a view toward urgent measures."[60]

The next morning, Friday, January 22, the

dawn sky above the Santa Ana Volcano was dark with gray ash. Three volcanoes across the border in Guatemala had erupted at once. All day the plumes were so thick that birds thumped into each other in midair, and the wintry fallout blanketed the trees and covered the ground around Santa Ana, six inches deep in spots.[61] It was clearly a sign, but no one could agree on the interpretation. In the evening firecrackers sliced bright gashes through the hazy darkness. Tremulous calls on conch shells sought each other out across the hillsides and ravines.[62]

Meanwhile, locked inside their embassies, American and British diplomats called for backup. "Situation hourly increasing in gravity," Consul Rodgers wrote to London. "British railway torn up and telegraph wires out." Rodgers suspected that the insurgents were trying to draw troops out of the capital before moving in to take it: "British lives and property are in danger owing to the imminent possibility of a general Communist uprising."[63] The head of the U.S. legation in San Salvador agreed: "The presence of war vessels," he cabled to Washington, "would have a great moral effect and prevent much bloodshed."[64]

In response, a British cruiser, HMS *Dragon,* set out from Jamaica, and the U.S. Navy "rushed" a cruiser and two destroyers from Panama. Closer than both the U.S. Navy and the Royal Navy, however, were twin Canadian destroyers, the *Skeena* and the *Vancouver,* which happened to be steaming down the Pacific coast from western Canada toward the Panama Canal.[65]

21.
AN EXCEEDINGLY GOOD LUNCH

At about eight o'clock on the evening of Friday, January 22, the telegrapher for the twin Canadian destroyers *Skeena* and *Vancouver* intercepted an urgent message from the commander in chief of the America and West Indies squadron of the Royal Canadian Navy to the chief of the Naval Staff in Ottawa. The message, which was passed quickly on to the ships' ranking officer, Commander Victor Brodeur, "stated that information has been received from the British Foreign Office that British lives and property in the Republic of El Salvador were in danger owing to the imminent possibility of a general Communist uprising," and that the nearest British ship, the HMS *Dragon,* was five days out at best.[1]

By 8:30, Commander Brodeur had established communication with Ottawa. By 9:00, the ships had turned toward the Salvadoran port of Acajutla and increased their speed, with the hope of arriving by daylight.

Less than three hours later, the fears of El Salvador's planters came true. Between five and seven thousand people, divided into loosely coordinated battalions and armed primarily with machetes, rose up at the peak of the harvest season to overturn the order of coffee production, to "make the workers the owners." Some of the revolutionaries were members of the Communist Party of El Salvador; the "great majority" were people who had worked on coffee plantations and had decided that they would not live that way another day.[2]

"In a revolution," wrote historian C. L. R. James in his classic study of Haiti, *The Black Jacobins,* "when the ceaseless slow accumulation of centuries bursts forth into volcanic eruption, the meteoric flares and flights above are a meaningless chaos and lend themselves to infinite caprice and romanticism unless the observer sees them always as projections of the sub-soil from which they came."[3]

In El Salvador in January 1932, revolution ran through the center of the coffee economy as surely as the railroad tracks and telegraph lines ringing the Santa Ana Volcano. In Izalco, insurgents took control of the town hall. They installed in power the man who had been the communist candidate for mayor in the recent

442

elections, rounded up and jailed fourteen of the town's wealthiest residents, and then headed for Sonsonate, where they stormed the customs building, a monument to the rise of coffee, and killed four guards. Nearby, in Nahuizalco, insurgents burned land titles recorded after privatization, broke into stores and took food, and forced the grander women of the town to make tortillas for them.[4]

Other attacks were personal.[5] In Juayúa, across the volcano from Las Tres Puertas, hundreds of insurgents armed with shotguns and machetes converged on the house of Emilio Redaelli, the town's former mayor, who owned a store, ran a large coffee mill, and exported coffee he bought by advancing cash to small growers before the harvest. Redaelli confronted the mob from his balcony, pistol in hand.

He could not have been completely surprised to find himself in such a position. The possibility lived somewhere in the mind of everyone who profited from coffee. Several months later, one planter admitted that he had often imagined what would happen if his workers confronted him. In his fantasies, he always got the best of them: "I, who always felt I could dispose of ten Indians in a row, they with their machetes and I with my revolver and fifty bullets; I who have not trembled before these wicked men because I saw them as humble little lambs . . ." Yet when the imagined confrontation finally arrived, it went quite differently: "When I made out the throng, the mob of two hundred that was coming after me, I had to mount my horse and I broke into a dizzying race over rocky ground and precipices, tearing apart fences, until I joined up with a brother of mine on his hacienda."[6]

Stranded on his balcony with nowhere to flee, Emilio Redaelli tried to bargain for his life. "What do you want?" he asked from above. "Money," came the answer, and Redaelli must have been hopeful as he turned inside. "Wait, I'll bring it," he promised. The crowd waited only long enough for Redaelli to return with the cash. Before he could give it up, a volley of stones knocked him down, and the crowd was on top of him.

After they killed Redaelli, the insurgents took the town he had governed. They ran a red flag up the pole in the center of town and made residents wear red ribbons and call each other comrade. They ordered women who were accustomed to being served to make them tortillas. They looted stores, collected all the goods in the town hall, and began to hand them out, inaugurating a regime of provision with clothes, blankets, tools, and corn. Children were given pocketfuls of candy.[7]

But even then, the counterinsurgency was already under way. The arrests, in fact, had begun before the uprising itself — Farabundo Martí, Miguel Mármol, and other leaders of the Salvadoran Communist Party were in jail when the fighting started. At the first reports of open insurrection, the army and the National Guard had set out from San Salvador and Santa Ana toward the smaller towns that were under siege. Taking over the job of protecting the larger cities was an irregular though well-armed force. On the suggestion of a "prominent banker," Rodolfo Duke, "adult citizens were equipped with rifles and revolvers and received carte blanche to shoot any Communist on sight." More than "300 sons of the first families" — the "flower of Salvadoran aristocracy," as the New York Times put it — "were armed and turned loose to snare any radicals."[8]

The next morning, Saturday, January 23, the Canadian sailors awoke at sea to find themselves in the middle of a cloud of volcanic ash, "causing a haze which reduced the visibility to about 2 1/2 miles, and making a landing difficult." A layer of fine brown silt stuck to the fresh paint on the ships, and it would be "several weeks before the last traces of it were finally removed." Slowed by low visibility, the Skeena and Vancouver dropped anchor about a mile off the pier of Acajutla around noon, six hours later than planned. Two armed men were sent into the engine room on each ship, "out of sight, but available in case of necessity." The executive officer, Commander Brodeur's deputy, went ashore by motor launch to assess the situation.

Once he had been lifted from the launch up to the "high, steel trestle-pier" in a kind of chair attached to a crane, the executive officer was met by the British vice-consul, H. B. Towning, "the only white man in Acajutla." Towning "at once stated that at present all was quiet in the port itself, but that trouble had broken out generally in the Republic on the previous night." He hadn't picked up any immediate threats locally, but regardless, Brodeur began to make preparations to land two platoons and two machine-gun sections, perhaps a hundred men in total, so they could deploy on short notice if needed. Once the port itself was determined to be secure, Commander Brodeur and a signalman, equipped with a lamp, hand flags, and a pistol, went ashore.

From the pier Brodeur "spoke over the telephone to the British Consul . . . Mr. D. J. Rodgers in San Salvador, who stated that the situation was becoming increasingly grave, and urging him to visit the capital in order to see things for himself." Brodeur made plans to do so the following day, and then he arranged for "five lady refugees," four from the town of Sonsonate and one "who was spending a few days at Acajutla," to be "taken on board" the *Skeena,* where they were put up in officers' cabins.

The next day, Brodeur went ashore as planned, heading for the capital and accompanied, "at the urgent recommendation" of Consul Rodgers, by a petty officer carrying a machine gun concealed inside a hammock. As soon as they set foot on the pier, Brodeur and his escort heard that "a telephone message had just been received from the capital requesting that an armed party should be sent there at once to protect British interests." Brodeur called back and said that nothing "would be done except by a direct personal request from Consul Rodgers himself," and hung up to wait. When no response from Rodgers was forthcoming, Brodeur and his escort prepared to depart Acajutla at 2:00 to track down the consul in San Salvador.

They climbed into a 1919 Overland touring car that had been retrofitted to run on railway tracks, reaching speeds of nearly forty-five miles an hour. At the switching station in Sonsonate — a right turn would lead to the capital, a left to Santa Ana — the driver refused to go any farther, "having been persuaded by his friends that he would be unlikely to get through the danger area alive." Fortunately "another driver was found willing to risk it."

The run to San Salvador took three and a half tense hours. On the way the party stopped in the village of Armenia, where Brodeur was finally able to reach Rodgers by phone. In the interim Rodgers had phoned back to the port of Acajutla, personally requesting that "an armed party be sent to San Salvador at once to protect British lives and property," and he reiterated the request to Brodeur, who in turn ordered one platoon and two machine-gun sections to come ashore. The soldiers were on the pier within an hour, by 4:30. But no sooner had they landed than contradictory word arrived from Rodgers: "Platoon is not to be landed until further instructions." So the platoon and the gunners motored back to the ships, and had just reboarded when, at 5:00, Rodgers cabled again: "Please send landing party immediately." The soldiers were already back on the pier, mustered into formation, and about to march toward the railroad station for transport to the capital, when the British vice-consul stopped them. President Martínez had decreed that "on no account was a foreign armed party to be allowed to land." Stuck on the pier, the Canadian sailors set to work filling sandbags that they could use to fortify railcars to take them to San Salvador, should they be permitted to proceed there.

Commander Brodeur heard about this confusion from Rodgers only after the old

Overland pulled into San Salvador station around 5:45 in the evening, the sun already setting. He was surprised to learn that Rodgers had made the request for a landing without the approval of the Salvadoran government, but he was relieved that it had been cleared with the United States. In consideration of the fact that neither the U.S. nor Great Britain had recognized Martínez's regime, that was "obviously the correct procedure." Consul Rodgers explained that he had called for the troops to land because Martínez had not been able to give him a "definite guarantee" of the protection of British lives and property — a category that included, of course, the Hill family, their plantations, and Las Tres Puertas. Hearing this, Brodeur ordered his men to remain on the pier while he went to speak with the president himself.

President Martínez granted Brodeur an immediate audience in the national palace, with Rodgers serving as interpreter. Martínez steadfastly refused "to allow foreign armed parties to land, stating very definitely that he had the situation perfectly well in hand." Brodeur assured the president that the idea was only to assist. Martínez thanked him and again refused assistance. Brodeur replied that "under the circumstances he must insist upon the immediate and thorough protection of all British interests." Martínez promised such protection without hesitation, and arranged it so that before long "all British property" was under armed guard and "various British refugees" were holed up at the British legation.[9] Satisfied that his insistence had "strengthened the president's stand considerably," Brodeur ordered his men off the pier at Acajutla and back to the ships. But because he had heard rumors of attacks on San Salvador, and because passage from the capital to the coast by moonlight was "considered a rather risky proceeding," Brodeur and his Petty Officer decided to stay the night. Martínez had imposed a 9:00 curfew on the capital. After that hour San Salvador was deserted except for "about 500 volunteers . . . raised from the younger members of the middle-class landowners." Brodeur, who kept the machine gun with him, heard "sporadic rifle fire" through the night. The next morning, Monday, January 25, he left the capital to return to the ships, which he planned to keep anchored off Acajutla for the rest of the week, to see if President Martínez did in fact have the situation in hand.

Later that day, the U.S. Navy arrived, having made the extraordinary speed of twenty-five knots on the way from Panama. Plans had been made for an operation deploying "maximum available force," but when the American officers went ashore, they were barred from leaving the pier at Acajutla even to talk with the port commander, and they turned around. Tuesday and Wednesday, so far as Brodeur could tell, "nothing of importance took place." Train transportation and telephone communications were practically normal, and the Salvadoran army and National Guard had seized the initiative and "were killing rebels left and right."

On Thursday, Brodeur went up to a British plantation with its "part-owner," a Mr. Plynn. Plynn had reported "many attacks," and Brodeur wanted to investigate the matter for himself. He found men "working surrounded with flies and dirty water," while others lurked ominously in the bushes nearby. No serious threat, Brodeur concluded, but he could see the problem.

> During normal times about 150 men are employed; but during the picking season . . . about 500 extra workers, including children of 15 years old and upwards and many women, are taken on. These common labourers work as much as ten hours a day in some cases, for which they are paid . . . 12 cents U.S. currency. . . . In addition, they are given their food consisting of a handful of beans and a few "tortillas" (small, flat, and exceedingly indigestible cakes made of maize) and coffee to drink; the cost of feeding each worker per day is at the most 1 cent.

It appears that up to a short time ago, this low class of labourer was content with its lot, or at least indifferent to the appalling conditions under which it worked — low wages, incredible filth, utter lack of consideration on the part of the employers, conditions in fact not far removed from slavery. But where here and there a few managed to better themselves, realization began to dawn upon these latter of the unhappy, and indeed unjust, lot of their class. It was to these few slightly superior types that the principles of Communism . . . appealed most strongly, and it is they who helped to spread the gospel of "class warfare" amongst the workers.

Brodeur could sense the danger: "It would have been the easiest thing in the world to destroy the plantation due to its isolated location."

Yet he also found that "reports of attacks on British-owned plantations . . . in every case were found to be grossly overstated. . . . and it was clear that the Government's statement that they had the situation well in hand was fully justified." The evidence had been left out in the open to see. "Many dead bodies of Indians were observed along the railway lines specially round Sonsonate," Brodeur reported. As for the living, "nearly everyone walking around carried a small white flag which they waved continuously to show that they were not red." It was unclear "whether these white flags influenced the troops patrolling the country, as one body was observed lying dead with the white flag still in his hat."

On Friday morning, a group of Salvadoran generals traveled to the port of Acajutla to call Brodeur and tell him that "peace had been reestablished, that the Communists had been completely beaten and dispersed, and that 4,800 of them had already been killed." Hearing this news, Brodeur "immediately went ashore to verify the statement in a general way, and to pay his respects." When he landed, the generals embraced him enthusiastically and, "just to show that they were doing all they could to protect British property and lives," invited him to come with them to the countryside the following day, Saturday, to "witness a few executions."

The next day Brodeur and three deputies were treated to an "exceedingly good lunch," courtesy of President Martínez, "very delicious and abundant." After lunch they climbed into a car "full of armed officers including one on each mudguard." A trailing car was loaded "full of volunteers armed to the teeth," and the party went up into the coffee districts. In each settlement they passed through, Brodeur noticed that the targets of the insurrection had been the same:

town halls, holding the archives of land titles, and "residences of the rich plantation owners who had already fled" were badly damaged.[10] He saw one planter's house left "completely untouched, though properties on either side were completely destroyed, specially all articles of family value such as priceless old furniture and paintings." The planter whose house still stood, Brodeur was told, had "treated his hands in a far more generous way."

Near Sonsonate, Brodeur and his deputies "were shown five Indians who were about to be shot." Three of the condemned "had actually surrendered themselves," Brodeur was told, "under the impression that the death of a sufficient number of them will stimulate those that are left to carry on the fight for conditions and higher wages." It was "thought to be inadvisable" for Brodeur to witness the executions, but he got close enough to the bodies afterward to take note of the "very peaceful look on the faces of those dead. . . . All the Indians executed were apparently glad to sacrifice their lives in the hope that martyrdom might bring a brighter future for the next generation." He had heard of an "actual case in Sonsonate . . . of a young pregnant married woman who was informed her husband had just been executed by the troops," to which she replied that "she did not care as she was carrying his avenger."[11] There was nothing Brodeur could do about that, and that night the Canadian ships were given the all-clear to leave the following evening, Sunday, January 31.

On Brodeur's final day in El Salvador, he woke up early and traveled to the capital to inform British consul Rodgers of his plans to leave, observing on the way several "new bodies along the railroad line." Told of the impending withdrawal, Rodgers "could offer no objection," only gratitude, for the "presence of the destroyers was of the greatest help from the point of view of British interests." While Rodgers had initially failed to get a definite commitment out of Martínez, after the arrival of the Canadians, "every official of the Government . . . from President Martínez down" had gone out of his way to demonstrate "the energy and determination of the Government in protecting British lives and property."[12]

After the meeting, Brodeur and three of his officers were invited by the British manager of the Salvadoran railway to play golf in San Salvador, and a party of fifty men from the ships were invited to visit a sugar plantation a few miles inland. After the outings, at 10:40 that night, the *Vancouver* and the *Skeena* pulled up anchor and sailed away.

From everything he saw during his week in El Salvador, Brodeur could not help thinking that the newspapers had it wrong. He had come to believe that "the revolution was entirely due to the lack of consideration for the Indians," and this was different, he thought, from the reports of "Bolshevism" given so much attention in the press. "It is very doubtful if the Indians who took part in the revolution knew what bolshevism meant," Brodeur concluded in his after-action report. "To them it meant an organization to release them from slavery."[13]

The U. S. Navy left a day later, on February 1, 1932, which was also the last day of the life of Farabundo Martí. By then Martí had been in prison for nearly two weeks. He had been arrested in the early-morning hours of January 20, even before the final call to arms was issued, two days ahead of the start of the revolution he had planned to lead.[14]

Martí had been captured with Alfonso Luna and Mario Zapata, two younger organizers, leaders of student groups. At six o'clock on the evening of Saturday, January 30, the three of them were tried before a "council of war" on the charge of treason. The trial had only one possible outcome, and it took less than a day, with arguments concluding at one o'clock in the morning on January 31. Martí spoke last, taking responsibility for having led the insurrection and asking for clemency for the younger men. Then the three were taken back to jail for a sleepless night. Martí smoked, Zapata paced, Luna conferred with a priest. At dawn they were called back to the courtroom and sentenced to death.

For the rest of the day the condemned men were permitted to receive visitors. They were obliged to attend mass. The two younger men gave confession, but Martí, in lieu of confessing his sins, said that there were more than a thousand bombs planted around San Salvador, and many times that number of insurgents ready to keep fighting. The next morning the three revolutionaries were loaded into the back of an ambulance, driven to a cemetery, encouraged to die "in communion with God," marched up to a wall, and turned to face the firing squad.[15]

457

22.
THE SLAUGHTER

The moon waned after the warships left, and around the Santa Ana Volcano the dark nights were passed anxiously. The insurgency was largely under control, as Commander Brodeur had observed, but it was not yet dead. Instead it was changing shape, "developing toward guerilla warfare made by small bands operating at night." In this new phase, the "hilly well-wooded country" of the coffee plantations favored the insurgents, for they knew it well enough to fight after dark.[1] Each afternoon, as the sun went down, the citizens of the towns hurried home.[2]

The continued fighting posed a problem for the Salvadoran government, whose supply of ammunition was "becoming exhausted." Urgent restocking orders had been put through to the United States, but the larger problem was that because of low coffee prices, the unplanned interruption of the harvest season, and the obligation to pay down the American loan, the government had no money.[3] At the start of the insurgency, the Salvadoran Minister of Finance had alerted W. W. Renwick that the government, "owing to the present situation, will demand more funds," but Renwick was not disposed to give over any more money.[4] "Government under attack urgently needing funds to pay armed forces," British consul D. J. Rodgers had telegraphed to the British legation in Washington on Monday, January 25. Rodgers recommended that British diplomats work with the U.S. State Department to set up another private syndicate to lend to the Martínez government perhaps a quarter million dollars.[5] Otherwise, Rodgers understood, a "very unfortunate situation may arise."[6]

When international financing was not forthcoming, Martínez turned to his constituents. The idea of using customs revenue to make loan payments to the United States in the midst of a national crisis was reviled in all corners of Salvadoran society, but only the rich were now in a position to do anything about it, and they used their money to influence Martínez's response to the insurgency. Even before the departure of the Canadian and American navies, the president had invited a group of businessmen, "for the most part coffee growers," to the national palace for a meeting, at which he "expounded on the danger that society was facing with the reds." As evidence he presented some "documents found in the power of the conspirators," and asked the businessmen for "economic aid for the urgent purchase of machine guns."[7]

At that point in the meeting, Jaime Hill, who was to become a great friend of President Martínez, asked to speak.[8] He rose with confidence and "made the President see that the economic situation was so depressed that it was not possible to easily gather the sum of money necessary, but that the Government could suspend service on the foreign borrowing, quite rightly so, given that a primordial duty of the state is to conserve its existence." Then Ángel Guirola, the banker whose plantations Miguel Mármol had described in Moscow, spoke up to support Jaime Hill's proposal. After Guirola spoke, "the others present unanimously supported the idea . . . of the suspension on the service of the foreign debt." At the same time, "there was no lack of those who called for the death penalty for the communists." Martínez promised that he would "punish the revolutionaries with the full weight of the law." To this end, because the government was in "very urgent need of money to pay for the military operations . . . and for fresh supplies of arms and ammunition," he requested again "that funds be raised for the purchase of machine guns."[9]

Machine guns made the counterinsurgency

460

so efficient that the revolution itself has been buried in history under the name of its suppression: La Matanza, the slaughter.[10]

After retaking the towns, the military and the militias chased the insurgents into the countryside, where the revolutionary force blended into the population from which it had emerged. Often the government's soldiers did not bother to determine whether the people they hunted and shot were in fact insurgents. Instead they judged guilt by appearance: age, gender, and, most of all, race. Soldiers "made ample use of machine guns," some mounted on trucks, in the "indiscriminate killings of males over twelve years old." Women and young children were not always spared. The figure of 4,800 dead that had been supplied to Commander Brodeur on Friday, January 29, was likely accurate. But that was only the "first phase" of the government response.[11]

After the Canadian and U.S. navies left, the killing entered a new stage: it became "unequivocally genocidal" — "focused exclusively on self-identified Indians."[12] Identity became a trap. In early February the Martínez government began issuing identification cards that would allow the holder to travel through the countryside, still on lockdown. One planter who had been threatened in the insurgency told the Indians who lived and worked on his estate that he was going to give

461

them cards. More than five hundred showed up to get identification, but as they assembled they were penned in, and the machine guns of the National Guard came alive. The mayor of Nahuizalco, where the town hall had been burned in the insurrection, did the same on February 13, turning the central plaza into a killing pen for roughly four hundred Indians.[13] Across the coffee districts, markers of Indian identity were used as targets: machetes, the traditional tool of agricultural workers; the white cotton shirts and pants of peasants; "a strongly Indian cast of features."[14]

Indian identity was a death sentence because of what it was understood to mean. The racist origins of the coffee economy, founded on the privatization of communal lands and the eradication of "backward" ways of life, resurfaced in the collapse of "Indian" and "communist" into synonymous death sentences. "There is not one Indian who is not affiliated with the communist movement," wrote one planter in the Santa Ana newspaper on the first of February. "Good mozos whom I considered loyal and whom we had treated as part of the family were among the first to join up and to lend their contribution to the evil cause. . . . Now that they see themselves vanquished by the actions of the government, which has served to annihilate them . . . they want to evade the

462

danger. But that is the penalty they have imposed on themselves."

The writer spoke both to and for his fellow planters: "We want this plague exterminated by the roots; for if it is not, it will sprout forth and with new spirit. . . . It was well done in North America . . . they first killed the Indians, because those would never have good sentiments toward anything. Here, we treated them like family, with every consideration, and now you see them in action! Their instincts are savage." Indians, mozos, communists, savages: race was the modality through which class revolt was suppressed. "It would seem that they are going to exterminate the Indians," wrote an American Baptist missionary on the scene during the counterinsurgency.[15]

At the same time, the Martínez government turned Communist Party rolls and Red Aid charity registers into hit lists. Soldiers carried around "foot-long books" that held the names of those who had signed up for or donated to communist causes, tracking them down, arresting them, throwing them in jail for one or two days, and then "taking them out late at night . . . to some isolated spot where they are told to disperse and machine gun fire is opened on them," reported one young Wall Street attorney who was visiting El Salvador in January 1932. He knew the protocol because he himself had joined "a vigilance committee" while in-country.[16]

When the coffee plantations became killing fields, people who lived there did what they could to survive. Many fled east, away from the coast and the coffee districts, some of them crossing the border into Honduras and finding work on the banana plantations of the United Fruit Company.[17] Those who could not flee tried to hide. Families dug holes in the ground and buried their men to keep them alive. Young men took off their clothes and sat down on the dirt in their underwear to disguise themselves as children. Others sought shelter in the houses and barns of the plantations, only to be given up to the National Guard by planters.[18] One survivor reported going to mass near San Salvador. The priest "would ask us if we were involved in communism. I said no. But the others who admitted it, he put a little cross next to their name. They were shot."[19]

The executions continued through the end of February, when British consul Rodgers put the number of dead as high as twelve thousand. Teams of soldiers were still roaming the countryside, searching for "fugitives."[20] Even so, Rodgers reported, many coffee planters were "afraid to return to their estates, and the coffee planters in the west of the republic are subscribing large sums for the increase of the numbers of the National Guards stationed there." Rodgers could understand the planters' fears, for as much as the "Indians [have] been cowed by the severity of the repressive measures," he also saw "a danger." "The Indian is very docile," Rodgers reported to London, "but also very tenacious and he has a long memory."[21]

It has often been a point of speculation among historians that General Martínez's Theosophical beliefs empowered the genocide he commanded, that his belief in reincarnation and the transmigration of souls led him to conclude that it was a greater crime to kill an ant than a man, since a man would return to earth in a new body.[22] Whether or not Martínez believed in the reality of such magical things, he was keenly aware of the moment's political and economic context. He knew that the United States — wary of Bolshevism in the hemisphere, still fighting to suppress a nationalist rebellion in Nicaragua, and above all a creditor — was watching closely. He knew that Great Britain was highly concerned for the safety of its subjects and investments. Most of all, Martínez, of Indian heritage himself, and whose own features were darker than those of many of the Salvadoran planter-presidents who had preceded him, knew that political stability, and particularly anti-Bolshevism, had great international value in what would prove to be the worst year of an unprecedented global economic and social crisis, one that had shaken even the richest, strongest governments.[23]

While the killing was still under way, the Salvadoran government — probably Martínez himself — enlisted photographers to document its progress. The condemned were lined up against walls to be photographed. They were photographed while receiving last rites, wrists bound together. The dead were photographed hanging from trees and lying by roadsides. They were photographed bound to yokes for easy transportation, spilling out of oxcarts, piled at the bottom of mass graves. Like the tour and lunch arranged for Commander Brodeur, the photographs of the condemned and dead were evidence that the government had the situation well in hand, as Martínez claimed. Once the dead had been photographed, their work was done.[24]

After the massacre and its documentation, the Salvadoran army pulled back. Left to keep peace in the coffee districts were the volunteer units of the Civic Guard, funded by the rich. Their first task was burying the dead.[25] The job was so large that the usual procedures that govern such work, so ancient as to be instinctive, needed to be revised. New burial rites took shape under the direction of the state, which had researched the matter scientifically. During the second week of February 1932, the Salvadoran ministry of health sent out a work order:

> In regard to the necessary sanitary measures to be followed related to the new interments to be conducted . . . past burials were done in trenches of variable dimensions, up to thirty meters long, one to two meters wide, and one and a half to two meters deep. This office thinks it is necessary to make the dimensions uniform for reasons of health. The accumulation of no more than fifty corpses in a single grave allows for better decomposition and less absorption into the soil. Even better would be isolated graves, two cubic meters in size, in which no more than eight to ten corpses would be placed. This information is particularly important for the municipalities of Juayúa, Nahuizalco, and Izalco.[26]

"Everywhere they made big holes," remembered one survivor, who was nine years old in 1932. "They dropped the bodies, after they shot them, and heaved them as if they were bales made of sugar cane."[27] Yet despite the scientific approach and detailed instructions, not all burials went as planned.

"Mármol, to the courtyard!" The first time Miguel Mármol heard his name called, near ten o'clock on the night of January 22, 1932, he sat still and said nothing. He had been ar-

467

rested hours earlier, locked in a hot cell crowded with political prisoners on the top floor of police headquarters in San Salvador, far from the center of the insurgency. A friend and fellow prisoner told Mármol to stay quiet, because they were calling the names of those who would be executed. It was not difficult to believe. The jailers had mounted a machine gun on a tripod and aimed it at the middle of the cell, and every once in a while they would threaten to use it. "The collective feeling of being close to death" had sucked Mármol's strength right out of him.

But the second time his name was called, Miguel Mármol answered, because he was tired of being afraid: "Here I am, asshole!" He gave the food he had been served to those who remained in the cell — "a prison meal of tortillas and beans and some eggs that the families of some criminals managed to get in to us by the street" — and approached the door. When Mármol stepped out of the cell, his wrists were tied behind his back, and he was prodded down the stairs and out into the dark courtyard, which looked to him like the place his story would end.

A truck pulled into the courtyard and parked, and Mármol and seventeen other prisoners were herded toward its tailgate. The gate was too high for him to climb in on his own, so the jailers grabbed his bound arms and threw him inside. He landed in the bed

468

of the truck near the feet of a tall, fair Russian, who traveled around the countryside selling pictures of the saints, and on whose legs Mármol asked to rest his head. The Russian replied "very warmly" in strictly correct and heavily accented Spanish: "Lie down, comrade, don't be ashamed." Mármol lay down, and the truck drove out of the courtyard, out of the capital, and into the countryside in the direction of Lake Ilopango, where he had been born.

When the truck stopped, the moon was completely hidden behind the trees. Mármol and his fellow prisoners stepped down from the gate of the truck into profound darkness. Two of the prisoners were taken around to the front of the truck and lined up in the headlights. The officer in charge of the execution could hardly find the breath to give the order, rushing through all three words at once. After the first two prisoners fell, the executioner asked who would be next to die, and Mármol stepped forward again.

As he faced the firing squad, Miguel Mármol thought that above all he was lucky that he was going to die near his old village, close to where his umbilical cord had been buried. Then the tall Russian stepped forward, too, and said, "I will die alongside comrade Mármol." The men joined hands behind their backs, and so much blood built up in Mármol's arms from the ties around his wrists that when the first bullet hit him it was almost a relief. As he began to fall, he realized that he was going down, but not for good.

When the Russian's pale body fell on top of him, Mármol hid himself in the gore and breathed as shallowly as he could. After some time, the shooting stopped, and he heard the executioners drive off in their truck, leaving the bodies for gravediggers. When he thought he was finally alone, "in great pain and with the sensation of being born again," Miguel Mármol stood up.[28]

Later he would learn that he was not the only one who did not remain where he had been left for dead. Because the government had taken charge of interment, many families had no idea where their dead lay, but that was very different from not knowing what had become of them. In the areas where there had been the most killing, survivors knew better than to eat pork. "At the moment in the department of Sonsonate, and in many places in Ahuachapán and some in Santa Ana," one newspaper reported, "pork meat has become so discredited that it has almost no value. . . . All of this is the consequence of the pigs eating in great quantities the flesh of corpses that have been left in the fields."[29] Mármol heard too that "people in the countryside kept being unpleasantly surprised all the time on seeing the skeleton of a hand, a

470

foot, a skull cropping up out of the earth. And every now and then, the domestic animals, pigs, dogs, etc., showed up with a decayed hand or a human rib between their teeth. . . . The vultures were the best fed creatures of the year in El Salvador, they were fat, with shiny feathers like never before and, fortunately, never since," Miguel Mármol concluded, prematurely.[30]

Without international recognition from the United States and Great Britain, it was unlikely that Martínez's government could borrow enough money to pay its debt and the salaries of the army, the minimum necessary to sustain itself, especially with coffee prices so low. On the other hand, the killings Martínez had ordered made his staying in office a question not just of ambition but also of survival. Though his response to the insurgency had undoubtedly earned the support of the coffee elite, who feared for their lives, families, and businesses, there was also the possibility that, if Martínez were to resign, those who had supported the massacre in the terror of the moment would try to exculpate themselves by putting him on trial for the whole thing.

As long as he was in power, Martínez had plenty of backers. In El Salvador, reams of petitions were circulated to encourage him to stay in office.[31] And internationally, the fact

471

that the regime was illegitimate under the treaty designed to discourage coups in Central America was almost as disappointing for the United States as it was for Martínez himself. While the killing was still in its early stages, the United States had acknowledged Martínez's competence in the arts of government. On January 25, 1932, three days after the beginning of the insurgency, the first suppressive phase of the counterinsurgency well under way, U.S. secretary of state Henry Stimson lamented the formal diplomatic principles that stood in the way of American recognition of Martínez: "The man who is president and who is the only pillar against the success of what seems to be a nasty proletarian revolution . . . we are unable to recognize under the 1923 rule."[32] With popular discontent on the rise around the world amid the economic crisis of the Depression, the importance of the rule and the precedent was heightened, but so was the significance of Martínez's accomplishment.[33]

There remained the matter of the loan. Though the Martínez government was illegitimate in a diplomatic sense, its checks still had to be good: the U.S. refused to recognize El Salvador's government but insisted upon its debt. For Martínez, there was no way out of this dilemma but forward. The bargain struck during the counterinsurgency, the alliance among the government, the coffee planters, and the military, was locked into place. El Salvador became a military dictatorship dedicated to and sustained by the production and exportation of coffee. The military dictatorship enforced coffee production; coffee production funded the military dictatorship. The state was built on killing and coffee.

Yet if this was the only feasible path toward national stability, it was precarious terrain internationally. After all, it had been the coffee planters, led by Jaime Hill, who pushed Martínez toward the suspension of payments on the American loan. Martínez resumed payments on February 22, just ahead of the default deadline.[34] No more than a week later, he suspended payments again — the country was out of money.

With the interlocking problems of political legitimacy and financing centering on the United States, Martínez sent the most distinguished emissaries he could muster to Washington to argue his case. In January, he commissioned Luis Anderson, a distinguished Costa Rican jurist, to find a constitutional basis for his power. Concluding that Martínez had achieved a popular mandate that obliged him to govern, Anderson traveled to Washington in February to lobby diplomats, congressmen, and the press.[35] In March, Dr. Gustavo Guerrero, a Salvadoran who had served as president of the Assembly of the

League of Nations in 1929 and 1930, and who in 1932 was serving as a judge on the Permanent Court of International Justice in Geneva, requested an audience with the secretary of state to inquire about the possibility of the U.S.'s recognizing Martínez. Henry Stimson told Guerrero to tell Martínez that it was hopeless.[36]

Yet Martínez would not be discouraged, for his mind was already made up. In early June, Santa Ana banker Benjamin Bloom called at the Department of State in Washington and explained that he had come on behalf of General Martínez to request recognition — or, failing that, some assurance that Martínez might be permitted to stay in office unmolested. Bloom acknowledged that "Martínez had come into office through a coup d'etat," but emphasized that "Martínez had handled the situation in an excellent manner when the communist disturbances broke out . . . some months ago, and . . . is conducting a very good Government." After listening to Bloom's appeal, the American diplomat who received him explained that the United States "had nothing against Martínez personally and we took the stand as a matter of principle. I told him that after the labor outbreaks some months ago . . . we were inclined to feel that it was a pity that the man who appeared to handle the situation in such an able manner could not be recognized, but such was nevertheless the case and there was nothing we could do about it."[37]

A week later Martínez declared his "unshakable determination" to remain in office. In August the Salvadoran government paid back the money it had borrowed from local banks "for military purposes" in January.[38] By October it was clear that Martínez had consolidated his hold on the presidency. "It appears at the present time that [the Martínez government] has secured a permanence which will permit it to remain in control for the constitutional term," predicted the American consul in San Salvador, "unless future events prove unfavorable to it." No one would have said that such events were out of the question, but serious popular resistance did not seem likely. "While there is considerable latent dissatisfaction especially among the lower classes, danger from this opposition has been eliminated for the present by the extremely violent measures taken by the Government in the suppression of the so-called 'communistic' movement of last January," wrote the diplomat. "On the whole it may be stated that it seems to be generally the opinion of responsible people that General Martínez is administering the country in an honest and able manner and that the regime is above the average of those usually found in Central America."[39] Trade sanctions might have broken El Salvador's military-coffee complex, but any block on the coffee trade would have also made it impossible for the country to repay its State Department–guaranteed loan, and sanctions were never a serious possibility.[40] While in December 1931 and January 1932 the U.S. had tried to engineer Martínez's ouster, six months later the State Department had given up that campaign for good. Martínez had not won U.S. recognition, but he had won its approval.

That left the door open for Martínez and the planters to collaborate on an unconventional approach to solving El Salvador's economic problems: more coffee. In August 1932, six months after a harvest cut short by an attempted revolution and its genocidal suppression, in the middle of the worst year of the worst global economic crisis in the history of the modern world economy, an American diplomat noticed, to his surprise, an "actual increase in the acreage under coffee."[41] This was hardly a logical response to the market. Coffee sales had been very slow, and European sales in particular were vanishingly small, pushing prices even lower and forcing El Salvador to look almost exclusively to the U.S. market.[42] Nevertheless, backed by the military dictatorship, Salvadoran coffee planters "chose expansion," racing to the bottom.[43]

It was a risky strategy, with no guarantee of profit or personal safety, and not every planter had the resources or stomach for it. Yet while some of his neighbors gave up their plantations during the early years of the Depression, valuing their savings and their lives more than their coffee — and reasonably so, given the fall in prices — James Hill was emboldened by the arrival of the trouble he had predicted. During the insurgency, as other planters fled the coffee districts to the comparative safety of their city houses, Hill had gone in the other direction. Instead of retreating, on January 25, he went up to Las Tres Puertas, where he hunkered down with business and books, working all day and reading all night.[44] Five days later, according to a report in the *New York Times,* a band of twenty-five insurgents stormed his mill — though by that time reported attacks were often massacres in disguise.[45] In the aftermath of the killing, and in the face of the worst market conditions he had seen in his forty years on the Santa Ana Volcano, James Hill, who was already celebrated as "the king of coffee in El Salvador," did what he had learned to do better than anyone else, and reached out for more.

23.
PILE IT HIGH
AND SELL IT CHEAP

Even where there was nothing else there was coffee. "The prevailing greeting at that time," songwriter Yip Harburg told Studs Terkel about the United States in the early years of the Great Depression, "on every block you passed, by some poor guy coming up, was: 'Can you spare a dime?' Or: 'Can you spare something for a cup of coffee?' "[1] Harburg turned the question into the lyrics of a song that became "the anthem of the Great Depression."

Then as now, a cup of coffee was not what the poor and the hungry needed most, but it was something they thought they might get. At soup kitchens and in breadlines, "hours of waiting would produce a bowl of mush, often without milk or sugar, and a tin cup of coffee." Country families who lost their farms pitched tents on the roadside and lived on "pinto beans and black coffee."[2] At the Catholic Worker on the Lower East Side of Manhattan, Dorothy Day recalled, "men would

478

come in for clothes or a pair of shoes or socks or a coat and we didn't have any left, we'd say, 'Sit down anyway and have a cup of coffee. And a sandwich.' We kept making more and more coffee."[3]

All the coffee was something of a rebuke to President Hoover. As secretary of commerce, Hoover had made a point of fighting the Brazilian defense of coffee and the high prices it caused, but he had failed — or, worse, given up. And then after the economic crisis did what Hoover had not done, and broke the Brazilian coffee defense plan, it was precisely because of the planting done across Latin America under high prices in the 1920s that there was so much coffee to be had in the worst years of the Depression. "Mister Herbert Hoover says that now's the time to buy," the Irving Berlin lyric taunted in 1932, an election year, "So let's have another cup of coffee, and let's have another piece o' pie." What did Hoover know anyway?

By 1932, it was no longer possible to believe that the Depression that had begun three years earlier was going to clear up on its own — that it was just another phase in another economic cycle about to turn toward prosperity. Only Hoover himself seemed to harbor that fantasy. His policies were limited by the belief that the country and the world had not fundamentally changed. He held on to a vision of the way the United States fit into the global economy that was fast becoming obsolete, and he stayed faithful to that vision's central orthodoxies: the gold standard and the protective tariff.[4]

These commitments tied Hoover's hands. Bound by old rules, he vetoed a plan to create jobs through government spending that would have been the first federal relief program — the gold standard favored a balanced budget. He turned General Douglas MacArthur and six tanks on desperate, out-of-work veterans camping out in the mud in Washington to demand that Congress print money to pay them a bonus that wasn't in fact due for more than a decade — under the gold standard, the money supply was fixed. And over the opposition of more than a thousand economists, Hoover made good on the central promise of his 1928 campaign and signed the Smoot-Hawley Tariff into law in 1930. Designed with the idea of shielding American farmers, especially, from international competition, the tariff prompted retaliations by foreign governments that closed overseas markets to U.S. exports. Food rotted on farms even while Americans went hungry elsewhere. A roving "army of the unemployed" already occupied the cities, and now agrarian revolt threatened the American countryside.[5]

When New York governor Franklin Roosevelt accepted his party's presidential nomination at the Democratic National Convention in Chicago in July 1932, he pledged "a new deal" consisting of the two things that he believed the American people wanted "more than anything else": "work and security." Roosevelt proposed to deliver work and security by doing exactly what Hoover had not done, and throwing aside the limiting orthodoxies of the old American economic system. "Our Republican leaders tell us economic laws — sacred, inviolable, unchangeable — cause panics which no one could prevent," Roosevelt said. "But while they prate of economic laws, men and women are starving. We must lay hold of the fact that economic laws are not made by nature. They are made by human beings." Laws could — and should — be changed.

Though it has often been overlooked in the history of the New Deal, the first "economic law" Roosevelt promised to change was the tariff. "Out of all the tons of printed paper, out of all the hours of oratory, the recriminations, the defenses, the happy-thought plans in Washington and in every State," he said in Chicago, "there emerges one great, simple, crystal-pure fact that during the past ten years a Nation of 120,000,000 people has been led by the Republican leaders to erect an impregnable barbed wire entanglement around its borders through the instrumentality of tariffs which have isolated us from all the other human beings in all the rest of the round world . . . I propose an invitation to them to forget the past, to sit at the table with us, as friends, and to plan with us for the restoration of the trade of the world."[6]

Hoover heard in Roosevelt's calls for freer trade nothing less than "a violation of American principles" and an upheaval of the "American system" on which the country had been built.[7] He threatened that with the tariff wall down, "grass will grow in the streets of a hundred cities, a thousand towns; the weeds will overrun the fields of millions of farms."[8] Hoover would not permit himself to see that, from the perspective of the "forgotten" voters Roosevelt invoked in Chicago, the American system, based on a century of tariff protection of industry and agriculture, no longer seemed worth defending.

When it was signed into law in June of 1934, the Reciprocal Trade Agreements Act, the legislative crux of Roosevelt's freer trade program, did not lower taxes on imported goods by a single cent. It did not even repeal the vilified Smoot-Hawley Tariff. Instead, the RTAA — drawn up primarily in the office of

Roosevelt's secretary of state Cordell Hull, a longtime Democratic senator from Tennessee, where free trading was as old as the plantation houses — did something much more effective. It shifted the power to set tariff rates from the legislative to the executive branch. While Congress had traditionally been in charge of tariff making, inflecting foreign economic policy with whatever local concerns rose to the surface of the legislature, President Roosevelt now gained the power to unilaterally raise or reduce tariff rates by as much as half. In the hands of the president, the power to adjust tariffs became an instrument for refining America's relation to the world — both by reshaping the U.S. economy to support the strategic priorities of foreign policy, and by using access to the U.S. consumer market as a bargaining chip in negotiating favorable commercial relationships abroad. Increasing America's international trade promised work and security particularly for those employed in the country's leading industries, including mass-production manufacturing, in which the U.S. enjoyed an advantage over many of its potential trading partners.[9]

The president's new tariff power was an especially valuable tool during the Depression, as the U.S. was competing for global markets and resources against other ambitious empires, especially Britain, Germany,

Japan, and Italy. All had adopted recovery strategies that were quite different from Roosevelt's. Britain imposed restrictive imperial commerce on its colonies; Italy pursued Mussolini's vision of an Italian *imperium* into Africa; Japan added new conquests to its "Greater East Asia Co-Prosperity Sphere"; and Nazi Germany proclaimed "independence from the world economy" at large and instituted a barter system that paid trading partners not in cash but in scrip redeemable for German goods.[10] The stakes of the competition were heightened after Germany sealed new "coffee for machines" deals with Brazil and Colombia in 1934. It seemed to Secretary of State Hull that Germany was "straining every tendon to undermine United States trading relations with Latin America."[11]

But while rival powers retrenched within their empires or sought to expand them, the U.S. took a different approach.[12] With Latin America foremost in mind, Roosevelt renounced American aspirations to colonial empire, professed respect for the sovereignty of independent nation-states, announced a policy of military nonintervention, and promised to be, in these respects and others, a "good neighbor." Marines were withdrawn from Nicaragua and Haiti, and independence was planned for the Philippines. Early programs for multilateral international economic and social development were undertaken through the Inter-American Development Commission, chaired by Nelson Rockefeller.[13] The premise for this good neighborliness was increased trade in the hemisphere, and coffee was the obvious "bargaining device" for making that happen.[14]

The effective outsourcing of coffee production from the new U.S. colonies to Latin America after the Spanish-American War in 1898 had cemented coffee's status as the prototypical "good-neighbor product" — the most important commodity that Latin America had to sell and the U.S. had to buy.[15] In 1934, the Roosevelt administration began working to rebuild America's international commerce along the coffee trade routes, for that "was the path of least resistance and most profit," and the path on which the U.S. was shadowing Germany.[16] While Germany's trade deals with Latin America offered barter, not cash, and the Third Reich's ability to consume coffee was limited by revenue-generating taxes levied on imports, the U.S. turned in the other direction. The Roosevelt administration approached tariff negotiations with Brazil and Colombia in 1934, and then, with what the president's strategists called "the minor coffee countries," through the promise that it would not tax coffee imports, preserving the free movement of coffee into the U.S. market precisely when European markets were shrinking.[17] More than half of the twenty-nine new U.S. trade agreements signed in the decade after 1934 were with Latin American republics, and patterns of trade and commerce shifted to match the new agreements, shoring up the hemispheric foundation of U.S. international power.[18]

Before this shift toward freer trade could begin, Roosevelt reversed two years of U.S. policy and officially recognized General Maximiliano Hernández Martínez as the president of El Salvador in January 1934, clearing the way to make trade deals with not only El Salvador itself but also the other Central American republics that had, in violation of the 1923 treaty and in defiance of the United States, already gone ahead and recognized Martínez. In the long term, the formal recognition of Martínez opened a "new era" of Latin American politics, one in which "any strong-willed leader could seize office and retain it."[19] In the short term, coffee planters in El Salvador and across Latin America resigned themselves to selling in the U.S. even though it meant accepting significantly lower prices than Germany was offering — at least in the U.S. they could get paid in cash, and cash was badly needed.[20]

In October 1932, the staff of the green coffee department inside the Hills Bros. plant in San Francisco detected a "peculiar" shift in the world coffee market.[21]

Coffee prices had fallen across the board in February 1929, even before the U.S. stock market crash in October, and by November of the same year the declines had "become sharp."[22] At first, prices for Brazilian coffee — propped up by years of coffee defense no longer sustainable amid the economic crisis — fell more than prices of high-quality mild coffees from Central America and Colombia.[23] As a result, low-price brands that relied on Brazilian beans were especially cheap at the grocery store. Unwilling to use cheaper Brazilian beans, Hills Bros. could only emphasize quality. They were proud to be "the one brand which may be depended on to supply the wants and needs of those who demand the best in coffee without regard to fluctuations of the market."[24]

Yet by 1931, with coffee prices less than half of what they had been two years earlier, Brazil found a new approach to coffee defense. There was far too much worthless coffee to store in warehouses, so instead each bag of coffee exported was taxed to pay the cost of destroying another. Coffee was loaded onto ships, sent out to sea, and dumped in the ocean. Coffee was piled into great heaps as tall as buildings and torched in acrid bonfires.[25] In all, nearly seventy-five million bags of coffee — about ten billion pounds — were destroyed, cutting back supplies to the point where prices began to stabilize.[26]

The mild-coffee countries, much smaller and lacking central coordination, could not move the market by controlling supply. Their only hope for meeting financial obligations — which did not change with the collapse of prices — was to sell more to make up for earning less. This was precisely the course of action pursued by Salvadoran planters, working hand in hand with Martínez's military dictatorship, who pushed for expanded production after the massacre of 1932, despite the fact that their options for selling coffee abroad were narrowing. As a result, even after the market for Brazilian coffees started to bounce back, prices for mild coffees continued to fall. High-quality mild coffees used in premium brands such as Hills Bros. became relatively, and surprisingly, cheap.

These unusual conditions changed the way Hills Bros. bought coffee. After 1932 they moved to take advantage of the surprising prices, and the increasing dependence of Salvadoran coffee planters on the U.S. market, by turning the Santa Ana Volcano into an annex of their San Francisco factory. Leveraging their new buying power, they made greater demands on coffee planters and millers to meet their particular specifications, even if it meant abandoning old and established ways of working. They told James Hill exactly how they wanted coffee prepared:

dried slowly under the sun on the patios, and never sent through dryers after the milling process, for the heat applied by the dryers cooked the coffee beans slightly, just enough to change their flavor and skew Hills Bros.' automated blending and roasting process in San Francisco. They told Hill that they didn't want coffee beans run through polishers after they were sorted and inspected, because the polishers created friction and the friction created heat that brought out oils that made the coffee go rancid even before it arrived in San Francisco. And once James Hill had agreed to these specifications, Hills Bros. bought everything he produced in Las Tres Puertas in 1933–1934, more than two million pounds, at nine cents a pound — about a third of what prices had been five years earlier.[27]

The unusual conditions in the world market also changed the way Hills Bros. sold coffee. In 1929, before the crash, retail prices for a pound of Hills Bros. Red Can had climbed above sixty cents. In 1931, the retail price was half that. In 1932, with world prices still falling, Hills Bros., who for much of the preceding two decades had worked to keep the retail price of their coffee high to signal its quality, "declared war" on high retail prices.[28] "To some firms, a declining market has meant ruination," wrote the head of the sales team, but "to us it only opens the doors wider for our admittance to new fields, new

489

users and a permanent foundation for future business."[29] These "peculiar" shifts in the market meant that "the price barrier" was "definitely down," and "the number of families using Hills Bros. Coffee and those that can and should use it is steadily increasing."[30] Continually cutting prices, Hills Bros. pushed their retail distribution from the Pacific coast into the Midwest: Chicago, Detroit, Indianapolis, and Cleveland. At the same time, they started making plans to stretch "Hills Bros. Coffeeland," as they called their sales territory, all the way to the East Coast by the end of the decade. The expansion was underwritten by the value — the high-quality, low-price coffee — they bought from El Salvador after 1932.

And as Hills Bros. sold the coffee they bought from James Hill and other Salvadoran planters in new places — new states and cities and towns — they also sold in new stores. These stores were not only new in that they sat within fresh sales territory. More than that, they were a new type of store altogether, one that transformed the entire landscape of American life.

One Saturday evening in 1938, the five members of the Muzak family were out driving in their fourth-hand car about three miles from their apartment when traffic snagged in front of what looked from the road like a

490

house on fire. When they pulled off the road, piled out of the car, and squeezed through the crowd already on the scene, the Muzaks saw that "the fiery glare" was coming from "banks of red and white floodlights, illuminating a square one-story white building of modernistic design. Its seventy-five-foot, plate-glass front was covered with banners. . . . Strings of pennants fluttered on the streamlined roof, and multicolored neon signs flamed from a triangular tower." The road they were on had led the Muzaks to their first "Supermarket Grand Opening."

When the Muzaks went in, "things began happening to them." They were given chocolate-coated ice cream bars for the children. Cigarettes for Poppa. A cut flower for Momma. Inside, the "huge building was completely filled with pile after pile of food, acres of it . . . [and] jammed with a thousand customers."

Momma pushed on and a young man in a green smock shoved at her a wheeled contraption resembling a foreshortened double-decked baby-buggy. It carried two large wire baskets. The young man snapped, "Put your groceries in it, lady," and shoved another of his baby buggies at a woman behind her.

Wheeling the cart, momma struggled through a crowd similarly encumbered. Her eyes widened, then narrowed shrewdly. "Look, Poppa," she cried. "My coffee! Only thirteen cents. Never did I buy it cheaper than nineteen cents at Schmaltz's. Maybe I should get a pound."

Poppa waved his cigarette expansively. "Maybe two pounds you should get. Or three."[31]

The vignette was a caricature dreamed up by the *Saturday Evening Post,* but it captured something real then happening in certain parts of the United States. The made-up Muzaks, with their funny name and stilted English, represented millions of second- and third-generation "new immigrants" from Southern, Central, and Eastern Europe who were giving up their neighborhood grocery stores and chain stores alike in favor of big new supermarkets.[32]

In 1932 there were fewer than 300 supermarkets in the United States.[33] By 1941 there were more than 10,000, and together they had a quarter of the nation's food on their shelves.[34] These new "supers" were twenty, thirty, or forty times larger than older food stores, including austere A&P Economy Stores. Supermarket shopping wasn't always fun or even pleasant — traffic jams, pushy crowds, and rude employees — yet it offered certain American shoppers things that were difficult to pass up, especially in the Depression decade. Set against "the hungry years" not yet past, these new stores of immense size and capacity not only symbolized prosperity and abundance, but also had real consequences for the way people shopped, ate, lived, and voted.[35]

The "supermarket revolution" in the United States stemmed from innovations in basic retail practices.[36] These innovations took root because they complemented deeper changes in the structure of the U.S. and global economy. As the Roosevelt administration pushed for freer trade abroad and mass consumption at home in the mid-1930s, supermarkets translated New Deal foreign and domestic policies into a compelling language of plenty. The organizing principle of the new "supers," in stark contrast to earlier grocery stores, was more for less: "Pile It High and Sell It Cheap," as the industry rule went.[37] Retailers wrapped this blunt principle in an appealing package of modernist style, domestic manners, and everyday value designed to lure the housewives and families, represented by the fictional Muzaks, who populated the growing mass-consumer class, and who were the greatest beneficiaries of the New Deal.[38]

The principles of supermarket selling, tailored to the shape of global markets in the 1930s, made coffee one of retailers' favorite products to pile high and sell cheap. It wasn't just that supermarkets sold coffee at low prices — chain stores, especially A&P Economy Stores, did that too. It was how supermarkets sold cheap coffee, and which coffees they sold. Chains had found cost savings that led to low prices by paring down shoppers' choices, but in the antimonopolistic political climate of the thirties they were, in part for this reason, attacked as cartels and penalized with new per-store taxes. In contrast, supermarkets found their cost savings by scaling up. The vast size of the new stores was a key factor in their low prices. Both chain and supermarket grocers bought from food manufacturers in great volume, earning savings over neighborhood grocers. But unlike small chain outlets, which, in the interest of keeping rents down, had minimal space to spare for stock, supermarkets served as their own warehouses. Stocks of food could be stored on-site, and this created additional savings on distribution costs. Ten-thousand-pound lots of wholesale merchandise did not have to be divided among and transported to many small stores, as was the case for chain grocers.

The greatest cost savings that size created for supermarket retailers was on labor. Each of the 16,000 A&P Economy Stores, though minimally staffed, still required a manager, a relatively skilled worker, to do the books, the ordering, and the oversight. A supermarket, even if it was twenty or forty times as large as an Economy Store, required the same number of managers, one, and perhaps one assistant manager.[39] The rest of the staff consisted of comparatively unskilled workers. By integrating the warehouse and the store, supermarkets replaced chains' armies of managers and clerks with armies of stock workers.[40]

Unlike neighborhood grocers and chain store clerks, the stock workers who staffed the new supermarkets didn't know much about selling food, but they didn't have to. Supermarkets stocked food that sold itself, food that shoppers had already been taught to want: brands that paid for their own advertising. And supermarkets had the space to stock enough brands to appeal to almost any taste, preference, and budget — in many cases, ten brands of coffee or more; in some cases, more than twenty.[41]

In many ways, coffee was the ideal supermarket product. First, quality advertised brands were usually packaged in brightly colored tin cans that were light by volume and perfect for piling into the "eye-filling" displays supermarket retailers favored.[42] Second, as a daily drink, coffee was a staple of weekly shopping lists, which made it an attractive bargain item to tout in newspaper ads and circulars.[43] And above all, coffee was

495

the most important branded staple of the American diet that was also produced almost exclusively outside the United States. As a result of dire conditions in the international market and in coffee-growing countries — and ultimately the ability of planters and governments to make people work under such conditions — coffee was unusually cheap in the United States during the Depression decade. This was especially true of the name-brand quality coffees, such as Hills Bros., that relied heavily on mild coffee beans from Central America and had once been comparatively expensive. That made coffee the perfect product to feature in weekly "extra-value" two- or three-pound deals designed to draw customers into the store and spit them out on the other side of the cash registers with more food than they would have carried home from an A&P Economy Store or from the corner market. In other words, Momma Muzak saw "her coffee" on sale when she stepped into the supermarket because that was exactly what she was supposed to see.

Broader changes in American domestic life, also nudged along by the New Deal, made the high-volume principles of supermarket shopping make sense — but only for some. Virtually everyone who shopped at the first supermarkets had one thing in common: a car. Car ownership was an essential condition for supermarket shopping because cars made it possible to carry more food home — "value" purchases of two pounds of coffee, or three, instead of the usual one.[44] Cars also opened up undeveloped tracts of relatively cheap land outside central cities and established commercial districts, where there was plenty of space to site a big new store. Unlike the rules of convenience and affinity that governed food shopping in close-knit urban neighborhoods, any site accessible from "a well-traveled highway" could work for a supermarket.[45]

Through car ownership, infrastructure, and real estate development, the supermarket revolution tracked economic recovery, especially in the manufacturing industries prioritized by the New Deal.[46] After emerging around Los Angeles and in the suburbs of New York City, supermarkets spread most quickly up the Pacific coast and around northern and eastern cities.[47] They lagged far behind in "the Old South and parts of the agricultural Middle West."[48] Of the roughly 7,500 supermarkets identified by the 1940 census, only 1.4 percent, or 113, were in the "East South Central" region — Kentucky, Tennessee, Alabama, and Mississippi. New England, though it had a smaller population than the East South Central region, was home to six times as many supermarkets.

California had fifteen times as many.[49] Tracking the geography of economic recovery, supermarkets both drew on the proceeds of the New Deal and helped to transform its core constituency, especially European immigrant families like the fictional Muzaks, from an ethnic industrial working class into a white American mass-consumer middle class loyal to the Democratic Party. Left behind, in the process, were many African, Asian, and Hispanic Americans who worked in agriculture, domestic service industries, and other sectors of the U.S. economy excluded from the core benefits of the new American welfare state: Social Security, collective bargaining, and the minimum wage.[50]

At the same time, New Deal programs supporting electrification, consumer credit, and home ownership and improvement also transformed American kitchens in the 1930s in ways that favored the larger purchases characteristic of supermarket shopping.[51] In 1930, only 8 percent of American households owned an electric refrigerator. By 1940, nearly half of Americans did.[52] A similar change happened with coffeemakers. In 1932, the stovetop percolator was still the most common method of home coffee preparation, used by well over 50 percent of households.[53] By 1939, percolator use was on the decline, while 39 percent of households used drip pots, and 7 percent used a newer appliance, electric Silex vacuum coffeemakers.[54]

American coffee roasters encouraged the change for reasons of quality and quantity. The oils that give brewed coffee its flavor and aroma can be extracted from coffee grounds very quickly by water at its boiling point. The longer the brewing time, the more elements are extracted from the beans. In a simple pan, a stovetop coffeepot, or a percolator that continually cycles boiling water over coffee grounds, it is possible to make a strong cup of coffee even with scant grounds simply by extending the brewing time. Yet longer extractions also release more tannins, which make coffee bitter and astringent. As a result, the flavor of boiled coffee is usually harsher than coffee made in a drip or Silex pot, in which water passes through the grounds only once, drawing out virtually no tannins. In the first third of the twentieth century, most American households made their coffee the old-fashioned way. They used methods that favored coffee economy, stretching and wringing flavor out of coffee beans by boiling them.[55] When that began to change, coffee roasters, especially those who dealt in mild coffee, approved. "It has been definitely determined that the most satisfactory way to prepare coffee is by the French Drip Method," one Hills Bros. pamphlet advised.[56] "If you are very particular about your coffee, use a good drip pot."[57]

There were also quantity implications. The shorter brewing times characteristic of drip and Silex pots also meant that more coffee grounds were needed to make the same intensity of brew.[58] On the basis of their own testing, Hills Bros. concluded that Silex makers required at least 5 percent more coffee to make an adequate-tasting cup than other methods.[59] Similarly, drip makers were built to make four to eight cups of coffee at a time. If they were filled with only enough coffee to make one or two or three cups, the water dripped through too fast, and the result was thin and weak.[60]

The increasing popularity of these new coffeemakers created "greater confusion in the mind of the consumer than any issue that has arisen in the coffee business in a long, long time."[61] In the first quarter of the twentieth century, *Good Housekeeping* had published articles on coffee such as "After-dinner Coffee," "Some Coffees of Today," "Some New Facts About Coffee," "Coffee as a Flavor," "Coffee Brewing in Variety," and "Children Should Not Drink Coffee or Tea."[62] The rise of new coffeemakers in the thirties changed the tone of the conversation. Readers were warned that "Perfect Coffee Is Not a Matter of Chance," treated to an industry-appointed expert explaining "What I Call Good Coffee!," nagged "Why Can't We Have Coffee Like This at Home?," and cautioned that

"You Can Tell a Hostess by Her Coffee."[63]

Domestic anxiety was an opportunity for instruction. The biggest obstacle to good coffee making, industry studies concluded, was parsimony. Coffee roasters pushed to establish a standard recipe of a "heaping tablespoon" of grounds per cup, and Hills Bros. took the idea a step further. Between 1935 and 1937 they set up displays in grocery stores and gave away, at no charge, the Hills Bros. coffee guide, a plastic measuring scoop that held two tablespoons of coffee, the recommended amount for each cup of water. In the first year alone they handed out nearly two million around the country.[64]

Imports of mild coffee from Central America into the U.S. climbed to new levels in the middle of the Depression decade. Salvadoran imports made the greatest gains in San Francisco, thanks in large part to Hills Bros.' increased purchases.[65] In turn, after 1936 Hills Bros. coffee was at its all-time lowest price, nationwide sales reached new highs and the company became the largest independent coffee roaster in the United States, selling around fifty million pounds.[66] "Never in the history of our business have we had such a value to offer to Mr. and Mrs. Consumer," one Hills Bros. executive wrote in 1938.[67] The same year, construction began on a million-dollar roasting and packing plant on

501

the Hudson River in Edgewater, New Jersey, complete with its own pier, to supply the company's new East Coast markets.[68]

Meanwhile, in San Francisco, the Bay Bridge was going up directly over the Hills Bros. factory on the Embarcadero. With the Golden Gate Exposition scheduled for 1939 to mark the completion of both of the city's new bridges, Hills Bros. planned to celebrate. The idea was to make a movie about where coffee came from, how it got to San Francisco, and how it became Hills Bros. coffee. They sketched out a budget north of $100,000, secured prime space on Treasure Island, the purpose-built fairground under construction in the middle of San Francisco Bay, and started to outline the film, which they were calling *Behind the Cup.*

Hills Bros. had made a film by the same title a decade earlier. Shot in Colombia, the old movie told the story of coffee with the black-and-white affect of a newsreel. They had something much more "sensational" in mind for Treasure Island: the new film would be shot in color, and set in a place that would highlight what made their coffee special.

Reuben Hills Jr., the son of the man who had pioneered cup testing and vacuum packing in San Francisco four decades earlier, had visited El Salvador after the harvest season in 1938, staying in Santa Ana as a guest of James Hill, and he liked what he saw.

During the trip, Reuben Hills had a pair of leather boots custom-made, and Hill lent him the cash to pay for the boots in local currency. When he returned to San Francisco, Reuben Hills mailed the money for the boots to James Hill, along with a note about sending his photographer Ken Allen down to Santa Ana with a movie camera.

When the letter arrived at Las Tres Puertas, James Hill's middle son, Eduardo, replied enthusiastically. "Father" was away, he reported, traveling on business in New York, but Eduardo was confident that he would approve.[69]

24.

BEHIND THE CUP

Salvadoran coffee planters sometimes imagined themselves to be great fathers, a self-image it was all the more important to cultivate after the 1932 massacre. The definitive statement comes from a 1936 editorial in *El Café de El Salvador,* the journal of the coffee planters' association:

A plantation is comparable to a small country, governed by its owner or whomever he appoints. In this small country develops the life of a great family that includes the owner and all who serve him, plus their respective relations. The workers earn wages, live on the plantation without paying rent, make use of many products: wood, fruit, pastures for raising animals, and other by-products. Cases are not rare in which the owner, in consideration of his social duties, concerns himself with the well-being of his servants and provides free medical care, over and above what the law requires.[1]

It is true that a plantation, like a country or a family, is made up of a set of relationships — it is something people do to each other. And it is also true that the history of El Salvador has often been written in terms of families. Yet the most common story about coffee and families in El Salvador itself is different from the one the coffee planters told in their magazine. Instead of "social duties," it has focused on the exclusive rather than the inclusive power of the family, and particularly of the oligarchical "Fourteen Families" — the coffee planters, exporters, and financiers who emerged from the crisis of 1932 as President Martínez's partners in the business of governing, a virtual "state within a state."[2] There are many versions of the list of fourteen families, but always it comprises a mix of native and immigrant names: "Regalados, de Solas, and Hills," as one historian sums it up.[3] The perpetual question of whether the precise number of ruling families is greater than, less than, or equal to fourteen — a number large enough to be plausible and small enough to be terrible — is merely an academic footnote to the history that motivates and justifies the impulse to count: the transformation of a relatively equal, peaceful place into one of the most unequal and violent countries in the history of the modern world.

After the massacre, James Hill pushed to

expand his coffee empire farther out across the Santa Ana Volcano, and even out beyond El Salvador into the United States. In the boom years before the world depression, from 1925 to 1930, Hill had planted an average of 80,000 new trees each year. From 1930 to 1935 he planted an average of almost 137,000 trees each year; and from 1935 to 1940 he planted 300,000 trees per year.[4] Between 1929 and 1941, Hill nearly doubled the area of land he had under cultivation, from 1,600 acres to 3,000.[5] As he expanded his plantations, Hill, who had turned sixty in 1931 and had his share of health problems — heart trouble serious enough that William H. Ukers had reported on it in the *Tea and Coffee Trade Journal* — brought his family in closer to the center of his business.[6] In the process, Hill's three sons, Jaime, Eduardo, and Federico, became more than heirs — they became their father's progenitors, the means by which the name James Hill would live on long after "the king of coffee in El Salvador" had died.

There was also one person outside his family whom James Hill brought into his coffee business after 1932, someone who helped him do what Hills Bros. had done, but in reverse: turn San Francisco into an annex of Las Tres Puertas.

Among the new businesses that opened in San Francisco in the Depression year of 1933 was Ortega & Emigh, a firm dedicated to the importation of coffee. They took offices on California Street, in San Francisco's "green coffee district," just off the Embarcadero. The principals were forty-year-old Paul Ortega and his partner, Milton Emigh, though the latter didn't last long. By 1934, which was the first year the firm bought any coffee to import, Emigh was gone. But still Ortega & Emigh stayed open as a one-man shop, thanks in part to the firm's other, silent partner.

Before he went out on his own, Paul Ortega had worked for Otis McAllister, traveling through Central America, getting to know the planters and the plantations, buying coffee for the firm's import account. With Ortega's help, Otis McAllister had been growing rapidly. The firm had come to rank among the leading importers in San Francisco and was on the way to becoming the largest independent importer of coffee in the United States. During the harvest season of 1932–1933, Ortega had been on an extended trip in Central America, returning to San Francisco early in the new year.[7] Soon after he got back, he cut ties with Otis McAllister and went into partnership with Milton Emigh and James Hill.

For Ortega the deal was a good one. In the crop year of 1933–1934 the only thing he had to do to earn his commission was coordinate the deal James Hill had made to sell all of his coffee to Hills Bros. Soon Ortega was buying from other Salvadoran planters and exporters to almost the same extent.[8] In 1934, Ortega & Emigh had been the sixth-ranking importer of coffee into San Francisco, with 109,000 bags, more than ten million pounds of coffee, 75,000 bags of which came from El Salvador. One spot behind in the rankings was Ortega's old employer, Otis McAllister, whose imports from El Salvador were notably lower. The following year, Ortega was the leading importer on the Pacific coast, taking 165,000 bags of coffee from El Salvador and 211,000 over-all. For 1936, 1937, and 1938, Ortega stayed on top, taking as many as 233,000 bags from El Salvador, including much of the coffee that James Hill produced specifically for the San Francisco trade, the mark he called — perhaps with his three boys in mind — "Three Crowns."[9]

For James Hill, setting up Paul Ortega in business in San Francisco was simply another way of reaching out for more, of gaining more control over the relationships that shaped the production and sale of his coffee. Just ahead of the harvest season of 1935, his focus squarely on the U.S. market, Hill again sent his three boys, now grown men, to San Francisco to study the "requirements" of coffee roasters there.[10]

The same year, Hill split his coffee business, J. Hill y Cía., into unequal shares and distributed them to his new partners: his wife and children. Hill was nearing sixty-five, but he was not ready to quit. On the contrary, the terms on which Hill's children became his partners vested them in the continued growth of the family business. Rather than give his children individual plantations, as his wife's father, Dionisio, had done, Hill gave out parts of the whole. He took 22 percent for himself. He gave his wife, Lola, 20 percent. He gave each of his sons 10 percent, and each of his daughters 7 percent. The girls received less because they were free to play golf at the country club in San Salvador, while the boys were expected to work in the business, on the plantations, in the mill, and in the offices.[11] The gifts were incentive deals, based on the idea that each of his seven children should net the benefit of the sale of at least 200,000 pounds of coffee each year. In a good year, they might get as much as 300,000 pounds each. The more coffee the family produced, and the greater the difference between their revenue and their costs, the more their shares were worth.

Vesting his sons in this way also carried the promise of securing the national politics of coffee, for the boys, as citizens of El Salvador, could hold office — as Hill expected that they would. And indeed, while James Hill hunkered down at Las Tres Puertas during the revolution and massacre of 1932, it was Jaime Hill who went to meet with President Martínez. When his father declined to serve as an officer of the coffee planters' association, it was Jaime Hill who was elected secretary, and then vice president, and then president, and then minister of agriculture for El Salvador.[12]

As his sons took on larger roles in the family business, James Hill's own job changed. While for many years his travels abroad had been irregular and unpredictable, now Hill began to travel to the United States every year, arriving in San Francisco in the summer, three or four months in advance of the year's harvest. Even in July and August of 1932, a year when there were very few visitors from Central America, Hill was in San Francisco, staying at the Palace Hotel.[13] In 1933 he spent "four weeks in San Francisco on business and pleasure," and then he went on to Chicago and New York before returning to Santa Ana.[14] In 1934 he was again a "popular visitor" in San Francisco.[15] In 1935 he started in San Francisco and went on to Seattle, Portland, Los Angeles, and New York.[16] In 1936 Hill sailed to San Francisco and then traveled by train across the country to New York, stopping in Pittsburgh for the annual convention of the Associated Coffee Industries of America, a trade group promoting coffee consumption, where he was giving a speech.[17]

Hill had prepared remarks for his address in Pittsburgh, but when he stood to speak he veered off script. He felt compelled to address the question that had emerged as the leading issue of the convention: subsidies from Latin American countries to pay for advertising to encourage coffee drinking in the United States. Delegates from Colombia had taken a stand against subsidies, but Hill spoke up for the other side. He said that he personally did not have the slightest objection to paying a tax of ten cents a bag to fund promotion in the U.S. — and he said that he could persuade the other members of the Salvadoran coffee planters' association to agree, too.[18] And then Hill read the paper he had prepared, elaborating on the idea that "the days of cheap labor in the tropics were finished," and warning that if coffee planters "ever had to pay our people the equivalent of American labor prices," the price of coffee would more than quadruple. The message was that everyone vested in the coffee trade — governments, planters, millers, bankers, brokers, importers, shippers, roasters, and retailers — should get together and "stabilize conditions in behalf of better profits" — meaning find a way to increase prices and pay working people enough to preempt future attempts to take much more.[19]

At the national level, El Salvador had already begun to move in the direction Hill

511

suggested. The marriage of the military dictatorship and the coffee planters gave rise to new state institutions dedicated to coffee — institutions for research, education, and publicity. In 1935 the Salvadoran government hired an American coffee cup-testing expert, and he began sampling and rating all shipments, shaping the country's economy to the standards of Hills Bros. and other San Francisco roasters.[20] The government also established a school for plantation overseers in Santa Ana, and James Hill made important contributions to the curriculum, writing books and pamphlets on coffee agronomy that were used as texts in Salvadoran agricultural schools.[21] At the same time, to build on the increasingly strong position Salvadoran coffee enjoyed in San Francisco, the coffee planters' association established an office for the promotion of the country's coffee in New York, as Colombia and Brazil had also done. The office was headed by Roberto Aguilar, who left his plantations in Sonsonate and sailed for New York City in January 1937.[22]

Aguilar's arrival in New York was well-timed, for not long after he began his new job, Brazil again gave up its attempts to support the price of coffee by destroying surpluses, instead adopting a business model based on exporting as much coffee as possible for whatever price could be had. With exports from Brazil rising, and prices falling again after what had been a rather anemic recovery to begin with — and falling this time lower than they had been since the turn of the twentieth century — all that coffee planters could do was try to stimulate more coffee drinking in what was by far the world's largest open market, the United States. Roberto Aguilar became the chairman of a new international organization created for that purpose, the Pan American Coffee Bureau, funded by a tax of five cents on every bag of coffee exported from member countries, including Brazil, Colombia, El Salvador, and others. Quickly the coffee bureau began planning its first major advertising campaign for the summer of 1938. Designed to introduce American coffee drinkers to a form of the beverage that had been promoted by the Brazilian-American committee in the 1920s, but was still not as popular as marketers thought it could be during the hot months, the campaign was called Iced Coffee Week.[23]

El Salvador's substantial investment in promoting American coffee consumption — combined with the increasing amounts of Salvadoran coffee imported through San Francisco — made Santa Ana seem like a promising setting for *Behind the Cup,* the movie Hills Bros. was producing for the 1939 Golden Gate Exhibition.

Ken Allen, who had also directed Hills

513

Bros.' earlier film, was coming down with a cold as he left San Francisco on the Johnson Line steamer *Portland* in October 1938. The illness felt like a bad omen, but when the ship reached "very hot" El Salvador, representatives of the coffee planters' association were on hand as promised to meet Allen at the port and shepherd him and his assistant, plus their cameras, film, and Ford station wagon, through customs.

Despite the extraordinary heat, and the fact that "very annoying but necessary police records . . . have to be kept, on moving in and out of various townships" in the coffee districts, Allen was optimistic. The coffee planters were "very appreciative" that Hills Bros. had chosen to set their picture in El Salvador and were "going out of their way to fix things for me," Allen reported to San Francisco. The planters had provided a guide to show him around the country, and Allen had already hit on a theme for the picture. The narrative would be a story of contrasts, which Allen sketched out in a letter to his bosses: "The general idea is this. High in the mountains of Central Americas lies the little republic of San Salvador but over its modern roads move much of the world's fine coffee. Surrounded by volcanoes on whose shaded slopes coffee grows almost to the summit, it is nevertheless a city of strange contrasts. Here Cadillacs and Carettas (oxcarts) move

514

side by side, etc., etc."[24] The difference between an oxcart and a Cadillac would frame the story of coffee in El Salvador and San Francisco.

There were a couple of unforeseen flaws in the plan. The first was that the "modern roads" were not actually so modern. At times Allen and his assistant had to get out and push their Ford through rough patches. And the second problem was that even in the city, the movie camera, mounted on a tripod, with Allen crouching behind and peering down the lens, unsettled the Salvadorans who found themselves in its sights. "Most of the natives duck," Allen reported. Others stood "like statues directly in front of the lens."[25]

After a few days of filming in the capital, Allen headed up into the heart of the coffee districts, where he found the planters eager to help. At first this help was of the kind Allen had learned to dread during the shoot in Colombia a decade earlier. After making a circuit of Santa Ana plantations, he reported that "everything is running about as expected," which was not a good thing. "I have been taken on a couple of 12-hour rides, as each [plantation] owner has to show me *all* of his property." Fixed on the story of contrasts, Allen could not see the relevance of every part to the whole. "Fortunately," he reported, "the President of the coffee association is very interested in the picture, so whenever I need him he is more than willing to be at my service. . . . We now have things on a working basis."[26]

The working basis Allen established was a movie set of plantation coffee production, staged in cooperation with planters. Allen had arrived in El Salvador at the beginning of the harvest season, but he wanted to shoot coffee's complete life cycle, from planting to milling. The coffee planters' association arranged everything, building a nursery specifically so that Allen could film the work of raising a coffee tree from seed. For footage of a coffee mill, Allen was "planning to shoot the patios at Mr. Hill's place in Santa Ana, as they are very nice."

Even in the process of developing a make-believe plantation, Allen got a taste of the strain that tensed the daily life and work of a coffee planter. Building the nurseries "takes time," he complained to San Francisco, which he didn't have. Then the coffee trees weren't cooperating — they needed another week at least before the cherries were good and ripe. And then, just as Allen thought he was ready to shoot on the plantations, it rained unexpectedly, and the nursery beds that had been built for him were washed out. Allen had new ones built on the plantations of Miguel Dueñas, another friend of Reuben Hills Jr., and "shot like the dickens when the sun came out for a few moments."[27]

Whenever Allen couldn't get the shot he wanted, planters helped stage it for him. He found that the dense thatch of a mature coffee plantation was impenetrable with a camera, and inside it was too dark to see what he was shooting anyway, and there were spiders everywhere: "Every [tree] has dozens on it . . . and it is hard not to bash into them once in a while." Plus, Allen complained, a thick layer of dust covered everything around Santa Ana, dulling the appeal of the scenery and making the trees look like mere "shrubs." But again the coffee planters fixed it: "The boys are arranging to leave a few coffee trees unpicked — and we are going to wash them so you can recognize the coffee." Allen set up his camera in the roads between the groves and shot just the edges, where the washed coffee cherries gleamed ripe red.

The planters also provided a cast for the film, who performed out-of-season dramatizations of plantation work: digging holes, planting seeds in the nursery, carrying seedlings, replanting seedlings, harvesting cherries, and processing coffee beans in the mill. To add some color, the planters were also "arranging an Indian dance to film," Allen reported. They rounded up a group of working people, dressed them in traditional-looking costumes, and lined them up so that the peak of the Santa Ana Volcano rose in the background. From behind his camera, Allen shot them while they danced.

On a real plantation, dedicated to the production of coffee rather than movies, the work of the harvest was very different, but it was coordinated and managed just as strictly.

A coffee tree in full fruit, ropy veins of red cherries shining through its dark green leaves, shares certain properties with a Christmas tree. After a steady buildup to the peak of the season comes a quick decline into irrelevance. Coffee profits were exceptionally time-sensitive, especially in Central America. A worker picking coffee in Brazil on the high-volume, low-price model could move through a plantation at harvest time on a steady forward path: encircling a branch in his palm or between his first finger and thumb and stripping it clean with a single pass, shedding leaves, twigs, and cherries all at once into a screen or onto the ground. Yet this rough method, though time-efficient, would damage the tree and yield a harvest of uneven ripeness.[28] Damage to the trees was never such a problem in Brazil, full of more coffee trees than anyone could ever figure out what to do with, but it was costly in El Salvador, where prime coffee land had always been scarce, and quality rather than volume was the rule. In mild coffee countries such as El Salvador, the emphasis on quality, and the measurement of quality in terms of "sweetness in the cup," made ripeness the crux of plantation coffee production.

Even within the small annual window of ripeness, not all the cherries on a tree or even on a single branch mature at the same rate, so the premium on ripeness imposes on the coffee harvest dual mandates of care and speed. Every harvest season, these twin priorities became work orders that shaped each moment of each day. It was the urgent business of the coffee planter with ripe cherries on his trees to make people work quickly and precisely. This meant moving harvest workers through the plantations tree by tree, to the branches where the fruit was fully ripe, in multiple waves of picking to be done selectively and delicately: one hand reaching out to hold the branch in place, the other hand seeking out the ripe red cherries and plucking them off the branch by the contraction of the thumb and the first two or three fingers around one or two cherries at a time, each contraction augmented and completed by a quick quarter-turn of the wrist, and then dropping the cherries into a basket or sack worn over the shoulders or belted around the waist.[29] James Hill expected each of his harvest workers to collect 20,000 cherries in exactly this way in the course of a ten-hour workday, six in the morning to five in the evening, with an hourlong break for lunch at noon. After six full days of picking, a harvest worker collecting 20,000 cherries a day would have finally gathered enough coffee to produce one sack, about 135 pounds, of export-ready beans.[30]

As the harvest season advanced and more and more cherries ripened, Hill employed more and more people to pick coffee — as many as five thousand at the peak of the season, often ten times as many people as he employed during the rest of the year. With his workforce swollen by thousands, including many migrant workers from around the country, Hill increased the number of supervisors and overseers he employed: one supervisor for every twenty people working. The harvest also required extra clerks, messengers, waterboys, cooks, and dozens of truckers and loaders who transported hundreds of thousands of pounds of fresh-picked cherries down the volcano to Las Tres Puertas at the end of each workday.

As soon as there were ripe coffee cherries coming in, James Hill began to keep his mill open late into the night, until eleven if not later, for he found that people working at night were more than twice as efficient as people working during the day, perhaps motivated by the hope of getting to bed before the predawn hour when the next workday began.[31] Hundreds of men worked in Las Tres Puertas shepherding coffee through the successive stages of milling, delivering it ultimately into the hands of the hundreds of limpiadoras who sorted and inspected the coffee beans before they were bagged up and shipped out.

Behind these seasonal workers followed a train of vendors and entertainers who set up shop wherever people were being paid. To watch over everyone, including his managers, Hill employed extra security guards for the harvest, plus an unknown number of spies.

Even so, close supervision was impossible amid the dense thickets of a mature coffee grove, where visibility topped out at about ten feet in every direction. There was always the possibility that harvest workers might leave a sack of picked coffee hidden among the trees; or bury a sack in the ground and return at night to carry it away; or secrete a handful of cherries every now and again in a bag hidden under their clothes; or continue to pick for their own account while the others gathered to weigh their sacks and collect their pay.[32] Thefts were most common in the late afternoon, as picking wound down and weighing started, and especially after six in the evening, after the tortillas and beans had been served and the sun had set, so Hill told his managers never to leave the groves without making sure that everyone else had left, too — yet another rule that was impossible to enforce.[33]

Along with extra overseers and security

guards, Hill used food to direct thousands of people to the places he needed them to be at the times he needed them to be there. He scheduled meals to coincide with the beginning and end of the workday. Hungry people showed up to work on time and left on time or they did not eat.[34]

Some plantation owners sponsored entertainment, often nighttime puppet shows or carnivals, to draw workers to their farms during the harvest and manage them during off-hours. For his part, Hill insisted that his managers not skimp on the rations, that they serve each person the full appointed amount: ten ounces of corn for tortillas, five ounces of beans, plus one cup of coffee, at a total cost of six cents for three meals a day.[35] Managers were instructed to give half a ration to small children if they arrived as part of a family — even though Hill didn't want children under fourteen picking, for fear they would damage the trees.[36] And he required managers to visit the kitchens of their plantations regularly to make sure that all the food served was clean and healthful.[37] By maintaining these standards, Hill hoped to set his plantations apart from his neighbors' and make them widely known as places where workers could expect to eat comparatively well, be treated comparatively well, and be paid promptly and wholly.[38] The farther this reputation spread across the volcano, the more working people Hill could expect to attract, and the more care they could be made to take with the work.[39] And as soon as the harvest season was over, as many people as possible were to be fired.

These calculations and anxieties, banal and urgent and never-ending, were the facts of a real planter's life, the keys to making people work coffee not featured in any movie. By the end of the Depression decade and the start of World War II, James Hill and his fellow planters on the Santa Ana Volcano had mastered them to an extraordinary degree — as thoroughly as planters in any coffee district in the world. "El Salvador has a distinctly American talent for stubborn self-development," wrote the American agricultural expert Charles Morrow Wilson in 1941 after a trip around the country, "for use of brawn and planning to change dormant natural resources into the goods and assets of a more abundant life. It is an Indian country which has effected a relatively successful transition to the ways and needs of white men."[40]

Ken Allen was still cutting *Behind the Cup* in early February 1939, a mere ten days before the Golden Gate Exposition was set to open on Treasure Island. The challenge was splicing together the footage he had shot in El Salvador with footage from the Hills Bros.

factory in San Francisco, and his bosses were getting anxious about the premiere. "Don't forget to get plenty of red pumped into the ripe coffee cherries — particularly in some of those basket scenes," one executive wrote to Allen, who was busy tinkering with the colors in Los Angeles, "and of course the color of our cans is important."[41] Red was the whole point of shooting the film in color, the unifying motif of "the story of contrasts." Allen pumped the footage full of so much red — the cherries, the lips of the women picking coffee, the cans — that it saturated and bled through the film.

"Coffee is America's favorite beverage," announced the narrator, Hills Bros. executive Carroll Wilson, finely suited and primly seated behind an immaculate desk, as the camera tracked in for the opening scene. "The United States alone consumes nearly 60 billion cups and is the world's largest customer. Have you ever wondered where coffee comes from, or what happens to coffee before it reaches your cup? Join us in a hurried trip to Coffeeland. Let us show you what goes on behind the cup." The shot dissolved to a map of Central America, with the city of Santa Ana marked prominently: "Far to the south, high in the mountains of Central America . . . studded with volcanic peaks, rich in tropical grandeur. . . . Here at the beginning of the coffee season we find gaiety

524

and laughter" — cut to Indians dancing under the volcano.

After the film showed coffee plantations and mills at harvest time in Santa Ana, the setting shifted back to the Hills Bros. plant on the Embarcadero, at the foot of the Bay Bridge: the green coffee department and the cupping room; a stream of sacks moving through the frame along a conveyor, all emblazoned with the importer's mark — O. & E., San Francisco, Ortega & Emigh — and then moving on to the big hot roasters; the bright red cans rolling through the vacuum-sealing machine. It was a story of contrasts, but also of continuity and collaboration — the story of how the "coffee grower and coffee roaster join hands to bring real coffee delight to your table."[42]

More than 90,000 people saw the forty-minute film in the first ten weeks of its run on Treasure Island, a "tremendous" total.[43] The reviews coming in to the Hills Bros. office suggested the expense had been worth it. "Saturday, while attending the Exposition, I had the pleasure of visiting your exhibit seeing the Motion Picture entitled 'Behind the Coffee Cup,' " wrote Victoria Paganini of San Francisco. "It was indeed a very interesting story. I have never used Hills Bros. coffee, but your motion picture has won me over and I have purchased my first can of Hills Bros. coffee today."[44] George Goodman of Oakland

525

wanted to share it with his lunch club. "Before seeing this picture little did I think about the time and effort spent to make that delicious beverage," he wrote. "I now understand and appreciate the perfection of Hills Bros. Coffee."[45]

25.
THE WAR

"Coffee-rich Salvador lacks Indians and romance," reported *New York Times* correspondent Arthur Goodfriend in 1947. Goodfriend was on assignment, driving the Pan American Highway down the isthmus to see what the Good Neighbor policy in the Western Hemisphere combined with total war in Europe and Japan had won.

Latin America had provided key support to the Allied forces: it was the source of hemp for rope, tin for munitions, cinchona for quinine, and especially coffee. Coffee accounted for nearly 10 percent of all U.S. imports between 1941 and 1945, and much of it was funneled toward strategic "defense areas" and into rations.[1] Hills Bros. won a government contract to deliver eighteen million pounds of coffee vacuum-packed in twenty-pound cans painted army drab.[2] American soldiers deployed abroad consumed more than 32.5 pounds of coffee beans per capita per year, double the civilian rate.[3]

Latin America was central to the making of the U.S.-led postwar order, too. The institutional foundation of American global power constructed between 1945 and 1948 adapted the Good Neighbor policy to the world. The Organization of American States, the North Atlantic Treaty Organization, the World Bank, the International Monetary Fund, the General Agreement on Trade and Tariffs, the United Nations: these postwar trade and aid programs, enthroning the U.S. as a global superpower, built on the economic and diplomatic strategies and institutions the Roosevelt administration had pioneered in Latin America in the thirties and forties.[4] In economic terms, the new global order made more things like coffee: abundantly available for import into the United States at low prices and in large quantities from a growing number of places around the world where everyday life and work were being precisely and painstakingly shaped to fit the American consumer market.

Yet in return for its contributions to the making of the "American Century," Latin America got nothing like a Marshall Plan. Promises of support for industrial development made during the Depression and the war were rescinded. Instead, Latin Americans were invited to help with redevelopment in Europe and Asia by continuing to focus on export agriculture — coffee and the old tropical staples could again be sold on the world market, and prices rose accordingly. The recovery of coffee prices was certainly welcome, but the memory of the strain of the past two decades had not faded, and even those countries and families most deeply invested in coffee were looking for a wider path forward.[5] The Latin Americans, after half a century of volatility in the coffee market and fifteen years of uninterrupted economic crisis, wanted more — they wanted industrialization, plus the loans, trade policies, and social programs that would pay for it.

From El Salvador, Arthur Goodfriend reported his findings as through the window of a car traveling down the Pan American Highway: "Gasoline at 43 cents a gallon, 10 cents cheaper than in Guatemala City. . . . La Cruzadilla, roadside rest vending the best pupusas in town. . . . Casas Clark, Oberholzer and Duena, the town's three best boarding houses, where food and lodging cost $60 to $70 a month, complete. . . . The balmy temperature, 80 degrees hot at noon, a cool 60 come evening . . . the heart-warming hospitality of John and Caroline Simmons, United States Ambassador and wife — only diplomat who delivers a citizen's mail personally to the citizen's pension. . . . The Casino Salvadoreno, home of the hotshots, where roof garden dances ooze swank and basement bowling alleys yield high scores for the players."[6]

Despite broader dissatisfaction with the postwar economic order, the mood inside the Casino Salvadoreño was celebratory when the coffee planters of El Salvador gathered in the spring of 1948 to honor one of their own. With the reopening of the European market, mild coffee prices had risen to all-time highs, around thirty cents a pound, roughly four times what they had been in 1940, and there was good reason to think that the prosperity would continue, for coffee drinking in the United States had also reached new highs — almost twenty pounds per person per year, more than triple what it had been at the start of James Hill's life.[7]

Six months earlier, in September 1947, before the start of the harvest season, the coffee planters of Central America and Mexico, who had organized to promote their interests after the war, held their second annual convention in Fortín de las Flores, Mexico. The town was on "the English road," the railway that had carried Hill from the port of Veracruz to Mexico City some sixty years before. As part of the annual meeting's business, the planters discussed the question of who should receive the group's Diploma of Merit, and one candidate stood out from the others in the eight member countries.

So, six months later, after the year's harvest

530

was over, the white-haired James Hill sat onstage in the banquet room at the Casino Salvadoreño. Wearing a dark blue suit and white
shirt, his thick necktie done in a neat Windsor
knot, Hill listened as his fellow planters
celebrated his life and work. They honored
his dedication to coffee, the growth and
development of his mill, the work he had
done to promote scientific methods of cultivation in El Salvador, especially soil preparation and shade tree selection. They honored
his contributions to the school for plantation
overseers in Santa Ana, his authority on questions of agricultural economics, and especially
his introduction of Bourbon coffee into El
Salvador, which "had made possible the current strength of the country as a producer of
coffee" — ranking behind only Brazil and
Colombia in volume, and ahead of even those
in yield per acre. And they honored James
Hill because, in light of these accomplishments, he was considered by his brother
planters to be a true son of El Salvador, the
country he transformed in the image of his
birthplace.[8]

After the citation was read, James Hill rose
from his chair and accepted the award. At six
feet, he stood above most of the other men
on stage, including his forty-seven-year-old
son, Jaime, who had dressed for the evening
in a gray suit and round metal eyeglasses
almost identical to his father's. Jaime Hill

531

was then serving concurrent terms as El Salvador's minister of agriculture and president of the coffee planters' association, and in his middle age he had become so focused on the family business that even his father mocked his single-mindedness. After shaking hands with the men onstage and receiving the diploma, James Hill turned to his son and handed him the award, and then turned to face the crowd. He spoke of his life in El Salvador with emotion and gratitude — but he also remembered how, when he had first planted Bourbon coffee trees in a corner of one of his plantations, all the planters and bankers in Santa Ana thought he had gone mad, and claimed that he would ruin his business and theirs, too.[9]

Later that year, James Hill's blood pressure rose to twice the normal level, 240 systolic. His doctor gave him a prescription and sent him to bed for a week, canceling a trip to Chile and Brazil that Hill had planned to take with his wife, Lola. At best, if his blood pressure came down, they might go to Miami for a change of scenery.

When Hill's health didn't improve, his doctor put him on the first boat to Los Angeles, with orders to check in to the Sansum Clinic, in Santa Barbara, where doctors were pioneering treatment of circulatory diseases. Yet even in Santa Barbara there was little to be done for hypertension, seen in the middle of the twentieth century to be a sign of imminent stroke or heart failure. Mental and psychological factors were thought to play a primary role in the disease, so heavy meals, hard work, and stress were to be avoided, and rest was prescribed.[10] A diet based on rice and fruit was among the most promising treatments.[11]

A year after his hospital stay, in December 1950, James Hill was still sick enough that for perhaps the first time in half a century he was not able to be where he usually was at the end of the year, up on the Santa Ana Volcano, where the coffee harvest was reaching its peak. Already the nearly four thousand people working on the family's plantations had picked and processed a million pounds of coffee for export. The season was only half over, and Hill expected to harvest at least that much again before it was done, which would be a good year indeed, though by no means out of line with what he had come to expect, and by no means the largest crop his plantations had produced. The harvest itself was going well, but there were real questions about what would become of the crop. So far Hill and his sons had sold exactly nothing. Sacks of coffee were piling up in port while the world waited for news from the United States.

The start of the Korean War that summer

had nearly doubled coffee prices, to over fifty cents a pound. But then, in the fall, overwhelmed by the arrival in North Korea of hundreds of thousands of Chinese troops, U.S. and United Nations forces had beaten a humiliating retreat south of the 38th parallel, the prewar boundary. Hill thought the U.S. had seriously underestimated the Soviet determination to spread communism, and he was eager to hear how President Truman would respond in his State of the Union Address on January 8, 1951.

But Hill would not live to see how it turned out. He would not live to see how the war in Korea metastasized across the second half of the twentieth century into other wars in other places until, three decades later, it reached El Salvador, too. He would not see how it became linked there to an old conflict, the coming of which he had predicted, or how the U.S. government judged the Soviet role in El Salvador in the 1980s. He would not see how this future war made of past wars claimed as its casualties members of his own family, even as it saved, in a roundabout way, the coffee dynasty he built.

Instead, at the end of May 1951, two weeks after his eightieth birthday, Hill sailed again to California. He traveled on a new Salvadoran diplomatic passport, in the company of his wife; his eldest son, Jaime; his doctor, a specialist in heart disease; and the young

534

doctor's wife. The party arrived in San Francisco on June 13, a mild Wednesday, and checked into the Hotel St. Francis on Union Square with a mountain of luggage: four trunks, fourteen bags, and four boxes.[12] They were prepared for a long stay.

Two and half months later, on Tuesday, August 29, 1951, James Hill had a heart attack at the Pebble Beach home of his youngest daughter, Julia Hill O'Sullivan. He died at Stanford-Lane Hospital in San Francisco, leaving his eldest son, Jaime — himself the father of a fourteen-year-old son named Jaime — in charge.[13]

"The war, the war, it is all because of the war," one American employer complained in 1951. World War II had done what coffee's promoters in Latin America and the United States had been trying to do for three decades: reshaped the American workday, rooting the coffee break as deeply in American life as "the seventh-inning stretch and the banana split." One congressman described the scene in postwar Washington, D.C., "like recess time in school. The boys & girls dash off for coffee as if rehearsing for fire drill." As *Time* magazine put it, "clerks, secretaries, junior executives and salesgirls" had come to consider coffee breaks "an inalienable right of the American office worker."[14]

The war had reshaped the American work-

535

day by changing the workforce. As more and more troops shipped out, competition for employees was tight, and employers were compelled to be flexible. Before the war, Phil Greinetz, owner of Los Wigwam Weavers in downtown Denver, makers of fine neckwear, "every thread woven by hand of fine virgin wools," had employed young men to operate his twenty looms. The looms were "primitive" and the work was draining, requiring weavers to step heavily on foot treadles while throwing shuttles of thread back and forth. Many of the neckties were brightly colored and elaborately patterned, so there were often many shuttles in play for a single piece of cloth. Weaving neckties required strength, coordination, and constant attention, and a few hours of it was a lot for anyone.

When the young men he employed went off to fight, Greinetz hired older men, but he found that they couldn't do the job up to his standards. To replace them, Greinetz hired a group of middle-aged women. They had the dexterity, but by the time they left at the end of the workday their cheeks were sunken with fatigue, and they were still tired when they came to work the next morning. Before long the women "broke down" altogether, and Greinetz didn't know what to do about it. When he called a company-wide meeting to discuss the problem, his employees suggested something he hadn't thought of: fifteen-

536

minute breaks twice a day, once in the morning and once in the afternoon, with coffee.[15]

"Break" did not always imply "coffee," nor vice versa. One historian has studied the case of industrial Buffalo in the first decades of the twentieth century. At the Barcolo factory, later BarcaLounger, there were breaks, but employees had to bring their own coffee if they wanted it. At the nearby Larkin Soap factory, there was free coffee for employees, but no authorized breaks when they could drink it.[16]

This was consistent with modern approaches to industrial organization around the world at the time. During World War I, the British minister of munitions and the Office of the Home Secretary in the UK had begun studies of the physical efficiency of workers in weapons factories. One experiment paused work for ten minutes in the morning and afternoon, during which time men stayed at their machines and "took tea and other nutriment." Though this "tea interval" was found to be a "valuable aid to output," it did not become standard practice. On the contrary, it was "normally allowed for men only when overtime is worked."[17]

Though coffee had been promoted as an "aid to factory efficiency" in the United States since the 1920s, the "coffee break" remained a few steps away. In the case of the

Tyler metalworks in Cleveland, coffee was served out of the plant's "coffee kitchen" only at lunchtime, and there was no suggestion of expanding the service to other times of the day. One ad created by N. W. Ayer for the Brazilian-American coffee committee in the 1920s suggested that "right at the peak of the day's duties it pays to pause for a chummy, cheery cup of Coffee. It is a stimulus to effort in the office or in the home — it coaxes cheerful spirits and clear-thinking for the rest of the day. As regularly as the clock swings 'round to four, drink an appetizing, reviving cup of Coffee."[18] Other industry promotions suggested a "fourth meal," or an "afternoon coffee hour . . . psychologists having decided that 4 in the afternoon is the zero hour of clerical energy."[19] Because experiments had proven that its energizing effects started within minutes, coffee was especially well suited to the "zero hour" of energy that came toward the end of the workday.

For all the coffee industry's promotional efforts, the decisive step toward a full-fledged coffee break came from working people themselves. Employees who got used to drinking coffee on breaks during the war were reluctant to give it up afterward, even when the breaks were no longer authorized. The "coffee sneak" became a daily ritual in postwar factories and offices, and it "knocked many a production schedule silly," as *Forbes* put it.[20] It was not until this interruption of regular work for coffee drinking became something that employers stopped trying to prevent, something that was incorporated into the workday as one of its standard features, that the practice became known as the "coffee break," a phrase that came into use in the early 1950s to seal the new consensus that time off for coffee was a natural part of a good day's work.

So authorized, the coffee break became the "office worker's national institution." One survey polled more than a thousand companies that had incorporated ten- or fifteen-minute coffee breaks into the working day, finding "less worker fatigue in 82 percent of the companies; better employee morale in 75 percent; increased productivity in 62 percent; fewer accidents in 32 percent; less labor turnover in 21 percent." One firm, Mutual Life Insurance of New York, calculated that coffee breaks saved them "$130,000 a year in over-all labor costs when the coffee is delivered to the workers' desks."[21] For American business, coffee was an easy sell: spending money to give out free coffee was actually a way to make money by increasing productivity. In 1952, the Pan-American Coffee Bureau, funded by coffee-producing countries of Latin America, started a new advertising campaign that fixed the phrase in American English for good: "Give yourself a coffeebreak . . . and get what coffee gives to you!"

The advent of the coffee break highlighted a larger change in American life. While the first half of the twentieth century, and the Depression years especially, had been characterized by dramatic conflict between employers and employees, by midcentury the "labor question" had been answered by prosperity. "Today there is no real proletariat in California," wrote historian and economics professor Rockwell D. Hunt in 1954. "The workday often is below the eight-hour standard, and more and more the five-day work-week is being ushered in. But atop all these there are important workers' benefits — insurance, medical aid, vacations with pay, pension, and all the rest, including the 'coffee break' at mid-morning."[22] Sociologist David Riesman noted that the workweek had shrunk by nearly 50 percent in half a century: "from 64 hours in Henry James's day to around 40 in ours, not including the mid-morning coffee break and the other sociabilities which have crept into the hours which the census registers as working ones."[23] It was precisely this ambiguity about whether the coffee break counted as recreation or working time that was the source of the trouble at Los Wigwam Weavers.

Taking his employees' suggestion, Phil Greinetz set up a break room furnished with a table and chairs, a coffeemaker, a kettle for tea, plus all the necessary supplies, and instituted fifteen-minute break periods, one in the morning and one in the afternoon. Soon Greinetz noticed a change in his workers. Four women who had been among the worst performers were now among the best. Altogether the middle-aged women began to do as much work in six and half hours as the older men had done in eight. Encouraged, Greinetz made the breaks compulsory. He considered the two fifteen-minute coffee breaks as time away from work — after all, employees were required to leave their stations, to "insure that they relaxed" — so he didn't pay his employees for that half hour. But because the half hour of uncompensated break time built into the workday at Los Wigwam regularly caused wages to fall below the minimum established in the Fair Labor Standards Act of 1938, the U.S. Department of Labor sued Greinetz in 1955. The question was whether the breaks were a part of the working day, legally speaking — whether workers had to be compensated for coffee breaks. The question within the question, again, was how coffee was related to the capacity of the human body to work.

In court, Greinetz testified to the extraordinary changes he had observed in his employees. The coffee breaks had been so effective that he had written them into new employment contracts: two compulsory fifteen-minute periods during which workers were free to do anything they wished, so long as it wasn't work. To Greinetz, this provision left no doubt that the coffee breaks were free time rather than working time, and so not subject to the rules of wages and hours. In answer, the Department of Labor cited a 1940 order that indicated that short rest periods "up to and including twenty minutes should be compensated" as working time, on the logic that "they promote the efficiency of the employee," and so benefited the employer. Lawyers for the government backed up their argument with case law supporting the idea that "when time out is of such a nature that it bears a relationship to employment time and is beneficial to the employer," it was to be counted as working time and compensated duly. Nevertheless, on the question of the relationship of the coffee break and work, the trial court agreed with Greinetz: it was not working time, so it was not compensable time. The Department of Labor appealed.[24]

The appeal was heard on the Tenth Circuit, in Denver, with judge Alfred P. Murrah presiding. Murrah was from Oklahoma. He had run away from home at thirteen years old, hopping a train until the railroad police kicked him off, and then finding work on a family farm in exchange for room and board. Murrah worked his way through high school

542

and the University of Oklahoma, where he studied law. After college, he founded a law firm in the oil boomtown of Seminole, Oklahoma, where he specialized in workers' compensation.[25]

The Wigwam case was an important one, Murrah's court noted, because "coffee breaks" were "rapidly becoming an accepted part of employment generally." It was also a tricky one, for the relationship of rest to work was bound up not only with questions about the power of employers to dictate what their employees did at work and how, but also with questions about the capabilities and limits of the human body. The key issues, as the court defined them, were whether a given break was "of sufficient duration and taken under such conditions that it is available to employees for their own use and purposes" and, above all, "whether idle time is spent predominantly for the employer's or employee's benefit." In other words, it mattered what workers did during their break time — the coffee made a difference.

On both points, Murrah's court disagreed with the trial court and Greinetz. The decision noted that while the weavers at Los Wigwam were technically free to use the break time as they wished, in practice they were constrained by the nature of the workplace itself. Workers were required to leave their stations, but the factory was on the third floor of a building with no elevator, and fifteen minutes gave them nowhere to go but the bathroom or the break area. More important, Murrah's court also disagreed with the trial court on the question of who benefited from the coffee breaks. While the breaks were no doubt beneficial to workers, the court found, they were at least "equally beneficial to the employer" — if not more so — "in that they promote more efficiency and result in a greater output, and this increased production is one of the primary factors, if not the prime factor, which leads the employer to institute such break periods." Indeed, Greinetz had made the breaks mandatory — he wanted his employees to take coffee breaks more than he wanted them to keep working. He gave them enough time to drink a cup of coffee, but not enough time to do much else.

On those grounds, Murrah's court overturned the earlier decision. Coffee breaks bore "a close relationship" to work, and therefore counted as working time, to be compensated as such. In that way, the principle that physiologists and bosses had already discovered in practice — that coffee adds something to the working power of the human body independent of the processes and timescales of eating and digestion, something beyond what the science of energy and laws of thermodynamics say is possible — became itself a kind of law.

■ ■ ■ ■

At the same time the coffee break was on trial in the United States, coffee production was under the microscope in Latin America. The investigators in the latter case came from two divisions of the United Nations: the Food and Agriculture Organization, and the Economic Commission for Latin America, directed by the Argentinian economist Raúl Prebisch. Prebisch had been appointed to head ECLA after the publication of his 1950 study *Economic Development in Latin America and Its Principal Problems.* The study was a critique of the region's historical role as a producer of food and raw commodities for "the great industrial centers." Demonstrating how trading agricultural products for industrial goods had led to chronic poverty in Latin America, Prebisch gave empirical weight to the push for industrialization. At the UN, his job was to figure out what to do about it — how to achieve industrialization in Latin America, with the goal of finally claiming "a share of the benefits of technical progress and of progressively raising the standard of living of the masses."[26] It was an important project, for after eighty years of "ever greater global interconnectedness," it was observed that the world had broken into three unstable parts: first, second, and third.[27]

Prebisch's vision for Latin American industrial development did not completely forsake traditional agricultural commodities. Exports and trade had to continue to grow, he argued, in order to raise the "enormous amount" of money necessary to pay for industrialization.[28] As Latin America's most important export, coffee was instrumental to Prebisch's project. The point of the UN study was to figure out how to make coffee production more efficient, so that coffee exports could be used to fund industrialization. The group chose three sites for study: El Salvador because it was the most intensive coffee economy; Colombia because it was exemplary of a small-farm model of production; Brazil because it was the world's leading coffee producer, with the largest plantations by size and gross yield.

Planters conventionally measured their success in terms of money: sales less costs, including wages, which by 1954 had reached an average of fifty cents a day in El Salvador, incorporating rations of tortillas, beans, and salt. But the UN, concerned with the efficient use of economic resources, wanted to measure coffee production not in terms of money but rather in terms of "physical costs": all the material resources that went into producing export-ready coffee — human, animal, mechanical, chemical — aggregated and expressed in a single, common unit that would allow for easy analysis. The integer they came up with was a derivative measure of energy: the number of "man-hours" required to produce a pound of coffee. While employers in the U.S. had been interested in measuring the work that came out of coffee drinking, in Latin America the challenge was to measure the work that went into coffee production.

UN analysts began their work in El Salvador first, in October 1954. The small size of the country and the proximity of the plantations to one another created a good opportunity to test the research methods, which had been pioneered on North Carolina tobacco farms. The study carried extra weight in light of the recent CIA/United Fruit Company–engineered overthrow of Guatemalan president Jacobo Árbenz, who had put through reforms that, from the distance of Washington, appeared to be communist. The hope was that harnessing efficient coffee production to industrial development would preempt similar trouble elsewhere.

The investigators set up in the coffee districts around the Santa Ana Volcano and began tallying all the work that went into making a coffee plantation: work in the nurseries, digging holes, weeding, harvesting, work in the mills — everything until the point of shipment. Adding up all the man-hours worked, dividing by the total coffee produced, the study determined that in El Salvador, on the aggregate, three man-hours of work produced one kilogram of green coffee, or about two pounds of roasted coffee.[29]

If we put the UN's measurements of the man-hours required for coffee production together with the testimony about coffee's relation to work that served as evidence in federal court in the United States, it is possible to reach a rough understanding of the relationship between the work that goes into coffee and the work that comes out of it. Take as a starting point the UN calculation for Salvadoran production: three man-hours per kilogram of green coffee, or roughly two pounds of roasted coffee, accounting for some weight loss in the roasting process. Run that figure through the most generous recipes for coffee making — as recorded, for example, in the Hills Bros. Coffee Guide: a pound of coffee yielding about forty cups, which would be enough for each of Phil Greinetz's twenty weavers at Los Wigwam to have two cups a day. With two coffee breaks per day at Los Wigwam, a pound of coffee is a reasonable to conservative estimate of what that factory might have been using each workday.

Greinetz had testified that the coffee breaks enabled the women he hired to do what had been eight hours of work in six and half hours — saving, across the whole shop of twenty workers, thirty hours of labor each day. The one and a half hours of work required to produce one pound of coffee in El Salvador became thirty hours of working time at Los Wigwam. The work that went into coffee in El Salvador created twenty times as much work in the United States. In terms of monetary cost the difference was greater. One and a half hours of work in El Salvador in 1954 paid roughly six cents. Thirty hours of working time in the United States in that year paid, at a minimum wage of seventy-five cents per hour, $22.50.

The extraordinary difference between these numbers — between the very low cost of coffee production in money, time, and energy, and the much greater value of coffee consumption by the same metrics — is a measure of the power that James Hill and his fellow planters had harnessed and accumulated in the coffee factory they built on the Santa Ana Volcano, and that they wielded to make people work. The scale and nature of their accomplishment, a sense of how they did it day after day, is suggested by the fact that a quarter century later, El Salvador would again, for the second time in fifty years, erupt in revolution.

26.
PAST LIVES

Twenty-five years later, lying handcuffed and blindfolded in the bed of a speeding pickup truck, Jaime Hill could not help wondering if he would be better off dead. A year earlier, in 1978, he had been demoted from his position atop the family business when his father, the elder Jaime, decided that his polo playing and Scotch drinking had become liabilities. Then Hill and his wife, Roxana, separated, and he became alienated from her family and their friends. Jaime Hill could not say with any confidence what he was worth to the people who would be asked to pay his ransom.[1]

After two hours of driving the truck stopped. The smell of the air and the tone of the silence told Jaime Hill that they were in the country. The kidnappers unloaded him from the pickup, put him in a jeep, and took off again. After another hour on the road, the jeep stopped in front of a small house at the foot of the Santa Ana Volcano. They had arrived in Chalchuapa, a town about ten miles from Las Tres Puertas, and home to people who had worked on Hill family coffee plantations for years. Blindfolded, Jaime Hill had no idea where he was. The kidnappers hauled him out of the jeep, pushed him inside the house, and removed the covering from his eyes. A room the size of a closet had been furnished with a canvas cot. Inside the cell, for the first time in his life, Jaime Hill found himself alone.[2]

Jaime Hill had been kidnapped by the People's Revolutionary Army of El Salvador, one of five leftist groups fighting the Fourteen Families and the military dictatorship. With eerie symmetry, the conflict had taken shape along the lines drawn half a century earlier.

After the massacre of 1932, as Communist Party voter rolls were turned into hit lists, the Salvadoran left went underground. The terror of the killing kept even those organizers who continued working isolated from and suspicious of one another.[3] Many others fled abroad, including Miguel Mármol. Meanwhile, the alliance between the military dictatorship and the coffee planters was strengthened by the Cold War and the rise of U.S.-sponsored anticommunist measures in Central America after 1948.

The Salvadoran left began to reemerge after Fidel Castro's unlikely triumph in the 1959

Cuban Revolution. Castro's influence was half inspiration and half irritation. He had become an important symbol of possibility for working people across Latin America, but his victory also heightened the pressure and surveillance coming from the United States. In 1961, Latin America appeared to newly elected President John F. Kennedy as the "most dangerous area in the world."[4] New U.S. aid programs designed to snuff out communism finally provided long-sought support for industrialization, but also created rising expectations among the Salvadoran working classes. These rising expectations were met in turn with an uneven mixture of "concession and repression," the classic dictatorial formula in twentieth-century Latin America.[5]

In some cases it was hard to tell the difference. So distant and detached was the Salvadoran government from the majority of its citizens that even policies meant as concessions backfired and caused more suffering. A minimum-wage law for agricultural workers passed in 1965 unintentionally put many people out of work.[6] Programs for health and social development improved living standards, especially in the cities, leading to a spike in population, which doubled from roughly two million to four million in the twenty-five years after 1950. This population surge increased the economic pressure on working people by making resources even scarcer.[7] By 1980, less than 2 percent of the population would own more than half the country's arable land.[8] At the same time, increasing political protests were met with deadly force, student demonstrators were jailed or worse, and the national university was closed.[9] The contrast between life in El Salvador and the possibilities symbolized by Cuba was stark.

For many years the question of revolution had been put to the side. This was as the government had intended. While much of the killing in 1932 had been performed for the world to see, afterward it became crucial to purge the massacre from the official record in order to shore up the legitimacy of the government and the coffee planters. As a matter of policy, "candid public discussion of the events was suppressed, archives were off limits, documents were destroyed, lost, or stolen, and many people who witnessed the events were exiled or killed or remained silent."[10] Even speaking of revolution carried potentially deadly consequences. Nevertheless, in the early 1970s several groups on the left became convinced of the necessity of using force to attempt again to change their country.

The People's Revolutionary Army, which had taken Jaime Hill, was one of these groups. It had been founded in 1972 by young radicals, many with ties to the church, who were dedicated to military action and the belief that a small group of committed fighters could carry through a revolution even without mass participation.[11] To fund their plans, the People's Revolutionary Army kidnapped members of the Salvadoran elite and held them for ransom.

As in the run-up to the massacre of 1932, the Salvadoran government responded to the militarization of the left with escalating force. In 1975 the National Guard opened fire on thousands of students who gathered in Santa Ana and San Salvador to protest the government's plan to spend $30 million hosting the Miss Universe pageant, and thirty-seven protesters were killed. The military was given a free hand to arrest anyone suspected of "subversive" activity.[12] Covert paramilitary "death squads," funded by the oligarchy, formed on the right, their ranks filled out by moonlighting National Guardsmen and soldiers.[13] The most notorious of these was the White Warriors Union, led by Major Roberto D'Aubuisson, who had trained in the early seventies at the International Police Academy in Washington, D.C. Though secretive in certain ways, often operating under the cover of night and hiding behind masks, the death squads enjoyed effective sanction and impunity, and brazenly displayed their work for all to see when the sun came up. "Sometimes the bodies were headless, or faceless, their features having been obliterated with a shotgun blast or an application of battery acid," American journalist Mark Danner reported. But "cut into the flesh of a corpse's back or chest was likely to be" the signature of the group that had authored the death.[14]

Electoral politics also paralleled the run-up to the massacre of 1932. In 1977 the presidential election was stolen with voter suppression and fraud, and fifty of the demonstrators who gathered in the capital to protest the results were killed. Then, in July 1979, as if to prove that history was indeed repeating itself, a popular insurrection in Nicaragua, carried out by a leftist group that had named itself after Augusto César Sandino, overthrew the military dictatorship that had ruled for the half century since Sandino's defeat. After the triumph of the Sandinistas in Nicaragua, conservative hard-liners in El Salvador doubled down on repression, ready to fight. A more moderate faction on the right, including many younger army officers, began plotting to avoid civil war by overthrowing the hard-liners and attempting to bargain with the left.

The coup that followed on October 15, 1979, ended the five-decade run of military rule that had begun with the coup of January 1932, but split itself into two factions in the process. One faction, taking control of the government, pushed for conciliatory measures: land reform, social welfare, and human rights. The other faction, taking control of the military, went ahead with the crackdown, targeting the People's Revolutionary Army in particular.[15] The day after the coup, thirty-five people were killed in San Salvador's poor suburbs, and then forty more the next day. On October 29, seventy-five people were killed at a rally in the capital. On Halloween, the day Jaime Hill was kidnapped, seven protesters were killed by police, even as the government convened a human rights commission to investigate kidnappings and disappearances.[16] The split personality of the coup made it impossible to know what was coming next.

During Jaime's first night in his cell, he took the pills his captors gave him and fell dead asleep. The next morning he awoke in a world in which the most familiar things had become the strangest. His kidnappers had spent months getting to know him, studying his routines and habits, shooting photographs as he went about his life in San Salvador, and investigating the financial situation of his family. Now they took pictures of him holding a newspaper for proof of life. They asked Jaime to write detailed information about his family members to use in negotiations, and to make an accounting of his family's finances. They served him a big lunch of fish, vegetables, tortillas, and fruit. Hill started reading *Murder on the Orient Express*. At certain moments he allowed himself to think that he would make it home alive. But then his kidnappers said that everything depended on the response of his family and the government to their ransom demands, and Jaime Hill lost faith.[17]

Two weeks later, in the middle of November, the People's Revolutionary Army demanded a ransom of $8 million. Harold Hill, Jaime's younger brother, a graduate of Texas A&M and the Wharton School who oversaw the family's coffee business, led the negotiations. Weeks of phone calls and letters accomplished nothing. In early December, Harold Hill approached the archbishop of San Salvador, Óscar Romero, to ask him to intervene.

If anyone could have done so, it would have been Romero. In three years as the leader of El Salvador's Catholic Church, he had become the most powerful person in the country, and this was something of a surprise. When Romero was elevated to archbishop in 1977, the Salvadoran oligarchy had celebrated, expecting the priest to be a deferential ally of the government. Yet soon it was clear that the opposite was true. Already sympathetic to the struggles of his impoverished compatriots, among whom he had lived and worked, Romero was radicalized in 1977 by the killing of a fellow priest in what appeared to be a government assassination, and he pushed the church into politics. His Sunday-morning homilies calling for the "liberation of the people," broadcast on a church-owned radio station, were heard in almost three-quarters of the households in rural El Salvador. In 1978, Romero was nominated for the Nobel Peace Prize by a group that included twenty-three members of the U.S. Congress. In May 1979, he traveled to the Vatican to ask for the help of the new pope, John Paul II, in ending poverty and violence in El Salvador.[18]

After listening to Harold Hill's appeal, Archbishop Romero pleaded for Jaime Hill's life in a December 16 Advent mass: "In the name of this family, and in the name of the families of all those who have been abducted, I beg you, as the Pope did in Ireland, I beg you on my knees if it is necessary, to return freedom to these people, our sisters and brothers and thus restore tranquility to these beloved homes."[19] Jaime Hill dreamed of being home for Christmas, around the tree with his family, but the holiday passed with no news. Time became an affliction. Each hour Jaime spent in his cell was interminable, yet each day sped him toward the end of his life.

Early in January 1980, Jaime Hill's kidnappers told his family that they were ready to kill him if their demands were not met by the sixteenth of the month. It was harvest time, but violence had put El Salvador's economy in turmoil. The Hill family claimed to be unable to sell or borrow against their businesses to raise cash, and they begged for an extension of the deadline. Jaime Hill's estranged wife, Roxana, went to visit Archbishop Romero on the day of the deadline, and two days later she went on national television to plead for her husband's life.

Two months later, in March, Hill's family agreed to the terms of his release with his kidnappers: $4 million in cash, plus a couple of conditions.[20] The first condition was the handover of Hill's armored Mercedes to the People's Revolutionary Army. The second was that Hill's family pay for the revolutionaries to tell their story in some of the world's largest newspapers.

On March 12 a full-page manifesto ran in the New York Times, the Washington Post, and Le Monde, as well as papers in Venezuela, Mexico, and Spain. The Times charged $16,800 for the ad, which appeared on page A21, eleven pages after an explanatory article. "As a condition for the release of a Salvadoran executive held by leftist guerrillas," the paper reported, "the family of the hostage has paid for the publication of a long political statement today." A spokesperson for the paper's advertising department apologized for the deviation in standards: "Normally we would look at the ad and would delete descriptions that might be offensive to our readers. We would also ask for substantiation or documentation of factual matters." But in this case, the spokesperson explained, the *Times* had "no choice but to print it as it had come in, considering that a person's life was involved."[21]

The manifesto, dense with text printed in a typeface slightly different from the *Times'* usual font, was both history and prophecy: "The Salvadorian people are at present confronting a crucial moment in history, in search of their final liberation. The struggle that is now taking place in our country, expresses a people's right to be the author of its own destiny." It would not end until "the people take in their hands what legitimately belongs to them, the huge plantations of coffee, sugar, cotton; the huge factories, the banks and all the properties of the oligarchy; this is the definitive solution and no other that would keep us subjected to poverty and permanent repression is acceptable." The money raised from kidnappings — money "recuperated" from the oligarchy — would fund "the people's conquest of justice and peace."[22]

On March 14, Jaime Hill's kidnappers gave him back the clothes he had been wearing four and a half months earlier, plus twenty dollars in cash, drove him three hours to San Salvador, and dropped him off at the edge of the city. From there, he caught a taxi home.

Ten days later Archbishop Romero was giving mass at a hospital chapel in San Salvador when he was struck in the heart by a single shot fired out the window of a red Volkswagen; a UN truth commission later confirmed what most Salvadorans already knew, blaming Roberto D'Aubuisson and his White Warriors Union. On May 11, right-wing death squads published a hit list of 138 "traitor communists."[23] On May 22, the People's Revolutionary Army joined with four other leftist guerrilla groups, and by October the five factions had organized themselves into a single force, taking as their name the Farabundo Martí National Liberation Front, the FMLN. The new coalition numbered seven thousand guerrilla fighters, men and women both, plus 100,000 civilian militia, and was funded by millions of dollars raised from kidnappings, including Jaime Hill's. For more than a decade, the FMLN fought the Salvadoran military and the death squads, which were funded by $6 billion in aid, more than a million dollars a day, from the United States.

On the road from Vietnam to the Middle East, U.S. military history turns at El Salvador. The Sandinista Revolution in Nicaragua

561

in 1979, combined with revolution in Iran and the Soviet invasion of Afghanistan, prompted the Carter administration, and then the Reagan administration, to make a stand against communism in Central America. The Salvadoran civil war was the largest American counterinsurgency and nation-building campaign between the fall of Saigon and the fall of Baghdad.[24] The battle plan for El Salvador, shaped in contrast to Vietnam and later adapted to the war in Iraq, deployed a small ground force to train the Salvadoran army to fight the Salvadoran people. Over twelve years, the countryside was again transformed into a mass grave for as many as 75,000 people. "Life is the exception," concluded an Inter-American Commission investigating human rights abuses during the war, "and death the rule in El Salvador."[25] A million Salvadorans, a fifth of the country's population, rich and poor alike, fled their homes to escape the violence, many seeking refuge in the United States. Elites clustered in Miami, while expatriate communities of working-class Salvadorans formed in San Francisco, Los Angeles, Washington, D.C., and the Long Island suburbs.

The fighting went on until the fall of 1991, when the first Bush administration told the Salvadoran government that funding "was not going to continue forever."[26] Not long afterward, on January 16, 1992, sixty years to the day that Farabundo Martí and Miguel Mármol had initially chosen for the start of the first communist revolution in the Western Hemisphere, peace accords ended one of the last armed conflicts of the Cold War. After the peace agreement, the Farabundo Martí National Liberation Front moved to secure a permanent peacetime role in Salvadoran politics and society. Some FMLN leaders took courses through Harvard University, "a sort of Politics 101," to learn how to set up a political party.[27] Others wanted to go into business, in part to provide employment for their former soldiers. For help, they called Jaime Hill.

When his kidnappers called, Jaime Hill invited five of them to his house. They sat together on his back patio under a canopy of shade trees.[28] The former revolutionaries told Hill they wanted to start a construction company, and they asked him to introduce them to other businessmen. Jaime Hill, well aware that some of his friends thought him a traitor, agreed to help his kidnappers find a bookkeeper.[29]

Two decades later, in 2011, journalist Kelefa Sanneh flew to El Salvador for *The New Yorker*. He was looking for the origins of a coffee revolution under way in New York, where, he reported, "in a small but growing number of cafés, you can order coffee more or less the way you might order wine, specifying the varietal and the region and the farm; for the price of a glass of house red, you will receive, if you're lucky, a cup of drip coffee that is mellower and weirder than the astringent beverage most people know. Perhaps you will detect a hint of gingerbread, or a honeyed aftertaste, or a rich, tangy sweetness that calls to mind tomato soup. And perhaps you will find it difficult to go back to whatever you used to drink."

Sanneh was describing a "third wave" of American coffee drinking. The first was made up of big supermarket brands such as Hills Bros., Folgers, and Maxwell House. The second was coffee-shop chains such as the Berkeley-based Peet's and Seattle's Starbucks, which also grew out of the Pacific coast trade in high-quality mild coffee. And the third was a "farmer-obsessed coffee movement" made up of boutique roasters and stylish shops where "a twelve-ounce bag may cost twenty dollars or more and comes accompanied by a lyrical essay on provenance and flavor."[30] Thanks to an unanticipated consequence of the Salvadoran civil war, the Santa Ana Volcano had become an especially sought-after provenance.

Twelve years of fighting had crippled the country's coffee industry and transformed the national economy. Migrants fleeing the violence became El Salvador's leading export, and remittances from the United States became the nation's most important economic sector. Yet the war was beneficial to Salvadoran coffee in one way. Coffee mills and plantations, actual and symbolic forms of elite wealth and power, were frequent targets for the FMLN.[31] Many planters — whether they abandoned their plantations in fear, hesitated to invest in coffee, or simply lost workers to the revolution — held back from replacing their old Bourbon trees with "technified" fast-growing, high-yield, full-sun hybrids, as planters in other parts of Central America were doing at the time. In the process, Bourbon — the original high-yield, hot-climate tree in El Salvador — became a sort of heirloom, heritage varietal.[32] When Sanneh visited, El Salvador was exporting less than half as much coffee as it had exported in 1975, but prices for quality beans had never been higher.

In Santa Ana, Sanneh met up with Aida Batlle, heir to a Salvadoran coffee dynasty, Flo Rida fan, online player of Call of Duty: Modern Warfare 2, and something of a coffee celebrity in the United States. Batlle ferried him to her plantations on the Santa Ana Volcano in a four-wheel-drive Toyota FJ Cruiser. She kept a tight grip on the steering wheel with Harley-Davidson driving gloves as they motored up slopes so steep "that pickers sometimes have to be lowered on ropes," following the same route her great-grandfather used to take in a Buick in the days "when coffee ruled El Salvador."

Batlle traveled with "two armed guards and one extraordinarily well-trained German shepherd, Chief," along with some worst-case scenarios in her head. She had grown up in Miami, but trips back to El Salvador in the 1980s showed her what her family had escaped. "It sounds bad," she said, "but you get used to seeing dead bodies by the side of the road." After the war, her father struggled to keep the family coffee business going in Santa Ana, and eventually Batlle, who had struggled herself in the restaurant business in Nashville, decided she should help. She knew little about coffee trees but had a native sense of what American coffee drinkers wanted. Her "idea was to treat her coffee the same way her local Wild Oats supermarket . . . had treated fruit: she would grow the plants organically and pick only cherry . . . that was ripe and healthy-looking — the ones she would want to eat." The next year she produced "coddled coffee" that won a national competition and sold for $14.00 a pound — at the time, the open-market price was less than a dollar. After that, Batlle began to sell her crop to boutique roasters in the U.S., including Counter Culture and Stumptown.

Batlle showed Sanneh the two principal coffee varietals on her land, Bourbon and

Pacamara. Each had its own character: the Bourbons were "ballerinas — tall, elegant," Batlle explained. "These pacas are more like gymnasts, short and stumpy." The pacas were hardy, while the Bourbon trees were "temperamental but fertile." Pointing to some Bourbon seedlings, she addressed a supervisor in a camouflage Superman T-shirt strapped with dual machetes: "Treat them with love and kindness, please."

After the tour of the plantation, Batlle brought Sanneh down the volcano to her "local mill," Las Tres Puertas. Sanneh followed Batlle's coffee through the mill to her "favorite place in the compound," the cupping room. The cupping room at Las Tres Puertas, Sanneh reported, was "the closest thing in the area to a well-equipped café," for El Salvador, "like many coffee-producing countries . . . never really developed a coffee-drinking culture." The economics of plantation coffee production meant that there weren't enough Salvadorans who could afford to pay what the country's crop could bring in the United States and Europe. Instead, Salvadoran grocery stores were full of cheap instant coffee manufactured from beans of lower quality and value, and usually imported from Vietnam or Brazil, where coffee was a volume business.

In the cupping room, Batlle's "most trusted lieutenant" prepared a few of her coffees for testing. He roasted several samples of export-ready beans and shirred each into fine powder in a retail-quality German grinder worth thousands of dollars. He portioned twelve and a half grams of grounds into each of the white cups arrayed around the edge of a table. Batlle bent to smell the grounds deeply, and then her lieutenant added 250 milliliters of hot water to each cup and let the brew steep for four minutes.

The cupping room at Las Tres Puertas also housed a stainless Italian espresso maker — La Marzocco, $6,500 — an artifact of the wider world of Batlle's coffee, where tasting notes read as leading indicators of value. After four minutes of brewing, the cuppers skimmed the grounds off the top of each cup. They dipped their spoons and tasted, slurping loudly to aerate the coffee across the palate. Fruit cup, heavy syrup, earth, sweetness, juice: "I'm getting chocolate-covered cherries," Batlle said. This was her unique ability as a "producer who speaks fluent consumer" — she could translate one language into the other. So prized was this fluency that Batlle had become something more than a client to J. Hill. She had also been working as a consultant to Las Tres Puertas, and the beans she approved personally were sold as "Aida Batlle Selection" — in a sense, she had inherited the J. Hill name. "To someone who's really paying attention," Sanneh wrote, "coffee is a form of communication — each cup, even a bad one, tells the story of how it got that way."

Before he left, Sanneh toured the rest of the compound at Las Tres Puertas. He walked through a formal rose garden outside the main office and climbed the steps to the old white house. He went inside and up to the second floor, where the master bedroom was dark and cool against the blazing day. Sanneh stepped out onto the balcony off the bedroom, overlooking the vast patios where, for more than a century, drying coffee beans had been raked and turned under the white sun in preparation for sorting, cleaning, bagging, and shipment. To the edge of the balcony someone had affixed "rather ominously . . . an antiquated spotlight and loudspeaker."[33] But over these instruments Sanneh's eye did not linger as it had over the coffee grinder and espresso machine, for they seemed to be relics from another time. The war was over. Things had changed. "We needed to differentiate, to construct a story around our coffee," James Hill's great-grandson Diego Llach explained in 2005. "We have learned to see the farm as a living entity, not just a production machine."[34] Looking out across the patios and up to the plantations on the volcano above, Sanneh could not see the deeper history of the thing he had come to Santa Ana to find — "a drink that hadn't entirely forgotten its past life as a fruit."[35]

More than two hundred years ago, around the turn of the nineteenth century, the past lives of things were at the heart of a question of great consequence. At that time sugar was the product most often used to think about how the world economy worked, and it was not difficult to know what it meant to be connected to distant places and people through sugar: it meant slavery. On the other hand, slavery itself was the subject of an intense debate that went to the very core of the question of what it meant to be human.

In 1791, London bookseller and printer William Fox worked out a new way to think about the relation between slavery and sugar. He wrote up a pamphlet and published it himself. "We have ascertained," Fox wrote, "by a course of experiments in cruelty, the least portion of nourishment requisite to enable man to linger a few years in misery; the greatest quantity of labor which, in such a situation, the extreme of punishment can extort; and the utmost degree of pain, labor, and hunger united, that the human frame can endure." Fox's pamphlet was titled *An Address to the People of Great Britain on the Utility of Refraining from the Use of West India Sugar and Rum.* As a good pamphlet should be, it was both reasonable and sensational.

The sensational part of its argument was that eating sugar was tantamount to cannibalism. On the reasonable side, Fox had done the calculations: "So necessarily connected are our consumption of the commodity, and the misery resulting from it, that in every pound of sugar used, (the produce of slaves imported from Africa) we may be considered as consuming two ounces of human flesh." A family accustomed to eating five pounds of sugar a week could save the life of one "person called a slave" by giving up sugar for twenty-one months.[36]

Fox was not the only one thinking about sugar as converted human flesh.[37] He cited a French writer who claimed that " 'he cannot look on a piece of sugar, without conceiving it stained with spots of human blood:' and Dr. Franklin . . . adds, that had he taken in all the consequences, 'he might have seen the sugar not merely spotted but dyed scarlet in grain.' " As plantation slavery transformed human lives into sugar, it was easy to imagine a quantum of blood moving through the soil into the cane, through the refinery, across the ocean, and into the mouths of sugar eaters. Fox's argument shifted the problem of slavery beyond racial difference, emphasizing instead the intimate economic and physiological relation between production and consumption. "If we purchase the commodity we participate in the crime," Fox concluded, arguing that the "utility" of not eating sugar — of not participating in the violent transformation of human beings into a commodity — had to be figured against the sweetness of the product itself.[38] His pamphlet went through twenty-six editions in Great Britain and the United States in 1791 and 1792, a quarter million copies in all, making it the most popular pamphlet of the age, ahead of Thomas Paine's *Rights of Man*.[39] Assessing the importance of Fox's work, the pioneering anthropologist of food and labor Sidney Mintz wrote that "the end of the [slave] trade in Britain came soon after."[40]

In one way, the global triumph of emancipation in the second half of the nineteenth century made it harder to see "the relationship between commodity and person," as Mintz described the deeper theme of his 1985 book on "the English connection between sugar production and sugar consumption," *Sweetness and Power*.[41] The form of capitalism that emerged from the end of chattel slavery was based on both rude and technical ways of forcing people to work voluntarily to meet their basic needs. The simultaneous redefinition of the human being as an energy-based mechanism both authorized and sharpened wage labor's characteristic forms of coercion and control. Energy made work look like the natural,

572

inevitable function of the healthy human body, providing a universal answer to the question that confronted would-be planters and employers everywhere: What makes people work? As systems of production, exchange, and consumption were reorganized around the idea of energy — from the plantations and mills of the Santa Ana Volcano to the banks, factories, and kitchens of the United States and beyond — this question, once fundamental to important debates about economics, politics, and the good society, was pushed to the side.

Over the same time, coffee has replaced sugar as the commodity most often used to think about how the world economy works, about connections between consumers and producers, about economic fairness, equality, and justice. Like sugar, coffee comes from the work of poorer, darker-skinned people, Africans, Latin Americans, and Asians, on plantations in the global tropics, and it fuels the work of richer, lighter-skinned people, Europeans and Americans, in factories and offices far away. But while sugar's appeal was so elemental as to be almost instinctive to any creature, human or otherwise, raised on sweet milk, coffee's introduction into the West was greeted with disgust and suspicion, not least because its effects confounded existing concepts of the body.[42] The rise of coffee as a mass beverage and unrivaled work drug in the modern United States went hand in hand not only with the disruption of circadian and customary patterns of work and rest that followed industrialization, but also with the parallel redefinition of the human being around the idea of energy. Energy was flexible enough to accommodate lingering ambiguities about coffee's effects in the body — and it also obstructed the connection between producers and consumers. As the energy harnessed in coffee production was differentiated and isolated from the energy acquired in coffee consumption, coffee drinkers were separated from coffee workers by the thing that connects them. In this light, coffee came to appear as a godsend for those with no choice but to make themselves work.

It could have been otherwise. The idea of energy was a concept of connection that made it possible to establish the relationship between one person's work and another's in a newly direct way. Yet almost as soon as this possibility was raised, the calculations were deemed too complex, and it was abandoned. There was not enough to be gained — or there was too much to be lost — by evaluating things in terms of what it took to make them, rather than what could be taken from them.

As a result, there is a dark territory, still uncrossed, in the middle of the modern world. We have no shared idea of what it means to be connected to faraway people and places through things. We have no common language for talking about the world in terms of the lives ours depend on.

So it is possible to pick up a bag of coffee that depicts a planter's fantasy world, presenting itself to the coffee drinker in the manner of a land title: the name of the plantation, the owner's name, the plot's location, its elevation, its distinguishing features — as if the coffee in the bag were a simple outgrowth of that place, outside history and free of the problem of how to make people work, and therefore free to claim as its own essence the flavors and sweetness of the berries, tomatoes, cacao, stone fruit, and all the wild abundance rooted out long ago in order to make people work to produce it.

Yet people who work coffee are hardly invisible to those who drink it. For at least a century, coffee workers have been depicted in news reports, advertisements, and popular culture in the United States, often specifically to show that their lives are very different from those of coffee drinkers. On many occasions the lives of coffee workers have been the subject of concern at the highest levels of policy-making and international governance. Yet in the absence of the deeper question of what makes people work, people who work coffee have been ultimately seen by coffee drinkers as planters would wish them to be seen — as if working coffee were their fate and identity, as if they were in fact "workpeople" who might hope for and receive, at best, a better wage.

"Certified ethical" coffees, far and away the leading fair-trade product, have not helped in this regard. Created after World War II by a Mennonite missionary who wanted to help poor Puerto Rican women sell their needlework, fair trade came into the retail mainstream through Central American coffee in the 1980s. During its covert war against the Sandinistas, the Reagan administration imposed an economic embargo on Nicaragua, blocking the country's products, including coffee, from entering the United States. Importers sympathetic to the Sandinistas found a loophole: if coffee from Nicaragua was roasted in another country, it could be legally imported. The costs were too high for any conventional retailer, but church groups and specialty shops, including Equal Exchange, based in Cambridge, Massachusetts, sold "Café Nica," which had been roasted in Amsterdam, for seven dollars a pound, almost double the average retail price for coffee at that time. In 1987, its first full year in business, Equal Exchange sold 20,000 pounds and saw a demand for more.[43]

The following year, the ethical principles shaping such early "alternative trade organizations" were codified by a Dutch group selling coffee under the mark Max Havelaar — named for Multatuli's 1860 tale of starvation in Java — which became the first fair-trade label. The Max Havelaar certification guaranteed that the coffee had come from co-operatives paid a premium over the market price, with the idea that this would lead to better wages for people who worked to produce it. In 1997, Max Havelaar and other fair-trade labels in Europe and the United States established common guidelines for prices, wages, and certain social and environmental conditions. In 1999 the U.S. imported about two million pounds of fair-trade coffee. Now imports approach one hundred times that much, representing about 5 percent of the American consumer market. Fair trade's impact on consumer culture has been much greater, having worked the question of global economic ethics into the awareness of about half of the households in the United States.[44]

Fair trade has plenty of critics. Some contend that its definition of fairness, set by richer people for poorer people, is too tied to market prices to seriously address the "gross inequalities" of life expectancy, education, and health that divide coffee workers and drinkers.[45] Others argue that its emphasis on helping small farmers doesn't reach the poorest of the poor — coffee workers on large plantations — and that its guaranteed-price model doesn't value coffee for its cup qualities.[46] And others question who really benefits, given that fair-trade producers earn only about one-tenth of the final retail price of their coffee, hardly enough to break the long-standing cycle of poverty, while big for-profit multinational corporations use fair-trade certifications to make themselves look like charities.[47]

Yet the ultimate critique of fair trade must be that its distillation of ethics to prices — its baseline concept of fairness as an amount of money — has obscured a more fundamental issue, and not only from coffee drinkers but also from those who work in the industry. Rick Peyser, for example, spent decades as an executive with Green Mountain Coffee, one of the world's largest buyers of fair-trade coffee, and also served on the board of directors of Fairtrade International, the world's largest ethical-trade certifier. Still, he was surprised when he began visiting coffee-producing regions, inspecting plantations, trees, and cherries to identify the best possible sources for the best possible cup of coffee, and he learned that the people working to produce the coffee he bought were chronically hungry year-round and actually starving during the months between the end of one coffee harvest and the beginning of another: what they called *los meses flacos,* "the thin months."[48]

Until recently coffee drinkers have paid little attention to the relationship between coffee production and hunger.[49] The largest study of "food insecurity" in the world's coffee districts to date, completed in 2005, focuses on El Salvador, Guatemala, Nicaragua, and Mexico, generally thought to be a more prosperous producing area than comparable regions in Africa and Asia. Among the nearly five hundred households surveyed, almost two-thirds struggled to meet their most basic food needs. Another study focusing specifically on the coffee districts of western El Salvador found chronic hunger in 97 percent of households.[50]

The problem of hunger is often described as impossibly complex, a matter of historical, market, and environmental forces much larger than any single household, plantation, or government.[51] Yet it is also as simple as a problem can be. Because the people who work coffee are hungry, they adopt vexed strategies of survival. When food is scarce, they eat less. When money is short, they buy smaller amounts of cheaper food. When money runs out, they go into debt to eat. When credit dries up, there is only work. To live is to work on whatever terms can be had. The problem is not that there is not enough work in coffee to get families through the thin months. The problem is that there is nothing but work in coffee. And so when working conditions on ethically certified plantations are revealed to be something other than what has been promised, worse than everyone knows they should be, working people have a simple explanation for why: "There's no food unless you earn it."[52] There is no principle more fundamental to the way the modern world works, and making it so has been war. This is the world the planters made.

People who live on the line between work and hunger often leave home in hope of making a better life elsewhere — just as James Hill did in 1889; just as many Salvadorans did after land privatization at the end of the nineteenth century, during the Bourbon coffee boom of the 1920s, after the massacre of 1932, during the civil war of the 1980s and 1990s; and just as many do today, displaced once more by violence and environmental change. Since the rise of coffee more than a hundred years ago, the alternatives for many people in El Salvador have been plantations, migration, or revolution — starve, toil, move, or fight.[53]

On the other hand, there are visions of a different future that would write this whole story in reverse, turning what is now coffee back into food. To end "hunger in the coffeelands," the Specialty Coffee Association of America proposes unmaking monocultures by planting fruit trees for shade above the coffee trees, and cultivating corn and beans in the soil below.[54] At the same time, poor and hungry people around the world have come together behind bolder proposals for food security and food sovereignty. Food security, as defined by the UN, "exists when all people, at all times, have physical, social, and economic access to sufficient, safe, and nutritious food which meets their dietary needs and food preferences for an active and healthy life."[55] Food sovereignty, a concept developed by small farmers themselves, goes further, calling not only for a human right to sufficient, varied, and healthy food, but also for the production and distribution of food to be governed locally by the people who eat it.[56] Both principles have begun to be translated into new, ethical certifications for coffee that honor instead of exploit basic human needs, and make eating the precondition of working rather than its contingent consequence.

There are two ways to think about food sovereignty. One is as a direct rebuke to the core order of the modern world, a way of plowing under the history of globalization, pulling up the root of the international coffee economy, cutting off the principal mechanism of long-distance connection between people who work coffee and people who drink coffee. But the other, more empathetic way, is to think of food sovereignty as a humane proposal for peace: picking wild fruit, tending tomatoes and blackberries, cultivating corn and beans, raising chickens, hunting and fishing, cooking with family, feeding children, sharing with neighbors, welcoming friends, eating anytime, and going back for more, again.

Many years after his kidnapping, Jaime Hill sat in his large and sunny office in San Salvador talking with a writer who was interested in the human consequences of globalization, especially its effects on the family. He was trying to describe how his kidnapping had freed him, so he told her the story of the family whose name he carried. It began when his grandfather James sailed from Manchester to El Salvador as a young man. Jaime Hill recounted how his grandfather had married into a coffee family, how he had "industrialized" Salvadoran coffee, how he sent his seven children to study in California, how the three boys had returned to help manage the plantations and the mill, and how they had later expanded the family business into banking and insurance and manufacturing. Jaime Hill said that his own father, Jaime, was "an extremely good man," though also "very authoritarian," who never asked his son, his namesake, who he was or what he wanted.

Jaime Hill explained that everything

changed when he was kidnapped. Once a price was affixed to his life and negotiations over the number began, he lost all sense of himself — he no longer knew who he was. He realized that he had made no decisions of his own, that his life had been controlled by his father. In contrast, his kidnappers were full of purpose. They "knew that they were doing something wonderful, they were fighting for social justice. . . . They had food, and they had shelter, they had medicine, and they had clothes." They had what they needed. Jaime Hill recalled how, during his months as a prisoner, he would have traded all his money and possessions to be with his family "in a very humble home." And when he understood that he wanted something that had no price, which he could not get by the means he was accustomed to, he discovered for the first time "what it really means to be alone." In his cell, he had no familiar resources at hand. He had to save himself with what he could muster. What kept him alive past the deadline that his kidnappers set for his death, Jaime Hill believed, was the humility he found in solitude.

When he was freed after four and a half months, Jaime Hill was a different person. His understanding of his place in the world had changed, but he struggled to make sense of it. For years afterward, he was "nobody" — not the person he had been in the past, but not entirely the person he had discovered himself to be, either. He hid from his life by drinking too much and feeling sorry for himself. Yet by degrees Jaime Hill began to understand that his problems were not his alone. They were the problems of his time and place, inseparable from the problems of El Salvador itself, and of his fellow Salvadorans.

Recognition steadied him. Jaime Hill built a clinic in San Salvador to treat addiction and post-traumatic stress caused by the civil war, and he brought his daughter Alexandra to work with him. He found that doing this work, going into businesses and schools and poor neighborhoods and talking about drugs and alcohol, about overcoming violence and suffering, and about how to develop self-esteem, "helping to do something in order for the people of El Salvador to be happy," had made him in turn "one of the happiest men that ever existed."[57] And as he sat in his office in San Salvador, telling his family's story so it could be written in a book alongside the stories of other families in the age of global connection, Jaime Hill felt at peace, and he wished the same for his country.

ACKNOWLEDGMENTS

Ten years ago, James Hill's great-grandson Diego Llach, a renowned coffee producer in his own right, was the first person to call this a book. "You're writing a book," he told me enthusiastically the minute we met in San Salvador. It wasn't a question. Then he invited me to Las Tres Puertas to look through his great-grandfather's papers.

I had traveled to El Salvador without knowing anyone there. I had no concrete idea of what I was looking for or how to find it. The only reason I didn't leave as empty-handed as I had come is that people helped me, even when they had little reason to do so.

Before my trip, Aldo Lauría-Santiago and Héctor Lindo-Fuentes took the time to meet with me in New York, offering invaluable advice and introductions. Héctor asked me to contribute an article describing my research to the extraordinary online magazine *El Faro.* I wrote in English, he translated it into Spanish, and like that, thanks to him, I

585

was credible.

On my first full day in El Salvador, Federico Barillas and Johanna Butter de Barillas invited me to their home, served me coffee and pastries on the patio, told me about all the local plants, animals, sayings, and legends, and apparently decided that they would take care of me for the rest of my stay. They became true friends. So did Oscar Campos Lara, a tireless companion during endless mornings and afternoons in stifling and dusty archives, and, just as important, an intrepid lunch-hour explorer of coffee shops in the capital. Juan Francisco Aguilar took me to meet everyone I needed to know. Later, Guillermo Alvarez took me places on the Santa Ana Volcano that I could not have gone to on my own. And of course the Hill family, along with Mario Mendoza, the current director of J. Hill y Cía. and Las Tres Puertas, where I spent two extraordinary days, opened up the past.

My work in the United States has been equally favored by the kindness and generosity of others. During long research trips in San Francisco, James Everett Kochheiser of Otis McAllister introduced me to both the Tadich Grill and R&G. Herb Mills talked to me about the shipping business and waterfront work on a rainy Sunday morning in Oakland, and the way he pronounced the word "employers" helped me see the big questions in the whole thing. Harvey Schwartz's curiosity made me believe I was doing something worthwhile. Those trips were a perfect excuse to eat salt-and-pepper crab with Nick and Joy Ohler, who put me up, invited me to family dinners, and drove me around, too.

In Williamsburg, years ago, Bob Gross and Arthur Knight taught me how to be a student. In New York, Bill Crandall and Ken Baron showed me how to report, write, and edit. In Portland, Donna Cassidy, Joe Conforti, Kent Ryden, Ardis Cameron, and Richard Maiman gave me a chance to be a historian. And in Cambridge, Alex Keyssar, Jim Kloppenberg, Sven Beckert, Skip Gates, Jack Womack, and Walter Johnson challenged me to develop my own voice. Mae Ngai and Greg Grandin did extra duty, providing intellectual and professional support when I most needed it.

More recently, at the University of South Florida, Fraser Ottanelli, Julia Irwin, and Brian Connolly went out of their way to make me feel at home in Tampa. At the University of Toronto, Bob Gibbs convened a yearlong discussion about food that I was fortunate to join. Andrea Most, Bob Davidson, Amira Mittermaier, and Gabrielle Jackson kept the conversation lively, and Dan Bender was an exceptionally generous mentor.

Along the way, I have been sustained by friendships with Nick Bournakel, Bob Miller,

Adam Ewing, Brian Hochman, Adena Spingarn, Sam Howard, Jason Kozlowski, Paul Kramer, Andy Urban, Michelle Neely, David Singerman, and Eileen Corbeil. I wish I saw each one of them more often.

For early financial support, I am indebted to the Charles Warren Center for Studies in American History, the David Rockefeller Center for Latin American Studies, the Center for American Political Studies, and the Project on Justice, Welfare, and Economics, all at Harvard; the Jackman Humanities Institute of the University of Toronto; the Andrew W. Mellon Foundation; and the American Council of Learned Societies.

Audiences at Harvard, Roger Williams University, South Florida, Toronto, the University of California, Berkeley, Drexel University, the University of Chicago, New York University, the University of Cambridge, the University of Amsterdam, the Max Planck Institute for the History of Science, the Goodwin-Niering Center for the Environment at Connecticut College, and the Tepoztlán Institute for the Transnational History of the Americas offered important critiques, suggestions, and encouragement. Laura Correa Ochoa provided invaluable help with translations.

Deserving of special acknowledgment are staff archivists and librarians at the Baker Library of Harvard Business School; the

Archives Center of the Smithsonian Institution's National Museum of American History; the U.S. National Archives and Records Administration in College Park, Maryland, and San Bruno, California; the North Baker Research Library of the California Historical Society; the Daniel E. Koshland San Francisco History Center of the San Francisco Public Library; the Bancroft Library of the University of California; the Executive Offices of the International Longshore and Warehouse Union; El Salvador's Archivo General de la Nación; the Rockland (Maine) Historical Society; the British National Archives; the Manchester (UK) Central Library; the Special Collections division of the Charles E. Young Research Library of the University of California, Los Angeles; the Abplanalp Library of the University of New England; and the Mudd Manuscript Library of Princeton University.

Scott Moyers and Ann Godoff at Penguin Press gave me the opportunity to learn how to write a book. They told me when my first attempts fell short, didn't balk when I took twice as long as planned to finally get there, and have been wise advisors since. It has been my good fortune and a true pleasure to work closely with Christopher Richards, whose thoughtful edits, critical insights, and good humor have added so much. Copy editor Annie Gottlieb and production editor Anna

Jardine saved me from a thousand errors and made strong contributions of their own. Simon Winder at Penguin Press UK came along with fresh eyes and another set of sharp suggestions just in time. Wendy Strothman and Lauren MacLeod have been staunch representatives throughout.

This book is dedicated to my family. My brothers Michael and Christo, my sister-in-law Jenn, my nieces Eleanor and Emmeline have offered love, forgiveness, and humor. All along, Samantha Seneviratne has been a source of immeasurable inspiration, love, and joy. I am so pleased that there is so much of her in our son, Arthur. What a blessing that he has grandparents who care for him as Upali and Suneetha Seneviratne do.

More than anyone else, my parents, John Sedgewick and Deborah Keefe, are the reason I was able to write this book. Growing up, I watched my father advocate for working people, and his tenacious and empathetic attention to labor shaped the subjects I chose to study. Somehow, my mother read my dissertation, and she saw a story in it that no one else had seen. As I struggled to bring that story out, I asked for their help again and again, and they gave it. Even when I thought I had failed, I kept trying because they helped me. And now the worst moments, low as they were, are insignificant compared with this chance to write one more sentence to tell them how lucky and proud I am to be their son.

NOTES

Prologue: One Hundred Years of Coffee

1. Except where otherwise noted, the account of the kidnapping is based on Marvin Galeas, *El oligarca rebelde: Mitos y verdades sobre las 14 familias: La oligarquía* (San Salvador: El Salvador Ebooks, 2015).
2. Henry E. Catto Jr., *Ambassadors at Sea: The High and Low Adventures of a Diplomat* (Austin: University of Texas Press, 2010), 60.
3. Héctor Lindo-Fuentes, *Weak Foundations: The Political Economy of El Salvador in the Nineteenth Century, 1821–1898* (Berkeley: University of California Press, 1991), 1–2.
4. Quoted in E. Bradford Burns, "The Modernization of Underdevelopment: El Salvador, 1858–1931," *Journal of Developing Areas* 18, no. 3 (April 1984), 293.
5. *Pictures of Travel in Far-Off Lands: Central America* (London: T. Nelson and Sons, 1871), 92.

6. E. G. Squier, *The States of Central America* (New York: Harper & Brothers, 1858), 288–90.

7. Squier, *States of Central America,* 314–15.

8. Lindo-Fuentes, *Weak Foundations,* 3.

9. Regina Marchi, "Día de los Muertos, Migration, and Transformation to the United States," in *Celebrating Latino Folklore,* vol. 1, ed. María Herrera-Sobek (Santa Barbara, CA: ABC-Clio, 2012), 414–15.

10. Quoted in W. P. Lawson, "Along the Romantic Coffee Trail to Salvador," *The Spice Mill,* November 1928, 1976–82.

11. United Nations Food and Agriculture Organization, *Coffee in Latin America: Productivity Problems and Future Prospects* (New York: United Nations and FAO, 1958).

12. Ethan B. Kapstein, *Seeds of Stability: Land Reform and U.S. Foreign Policy* (New York: Cambridge University Press, 2017), 188; and William H. Durham, *Scarcity and Survival in Central America: The Ecological Origins of the Soccer War* (Stanford, CA: Stanford University Press, 1979), 7.

13. Interview with Jaime Hill, Perdita Huston Papers [PHP], Series 7, Box 7.3, Unedited Interview Transcripts, El Salvador (Tapes 11–22), Maine Women Writers Collection, University of New England, Portland, Maine.

14. Interview with Jaime Hill, PHP.
15. Quoted in Galeas, *Oligarca rebelde;* for "Coffeeland," see *Behind the Cup* (film, 1938), Box 6, Hills Bros. Coffee, Inc., Records, Archives Center, National Museum of American History, Smithsonian Institution, Washington, DC.
16. Eugene Cunningham, *Gypsying Through Central America* (London: T. Fisher Unwin, 1922), 191–92.
17. Arthur Ruhl, *The Central Americans: Adventures and Impressions Between Mexico and Panama* (New York: Charles Scribner's Sons, 1928), 202.
18. Descriptions of Las Tres Puertas from W. P. Lawson, "Along the Romantic Coffee Trail to Salvador," *The Spice Mill,* November 1928, 1976–82; "coffee king": *The Spice Mill,* December 1929, 2174.
19. For example, Cyrus Townsend Brady, *The Corner in Coffee* (New York: G. W. Dillingham, 1904).
20. Ruhl, *Central Americans,* 190.
21. Peter Radford, "Arthur Brown Ruhl, Rowing and Track Athletics, 1905," Athlos .com, www.athletics-archive.com/books/rowingandtrackathleticsextract.htm.
22. Ruhl, *Central Americans,* 3–5, 19–25, 178–206.
23. Steven C. Topik and Allen Wells, "Commodity Chains in a Global Economy," in *A*

World Connecting: 1870–1945, ed. Emily S. Rosenberg (Cambridge, MA: Belknap Press, 2012), 592; "Global, *adj.,* " *Oxford English Dictionary,* OED.com.

24. Emily S. Rosenberg, "Introduction," in Rosenberg, *World Connecting,* 3; "Interconnect, *v.,* " *Oxford English Dictionary,* OED.com.

25. Jürgen Osterhammel, *The Transformation of the World: A Global History of the Nineteenth Century,* trans. Patrick Camiller (Princeton, NJ: Princeton University Press, 2014), xv.

26. Eugene Anderson, cited in David T. Courtwright, *Forces of Habit: Drugs and the Making of the Modern World* (Cambridge, MA: Harvard University Press, 2001), 19.

27. Benoit Daviron and Stefano Ponte, *The Coffee Paradox: Global Markets, Commodity Trade and the Elusive Promise of Development* (London: Zed Books, 2005), xvi; United Nations Food and Agriculture Organization, *Coffee 2015,* FAO Statistical Pocketbook, www.fao.org/3/a-i4985e.pdf.

28. "Our Collective Coffee Craze Appears to Be Good for Us," Harvard T.H. Chan School of Public Health News, www.hsph.harvard.edu/news/hsph-in-the-news/coffee-health-benefits/.

29. *Fair Trade USA 2016 Almanac,* https://www.fairtradecertified.org/sites/default/

files/filemanager/documents/FTUSA_MAN
_Almanac2016_EN.pdf.

30. For example, Jeanette M. Fregulia, *A Rich and Tantalizing Brew: A History of How Coffee Connected the World* (Little Rock: University of Arkansas Press, 2019); Catherine M. Tucker, *Coffee Culture: Local Experiences, Global Connections* (New York: Routledge, 2010).

31. Rosenberg, *World Connecting.*

32. Steven C. Topik and Allen Wells, "Introduction: Latin America's Response to International Markets During the Export Boom," in *The Second Conquest of Latin America: Coffee, Henequen, and Oil During the Export Boom, 1850–1930,* ed. Topik and Wells (Austin: University of Texas Press, 1998), 3.

33. Deepak Nayyar, *The South in the World Economy: Past, Present and Future* (New York: United Nations Development Programme, Human Development Report Office, 2013), 1.

34. Topik and Wells, "Commodity Chains," 605.

35. John M. Talbot, *Grounds for Agreement: The Political Economy of the Coffee Commodity Chain* (Lanham, MD: Rowman & Littlefield, 2004), 2.

36. *Coffee 2015,* FAO Statistical Pocketbook; retail sales in the U.S. alone reached nearly

$50 billion in 2018: "The Retail Market for Coffee Industry in the U.S.," *IbisWorld,* Industry Market Research Report, August 2018, www.ibisworld.com/industry-trends/specialized-market-research-reports/retail-market-reports/the-retail-market-for-coffee.html.

Chapter 1. The Perfect Symbol of Islam

1. Quoted in Markman Ellis, *The Coffee-House: A Cultural History* (London: Weidenfeld & Nicolson, 2004), 12–13.
2. Michel Tuchscherer, "Coffee in the Red Sea Area from the Sixteenth to the Nineteenth Century," in *The Global Coffee Economy in Africa, Asia, and Latin America, 1500–1989,* ed. William Gervase Clarence-Smith and Steven Topik (New York: Cambridge University Press, 2003), 51.
3. Ellis, *The Coffee-House,* 13.
4. Kenneth Pomeranz and Steven Topik, *The World That Trade Created: Society, Culture, and the World Economy, 1400 to the Present,* 3rd ed. (Armonk, NY: M. E. Sharpe, 2013), 95.
5. Ellis, *The Coffee-House,* 15.
6. Ellis, 16–21.
7. Ellis, 1–11.
8. Quoted in William H. Ukers, *All About Coffee* (New York: Tea and Coffee Trade Journal Company, 1922), 38; and Ellis, *The*

Coffee-House, 22.

9. Ellis, *The Coffee-House,* 23.

10. Lorraine Boissoneault, "How Coffee, Chocolate and Tea Overturned a 1,500-Year-Old Medical Mindset," Smithsonian .com, May 17, 2017, https://www .smithsonianmag.com/history/how-coffee -chocolate-and-tea-overturned-1500-year -old-medical-mindset-180963339/.

11. Brian Cowan, *The Social Life of Coffee: The Emergence of the British Coffeehouse* (New Haven: Yale University Press, 2005), 47–53.

12. Cowan, 31.

13. As reported by John Houghton, a Fellow of the Royal Society, in his "Discourse of Coffee," *Philosophical Transactions of the Royal Society* 21, no. 256 (September 1699): 311–17; recounted in Ellis, *The Coffee-House,* 26–41.

14. Cowan, *Social Life,* 49; Ellis, *The Coffee-House,* 34–36.

15. For a searchable version, see *The Diary of Samuel Pepys,* www.pepysdiary.com.

16. Jürgen Habermas, *The Structural Transformation of the Public Sphere: An Inquiry into a Category of Bourgeois Society,* trans. Thomas Burger with Frederick Lawrence (Cambridge, MA: MIT Press, 1989), 32–33.

17. Cowan, *Social Life,* 215.

18. Quoted in Habermas, *Public Sphere,* 59.
19. Cowan, *Social Life,* 196–99.
20. Cowan, 44–46.
21. Houghton, "Discourse of Coffee."
22. Cowan, *Social Life,* 27.
23. Ellis, *The Coffee-House,* 123–25.
24. Pomeranz and Topik, *The World That Trade Created,* 90.

Chapter 2. Cottonopolis

1. Eric J. Hobsbawm, *The Age of Revolution: 1789–1848* (1962; reprint, New York: Vintage, 1996), 29.
2. Kimball quoted in Sven Beckert, *Empire of Cotton: A Global History* (New York: Alfred A. Knopf, 2014), 81.
3. Robert H. Kargon, *Science in Victorian Manchester: Enterprise and Expertise* (Baltimore: Johns Hopkins University Press, 1977; reprint, New York: Routledge, 2017), 2.
4. Carlyle quoted in Allen MacDuffie, *Victorian Literature, Energy, and the Ecological Imagination* (New York: Cambridge University Press, 2014), 44.
5. Alexis de Tocqueville, *Journeys to England and Ireland,* trans. George Lawrence and K. P. Mayer, ed. J. P. Mayer (1979; reprint, New Brunswick, NJ: Transaction, 1988; New York: Routledge, 2017), 107–8.
6. Richard D. Altick, *Victorian People and*

Ideas: A Companion for the Modern Reader of Victorian Literature (New York: W. W. Norton, 1973), 44.

7. Tocqueville, *Journeys*, 107–8.

8. Stephen Mosley, *The Chimney of the World: A History of Smoke and Pollution in Victorian and Edwardian Manchester* (Cambridge, UK: White Horse Press, 2001; reprint, New York: Routledge, 2008); Robert Angus Smith, *Air and Rain: The Beginnings of a Chemical Climatology* (London: Longmans, Green, 1872), vii.

9. "Manchester and Her Ship Canal," *Journal of the Manchester Geographical Society* 2, no. 1–3 (1886), 60–78; Topik and Wells, "Commodity Chains," 613.

10. For example, Beckert, *Empire of Cotton*, ix–xi.

11. Rosenberg, *World Connecting*.

12. Beckert, *Empire of Cotton*, 178–79.

13. Léon Faucher quoted in Kargon, *Science in Victorian Manchester*, 2.

14. Eric J. Hobsbawm, *Industry and Empire: From 1750 to the Present Day*, rev. updated ed. (New York: New Press, 1999), 65.

15. Friedrich Engels, *The Condition of the Working Class in England in 1844, with Preface Written in 1892*, trans. Florence Kelley Wischnewetzky (London: Swan Sonnenschein, 1892), 48–52.

16. James Hill and Alice Greenway, April 26,

1869, Manchester, England, Marriages and Banns, 1754–1930, Manchester Central Library, Manchester, UK.

17. *Slater's Directory of Manchester and Salford,* 1869, Manchester Central Library, Manchester, UK.

18. Altick, *Victorian People and Ideas,* 41–46.

19. Mary Turner, "A History of Collyhurst, Manchester, to 1900," submitted for a Certificate of Extra-Mural Education, Manchester University, May 1975, Manchester Central Library, Manchester, UK.

20. England Census, 1871 and 1881, Lancashire, Manchester, St. George, Dist. 7; *Slater's Directory,* 1869–1889, Manchester Central Library, Manchester, UK.

21. Hugh D. Hindman, ed., *The World of Child Labor: An Historical and Regional Survey* (Armonk, NY: M. E. Sharpe, 2009; New York: Routledge, 2014), 50.

22. School Diary, St. George's Infants, 1875, Manchester Central Library, Manchester, UK.

23. St. George's Infants School Report of the Diocesan Inspector, 1875, Manchester Central Library, Manchester, UK.

24. James Walvin, *A Child's World: A Social History of English Childhood, 1800–1914* (New York: Penguin, 1982), 77.

25. Michael Sanderson, *Education, Economic Change and Society in England, 1780–1870*

(London: Macmillan, 1991; 2nd ed., New York: Cambridge University Press, 1995), 62–63.

26. Interview with Jaime Hill, Perdita Huston Papers.

27. Galeas, *Oligarca rebelde.*

28. T. D. Olverson, *Women Writers and the Dark Side of Late-Victorian Hellenism* (New York: Palgrave Macmillan, 2009), 1–2.

29. Olverson, *Women Writers and the Dark Side,* 3.

30. Galeas, *Oligarca rebelde.*

31. Quoted in Eduardo Galeano, *Open Veins of Latin America: Five Centuries of the Pillage of a Continent,* trans. Cedric Belfrage (New York: Monthly Review Press, 1973; 25th anniv. ed., 1997), 173.

32. Walvin, *Child's World,* 130–33.

33. Robert Louis Stevenson, *Treasure Island* (Boston: Roberts Brothers, 1884), 33, 52.

34. Walvin, *Child's World.*

35. Stevenson, *Treasure Island,* 1.

36. Quoted in Cannon Schmitt, *Darwin and the Memory of the Human: Evolution, Savages, and South America* (New York: Cambridge University Press, 2009), 27.

37. See Robert D. Aguirre, *Informal Empire: Mexico and Central America in Victorian Culture* (Minneapolis: University of Minnesota Press, 2005), 103–34.

38. Henry Morley, "Our Phantom Ship:

Central America," *Household Words* 2, no. 48 (February 22, 1851): 516–22.

39. John L. Stephens, *Incidents of Travel in Central America, Chiapas, and Yucatan,* vol. 2 (London: John Murray, 1841), 78, 48; "best-selling": Aguirre, *Informal Empire,* 66.

40. Galeas, *Oligarca rebelde.*

41. Peter K. Andersson, *Streetlife in Late Victorian London: The Constable and the Crowds* (New York: Palgrave Macmillan, 2013), 61.

42. Alex Murray, " 'The London Sunday Faded Slow': Time to Spend in the Victorian City," in *The Oxford Handbook of Victorian Literary Culture,* ed. Juliet John (New York: Oxford University Press, 2016), 319–20; Andrew Whitehead, "Red London: Radicals and Socialists in Late-Victorian Clerkenwell," *Socialist History* 18 (2000), 1–31.

43. F. W. Farrar, review of *The Nether World, Contemporary Review,* September 1889, 370–71.

44. George Gissing, *The Nether World* (New York: Harper & Brothers, 1889), 14–15.

45. Galeas, *Oligarca rebelde.*

Chapter 3. A State of Constant Eruption

1. "Sights in Central America," *New York Times,* December 16, 1888, 13.

2. Leslie Bethell, "Britain and Latin American

in Historical Perspective," in *Britain and Latin America: A Changing Relationship,* ed. Victor Bulmer-Thomas (New York: Cambridge University Press, 1989), 1.

3. Steven C. Topik and Allen Wells, "Introduction: Latin America's Response to International Markets During the Export Boom," in Topik and Wells, *Second Conquest of Latin America,* 1.

4. Helen J. Sanborn, *A Winter in Central America and Mexico* (Boston: Lee and Shepard, 1886), 224–25.

5. Sanborn, *Winter in Central America,* 225–26, 228.

6. *Mexico,* prepared by Arthur W. Fergusson, Bulletin no. 9 of the Bureau of the American Republics (Washington, DC: Government Printing Office, 1891), 324.

7. Sanborn, *Winter in Central America,* 228–38.

8. Galeas, *Oligarca rebelde.*

9. "A Trip in San Salvador," *New York Times,* July 6, 1889, 2; Audley Gosling, "Central America and Its Resources," *North American Review* 162, no. 470 (January 1896), 101.

10. "Birth of a Volcano," *San Francisco Chronicle,* June 11, 1889, 6.

11. Alfred Russel Wallace, *The Malay Archipelago: The Land of the Orangu-tan and the Bird of Paradise,* 4th ed. (London: Macmillan, 1872), 286–87.

12. John Wesley Judd, *Volcanoes: What They Are and What They Teach* (New York: D. Appleton, 1881), 8.

13. William Eleroy Curtis, The *Capitals of Spanish America* (New York: Harper & Brothers, 1888), 188.

14. George Ripley and Charles Anderson Dana, eds., *The American Cyclopaedia: A Popular Dictionary of General Knowledge,* vol. 9 (New York: D. Appleton, 1881), 478.

15. E. G. Squier, *Notes on Central America* (New York: Harper & Brothers, 1855), 312.

16. M. M. de Montessus, "Earthquakes in Central America," *Popular Science Monthly* 28 (April 1886), 819.

17. Squier, *Notes on Central America,* 313.

18. Frederick Palmer, *Central America and Its Problems* (New York: Moffat, Yard, 1910), 113.

19. Bureau of American Republics, *Coffee in America: Methods of Production and Facilities for Successful Cultivation in Mexico, the Central American States, Brazil and Other South American Countries, and the West Indies* (Washington, DC: Bureau of the American Republics, 1893), 6.

20. Steven Topik and William Gervase Clarence-Smith, "Introduction: Coffee and Global Development," in Clarence-Smith and Topik, *The Global Coffee Economy.*

21. Many books review coffee's global disper-

sal. See for example Antony Wild, *Coffee: A Dark History* (New York: W. W. Norton, 2004); Mark Pendergrast, *Uncommon Grounds: The History of Coffee and How It Transformed the World,* rev. ed. (New York: Basic Books, 2010); and Steven Topik, "The Integration of the World Coffee Market," in Clarence-Smith and Topik, *The Global Coffee Economy,* 21–49, which argues for a "messier" story on the margins.

22. Warren Dean, *With Broadax and Firebrand: The Destruction of the Brazilian Atlantic Forest* (Berkeley: University of California Press, 1995), 179.

23. Curtis, *Capitals of Spanish America,* 176.

24. David Browning, *El Salvador: Landscape and Society* (New York: Clarendon / Oxford University Press, 1971), 149.

25. Browning, *El Salvador,* 163–65.

26. Quoted in Lindo-Fuentes, *Weak Foundations,* 134.

27. Lindo-Fuentes, 116.

28. Browning, *El Salvador,* 155; Lindo-Fuentes, *Weak Foundations,* 119.

29. Lindo-Fuentes, *Weak Foundations,* 117–19.

30. C. F. S. Cardoso, "Historia económica del café en Centroamérica (siglo XIX)," *Estudios Sociales Centroamericanos* 4, no. 10 (January 1975): 9–55.

31. Lindo-Fuentes, *Weak Foundations,* 125–31.

32. Browning, *El Salvador,* 157.

33. Browning, 179.

34. Aldo Lauria-Santiago, *An Agrarian Republic: Commercial Agriculture and the Politics of Peasant Communities in El Salvador, 1823–1914* (Pittsburgh: University of Pittsburgh Press, 1999), 136.

35. Quoted in Lauria-Santiago, *Agrarian Republic,* 95.

36. Browning, *El Salvador,* 158; Barrios quoted in Burns, "Modernization of Underdevelopment," 299.

37. For example, Lindo-Fuentes, *Weak Foundations,* 90, 135.

38. Cardoso, "Historia económica del café."

39. Lindo-Fuentes, *Weak Foundations,* 145, 135.

40. Quoted in Browning, *El Salvador,* 173.

41. Browning, 180, 203.

42. Quoted in Browning, 173.

43. Quoted in Lindo-Fuentes, *Weak Foundations,* 135.

44. Lindo-Fuentes, 135.

45. Lindo-Fuentes, 147.

46. Lauria-Santiago, *Agrarian Republic,* 163–221.

47. For a discussion of varying estimates, see Lindo-Fuentes, *Weak Foundations,* 128–31.

48. Quoted in Browning, *El Salvador,* 158.

49. Everett Alan Wilson, "The Crisis of National Integration in El Salvador, 1919–1935" (Ph.D. diss., Stanford University, 1969), 29.

50. Nora Hamilton and Norma Stoltz Chinchilla, "Central American Migration: A Framework for Analysis," in *Challenging Fronteras: Structuring Latina and Latino Lives in the U. S.,* ed. Mary Romero et al. (New York: Routledge, 1997), 84.

51. Browning, *El Salvador,* 216–18; also Rafael Menjívar Larín, *Acumulación originaria y desarrollo del capitalismo en El Salvador* (San José, Costa Rica: EDUCA, 1980).

52. Browning, *El Salvador,* 217.

53. Ana Patricia Alvarenga, "Reshaping the Ethics of Power: A History of Violence in Western Rural El Salvador, 1880–1932" (Ph.D. diss., University of Michigan, Ann Arbor, 1994), 182–84.

54. Browning, *El Salvador,* 217.

55. Robert G. Williams, *States and Social Evolution: Coffee and the Rise of National Governments in Central America* (Chapel Hill: University of North Carolina Press, 1994), 75.

56. Browning, *El Salvador,* 218.

57. Lauria-Santiago, *Agrarian Republic,* 134; Browning, *El Salvador,* 159.

58. Browning, 159.

59. Victor Bulmer Thomas, *The Political*

Economy of Central America Since 1920 (Cambridge: Cambridge University Press, 1987), 4.

60. Lauria-Santiago, *Agrarian Republic,* 215–18.

61. Williams, *States and Social Evolution,* 75.

62. Lindo-Fuentes, *Weak Foundations,* 135–36.

63. Report of J. Maurice Duke to U.S. Department of State, November 15, 1885, Dispatches from U.S. Consuls in San Salvador, RG 84.4, U.S. National Archives and Records Administration, College Park, MD.

64. Lauria-Santiago, *Agrarian Republic,* 165–66, 150.

65. "A Trip in San Salvador," 2.

Chapter 4. Eel

1. L. E. Elliot, *Central America: New Paths in Ancient Lands* (London: Methuen, 1924; New York: Dodd, Mead, 1925), 114–15.

2. "A Trip in San Salvador," *New York Times,* July 6, 1889, 2.

3. "A Trip in San Salvador," 2.

4. Galeas, *Oligarca rebelde.*

5. Derek Kerr, "The Role of the Coffee Industry in the History of El Salvador, 1840–1906" (master's thesis, University of Calgary, April 1977), 96–97; Stephen J. Nicholas, "The Overseas Marketing Perfor-

mance of British Industry, 1870–1914,"
Economic History Review, 2nd ser., 37, no.
4 (November 1984): 489–506; Eugene W.
Ridings, "Foreign Predominance Among
Overseas Traders in Nineteenth-Century
Latin America," *Latin American Research
Review* 20, no. 2 (1985): 3–27.
6. A. J. Marrison, "Great Britain and Her
Rivals in the Latin American Cotton Piece
Goods Market, 1880–1914," in *Great Britain
and Her World, 1750–1914: Essays in Honour of W. O. Henderson,* ed. Barrie M.
Ratcliffe (Manchester, UK: Manchester
University Press), 316.
7. W. H. Zimmern, "Lancashire and Latin
America," *Geography* 28, no. 2 (June 1943):
53.
8. Nicholas, "Overseas Marketing Performance," 493.
9. J. W. Boddam Whetham, *Across Central
America* (London: Hurst and Blackett,
1877), 210–11.
10. Brian William Clapp, *John Owens, Manchester Merchant* (Manchester, UK: Manchester University Press, 1965), 73.
11. Audley Gosling, "Central America and
Its Resources," *North American Review* 162,
no. 470 (January 1896): 102.
12. Notes of July 5, 1889, and July 12, 1889,
and related letters of Charles Sawyer,
Consular Records of Salvador, 1889, The

National Archives, Kew, Richmond, UK.

13. "Central American Advance," *New York Times,* December 28, 1889, 5.

14. Stanley J. Stein, *Vassouras: A Brazilian Coffee County, 1850–1900: The Roles of Planter and Slave in a Plantation Society* (Princeton, NJ: Princeton University Press, 1985), 230.

15. See Adam Hochschild, *Bury the Chains: Profits and Rebels in the Fight to Free an Empire's Slaves* (New York: Houghton Mifflin, 2005).

16. Stein, *Vassouras,* 294.

17. Warren Dean, *Rio Claro: A Brazilian Plantation System, 1820–1920* (Stanford, CA: Stanford University Press, 1976), 126.

18. Dean, *Rio Claro,* 142.

19. Dean, *Rio Claro,* 88–123.

20. For a survey, see Williams, *States and Social Evolution.*

21. Stein, *Vassouras,* 278.

22. Mario Samper and Radin Fernando, "Historical Statistics of Coffee Production and Trade from 1700 to 1960," in Clarence-Smith and Topik, *The Global Coffee Economy,* 422.

23. M. R. Fernando, "Coffee Cultivation in Java, 1830–1917," in Clarence-Smith and Topik, *The Global Coffee Economy,* 162.

24. Samper and Fernando, "Historical Statistics," 418, 451.

25. "Society in San Salvador," *New York Times,* November 3, 1889, 17.
26. Galeas, *Oligarca rebelde.*
27. "A Trip in San Salvador," 2.
28. "Society in San Salvador."
29. J. H. Vinter to Messrs Otis, McAllister & Co., March 21, 1904, uncollected papers of Otis McAllister, San Francisco [OMC].
30. "El Salvador Coffee Firm Observes 50th Anniversary," *Tea and Coffee Trade Journal,* November 1938, 42.
31. Vinter to Otis, McAllister & Co., March 21, 1904, OMC.
32. Galeas, *Oligarca rebelde.*
33. Vinter to Otis, McAllister & Co., March 14, 1904, OMC.
34. Williams, *States and Social Evolution,* 207; Kerr, "Role of the Coffee Industry," 94–104; D. B. Rae, "So the Ezetas Fell: The Last Upheaval in San Salvador," *San Francisco Chronicle,* July 29, 1894, 10.
35. Lauria-Santiago, *Agrarian Republic,* 126–27.
36. Kerr, "Role of the Coffee Industry," 94–104.
37. James Hill to "Jessie" [K. B. Crewe], March 11, 1949, uncollected papers of J. Hill y Cía., Las Tres Puertas, Santa Ana, El Salvador.

Chapter 5. The Hills Brothers

1. Roger L. Grindle, *Quarry and Kiln: The Story of Maine's Lime Industry* (Rockland, ME: Courier-Gazette, 1971).
2. Pendergrast, *Uncommon Grounds,* 117.
3. John Adams quoted in Steven C. Topik and Michelle Craig MacDonald, "Why Americans Drink Coffee: The Boston Tea Party or Brazilian Slavery?," in *Coffee: A Comprehensive Guide to the Bean, the Beverage, and the Industry,* ed. Robert W. Thurston et al. (Lanham, MD: Rowman & Littlefield, 2013), 236; John Adams to Abigail Adams, August 11, 1777, *Adams Papers Digital Edition,* Adams Family Correspondence, vol. 2, www.masshist.org/publications/apde2/view?id=ADMS-04-02-02-0245.
4. Michelle Craig MacDonald, "The Chance of the Moment, Coffee and the New West Indies Commodities Trade," *William and Mary Quarterly,* 3rd ser., 62, no. 3 (July 2005): 441.
5. Jefferson quoted in Topik and MacDonald, "Why Americans Drink Coffee," 237.
6. Pendergrast, *Uncommon Grounds,* 14–15.
7. Quoted in Topik and MacDonald, "Why Americans Drink Coffee," 235.
8. Michael F. Jiménez, " 'From Plantation to Cup': Coffee and Capitalism in the United States," in *Coffee, Society, and Power in*

Latin America, ed. William Roseberry et al. (Baltimore: Johns Hopkins University Press, 1995), 39.

9. Pendergrast, *Uncommon Grounds,* 43.

10. Topik and MacDonald, "Why Americans Drink Coffee."

11. Topik and Wells, "Commodity Chains in a Global Economy," 783.

12. For statistics, William H. Ukers, *All About Coffee* (New York: Tea and Coffee Trade Journal Company, 1922), 529.

13. Pendergrast, *Uncommon Grounds,* 40, 46.

14. Jon Grinspan, "How Coffee Fueled the Civil War," *New York Times,* July 9, 2014, https://opinionator.blogs.nytimes.com/2014/07/09/how-coffee-fueled-the-civil-war/.

15. Topik and MacDonald, "Why Americans Drink Coffee," 243.

16. "Industrial Topics," *San Francisco Chronicle,* October 21, 1886, 3.

17. "San Francisco's Coffee Trade," *Tea and Coffee Trade Journal,* October 1920, 423.

18. Bureau of American Republics, *Coffee in America,* 31–32.

19. "San Francisco's Coffee Trade," 423.

20. "Industrial Topics," 3.

21. "Industrial Topics," 3.

22. "San Francisco's Coffee Trade," 423.

23. "Industrial Topics," 3.

24. "Improvement in Central American Cof-

fees," *The Spice Mill,* March 1929, 510.

25. Rafael García Escobar, "Romance of Coffee with Observations on Salvador Coffee," *The Spice Mill,* January 1923, 32a–32c.
26. George L. Henderson, *California and the Fictions of Capital* (New York: Oxford University Press, 1998; reprint, Philadelphia: Temple University Press, 2003), xii.
27. Bruce Cumings, *Dominion from Sea to Sea: Pacific Ascendancy and American Power* (New Haven: Yale University Press, 2009), 227–29.
28. Francis Beatty Thurber, *Coffee: From Plantation to Cup* (New York: American Grocer Publishing Assn., 1881), 152.
29. *Otis, McAllister, & Co., San Francisco, California,* n.d. [1956], uncollected papers of Otis McAllister, San Francisco.
30. Rae, "So the Ezetas Fell," 10.

Chapter 6. The Sign of Apollo

1. For example, see bank records in Impuestos sobre la Renta, Banco Salvadoreño, Ministerio de Hacienda, Archivo General de la Nación, San Salvador, El Salvador.
2. Bureau of American Republics, *Coffee in America,* 6.
3. Ruhl, *Central Americans,* 202.
4. Edwin Lester Arnold, *Coffee: Its Cultivation and Profit* (London: W. B. Whittingham,

1886), v.

5. Robert Henry Elliot, *The Experiences of a Planter in the Jungles of Mysore,* vol. 1 (London: Chapman and Hall, 1871), 6.

6. Elliot, *Experiences,* vol. 1, 8–9.

7. J. H. Vinter to Otis, McAllister & Co., December 23, 1905, uncollected papers of Otis McAllister, San Francisco [OMC].

8. Arnold, *Coffee,* 35, vi.

9. Bureau of American Republics, *Coffee in America.*

10. William Roseberry, "La Falta de Brazos: Land and Labor in the Coffee Economies of Nineteenth-Century Latin America," *Theory and Society* 20, no. 3 (June 1991): 351–81.

11. Francis J. A. Darr, "Growing and Selling Coffee," *New York Times,* March 11, 1888, 10.

12. Darr, "Growing and Selling Coffee," 10.

13. Darr, 10.

14. Elliot, *Experiences,* vol. 1, 141.

15. On banks in El Salvador in 1894, see Charles A. Conant, *A History of Modern Banks of Issue: With an Account of the Economic Crises of the Present Century* (New York: G. P. Putnam's Sons, 1896), 428.

16. Vinter to Otis, McAllister & Co., December 16, 1904, OMC.

17. Julie A. Charlip, "At Their Own Risk:

Coffee Farmers and Debt in Nicaragua, 1870–1930," in *Identity and Struggle at the Margins of the Nation-State,* ed. Aviva Chomsky and Aldo A. Lauria-Santiago (Durham, NC: Duke University Press, 1998), 113.

18. Vinter to Otis, McAllister & Co., December 16, 1904, OMC; [James Hill], "Remarks from a Planter," in E. A. Kahl, *Coffee Prices — High or Low?,* printed by W. R. Grace & Co., San Francisco, May 26, 1926, Hills Bros. Coffee, Inc., Records, Archives Center, National Museum of American History, Smithsonian Institution, Washington, DC, Series 7, Box 11, Folder 5, [7, 11, 5].

19. Report of J. Maurice Duke to U.S. Department of State, November 15, 1885, Dispatches from U.S. Consuls in San Salvador, RG 84.4, U.S. National Archives and Records Administration, College Park, MD.

20. Darr, "Coffee," 10.

21. On the triskelion and coins, see Barclay V. Head, *A Guide to the Principal Gold and Silver Coins of the Ancients, from circ. B.C. 700 to A.D. 1* (London: Trustees of the British Museum, 1886); *Annual Report of the Board of Regents of the Smithsonian Institution* (Washington, DC: Government Printing Office, 1896), 871–75; on the Victorian view of Apollo, see Yisrael Levin, *Swin-*

burne's Apollo: Myth, Faith, and Victorian Spirituality (New York: Routledge, 2016), and Ted Underwood, *The Work of the Sun: Literature, Science, and Political Economy, 1760–1860* (New York: Palgrave Macmillan, 2005), 134.

22. Edward L. Youmans, "Preface," in *The Correlation and Conservation of Forces: A Series of Expositions,* ed. Youmans (New York: D. Appleton, 1865), v.

Chapter 7. A God on the Make

1. Biographical sketch distilled from Robert Bruce Lindsay, *Julius Robert Mayer: Prophet of Energy* (New York: Pergamon Press, 1973), and Kenneth L. Caneva, *Robert Mayer and the Conservation of Energy* (Princeton, NJ: Princeton University Press, 1993).

2. Robert Hewitt Jr., *Coffee: Its History, Cultivation, and Uses* (New York: D. Appleton, 1872), 56.

3. M. R. Fernando, "Coffee Cultivation in Java 1830–1917," in Clarence-Smith and Topik, *The Global Coffee Economy,* 157–72.

4. Quoted in Caneva, *Robert Mayer,* 7, 241.

5. Julius Robert Mayer, "On the Quantitative and Qualitative Determination of Forces," trans. Robert Bruce Lindsay, in Lindsay, *Julius Robert Mayer,* 59–66.

6. Julius Robert Mayer, "The Motions of Organisms and Their Relation to Metabolism: An Essay in Natural Science," trans. Robert Bruce Lindsay, in Lindsay, *Julius Robert Mayer*, 75–145.

7. Julius Robert Mayer, "On the Forces of Inorganic Nature," trans. Robert Bruce Lindsay, in Lindsay, *Julius Robert Mayer*, 67–74.

8. Caneva, *Robert Mayer*, 30.

9. Lindsay, *Julius Robert Mayer*, 8.

10. Mayer, "Forces of Inorganic Nature," 210.

11. Underwood, *Work of the Sun*, 179.

12. Youmans, *Conservation of Forces*, xiv.

13. Underwood, *Work of the Sun*, 179.

14. Henry John Steffens, *James Prescott Joule and the Concept of Energy* (New York: Science History Publications/USA, 1979), 1–17.

15. Steffens, *James Prescott Joule*, 39.

16. Kargon, *Science in Victorian Manchester*, 52.

17. Faraday and Spencer quoted in Underwood, *Work of the Sun*, 179.

18. Iwan Rhys Morus quoted in MacDuffie, *Victorian Literature*, 17; Underwood, *Work of the Sun*, 181–82.

19. Thomas Carlyle, *Sartor Resartus* (1831; London: J. M. Dent, 1902), 159.

20. Walter E. Houghton, *The Victorian Frame*

of Mind, 1830–1870 (New Haven: Yale University Press, 1957; reprint, 1953, 1985), 243.
21. MacDuffie, *Victorian Literature,* 37.
22. Anson Rabinbach, *The Human Motor: Energy, Fatigue, and the Origins of Modernity* (New York: Basic Books, 1990), 290.
23. Underwood, *Work of the Sun,* 179–90.
24. Quoted in Underwood, 189, 183.
25. Quoted in Rabinbach, *Human Motor,* 56.
26. Rabinbach, 46; Underwood, *Work of the Sun,* 173.
27. Rabinbach, *Human Motor,* 3.
28. Underwood, *Work of the Sun,* 134, 72.
29. Underwood, 144.

Chapter 8. The Mill

1. James Hill, "Raising Coffee in Salvador," *Tea and Coffee Trade Journal,* December 1936, 424.
2. Based on Report of J. Maurice Duke to U.S. Department of State, November 15, 1885, Dispatches from U.S. Consuls in San Salvador, RG 84.4, U.S. National Archives and Records Administration, College Park, MD; and various reports of J. H. Vinter, 1904–1907, uncollected papers of Otis McAllister, San Francisco.
3. James Hill to Juan F. Rivas, November 1, 1941, uncollected papers of J. Hill y Cía., Las Tres Puertas, Santa Ana, El Salvador.

4. Kara Newman, *The Secret Financial Life of Food: From Commodities Markets to Supermarkets* (New York: Columbia University Press, 2013), 80–83.
5. "History of the Importers' and Grocers' Exchange of New York," in *New York's Great Industries,* ed. Richard Edwards (New York: Historical Publishing Company, 1884), 79.
6. William H. Ukers, *All About Coffee,* 2nd ed. (New York: Tea and Coffee Trade Journal Company, 1935), 364.
7. Topik, "Integration of the World Coffee Market," 40.
8. Ukers, *All About Coffee,* 2nd ed. (1935), 357–62.
9. Ukers, *All About Coffee* (1922), 296.
10. Ukers (1922), 288.
11. John Bodnar, *The Transplanted: A History of Immigrants in Urban America* (Bloomington: Indiana University Press, 1985), 198.
12. Jacob A. Riis, *How the Other Half Lives: Studies Among the Tenements of New York* (New York: Charles Scribner's Sons, 1890).
13. Topik and MacDonald, "Why Americans Drink Coffee," 235.
14. Pan American Union, *Coffee: Extensive Information and Statistics* (Washington, DC: Government Printing Office, 1902), 56–57.
15. Lauria-Santiago, *Agrarian Republic,* 137.

Chapter 9. Bad Luck

1. Jeffrey Lesser, *Immigration, Ethnicity, and National Identity in Brazil, 1808 to the Present* (New York: Cambridge University Press, 2013), 96.
2. Mario Samper and Radin Fernando, "Historical Statistics of Coffee Production and Trade from 1700 to 1960," in Clarence-Smith and Topik, *The Global Coffee Economy*, 450–53.
3. Samper and Fernando, "Historical Statistics," 450–53; Williams, *States and Social Evolution*, 265–72.
4. [James Hill], "Remarks from a Planter," in E. A. Kahl, *Coffee Prices — High or Low?*, printed by W. R. Grace & Co., San Francisco, May 26, 1926, Hills Bros. Coffee, Inc., Records, Archives Center, National Museum of American History, Smithsonian Institution, Washington, DC, 7, 11, 5.
5. Quoted in Albert Bushnell Hart, *The Monroe Doctrine: An Interpretation* (Boston: Little, Brown, 1916), 190.
6. G. S. McMillan to Harold Stokes, January 29, 1926, RG 151:351.1, Folder: General File, 1926–1927, U.S. National Archives and Records Administration, College Park, MD.
7. "The Tariff and the Pan American Congress," *Chicago Tribune*, October 7, 1889, 4.

8. "Pan-American Exposition," *New York Times*, November 11, 1900, 14.

9. Robert W. Rydell et al., *Fair America: World's Fairs in the United States* (Washington, DC: Smithsonian Books, 2013); *Official Catalogue and Guide Book to the Pan-American Exposition, Buffalo, N.Y.* (New York: Charles Ehrhart, 1901), 17.

10. Jon Grinspan, "How Coffee Fueled the Civil War," *New York Times,* July 9, 2014, https://opinionator.blogs.nytimes.com/2014/07/09/how-coffee-fueled-the-civil-war/.

11. McKinley quoted in Kevin Phillips, *William McKinley,* The American Presidents Series (New York: Henry Holt, 2003), 116.

12. William McKinley, President's Day Address, September 5, 1901, Miller Center, University of Virginia, Presidential Speeches, www.millercenter.org/the-presidency/presidential-speeches/september-5-1901-speech-buffalo-new-york.

13. Pan American Union, *Coffee: Extensive Information and Statistics,* 45.

14. "Porto Rico Not Prospering Under United States Rule," *New York Times,* October 4, 1903, 27.

15. "Report of the Delegation from Porto Rico (On Behalf of the United States)," in *Proceedings of the International Congress for the Study of the Production and Consumption*

of Coffee (Washington, DC: Government Printing Office, 1903), 119–29.
16. Howard Wayne Morgan, *William McKinley and His America* (Kent, OH: Kent State University Press, 2003), 235.
17. Eric Rauchway, *Murdering McKinley: The Making of Theodore Roosevelt's America* (New York: Hill and Wang, 2003), x.
18. "President McKinley and the Pan-American Exposition of 1901: A Tragic Encounter," Library of Congress, www .loc.gov/collections/mckinley-and-the -pan-american-expo-films-1901/arti cles-and-essays/president-mckinley-and-the -panamerican-exposition-of-1901.
19. Walter LaFeber, *The New Empire: An Interpretation of American Expansion, 1860– 1898* (Ithaca, NY: Cornell University Press, 1963).
20. "Porto Rico Not Prospering."
21. "Awards Recommended by Jury on Division IV, Foods and Their Accessories," Box 7, Frederic William Taylor Papers, 1897– 1944, UCLA Special Collections, Los Angeles, California.

Chapter 10. The Taster

1. Thurber, *Plantation to Cup,* 19.
2. "How the DNC Tests Coffee Freshness," *The Spice Mill,* January 1937, 10–11, 16.
3. Ukers, *All About Coffee* (1922), 522.

4. Thurber, *Plantation to Cup,* 18–21.

5. Charles W. Trigg, "The Chemistry of the Coffee Bean," in Ukers, *All About Coffee* (1922), 156.

6. Thurber, *Plantation to Cup,* 19; Ukers, *All About Coffee* (1922), 357.

7. E. A. Kahl, "The Rise of Mild Coffees," *Tea and Coffee Trade Journal,* August 1922, 204.

8. Bureau of American Republics, *Coffee in America,* 31.

9. Thurber, *Plantation to Cup,* 20–21.

10. "The Green Coffee Trade," *Tea and Coffee Trade Journal,* April 1928, 526.

11. "Faber's" [advertisement], *San Francisco Chronicle,* December 21, 1901, 3; L. Lenbenbaum, *San Francisco Chronicle,* August 26, 1901, 3; Pan American Union, *Coffee: Extensive Information and Statistics,* 60–64.

12. J. H. Vinter to Messrs. Otis, McAllister & Co., April 3, 1904, uncollected papers of Otis McAllister, San Francisco [OMC].

13. Vinter to Otis, McAllister & Co., December 16, 1904, OMC.

14. "Coffee Planting in Brazil," *Los Angeles Times,* April 16, 1899, 16.

15. Remarks of Modesto Martinez at the 1930 meeting of the National Coffee Roasters Association, reprinted in "Stenographic Report of Those Portions of Conference Relating to Coffee," *The Spice Mill,* October

1930, 1519.

16. Quoted in Thurber, *Plantation to Cup,* 152.

17. Vinter to Otis, McAllister & Co., September 20, 1904, OMC.

18. Vinter to Otis, McAllister & Co., March 21, 1904, OMC.

19. Vinter to Otis, McAllister & Co. [date illegible, marked #135/376], OMC.

20. Vinter to Otis, McAllister & Co., January 8, 1906, OMC.

21. Vinter to Otis, McAllister & Co., January 8, 1906, OMC.

22. Vinter to Otis, McAllister & Co., January 12, 1906, OMC.

23. Vinter to Otis, McAllister & Co., January 15, 1906, OMC.

24. Vinter to Otis, McAllister & Co., January 21, 1906, OMC.

25. Benjamin J. Older, "Early History of the Pacific Coast Association as Recalled by Its First President," *Tea and Coffee Trade Journal,* June 1936, 19.

26. Ukers, *All About Coffee* (1922), 356–57.

27. Ukers, 488.

28. Oscar Willoughby Riggs, "The Coffee Trade of New York," *Frank Leslie's Popular Monthly* 23 (June 1887): 668.

29. "Coffee Exchange Adopts Contract 'F' for Mild Coffee," *The Spice Mill,* October 1929, 1746.

30. Ukers, *All About Coffee* (1922), 345.
31. Ukers, 341.
32. Kahl, "Rise of Mild Coffees," 204.
33. Hills Bros., Bulletin for Salesmen, San Francisco Division, December 15, 1913, Hills Bros. Coffee, Inc., Records, Archives Center, National Museum of American History, Smithsonian Institution, Washington, DC, 7, 10, 2.

Chapter 11. Special Work

1. Transcript of a Meeting of the Board of Special Inquiry, Angel Island Station, with attachments, in the matter of Frederick Hill, September 11, 1917, in File No. 16502/6-2, U.S. National Archives and Records Administration, Pacific Region, San Bruno, CA [NARA SB].
2. Transcript of a Meeting of the Board of Special Inquiry, Angel Island Station, in the matter of the application of Mauricio & Fermina Avila, September 11, 1917, File no. 16502/5-1 and 5-2, NARA SB.
3. List or Manifest of Alien Passengers for the United States, SS *Acapulco,* Acajutla, El Salvador, July 26, 1912.
4. "Harker History: Manzanita Hall," The Harker School, http://news.harker.org/harker-history-manzanita-hall/.
5. "How Marin Academy Began," *Heads and Tales at Marin Academy,* https://travisma

.wordpress.com/2012/09/10/how-marin-academy-began.

6. Carolyn V. Neal, "Montezuma Mountain School for Boys a Rustic Campus for Children of Privilege," *San Jose Mercury News,* August 1985, posted March 18, 2013, www.mercurynews.com/ci_22741 079/from-archives-montezuma-mountain-school-boys-rustic-campus/.

7. "Development of San Francisco as a Coffee Port, Part I," *The Spice Mill,* January 1923, 18; "Development of San Francisco as a Coffee Port, Part II," *The Spice Mill,* February 1923, 239; "San Francisco's Coffee Gains," *Tea and Coffee Trade Journal,* March 1922, 327.

8. "First Steamer of the Kosmos Line Arrives," *San Francisco Call,* December 15, 1899, 5.

9. Ukers, *All About Coffee* (1922), 489.

10. "The Green Coffee Trade," *Tea and Coffee Trade Journal,* April 1928, 534.

11. "San Francisco's Coffee Gains," *Tea and Coffee Trade Journal,* March 1922, 327–28.

12. "News from Montezumans," *Boy Builder* 5, no. 8 (January 1920), 13.

13. Walter E. Pittman, "Eugene W. Hilgard, A Confederate Scientist," presented at the Joint Annual Meeting of the North-Central and South-Central Section of the Geological Society of America, April 11–13, 2010,

Branson, Missouri.

14. Luther N. Steward Jr., "California Coffee: A Promising Failure," *Southern California Quarterly* 46, no. 3 (September 1964): 259–64.

15. Bruce Cumings, *Dominion from Sea to Sea: Pacific Ascendancy and American Power* (New Haven: Yale University Press, 2009), 219–37; George L. Henderson, *California and the Fictions of Capital* (1998; 2nd ed., Philadelphia: Temple University Press, 2003).

16. Benjamin J. Older, "Early History of the Pacific Coast Association Recalled by Its First President," *Tea and Coffee Trade Journal,* June 1945, 19; James Hill, "El cultivo del café Borbón en El Salvador," *El Café de El Salvador* 18, no. 209 (September 1948), 791–94.

17. Hill, "El cultivo del café Borbón en El Salvador."

18. Felix Choussy, *El café* (San Salvador: Asociación Cafetelera de El Salvador, 1934), 48–62.

19. United Nations Food and Agriculture Organization, *Coffee in Latin America: Productivity Problems and Future Prospects* (New York: United Nations and FAO, 1958), 108–9.

20. Notebook on Agronomy, uncollected papers of J. Hill y Cía., Las Tres Puertas,

Santa Ana, El Salvador [JHP].
21. Notebook on Agronomy, JHP.
22. Carey McWilliams, "Foreword [1971]," *Factories in the Field* (1939; reprint, Santa Barbara, CA: Peregrine Publishers, 1971), viii–vix, 3–10.
23. *Report of the College of Agriculture and the Agricultural Experiment Station of the University of California* (Berkeley: University of California Press, 1922), 148.
24. George L. Henderson, *California and the Fictions of Capital* (New York: Oxford University Press, 1998; 2nd ed., Philadelphia: Temple University Press, 2003), 91–96; "In Memoriam, Richard Laban Adams, Agricultural Economics: Berkeley," University of California, texts.cdlib.org/view?docId=hb3r29n8f4&doc.view=frames&chunk.id=div00001&toc.depth=1&toc.id=, last accessed January 10, 2017.
25. David Igler, *Industrial Cowboys: Miller & Lux and the Transformation of the Far West, 1850–1920* (Berkeley: University of California Press, 2001).
26. R. L. Adams, *Farm Management* (New York: McGraw-Hill, 1921), 520–25.
27. *Tea and Coffee Trade Journal,* March 1926, 328.
28. Meeting of the Board of Special Inquiry, Angel Island Station, in the matter of Frederick Hill, September 11, 1917.

Chapter 12. The History of Holes

1. Ordenes Generales para el Trabajo en las Fincas de J. Hill [OT], 22, uncollected papers of J. Hill y Cía., Las Tres Puertas, Santa Ana, El Salvador [JHP].
2. OT 63, JHP.
3. Mario Samper and Radin Fernando, "Historical Statistics of Coffee Production and Trade from 1700 to 1960," in Clarence-Smith and Topik, *The Global Coffee Economy*, 424–27.
4. Samper and Fernando, "Historical Statistics," 455–58.
5. Jeffrey L. Gould and Aldo A. Lauria-Santiago, *To Rise in Darkness: Revolution, Repression, and Memory in El Salvador, 1920–1932* (Durham, NC: Duke University Press, 2008), 7.
6. "Cosechas de café de fincas propias, 1917–1947," JHP.
7. Belarmino Suárez quoted in Wilson, "Crisis of National Integration," 45.
8. OT 20, JHP.
9. OT 119, JHP.
10. E. P. Thompson, "Time, Work-Discipline, and Industrial Capitalism," *Past and Present* 38 (December 1967), 60.
11. OT 22, JHP.
12. OT 90, 89, JHP.
13. José Luis Cabrera Arévalo, *Las controver-*

siales fichas de fincas salvadoreñas: Antecedentes, origen y final (San Salvador: Universidad Tecnológica de El Salvador, 2009).
14. Ivy Pinchbeck, *Women Workers and the
Industrial Revolution, 1750–1850* (1930;
reprint, New York: Frank Cass, 1969), 179.
15. Ruhl, *Central Americans,* 203.
16. Report of J. Maurice Duke to U.S.
Department of State, November 15, 1885,
Dispatches from U.S. Consuls in San
Salvador, RG 84.4, U.S. National Archives
and Records Administration, College Park,
MD.
17. Ruhl, *Central Americans,* 203.
18. OT 78, JHP.
19. James Hill to Jaime and Federico Hill,
February 28, 1938, JHP.
20. James Hill to Don Eduardo Guirola, July
12, 1921, JHP.
21. Alvarenga, "Ethics of Power," 90.

Chapter 13. The Glass Cage

1. "Occupants of the Wesleyan Glass Cage
Changed," *Chicago Tribune,* March 24,
1896, 10; "The Wesleyan Calorimeter: Account of the Tests to Which A. W. Smith
Was Subjected," *New York Times,* April 5,
1896, 5.
2. "Occupants of the Wesleyan Glass Cage,"
10; "Wesleyan Calorimeter," 5.
3. W. O. Atwater, "How Food Nourishes the

Body: The Chemistry of Foods and Nutrition, Part II," *Century Illustrated Magazine* 34 (June 1887): 237.

4. James L. Hargrove, "The History of the Calorie in Nutrition," *Journal of Nutrition* 136, no. 12 (December 2006): 2957–61.

5. Hermann von Helmholtz, "On the Interaction of Natural Forces," trans. John Tyndall, *American Journal of Science,* 2nd ser., 24, no. 71 (1857): 189–216.

6. Harold Francis Williamson, *Edward Atkinson: The Biography of an American Liberal, 1827–1905* (Boston: Old Corner Book Store, 1934).

7. Andrew F. Smith, "Wilbur O. Atwater," in *The Oxford Encyclopedia of Food and Drink in America,* ed. Smith, 2nd ed., vol. 2 (New York: Oxford University Press, 2013), 95–96; Nicolas Larchet, "Food Reform Movements," in *Oxford Encyclopedia of Food and Drink in America,* vol. 2, 798–800.

8. Atwater, "How Food Nourishes the Body," 237.

9. "The Wesleyan Calorimeter," 5.

10. "Historical Row: Counting Calories," *Wesleyan University Magazine,* Summer 2004, 60.

11. "Nine Days in a Sealed Box," *Chicago Daily Tribune,* March 21, 1899, 1.

12. "Occupants of the Wesleyan Glass Cage," 10.

13. Youmans, "Preface," in *Conservation of Forces,* v; "Introduction," xli.
14. John Fiske, *Edward Livingston Youmans: The Man and His Work* (Boston: James H. West, 1890).
15. Youmans, "Preface," in *Conservation of Forces,* v.
16. Youmans, "Introduction," in *Conservation of Forces,* xvii.
17. Youmans, "Introduction," xiv.
18. William Carpenter, "On the Correlation of the Physical and Vital Forces," in Youmans, *Conservation of Forces,* 403–6.
19. W. Carpenter, "Physical and Vital Forces," 432.
20. Youmans, "Introduction," xxxii–xxxiii.
21. Youmans, "Introduction," xxxvi–xxxviii.
22. Youmans, "Introduction," xxxi.
23. Ofelia Schutte, *Beyond Nihilism: Nietzsche Without Masks* (Chicago: University of Chicago Press, 1984), 204n13.
24. Quoted in R. J. Hollingdale, *Nietzsche: The Man and His Philosophy* (New York: Cambridge University Press, 2001), 226–27.
25. Quoted in Underwood, *Work of the Sun,* 160.
26. M. Norton Wise and Crosbie Smith, "Work and Waste: Political Economy and Natural Philosophy in Nineteenth Century Britain (I)," *History of Science* 27, no. 4

(1989): 263–301.

27. Eric Zencey, "Some Brief Speculations on the Popularity of Entropy as Metaphor," *North American Review* 271, no. 3 (September 1986): 7–10.

28. J. R. Mayer, "Celestial Dynamics," in Youmans, *Conservation of Forces*, 259.

29. MacDuffie, *Victorian Literature*, 66–86.

30. Balfour Stewart and J. Norman Lockyer, "The Sun as a Type of the Material Universe," part 1, *Macmillan's Magazine* 18 (July 1868): 246–57.

31. Atwater, "How Food Nourishes the Body," 237.

32. Smith, "Atwater," 95–96.

33. "Mystery of Body Read Like a Book," *Chicago Tribune,* December 21, 1908, 1.

34. "Science Measures the Energy Stores in Various Foods," *New York Times,* June 26, 1910, SM4.

35. "Mystery of Body," 1.

36. "Mystery of Body," 1.

37. Hargrove, "History of the Calorie."

38. "Mystery of Body," 1.

39. Henry Adams, *The Education of Henry Adams: An Autobiography* (Boston: Houghton Mifflin, 1918), 426.

40. Henry Adams to Edward E. Hale, February 8, 1902, *Letters of Henry Adams,* vol. 5 (Cambridge, MA: Belknap Press, 1982), 336–37.

Chapter 14. The Hunger Plantation

1. Report of J. Maurice Duke to U.S. Department of State, November 15, 1885, Dispatches from U.S. Consuls in San Salvador, RG 84.4, U.S. National Archives and Records Administration, College Park, MD.
2. Report of J. Maurice Duke.
3. Alvarenga, "Ethics of Power," 79.
4. Criminal contra Enecón Godoy por homicidio en Eulalio Ventura, Fondo Judicial, Departamento de Santa Ana, 1930, Box 101, Archivo General de la Nación, San Salvador, El Salvador.
5. Gould and Lauria-Santiago, *To Rise in Darkness,* 200.
6. Alvarenga, "Ethics of Power," 82.
7. Ruhl, *Central Americans,* 203.
8. Ordenes Generales para el Trabajo en las Fincas de J. Hill [OT], 77, uncollected papers of J. Hill y Cía., Las Tres Puertas, Santa Ana, El Salvador [JHP]; OT 85, JHP.
9. Alvarenga, "Ethics of Power," 99–101.
10. Alvarenga, 174–77.
11. Galeas, *Oligarca rebelde.*
12. William R. Fowler Jr., *The Cultural Evolution of Ancient Nahua Civilizations: The Pipil-Nicarao of Central America* (Norman: University of Oklahoma Press, 1989), 85.
13. W. P. Lawson, "Along the Romantic Coffee Trail to Salvador," *The Spice Mill,* No-

vember 1928, 1976–82.

14. OT 38, JHP.

15. OT 98, JHP; OT 63, JHP.

16. Daniel Buckles, Bernard Triomphe, and Gustavo Sain, *Cover Crops in Hillside Agriculture: Farmer Innovation with Mucuna* (Ottawa: International Development Research Centre, 1998).

17. Fowler, *Cultural Evolution,* 114–30.

18. William R. Fowler Jr., " 'The Living Pay for the Dead': Trade, Exploitation, and Social Change in Early Colonial Izalco, El Salvador," in *Ethnohistory and Archaeology: Approaches to Postcontact Change in the Americas,* ed. J. Daniel Rogers and Samuel M. Wilson (New York: Plenum, 1993), 181–87.

19. Browning, *El Salvador,* 15–87.

20. Jeffrey M. Pilcher, *Planet Taco: A Global History of Mexican Food* (New York: Oxford University Press, 2012), 25.

21. Paula E. Morton, *Tortillas: A Cultural History* (Albuquerque: University of New Mexico, 2014), 12.

22. Browning, *El Salvador,* 7.

23. Pilcher, *Planet Taco,* 24–25.

24. Roberto Cintli Rodríguez, *Our Sacred Maíz Is Our Mother: Indigeneity and Belonging in the Americas* (Tucson: University of Arizona Press, 2014), 114.

25. Pilcher, *Planet Taco,* 26–27.

26. James C. Scott, *Against the Grain: A Deep History of the Earliest States* (New Haven: Yale University Press, 2017), 129–58.
27. OT 85, JHP.
28. OT 4, JHP.
29. OT 86, JHP.
30. OT 43, JHP.
31. OT 36, JHP.
32. OT 2, JHP.

Chapter 15. Love in the Time of Coffee

1. Ruhl, *Central Americans,* 202.
2. Ruhl, 203.
3. Ordenes Generales para el Trabajo en las Fincas de J. Hill [OT], 62, 66, uncollected papers of J. Hill y Cía., Las Tres Puertas, Santa Ana, El Salvador [JHP].
4. OT 66, JHP.
5. OT 78, JHP.
6. OT 92, JHP.
7. OT 70, JHP.
8. "Para agregar al libro de 'ORDENES GENERALES,' " JHP.
9. OT 41, JHP.
10. OT 63, JHP.
11. OT 78, JHP.
12. OT 83, JHP.
13. OT 126, JHP.
14. OT 85, JHP.

Chapter 16. The Truth About Coffee

1. Ukers, *All About Coffee* (1922), 527.
2. Ukers, 538–39.
3. Charles W. Trigg, "The Chemistry of the Coffee Bean," in Ukers, *All About Coffee,* 155.
4. Charles W. Trigg, "The Pharmacology of the Coffee Drink," in Ukers, *All About Coffee,* 174.
5. Pendergrast, *Uncommon Grounds,* 92–99.
6. Ukers, *All About Coffee* (1935), 489–91.
7. Trigg, "Pharmacology," 176.
8. Trigg, "Pharmacology," 177.
9. Trigg, "Pharmacology," 188, 174.
10. Ukers, *All About Coffee* (1922), xi.
11. Bennett Alan Weinberg and Bonnie K. Bealer, *The World of Caffeine: The Science and Culture of the World's Most Popular Drug* (New York: Routledge, 2002), xi–xii. Estimates of use vary. See for comparison Stephen Cherniske, *Caffeine Blues: Wake Up to the Hidden Dangers of America's #1 Drug* (New York: Grand Central, 1998).
12. Astrida Orle Tantillo, *The Will to Create: Goethe's Philosophy of Nature* (Pittsburgh: University of Pittsburgh Press, 2002), 14.
13. *Conversations of Goethe with Eckermann and Soret,* vol. 1, trans. John Oxenford (London: Smith, Elder, 1850), 265–66.
14. MacDuffie, *Victorian Literature,* 38.
15. Richard L. Myers, *The 100 Most Important*

Chemical Compounds: A Reference Guide
(Westport, CT: Greenwood Press, 2007),
55–56.

16. Compare Jonathan Pereira, *The Elements of Materia Medica and Therapeutics,* vol. 2, part 2 (1857; reprint, New York: Cambridge University Press, 2014), 551; and Thurber, *Plantation to Cup,* 223.

17. Weinberg and Bealer, *World of Caffeine,* xix.

18. Thurber, *From Plantation to Cup,* 171.

19. Honoré de Balzac, *Treatise on Modern Stimulants,* trans. Kassy Hayden (Cambridge, MA: Wakefield Press, 2018), 20.

20. Samuel C. Prescott, *Report of an Investigation of Coffee* (New York: National Coffee Roasters Association, 1927), 5.

21. W. O. Atwater, "How Food Nourishes the Body: The Chemistry of Foods and Nutrition, II," *Century Illustrated Magazine,* June 1887, *239.*

22. W. O. Atwater, "Foods and Beverages: The Chemistry of Foods and Nutrition, VI," *Century Illustrated Magazine,* May 1888, 136; W. O. Atwater, *Methods and Results of Investigations on the Chemistry and Economy of Food* (Washington, DC: Government Printing Office, 1895), 16.

23. Atwater, "Foods and Beverages," 136–37.

24. Frank Barkley Copley, *Frederick W. Taylor: Father of Scientific Management,* vol. 1

(New York: Harper & Brothers, 1923), 83.
25. Ukers, *All About Coffee* (1922), 446.
26. Micol Seigel, *Uneven Encounters: Making Race and Nation in Brazil and the United States* (Durham, NC: Duke University Press, 2009), 13–43.
27. "Your Uncle Sam," N. W. Ayer Advertising Agency Records, Box 28, Folder 2, Archives Center, Smithsonian National Museum of American History, Washington, DC.
28. Quoted in Seigel, *Uneven Encounters,* 24–35.
29. *Coffee as an Aid to Factory Efficiency,* reprinted in *Tea and Coffee Trade Journal,* February 1920, 186–88.
30. "Plant, *n.,*" OED.com.
31. *Factory Efficiency,* 186–88.
32. Larry Owens, "Engineering the Perfect Cup of Coffee: Samuel Prescott and the Sanitary Vision at MIT," *Technology and Culture* 45, no. 4 (October 2004), 801.
33. Prescott, *Investigation of Coffee,* 3.
34. Owens, "Perfect Cup," 800.
35. Prescott, *Investigation of Coffee,* 5.
36. Prescott, 10–11.
37. Murray Carpenter, *Caffeinated: How Our Daily Habit Helps, Hurts, and Hooks Us* (New York: Plume, 2015), 81–88.
38. Weinberg and Bealer, *World of Caffeine,* 189.

39. Ludy T. Benjamin, "Pop Psychology: The Man Who Saved Coca-Cola," *Monitor on Psychology* 40, no. 2 (February 2009), 18.
40. H. L. Hollingworth, *The Influence of Caffein on Mental and Motor Efficiency* (New York: Science Press, 1912), 6.
41. Hollingworth, 164–65.
42. Quoted in M. Carpenter, *Caffeinated,* 84.
43. Prescott, *Investigation of Coffee,* 13, 20–22.
44. "During 1929–1930 we've done these things for you," N. W. Ayer Advertising Agency Records, Box 75, Folder 2.
45. See Jiménez, " 'From Plantation to Cup,' " 38; "Comstock Record Defines Him as Guzzling Gus," *Daily Journal* (Fergus Falls, MN), February 21, 2009, www.fergusfallsjournal.com/2009/02/comstock-record-defines-him-as-guzzling-gus.

Chapter 17. The American Cure

1. Dana Gardner Munro, *The United States and the Caribbean Republics, 1921–1933* (Princeton, NJ: Princeton University Press, 1974), 145–46.
2. Paul W. Drake, *The Money Doctor in the Andes: The Kemmerer Missions, 1923–1933* (Durham, NC: Duke University Press, 1989), 13.
3. Emily S. Rosenberg, *Financial Missionaries to the World: The Politics and Culture of Dol-*

lar Diplomacy, 1900–1930 (Cambridge, MA: Harvard University Press, 1999), 109–10.

4. Rosenberg, *Financial Missionaries,* 110–11.

5. "Sick Nations Take the American Cure," *New York Times,* December 9, 1928, SM4.

6. Drake, *Money Doctor,* 24.

7. "Historical Row: Counting Calories," *Wesleyan University Magazine,* Summer 2004, 60, http://magazine.blogs.wesleyan.edu/2004/09/20/historical-row-counting-calories/.

8. "The Postmaster General to College Men," *Postal Record* 9, no. 4 (April 1896): 91.

9. *Diaries of Edwin Kemmerer,* Edwin W. Kemmerer Papers, Public Policy Papers, Department of Rare Books and Special Collections, Princeton University Library.

10. See Drake, *Money Doctor.*

11. Rosenberg, *Financial Missionaries,* 102–5.

12. See, for example, Drake, *Money Doctor.*

13. For example, Douglas Vickers, *Economics and Ethics: An Introduction to Theory, Institutions, and Policy* (Westport, CT: Prager, 1997), 5–8.

14. Philip Mirowski, *More Heat than Light: Economics as Social Physics, Physics as Nature's Economics* (New York: Cambridge University Press, 1989), 193–275.

15. Roger E. Backhouse, *The Ordinary Business of Life: A History of Economics from the Ancient World to the Twenty-First Century*

(Princeton, NJ: Princeton University Press, 2004), 4.

16. William Stanley Jevons, *The Principles of Science: A Treatise on Logic and Scientific Method,* 2nd ed. (London: Macmillan, 1905), 735–37.

17. Mirowski, *More Heat than Light.*

18. Irving Fisher's table of equivalency or "translations" between mechanics and economics terms, cited in Mirowski, 224.

19. Rosenberg, *Financial Missionaries,* 109–14.

20. Quoted in Munro, *The United States and the Caribbean Republics,* 146–47.

21. "El Salvador Seeks Loan of $2,000,000," *New York Times,* October 18, 1931, 45.

22. W. B. Schott to the Secretary of State, May 6, 1930, RG 84, Records of the Foreign Service Posts of the Department of State, 1862–1958: El Salvador, vol. 106, U.S. National Archives and Records Administration, College Park, MD.

23. Ruhl, *Central Americans,* 187–88.

24. Rosenberg, *Financial Missionaries,* 229.

25. Edwin W. Kemmerer, "The Work of the American Financial Commission in Chile," *Princeton Alumni Weekly* 26, no. 12 (December 16, 1925): 295.

26. Ruhl, *Central Americans,* 188.

27. F. W. Taylor to Family, September 14, 1923, Correspondence, Box 3, Folder 1,

Frederic William Taylor Papers, 1897–1944, UCLA Special Collections, Los Angeles, California [FWT].

28. Marcos A. Letona to Carlos Milner, March 21, 1923, Salvador Letters and Reports, FWT.

29. David Browning, *El Salvador: Landscape and Society* (New York: Clarendon Press, 1971), 222.

30. F. W. Taylor to Marcus A. Letona, April 14, 1923, Salvador Letters and Reports, Box 3, Folder 2, FWT.

31. F. W. Taylor to Marian Taylor, n.d. [1923], F. W. Taylor & Family Correspondence, 1923–1927, FWT.

32. Report of the Director General of Agriculture for 1923, Salvador Letters and Reports, Box 3, Folder 2, FWT.

33. F. W. Taylor to Harry Humberstone, April 17, 1926, FWT.

34. "From an Old Farm Congress Friend," *Agricultural Review,* September 1924, collected in Salvador Letters and Reports, FWT.

35. Report of the Director General of Agriculture for 1925, Salvador Letters and Reports, Box 3, Folder 2, FWT.

36. Reports of the Director General of Agriculture for 1924, 1925, and 1926, Salvador Letters and Reports, Box 3, Folder 2, FWT.

37. "From an Old Farm Congress Friend."

38. F. W. Taylor to Marcos Letona, date illegible [1924], Salvador Letters and Reports, Box 3, Folder 2, FWT.
39. Report of the Director General of Agriculture for 1924.
40. F. W. Taylor to My Dear Peoples, October 17, 1923, Correspondence, Box 3, Folder 1, FWT.
41. Gould and Lauria-Santiago, *To Rise in Darkness,* 8.
42. Durham, *Scarcity and Survival,* 36.
43. Marcus Letona to F. W. Taylor, February 14, 1924, Salvador Letters and Reports, Box 3, Folder 2, FWT.
44. Admor. Casino Salvadoreño to F. W. Taylor, n.d., Salvador Letters and Reports, Box 3, Folder 2, FWT.
45. F. W. Taylor to Dear Family, n.d., Correspondence, Box 3, Folder 1, FWT.
46. F. W. Taylor to Dear Family, January 18, 1927, Correspondence, Box 3, Folder 1, FWT.
47. F. W. Taylor to Marion, January 18, 1927, Correspondence, Box 3, Folder 1, FWT.
48. F. W. Taylor to My Dear Wife, September 12, 1924, Box 3, Folder 1, FWT.
49. Telegram from F. W. Taylor, April 1, 1927, Correspondence, Box 3, Folder 1, FWT.
50. Drake, *Money Doctor,* 13.
51. Thomas M. Leonard, "Central American Conference, Washington, 1923," in *Encyclo-*

pedia of U.S.–Latin American Relations, vol. 1, ed. Leonard et al. (Thousand Oaks, CA: CQ Press / SAGE, 2012), 156–57.

52. Alvarenga, "Ethics of Power," 175.

53. Drake, Money Doctor, 1.

54. Samuel Guy Inman, "Imperialistic America," Atlantic Monthly, July 1924, 107–16.

55. Rosenberg, Financial Missionaries, 134.

56. Rosenberg, Financial Missionaries, 135–36.

Chapter 18. The Coffee Question

1. Samper and Fernando, "Historical Statistics," 450–53.

2. "Cosechas de las fincas propias, 1922–1926" and "Cosechas de café de fincas propias, 1917–1927," uncollected papers of J. Hill y Cía., Las Tres Puertas, Santa Ana, El Salvador.

3. [James Hill], "Remarks from a Planter," in E. A. Kahl, Coffee Prices — High or Low?, printed by W. R. Grace & Co., San Francisco, May 26, 1926, Hills Bros. Coffee, Inc., Records, Archives Center, National Museum of American History, Smithsonian Institution, Washington, DC [HBC], 7, 11, 5; "Salvador Conditions Good," Tea and Coffee Trade Journal, June 1928, 791.

4. Ukers, All About Coffee (1935), 460–61.

5. Trygge A. Siqueland, "The Romance of

Coffee," *The Spice Mill,* November 1932, 1253–57; Ukers, *All About Coffee* (1935), 462–63.

6. Samper and Fernando, "Historical Statistics," 450–53.

7. Herbert Hoover, *Memoirs: Years of Adventure, 1874–1920* (New York: Macmillan, 1951), 132–33.

8. Hoover, *Memoirs,* 257.

9. Bertrand M. Patenaude, *The Big Show in Bololand: The American Relief Expedition to Soviet Russia in the Famine of 1921* (Stanford, CA: Stanford University Press, 2002).

10. Quoted in Pendergrast, *Uncommon Grounds,* 160.

11. Quoted in Seigel, *Uneven Encounters,* 48.

12. Quoted in Seigel, 51.

13. "Coffee Planters Ask for Tariff," *Chicago Tribune,* December 31, 1908, 6.

14. William H. Ukers to Herbert Hoover, January 19, 1926, RG 151:351.1, Folder: General File, 1926–1927, U.S. National Archives and Records Administration, College Park, MD [NARA CP].

15. G. S. McMillan to H. P. Stokes, January 29, 1926, RG 151:351.1, Folder: General File, 1926–1927, NARA CP.

16. Joseph Brandes, *Herbert Hoover and Economic Diplomacy: Department of Commerce Policy, 1921–1928* (Pittsburgh: University of Pittsburgh Press, 1962), 137.

17. James M. Mayo, *The American Grocery Store: The Business Evolution of an Architectural Space* (Westport, CT: Greenwood Press, 1993), 51–76; Bureau of Foreign and Domestic Commerce, *Merchandising Characteristics of Grocery Store Commodities: General Findings and Specific Results,* Distribution Cost Studies no. 11 (Washington, DC: Government Printing Office, 1932), 25.

18. Bureau of Foreign and Domestic Commerce, *Merchandising Characteristics of Grocery Store Commodities: Dry Groceries,* Distribution Cost Studies no. 13 (Washington, DC: Government Printing Office, 1932), 59–68.

19. Marc Levinson, *The Great A&P and the Struggle for Small Business in America* (New York: Hill and Wang / Farrar, Straus and Giroux, 2011), 19.

20. Richard S. Tedlow, *New and Improved: The Story of Mass Marketing in America* (New York: Basic Books, 1991), 189–94.

21. Godfrey M. Lebhar, *Chain Stores in America, 1859–1950* (New York: Chain Store Publishing, 1952), 25.

22. Waldon Fawcett, "The General Trend to the Small Package," *The Spice Mill,* March 1929, 476, 478.

23. "Importations of Brazil Coffee Through New York — 1929," *The Spice Mill,* Febru-

ary 1930, 204. For A&P's move into manufacturing, see Tedlow, *New and Improved,* 210.

24. For an overview, Edwin J. Perkins, *Wall Street to Main Street: Charles Merrill and Middle-Class Investors* (New York: Cambridge University Press, 1999), 109–26; in more detail, "San Francisco and Denver Roasting Plants of the Dwight Edwards Co.," *The Spice Mill,* March 1933, 240.

25. "The Louisville Conference," *Tea and Coffee Trade Journal,* March 1929, 442.

26. Brandes, *Hoover and Economic Diplomacy,* 132.

27. Levinson, *The Great A&P,* 133.

28. Levinson, 96–97.

29. Salesman's Reference Book (1912), HBC 8, 1, 1.

30. B. D. Balart, "Coffee Profits of the Past — Where Are They?," *Tea and Coffee Trade Journal,* May 1937, 270, 315.

31. Hills Bros [HB]., Bulletin for Salesmen, San Francisco Division, April 5, 1923, HBC 7, 10, 12.

32. HB Bulletin for Salesmen, San Francisco Division, August 5, 1914, HBC 7, 10, 3; HB Bulletin for Salesmen, San Francisco Division, September 7, 1916, HBC 7, 10, 5; HB Bulletin for Salesmen, November 19, 1918, HBC 7, 10, 7; HB Correspondence to Salesmen, General Letter 3, December

1918, HBC 7, 10, 7.

33. HB Bulletin for Salesmen, Chicago Division, March 6, 1937, HBC 7, 1, 2.
34. Folgers ad quoted in Seigel, *Uneven Encounters,* 52.
35. J. H. Polhemus to Sec. Herbert Hoover, August 24, 1925, RG 151:351.1, Folder: General File, 1919–1925, NARA CP.
36. Memorandum from Hector Lazo, September 19, 1925, RG 151:351.1, Folder: General File, 1919–1925, NARA CP; "Moves to Reform Brazil Coffee Plan," *New York Times,* November 2, 1930, 17.
37. L. E. Robinson, "Books Worth While," *The Rotarian,* November 1926, 31.
38. George Palmer Putnam, *The Southland of North America: Rambles and Observations in Central America in the Year 1912* (New York: G. P. Putnam's Sons, 1914), 1.
39. Putnam, *Southland,* 1.
40. Putnam, 233–35.
41. Putnam, 114, 194.
42. E. A. Kahl, "If Coffee Labor Went Up," *Tea and Coffee Trade Journal,* January 1925, 45.
43. Kahl, *Coffee Prices — High or Low?,* HBC 7, 11, 5.
44. Kahl, *Coffee Prices.*
45. Multatuli, *Max Havelaar,* trans. W. Siebenhaar (New York: Alfred A. Knopf, 1927), 74.

46. Multatuli, "Introductory Note by Multatuli to the Edition of 1875," *Max Havelaar*, 321–27.

47. D. H. Lawrence, "Introduction," in Multatuli, *Max Havelaar*, 11–15.

48. Simeon Strunsky, "About Books, More or Less: White Man's Burden," *New York Times Book Review*, January 23, 1927, 4.

49. Ruhl, *Central Americans*, 40.

50. [James Hill], "Poor Outlook in Salvador," *Tea and Coffee Trade Journal*, April 1927, 420.

51. Ruhl, *Central Americans*, 203–4.

52. "Salvadoran Conditions Good," *Tea and Coffee Trade Journal*, June 1928, 791.

53. Brandes, *Hoover and Economic Diplomacy*, 137.

Chapter 19. The Paradise of Eating

1. Miguel Mármol's story is based on Roque Dalton, *Miguel Mármol*, trans. Kathleen Ross and Richard Schaaf (Willimantic, CT: Curbstone Press, 1987), except where noted otherwise.

2. Dalton, *Miguel Mármol*, 53, 47.

3. Dalton, 58, 71.

4. Dalton, 79–80, 109.

5. Dalton, 115.

6. Account of Martí's life based on Thomas P. Anderson, *Matanza: El Salvador's Com-*

munist Revolt of 1932 (Lincoln: University of Nebraska Press, 1971), except where noted otherwise.

7. Quoted in Anderson, *Matanza,* 57.

8. Erik Ching, "In Search of the Party: The Communist Party, the Comintern, and the Peasant Rebellion of 1932 in El Salvador," *The Americas* 55, no. 2 (October 1998): 216.

9. Alejandro D. Marroquín, "Estudio sobre la crisis de los años treinta en El Salvador," *Anuario de Estudios Centroamericanos* 3, no. 1 (1977): 122.

10. "Libro de planillas de la Finca de la propiedad de Antonio Flores Torres," [1926–1931], uncollected manuscript. Original in possession of Federico Barillas, Intercorp S.V., San Salvador, El Salvador.

11. Michael McClintock, *The American Connection,* vol. 1: *State Terror and Popular Resistance in El Salvador* (London: Zed Books, 1985), 106; Gould and Lauria-Santiago, *To Rise in Darkness,* 18–20.

12. Gould and Lauria-Santiago, *To Rise in Darkness,* 2–3.

13. Quoted in Héctor Pérez Brignoli, "Indians, Communists, and Peasants: The 1932 Rebellion in El Salvador," in *Coffee, Society, and Power in Latin America,* ed. William Roseberry et al. (Baltimore: Johns Hopkins University Press, 1995), 244–45.

14. Masferrer quoted in Gould and Lauria-Santiago, *To Rise in Darkness,* 301n92.
15. Hamilton and Chinchilla, "Central American Migration," 84–85.
16. Robert G. Williams, *States and Social Evolution: Coffee and the Rise of National Governments in Central America* (Chapel Hill: University of North Carolina Press, 1994), Table A-1, 265–74.
17. James Dunkerley, *Power in the Isthmus: A Political History of Modern Central America* (London: Verso, 1988), 59.
18. Quoted in E. Bradford Burns, "The Modernization of Underdevelopment in El Salvador, 1858–1931," *Journal of Developing Areas* 18 (April 1984): 293.
19. Quoted in Wilson, "Crisis of National Integration," 122; see also Karen Racine, "Alberto Masferrer and the Vital Minimum: The Life and Thought of a Salvadoran Journalist, 1868–1932," *The Americas* 54, no. 2 (October 1997): 209–37.
20. Biographical sketch based on Racine, "Vital Minimum."
21. Racine, 216, 209.
22. Racine, 231.
23. Racine, 225–26.
24. Racine, 225–29, 234n79.
25. Dalton, *Miguel Mármol,* 224.
26. Gould and Lauria-Santiago, *To Rise in Darkness,* 32–62.

27. Dalton, *Miguel Mármol,* 118.
28. Dalton, 154.
29. Dalton, 194–95.
30. Dalton, 196–97.
31. For La Constancia, Gould and Lauria-Santiago, *To Rise in Darkness,* 55; for agricultural workers, Anderson, *Matanza,* 61.
32. Gould and Lauria-Santiago, 56–57.
33. Quoted in Anderson, *Matanza,* 90.
34. Anderson, *Matanza,* 90–91.
35. Racine, "Vital Minimum," 221.
36. Racine, 234.
37. "The Declaration of the President of the Republic, Engineer Arturo Araujo," enclosed in Dispatch to the Secretary of State, March 11, 1931, RG 84, Records of Foreign Service Posts: El Salvador, vol. 114, U.S. National Archives and Records Administration, College Park, MD [NARA CP].
38. W. W. Renwick to J. T. Monahan, November 7, 1930, RG 84, El Salvador, vol. 106, NARA CP.
39. W. W. Renwick to J. T. Monahan, November 7, 1930, RG 84, El Salvador, vol. 106, NARA CP.
40. Gould and Lauria-Santiago, *To Rise in Darkness,* 91–92.
41. Anderson, *Matanza,* 101–2.
42. Gould and Lauria-Santiago, *To Rise in Darkness,* 92–93.

43. Anderson, *Matanza,* 101–2.
44. Dalton, *Miguel Mármol,* 218.
45. Gould and Lauria-Santiago, *To Rise in Darkness,* 95.
46. Harold D. Finley to the Secretary of State, May 12, 1931, RG 84, El Salvador, vol. 111, NARA CP.
47. Harold D. Finley to Secretary of State, May 20, 1931, RG 84, El Salvador, vol. 111, NARA CP.
48. Anderson, *Matanza,* 102–6.
49. Eugene Cunningham, "Snake Yarns of Costa Rica," *Outing* 80, no. 6 (September 1922): 266.
50. Dalton, *Miguel Mármol,* 216–17.
51. Gould and Lauria-Santiago, *To Rise in Darkness,* 76.
52. Dalton, *Miguel Mármol,* 135.
53. Quoted in Gould and Lauria-Santiago, *To Rise in Darkness,* 76.
54. Dalton, *Miguel Mármol,* 223.
55. Gould and Lauria-Santiago, *To Rise in Darkness,* 73–74.
56. Collected as an appendix to Jorge Schlesinger, *Revolución comunista: Guatemala en peligro . . . ?* (Guatemala City: Editorial Unión Tipográfica Castañeda, Ávila, 1946); two are reproduced and discussed in Gould and Lauria-Santiago, *To Rise in Darkness,* 65–69.
57. Gould and Lauria-Santiago, *To Rise in

Darkness, 67–68.
58. See especially Gould and Lauria-Santiago, 91; and Jeffrey L. Gould, "On the Road to 'El Porvenir': Revolutionary and Counterrevolutionary Violence in El Salvador and Nicaragua," in *A Century of Revolution: Insurgent and Counter-insurgent Violence During Latin America's Long Cold War,* ed. Greg Grandin and Gilbert M. Joseph, 88–120 (Durham, NC: Duke University Press, 2010).

Chapter 20. Inside the Red Circle

1. Schott to the Secretary of State, January 31, 1930, RG 84, Diplomatic Posts: El Salvador, vol. 106, U.S. National Archives and Records Administration, College Park, MD [NARA CP].
2. "Una carta muy importante del consocia señor J. Hill," *El Café de El Salvador,* December 1929, 23.
3. "Fundacíon de la 'Sociedad de Defensa del Café," *El Café de El Salvador,* February 1930, 5–8.
4. Schott to the Secretary of State, January 20, 1930, RG 84, Diplomatic Posts: El Salvador, vol. 106, NARA CP.
5. "Central American Coffee Countries Hold Congress in Guatemala City," *The Spice Mill,* May 1930, 701.
6. W. W. Renwick, "Memorandum to the

American Legation," September 19, 1931, RG 84, Diplomatic Posts: El Salvador, vol. 114, NARA CP.

7. Warren D. Robbins to the Secretary of State, January 3, 1931, RG 84, Records of Foreign Service Posts: El Salvador, vol. 114, NARA CP.

8. Harold D. Finley to the Secretary of State, September 30, 1931, RG 84, Diplomatic Posts: El Salvador, vol. 114, NARA CP.

9. Samper and Fernando, "Historical Statistics," 452.

10. W. J. McCafferty to the Secretary of State, January 16, 1932, RG 84, El Salvador, vol. 116, NARA CP.

11. See, among other sources, Joan Didion, *Salvador* (New York: Simon & Schuster, 1983; reprint, Vintage, 1994), 54; Robert Armstrong and Janet Shenk, *El Salvador: Face of Revolution* (Boston: South End Press, 1982), 26.

12. Kenneth J. Grieb, "The United States and the Rise of General Maximiliano Hernández Martínez," *Journal of Latin American Studies* 3, no. 2 (November 1971): 151.

13. McCafferty to the Secretary of State, January 16, 1932.

14. McCafferty to the Secretary of State, January 16, 1932.

15. Gould and Lauria-Santiago, *To Rise in*

Darkness, 139.
16. Dalton, *Miguel Mármol,* 229.
17. Dalton, 233.
18. Gould and Lauria-Santiago, *To Rise in Darkness,* 141–42.
19. Gould and Lauria-Santiago, 143.
20. Gould and Lauria-Santiago, 141–44.
21. Philip F. Dur, "U.S. Diplomacy and the Salvadorean Revolution of 1931," *Journal of Latin American Studies* 30, no. 1 (February 1998): 104–5.
22. McCafferty to the Secretary of State, January 16, 1932; Grieb, "Rise of Martínez," 160; C. B. Curtis to the Secretary of State, December 11, 1931, RG 84, El Salvador, vol. 111, NARA CP.
23. Major A. R. Harris to War Department, December 22, 1931, RG 59, 816.00/828, NARA CP.
24. Gould and Lauria-Santiago, *To Rise in Darkness,* 144–47.
25. Gould and Lauria-Santiago, 151.
26. D. J. Rodgers to Sir John Simon, January 7, 1932, Foreign Office [FO] 813/22, Central American Politics: 1932, The National Archives, Kew, Richmond, UK [TNA].
27. D. J. Rodgers to H. A. Grant Watson, January 12, 1932, FO 813/22, Central American Politics: 1932, TNA.
28. Rodgers to Simon, January 7, 1932.

29. Dalton, *Miguel Mármol,* 237.
30. Gould and Lauria-Santiago, *To Rise in Darkness,* 154.
31. Dalton, *Miguel Mármol,* 238–39.
32. Dalton, 240.
33. Gould and Lauria-Santiago, *To Rise in Darkness,* 160–64.
34. Gould and Lauria-Santiago, 65.
35. Tristram Hunt, *Marx's General: The Revolutionary Life of Friedrich Engels* (New York: Metropolitan / Henry Holt, 2009), 96–98, 123.
36. Hunt, 116.
37. Hunt, 190–99, 235.
38. Friedrich Engels, *Landmarks of Scientific Socialism: "Anti-Duehring,"* trans. and ed. Austin Lewis (1877; Chicago: Charles Kerr, 1907), 225–26; Ernest Mandel, *The Formation of the Economic Thought of Karl Marx, 1843 to* Capital, trans. Brian Pearce (New York: Monthly Review Press, 1971), 83*n*17.
39. David Harvey, "Revolutionary and Counter-Revolutionary Theory in Geography and the Problem of Ghetto Formation," in *The Ways of the World* (New York: Oxford University Press, 2016), 15–16.
40. Peter Linebaugh, "Karl Marx, the Theft of Wood, and Working-Class Composition," in *Stop, Thief! The Commons, Enclosures, and Resistance* (Oakland, CA: PM Press,

2014), 56.

41. Quoted in Underwood, *Work of the Sun,* 7; see also Paul Burkett and John Bellamy Foster, "Metabolism, Energy, and Entropy in Marx's Critique of Political Economy: Beyond the Podolinsky Myth," *Theory and Society* 35, no. 1 (February 2006): 112.

42. Quoted in Jonathan Sperber, *Karl Marx: A Nineteenth-Century Life* (New York: Liveright, 2013), 537–38.

43. Sergei Podolinsky, "Socialism and the Unity of Physical Forces," trans. Angelo Di Salvo and Mark Hudson, *Organization and Environment* 17, no. 1 (March 2004): 61–75.

44. John Bellamy Foster, *Marx's Ecology: Materialism and Nature* (New York: Monthly Review Press, 2000), 166.

45. Quoted in Burkett and Foster, "Metabolism, Energy, and Entropy," 123.

46. Stephen Kotkin, *Stalin,* vol. 1: *Paradoxes of Power, 1878–1928* (New York: Penguin Press, 2014), 87.

47. Quoted in Zenovia A. Sochor, *Revolution and Culture: The Bogdanov-Lenin Controversy* (Ithaca, NY: Cornell University Press, 1988), 72.

48. V. I. Lenin, *Materialism and Empirio-Criticism: Critical Comments on a Reactionary Philosophy* (1927; reprint New York: International Publishers, 1970), 279.

49. V. I. Lenin, "A 'Scientific' System of Sweating," in *Collected Works of Lenin*, vol. 18 (Moscow: Progress Publishers, 1975), 594–95.

50. Quoted in Kotkin, *Stalin*, 79.

51. Ching, "In Search of the Party," 227.

52. See *El Café de El Salvador*, 1929–1932.

53. Louis A. La Garde, *Gunshot Injuries: How They Are Inflicted, Their Complications and Treatment* (New York: William Wood, 1914), 67.

54. La Garde, *Gunshot Injuries*, 62–66, 72–73.

55. D. J. Rodgers to Sir John Simon, January 13, 1932, No. 22, FO 420/283, Further Correspondence Respecting South and Central America, Part 34, Jan-June 1932, TNA.

56. Dalton, *Miguel Mármol*, 244.

57. Gould and Lauria-Santiago, *To Rise in Darkness*, 167–68.

58. Telegram to Foreign Office No. 2, January 20, 1932, FO 813/22, Central American Politics: 1932, TNA.

59. Telegram to Foreign Office No. 1, January 20, 1932, FO 813/22, Central American Politics: 1932, TNA.

60. Telegram to Foreign Office No. 3, January 21, 1932, FO 813/22, Central American Politics: 1932, TNA.

61. "Volcanoes Blanket Guatemalan Towns,"

New York Times, January 23, 1932, 1.
62. Gould and Lauria-Santiago, *To Rise in Darkness,* 170.
63. General Resume of the Proceedings of H.M.C. Ships while at Acajutla, Republic of San Salvador, January 23–31, 1932, reprinted in Leon Zamosc, "The Landing That Never Was: Canadian Marines and the Salvadorean Insurrection of 1932," *Canadian Journal of Latin American and Caribbean Studies* 11, no. 21 (1986): 133.
64. McCafferty quoted in Philip F. Dur, "U.S. Diplomacy and the Salvadorean Revolution of 1931," *Journal of Latin American Studies* 30, no. 1 (February 1998): 111.
65. "Red Revolt Sweeps Cities in Salvador," *New York Times,* January 24, 1932, 1.

Chapter 21. An Exceedingly Good Lunch

1. General Resume of the Proceedings of H.M.C. Ships while at Acajutla, Republic of San Salvador, January 23–31, 1932, reprinted in Leon Zamosc, "The Landing That Never Was: Canadian Marines and the Salvadorean Insurrection of 1932," *Canadian Journal of Latin American and Caribbean Studies* 11, no. 21 (1986): 131–47.
2. Gould and Lauria-Santiago, *To Rise in Darkness,* 170–71.
3. C. L. R. James, *The Black Jacobins: Tous-*

saint L'Ouverture and the San Domingo Revolution* (1938; rev. ed., New York: Random House, 1963), x.

4. Gould and Lauria-Santiago, *To Rise in Darkness,* 174–82.

5. Héctor Lindo-Fuentes et al., *Remembering a Massacre in El Salvador: The Insurrection of 1932, Roque Dalton, and the Politics of Historical Memory* (Albuquerque: University of New Mexico Press, 2007), 41.

6. "A Landowner's Account" (1932), in Appendix, Document 6-1, of Lindo-Fuentes et al., *Remembering a Massacre,* 336.

7. Gould and Lauria-Santiago, *To Rise in Darkness,* 180.

8. "Martial Law Set Up in Salvador Revolt," *New York Times,* January 25, 1932, 10; "Youths Armed in San Salvador," *New York Times,* January 26, 1932, 10.

9. Telegram to Foreign Office No. 8, January 26, 1932, Foreign Office [FO] 813/22, Central American Politics: 1932, The National Archives, Kew, Richmond, UK [TNA].

10. See also Erik Ching, *Authoritarian El Salvador: Politics and the Origins of Military Regimes, 1880–1945* (South Bend, IN: University of Notre Dame Press, 2014), 290.

11. Photographs published in Gould and Lauria-Santiago, *To Rise in Darkness,* 228.

12. D. J. Rodgers to Sir John Simon, February 2, 1932, No. 25, FO 420/283, Further Correspondence Respecting South and Central America, Part 34, Jan-June 1932, TNA.
13. Brodeur's story compiled from documents reprinted in Zamosc, "The Landing That Never Was."
14. On the basis of anecdotal evidence, Anderson, *Matanza,* 125–26, has Martí arrested on the 18th. Dispatches from British diplomats indicate the 19th/20th. See D. J. Rodgers to Sir John Simon, January 22, 1932, No. 22, FO 420/283, Further Correspondence Respecting South and Central America, Part 34, Jan-June 1932, TNA.
15. Anderson, *Matanza,* 179–86.

Chapter 22. The Slaughter

1. Telegram to Foreign Office No. 11, January 28, 1932, Foreign Office [FO] 813/22, Central American Politics: 1932, The National Archives, Kew, Richmond, UK [TNA].
2. D. J. Rodgers to Sir John Simon, January 26, 1932, No. 23, FO 420/283, Further Correspondence Respecting South and Central America, Part 34, Jan-June 1932, TNA.
3. Telegram to Foreign Office No. 9, January 2, 1932, FO 813/22, Central American

Politics: 1932, TNA.

4. "Fiscal Representative has received advice
. . . ," n.d., FO 813/22, Central American
Politics: 1932, TNA.

5. Telegram to Washington, January 25, 1932,
FO 813/22, Central American Politics:
1932, TNA.

6. D. J. Rodgers to Sir John Simon, January
30, 1932, No. 24, FO 420/283, Further
Correspondence Respecting South and
Central America, Part 34, Jan-June 1932,
TNA.

7. Enrique Córdova, "General Maximiliano
Hernández Martínez" (memoir, 1960s), in
Appendix, Document 6-6, of Lindo-
Fuentes et al., *Remembering a Massacre,*
353–55.

8. Galeas, *Oligarca rebelde.*

9. Córdova, "General Maximiliano Hernández Martínez," 354–55.

10. Lindo-Fuentes et al., *Remembering a Massacre,* 38.

11. Gould and Lauria-Santiago, *To Rise in
Darkness,* 211.

12. Gould and Lauria-Santiago, 221.

13. Gould and Lauria-Santiago, 221–27.

14. Anderson, *Matanza,* 170; Tilley, *Seeing
Indians,* 159.

15. Quoted in Tilley, Seeing Indians, 161–63,
164.

16. Quoted in Gould and Lauria-Santiago,

To Rise in Darkness, 227.

17. Hamilton and Chinchilla, "Central American Migration," 85.

18. Tilley, *Seeing Indians,* 155–56.

19. Quoted in Gould and Lauria-Santiago, *To Rise in Darkness,* 230.

20. Lindo-Fuentes et al., *Remembering a Massacre,* 38.

21. D. J. Rodgers to Sir John Simon, February 25, 1932, No. 33, FO 420/283, Further Correspondence Respecting South and Central America, Part 34, Jan-June 1932, TNA.

22. William Krehm, *Democracies and Tyrannies of the Caribbean in the 1940s* (Toronto: Lugus, 1999), 3–17; Lindo-Fuentes et al., *Remembering a Massacre,* 63; and Roque Dalton, *Historias prohibidas del Pulgarcito* (1974), excerpted as "People, Places, and Events of 1932," in Appendix, Document 3-6, of Lindo-Fuentes et al., *Remembering a Massacre,* 282–83.

23. Tilley, *Seeing Indians,* 143–44.

24. Photographs published in Schlesinger, *Revolución comunista,* and supposedly provided to him by Martínez. Lindo-Fuentes et al., *Remembering a Massacre,* 123 and 368n48.

25. Erik Ching, *Authoritarian El Salvador,* 292–93.

26. Lindo-Fuentes et al., *Remembering a Mas-*

sacre, 39.
27. Gould and Lauria-Santiago, *To Rise in Darkness,* 213.
28. Dalton, *Miguel Mármol,* 255–61.
29. Gould and Lauria-Santiago, *To Rise in Darkness,* 244.
30. Dalton, *Miguel Mármol,* 308.
31. Grieb, "Rise of Martínez," 165.
32. Stimson quoted in Lindo Fuentes et al., *Remembering a Massacre,* 66.
33. Grieb, "Rise of Martínez," 164.
34. D. J. Rodgers to Sir John Simon, February 25, 1932, No. 33, FO 420/283, Further Correspondence Respecting South and Central America, Part 34, Jan-June 1932, TNA.
35. Grieb, "Rise of Martínez," 165–66.
36. "General Conditions Prevailing in El Salvador, 4/1/32 to 4/30/32," RG 84, Diplomatic Posts: El Salvador, vol. 116, U.S. National Archives and Records Administration, College Park, MD [NARA CP].
37. "Memo of Conversation, Mr. Benjamin Bloom: Recognition of Martínez regime in Salvador," June 2, 1932, RG 84, vol. 118, NARA CP.
38. "General Conditions Prevailing in El Salvador, 8/1/32 to 8/31/32," RG 84, Diplomatic Posts: El Salvador, vol. 116, NARA CP.
39. W. J. McCafferty to the Secretary of State,

General Conditions Report for September 1932, October 4, 1932, RG 84, El Salvador, vol. 116, NARA CP.

40. Grieb, "Rise of Martínez," 171.

41. A. E. Carleton, "Trade Policy of El Salvador," August 17, 1932, RG 84, Records of Foreign Service Posts: El Salvador, vol. 116, NARA CP.

42. "General Conditions Prevailing in El Salvador, 2/1/32 to 2/29/32," RG 84, Diplomatic Posts: El Salvador, vol. 116, NARA CP.

43. "General Conditions Prevailing in El Salvador, July 1933," RG 84, Diplomatic Posts: El Salvador, vol. 122, NARA CP.

44. James Hill to Enrique Borja, April 6, 1932, uncollected papers of J. Hill y Cía., Las Tres Puertas, Santa Ana, El Salvador.

45. Gould and Lauria-Santiago, *To Rise in Darkness*, 187, 328–29n50.

Chapter 23. Pile It High and Sell It Cheap

1. Yip Harburg, quoted in Studs Terkel, *Hard Times: An Oral History of the Great Depression* (New York: Pantheon, 1970; reprint, New Press, 2005), 20.

2. Arthur M. Schlesinger Jr., *The Age of Roosevelt,* vol. 1: *The Crisis of the Old Order, 1919–1933* (New York: Houghton Mifflin, 1957; reprint, Mariner / Houghton Mifflin, 2003), 171, 3.

3. Dorothy Day quoted in Terkel, *Hard Times,* 305.

4. On Hoover's strict economic orthodoxy, see David M. Kennedy, *Freedom from Fear: The American People in Depression and War, 1929–1945* (New York: Oxford University Press, 1999), 82.

5. David E. Hamilton, *From New Day to New Deal: American Farm Policy from Hoover to Roosevelt, 1928–1933* (Chapel Hill: University of North Carolina Press, 1991; reprint, 2011).

6. Franklin D. Roosevelt, "Address Accepting the Presidential Nomination at the Democratic National Convention in Chicago," *The American Presidency Project,* https://www.presidency.ucsb.edu/documents/address-accepting-the-presidential-nomination-the-democratic-national-convention-chicago-1.

7. Schlesinger, *Crisis of the Old Order,* 234.

8. Quoted in William E. Leuchtenburg, *Herbert Hoover* (New York: Henry Holt, 2009), 141.

9. Thomas Ferguson, "From Normalcy to New Deal: Industrial Structure, Party Competition, and American Public Policy in the Great Depression," *International Organization* 38, no. 1 (Winter 1984): 41–94.

10. Charles P. Kindleberger, *The World in Depression: 1929–1939* (1973; rev. ed.,

Berkeley: University of California Press, 1986), 278–80; Dietmar Rothermund, *The Global Impact of the Great Depression, 1929–1939* (New York: Routledge, 1996), 100–105; on Japan, see Yûzô Yamamoto, "Japanese Empire and Colonial Management," and Takafusa Nakamura, "The Age of Turbulence: 1937–1954," in *The Economic History of Japan, 1914–1955: A Dual Structure,* ed. T. Nakamura and Kônosuke Odaka, trans. Noah S. Brannen (New York: Oxford University Press, 2003); on Germany, see Avraham Barkai, *Nazi Economics: Ideology, Theory, and Policy,* trans. Ruth Hadass-Vashitz (New Haven: Yale University Press, 1990), 172–83.

11. Hull quoted in Murray N. Rothbard, "The New Deal and the International Monetary System," in *Watershed of Empire: Essays on New Deal Foreign Policy,* ed. Leonard P. Liggio and James J. Martin (Colorado Springs: Ralph Myles, 1976), 46.

12. David Green, *The Containment of Latin America: A History of the Myths and Realities of the Good Neighbor Policy* (Chicago: Quadrangle Books, 1971).

13. Lloyd C. Gardner, *Economic Aspects of New Deal Diplomacy* (Madison: University of Wisconsin Press, 1964), 194–99.

14. Minutes of the Meeting of the Inter-

Departmental Advisory Board on Reciprocity Treaties, July 17, 1933, Records of the Interdepartmental Advisory Board on Reciprocity Treaties: Memoranda and Records of Meetings, RG 353, Box 1, U.S. National Archives and Records Administration, College Park, MD [NARA CP].

15. *Coffee: The Story of a Good Neighbor Product* (New York: Pan-American Coffee Bureau, 1954).

16. Dick Steward, *Trade and Hemisphere: The Good Neighbor Policy and Reciprocal Trade* (Columbia: University of Missouri Press, 1975), 208; Michael A. Butler, *Cautious Visionary: Cordell Hull and Trade Reform, 1933–1937* (Kent, OH: Kent State University Press, 1998), 112.

17. Minutes of the Meeting of 2 July 1934, Records of the Interdepartmental Committee on Trade Agreements, Committee Meeting Minutes, 1934–1961, RG 353.5.7, Box 1, Folder 1, NARA CP.

18. Kindleberger, *World in Depression,* 234.

19. Grieb, "Rise of Martínez," 170–72.

20. "Monthly Economic Report on El Salvador," December 22, 1934, RG 84, Records of Foreign Service Posts: El Salvador, vol. 127, NARA CP; "Sobre la venta del café salvadoreño en Alemania," *El Café de El Salvador,* July 1936, 335–37; "Alemania y el comercio internacional," *El Café de El*

Salvador, November 1936, 520.
21. Hills Bros., [HB] Bulletin for Salesmen, Chicago Division, October 10, 1932, Hills Bros. Coffee, Inc., Records, Archives Center, National Museum of American History, Smithsonian Institution, Washington, DC [HBC], 7, 1, 2.
22. "Coffee Prospects in El Salvador," *The Spice Mill,* February 1930, 220.
23. HB Bulletin for Salesmen, San Francisco Division, June 17, 1930, HBC 7, 12, 1.
24. HB Bulletin for Salesmen, San Francisco Division, March 1931, HBC 7, 12, 2.
25. H. E. Jacob, *Coffee: The Epic of a Commodity,* trans. Eden and Cedar Paul (1935; Short Hills, NJ: Burford Books, 1998), 267.
26. Pendergrast, *Uncommon Grounds,* 171.
27. James Hill to Oliva, November 17, 1934, uncollected papers of J. Hill y Cía., Las Tres Puertas, Santa Ana, El Salvador [JHP]; "Cosecha 1933/1934," JHP.
28. HB Bulletin for Salesmen, San Francisco Division, December 21, 1931, HBC 7, 12, 2.
29. HB Bulletin for Salesmen, Chicago Division, January 7, 1933, HBC 7, 1, 2.
30. HB Bulletin for Salesmen, Chicago Division, October 10, 1932, HBC 7, 1, 2.
31. Craig Davidson, "What About Supermarkets?," *Saturday Evening Post,* September 17, 1938, 23.

32. Lizabeth Cohen, *Making a New Deal: Industrial Workers in Chicago, 1919–1939* (New York: Cambridge University Press, 1990), 234–38; Tracey Deutsch, *Building a Housewife's Paradise: Gender, Politics, and American Grocery Stores in the Twentieth Century* (Chapel Hill: University of North Carolina Press, 2010).

33. M. M. Zimmerman, "The Supermarket and the Changing Retail Structure," *Journal of Marketing* 5, no. 4 (April 1941), 402–3; M. M. Zimmerman, *The Super Market: A Revolution in Distribution* (New York: McGraw-Hill, 1955), 131.

34. "Super Markets," *Time,* September 29, 1941.

35. T. H. Watkins, *The Hungry Years: A Narrative History of the Great Depression* (New York: Henry Holt, 1999).

36. Tedlow, *New and Improved,* 226–38; Mayo, *American Grocery Store,* 117–55.

37. Zimmerman, *The Super Market,* 31–68.

38. Deutsch, *Housewife's Paradise;* Adam Mack, " 'Speaking of Tomatoes': Supermarkets, the Senses, and Sexual Fantasy in Modern America," *Journal of Social History* 43, no. 4 (Summer 2010), 815–42; Richard Longstreth, *The Drive-In, the Supermarket, and the Transformation of Commercial Space in Los Angeles, 1914–1941* (Cambridge, MA: MIT Press, 1999), 77–126.

39. See Michael Cullen's 1930 business plan, reprinted in Zimmerman, *The Super Market,* 32–35.
40. "Getting the Most out of the Super Market," *Super Market Merchandising,* December 1936, 5.
41. See, for example, "Ralphs Summer Sale" [advertisement], *Los Angeles Times,* July 11, 1932, A3; "The Super Market Aims at Mass Sales of Tea and Coffee," *Tea and Coffee Trade Journal,* June 1937, 330.
42. "How Mass Displays Help Sell Nationally Advertised Brands," *Super Market Merchandising,* December 1937, 1.
43. See "Super Markets and Coffee," *The Spice Mill,* December 1937, 744–45; Harry S. Kantor, *Price Control in the Coffee Industry,* Work Materials No. 55, Trade Practice Studies Section, National Recovery Administration (Washington, DC: National Recovery Administration, 1936), 12, 19–21. For representative promotions and advertisements, see "Ralphs," *Los Angeles Times,* June 7, 1935, 4; "Storewide Christmas Sale" [Safeway], *Los Angeles Times,* December 22, 1937, 7; "Learn About Safeway Coffee Values!," *Los Angeles Times,* November 11, 1938, 4; "33rd Anniversary & Grand Opening Sale" [Vons], *Los Angeles Times,* December 28, 1939, B10.
44. For example, Edward L. Anderson, "Sell-

676

ing Self-Service to the Classes as Well as to the Masses," *Super Market Merchandising,* October 1938, 40.

45. "Super Pledges Community Aid," *Super Market Merchandising,* July 1941, 6.

46. Jane Holtz Kay, *Asphalt Nation: How the Automobile Took Over America, and How We Can Take It Back* (New York: Crown, 1997), 196–207; for Southern California in detail, Scott L. Bottles, *Los Angeles and the Automobile: The Making of the Modern City* (Berkeley: University of California Press, 1987), 175–234.

47. "The Industry in 1941 — A Panoramic Review," *Super Market Merchandising,* January 1941, 6–8.

48. "The Present and Future of the Super Market," *Tea and Coffee Trade Journal,* October 1937, 250.

49. "Mapping the Nation's Super Market Growth," *Super Market Merchandising,* February 1941, 22–30.

50. For example, Ira Katznelson, *When Affirmative Action Was White: An Untold History of Racial Inequality in Twentieth-Century America* (New York: W. W. Norton, 2005), 25–79; and David R. Roediger, *Working Toward Whiteness: How America's Immigrants Became White: The Strange Journey from Ellis Island to the Suburbs* (New York: Basic Books, 2005), 199–244.

51. Kenneth T. Jackson, *Crabgrass Frontier: The Suburbanization of the United States* (New York: Oxford University Press, 1985), 190–218; Louis Hyman, *Debtor Nation: A History of America in Red Ink* (Princeton, NJ: Princeton University Press, 2011), 45–97.

52. Matt Novak, "The Great Depression and the Rise of the Refrigerator," *Pacific Standard,* updated June 14, 2017, https://psmag.com/environment/the-rise-of-the-refrigerator-47924.

53. O. Q. Arner, "Coffee Habits Survey No. 4," *Tea and Coffee Trade Journal,* September 1932, 250–51.

54. J. S. Millard, "Coffee Habits Surveyed," *The Spice Mill,* September 1939, 10.

55. Ukers, *All About Coffee* (1922), 723. The discussion of brewing methods is based on Ukers's chapter "Preparation of the Universal Beverage," 693–724.

56. *Coffee: How It's Grown and How to Make It* (1932), HBC 2, 2, 9.

57. *Use the Hills Bros. Coffee Guide for Coffee Economy and Coffee Goodness* (1934), HBC 2, 2, 9.

58. "The Proper Grind for Coffee," *Tea and Coffee Trade Journal,* April 1937, 243.

59. H. G. Hills, "The Correct Grind for Coffee," *Tea and Coffee Trade Journal,* March 1937, 144–45, 170–72.

60. *How to Make Good Coffee* [1940], HBC 2, 2, 9.
61. Hills, "Correct Grind," 144.
62. All articles in *Good Housekeeping,* by dates as noted: T. Coe, "After-dinner Coffee," March 1912, 381–82; W. B. Harris, "Some Coffees of Today," August 1913, 264–68; H. W. Wiley, "Some New Facts About Coffee," October 1917, 144; D. B. Marsh, "Coffee as a Flavor," May 1920, 83; H. Conklin et al., "Coffee Brewing in Variety," November 1922, 79; O. T. Osborne, "Children Should Not Drink Coffee or Tea," October 1924, 284.
63. All articles in *Good Housekeeping,* by dates as noted: P. W. Punnett et al., "Good Cup of Coffee," October 1931, 88–89; "Perfect Coffee Is Not a Matter of Chance," July 1935, 109; B. MacFayden, "What I Call Good Coffee!," April 1938, 82–83; A. N. Clark and P. W. Punnett, "Why Can't We Have Coffee Like This at Home?," September 1940, 89; P. W. Punnett, "You Can Tell a Good Hostess by Her Coffee," December 1941, 168.
64. Hills Bros. Bulletin for Salesmen, San Francisco Division, November 16, 1920, HBC 7, 10, 9.
65. Covington Janin, "Coast's Coffee Importers Buying Larger Quantities from Central America; Takings from Brazil Off," *Wall Street Journal* [Pacific Coast Edition],

September 11, 1935; "Receivers of Coffee from Foreign Countries by Sea," *The Spice Mill,* March 1939, 40; "San Francisco News," *The Spice Mill,* February 1941, 35.
66. *The Art of Coffee Making,* HBC 2, 2, 9; Arthur F. Thomas to H. G. Hills, July 3, 1935, HBC 1, 6: HGH 35; HB Bulletin for Salesmen, San Francisco Division, September 10, 1936, HBC 7, 12, 5.
67. HB Bulletin for Salesmen, Los Angeles Division, January 6, 1938, HBC 7, 6, 2.
68. T. Carroll Wilson, "A Chronological Review of Hills Bros. Coffee," HBC 2, 1, 2.
69. Eduardo Hill to Reuben W. Hills Jr., September 30, 1938, HBC 11, 6.

Chapter 24. Behind the Cup

1. "Conveniencia de proteger la agricultura," *El Café de El Salvador,* June 1936, 299.
2. Jeffery M. Paige, "Coffee and Power in El Salvador," *Latin American Research Review* 28, no. 3 (1993): 11.
3. Jeffery M. Paige, *Coffee and Power: Revolution and the Rise of Democracy in Central America* (Cambridge, MA: Harvard University Press, 1997), 18–19.
4. "Siembras cafetos de año," n.d. [1945–1946], uncollected papers of J. Hill y Cía., Las Tres Puertas, Santa Ana, El Salvador [JHP].
5. James Hill to Jaime and Federico Hill,

October 23, 1941, JHP.

6. *Tea and Coffee Trade Journal,* September 1929, 330.

7. "San Francisco Trade," *Tea and Coffee Trade Journal,* February 1933, 146.

8. For example, Impuestos sobre la Renta, 1939, Soc. Concha G.v. de Regalado y Hijos, Ministerio de Hacienda, Archivo General de la Nación, San Salvador, El Salvador.

9 James Hill to Oliva, November 17, 1934, JHP. For San Francisco import totals, see yearly trade-journal reports, for example, "Receivers of Coffee from Foreign Countries by Sea During 1938," *The Spice Mill,* March 1939.

10. "San Francisco Trade," *Tea and Coffee Trade Journal,* September 1935, 216.

11. Interview with Jaime Hill, Perdita Huston Papers.

12. "Se nombra a don Jaime D. Hill primer vocal de la junta gobierno de la ACDES," *El Café de El Salvador,* August 1932, 53; "Growers of El Salvador Elect," *The Spice Mill,* May 1938, 345.

13. "Viaje de James Hill," JHP; *Tea and Coffee Trade Journal,* September 1932.

14. "San Francisco News," *The Spice Mill,* August 1933, 757.

15. *Tea and Coffee Trade Journal,* July 1934, 45.

681

16. *Tea and Coffee Trade Journal,* July 1935, 43.
17. *Tea and Coffee Trade Journal,* May 1936, 398.
18. On Brazil and Colombia, "Coffee Industries End Convention," *Pittsburgh Press,* September 24, 1936, 21.
19. J. Hill, "Raising Coffee in Salvador," *Tea and Coffee Trade Journal,* December 1936, 424; "Salvador Grower Speaks," *The Spice Mill,* July 1936, 658.
20. Monthly Economic Report on El Salvador, July 19, 1935, RG 84, vol. 132, U.S. National Archives and Records Administration, College Park, MD [NARA CP].
21. "Diploma al Mérito Agricola Cafetalero," *El Café de El Salvador,* May 1948, 341–42.
22. Monthly Economic Report on El Salvador, November 18, 1935, RG 84, vol. 132, NARA CP; William H. Ukers, *Ten Years of Coffee Progress: The Highlights of Coffee Development During the Decade, 1935–1944* (New York: Pan American Coffee Bureau, 1945), 5; "Pan American Coffee Bureau Activities," *The Spice Mill,* January 1937, 103.
23. "The Coffee Industry Holds Big Convention," *The Spice Mill,* October 1937, 674; "Coffee Campaign Gets Under Way," *The Spice Mill,* May 1938, 262.
24. Allen to Wilson, November 12, 1938,

Hills Bros. Coffee, Inc., Records, Archives Center, National Museum of American History, Smithsonian Institution, Washington, DC [HBC], 10, 5, 2.

25. Allen to Wilson, October 31, 1938, HBC 10, 5, 2.

26. Allen to Wilson, October 31, 1938, HBC 10, 5, 2.

27. Allen to Wilson, November 17, 1938, HBC 10, 5, 2.

28. For the "carelessness" of Brazilian production, see Warren Dean, *Rio Claro: A Brazilian Plantation System, 1820–1920* (Stanford, CA: Stanford University Press, 1976), 36–38.

29. Choussy, *El café,* 54.

30. Untitled notes, December 30, 1944, JHP.

31. James Hill to Juan F. Rivas, November 1, 1941, JHP.

32. Alvarenga, "Ethics of Power," 96–97, 176.

33. Ordenes Generales para el Trabajo en las Fincas de J. Hill, 122, JHP.

34. "Ordenes mandadores fincas respecto de corte de café," JHP.

35. "Calculos sobre la manutención diaria de la gente . . . ," November 13, 1944, JHP.

36. "Ordenes mandadores fincas."

37. James Hill to Juan F. Rivas, November 1, 1941, JHP.

38. "Ordenes mandadores fincas."

39. James Hill to Mandador de la Finca, November 9, 1940, JHP; "Ordenes manda-

dores fincas."
40. Charles Morrow Wilson, *Central America: Challenge and Opportunity* (New York: Henry Holt, 1941), 52.
41. Wilson to Allen, February 8, 1939, HBC 10, 5, 2.
42. "Among the highly interesting novelties . . . ," *Oakland Post Enquirer,* June 20, 1939, HBC 10, 1, 6.
43. Hills Bros. to Joseph C. Harth, May 5, 1939, HBC 10, 6, 2.
44. Victoria Paganini to Hills Bros. Coffee, August 29, 1939, HBC 10, 1, 4.
45. George Goodman to Hills Bros. Coffee, July 18, 1939, HBC 10, 1, 4.

Chapter 25. The War

1. Pendergrast, *Uncommon Grounds,* 210.
2. H. W. Clark to T. C. Wilson, May 25, 1945, Hills Bros. Coffee, Inc., Records, Archives Center, National Museum of American History, Smithsonian Institution, Washington, DC [HBC], 8, 3, 3; War Department Purchase Order, March 7, 1945, HBC 8, 3, 3; War Department Government's Order and Contractor's Acceptance, June 14, 1945, HBC 8, 3, 3.
3. Michael Haft and Harrison Suarez, "The Marine's Secret Weapon: Coffee," *New York Times,* August 16, 2013, https://atwar.blogs.nytimes.com/2013/08/16/the-marines

-secret-weapon-coffee/.
4. Jules R. Benjamin, "The New Deal, Cuba, and the Rise of a Global Foreign Economic Policy," *Business History Review* 51, no. 1 (Spring 1977): 57–78; Carolyn Rhodes, *Reciprocity, U.S. Trade Policy, and the GATT Regime* (Ithaca, NY: Cornell University Press, 1993), 53–78; Claude C. Erb, "Prelude to Point Four: The Institute of Inter-American Affairs," *Diplomatic History* 9, no. 3 (July 1985): 250–67.

5. Green, *Containment of Latin America,* 201–8; Leslie Bethell and Ian Roxborough, "The Postwar Conjuncture in Latin America: Democracy, Labor, and the Left," in *Latin America Between the Second World War and the Cold War, 1944–1948,* ed. Bethell and Ian Roxborough (New York: Cambridge University Press, 1992), 20–22.

6. Arthur Goodfriend, "Latin American Log: El Salvador: Good Roads in a Small Country, Good Food in Its Capital," *New York Times,* May 11, 1947, X15.

7. Samper and Fernando, "Historical Statistics," 453.

8. "Diploma al Mérito Agricola Cafetalero," *El Café de El Salvador,* May 1948, 341–42.

9. "Diploma al Mérito."

10. Mark E. Silverman, "A View from the Millennium: The Practice of Cardiology Circa 1950 and Thereafter," *Journal of*

American College of Cardiology 33, no. 5 (1999): 1141–51.

11. Vincent P. Dole et al., "Dietary Treatment of Hypertension: Clinical and Metabolic Studies of Patients on the Rice-Fruit Diet," *Journal of Clinical Investigation* 29, no. 9 (September 1950): 1189–1206.

12. Manifest of In-Bound Passengers (Aliens), SS *Guyana* dep. La Libertad, El Salvador, May 31, 1951, arr. San Francisco, CA, June 13, 1951.

13. "Hill, Noted S.F. Coffee Man, Dies," *San Francisco Call,* August 30, 1951.

14. "The Coffee Hour," *Time,* March 5, 1951.

15. "The Unpaid Coffee Break," *Time,* October 10, 1955; *Mitchell v. Greinetz,* U.S. Court of Appeals, 10th Circuit, July 24, 1956.

16. Susan Stamberg, "Present at the Creation: The Coffee Break," NPR.org, December 2, 2002, http://news.npr.org/programs/morning/features/patc/coffeebreak/index.html.

17. *Bulletin of the U.S. Bureau of Labor Statistics 221: Hours, Fatigue, and Health in British Munition Factories* (Washington, DC: Government Printing Office, April 1917), 10, 29.

18. Illustration in "Publicity Campaign Resumed," *Tea and Coffee Trade Journal,*

September 1921, 327.

19. " 'Afternoon Coffee Hour' Inaugurated," *The Spice Mill,* February 1929, 194.

20. *Forbes,* December 15, 1952, 20. On "coffee sneak" versus "coffee break," see "Coffee Break," an etymology by Barry Popik, December 26, 2008, www.barrypopik.com/index.php/new_york_city/entry/coffee_break.

21. "Three Cheers for the Coffee Klatsch," *Challenge Magazine,* August 1953, 40.

22. Rockwell D. Hunt, "Changes in California in My Time," *Historical Society of Southern California Quarterly* 36, no. 4 (December 1954): 267–86.

23. David Riesman, "Some Observations on Changes in Leisure Attitudes," *Antioch Review* 12, no. 4 (Winter 1952): 417–36.

24. *Mitchell v. Greinetz.*

25. "Murrah, Alfred Paul (1904–1975)," Oklahoma Historical Society, www.okhistory.org/publications/enc/entry.php?entry=MU010.

26. Raúl Prebisch, *Economic Development in Latin America and Its Principal Problems* (New York: United Nations, 1950), 2.

27. Rosenberg, "Introduction," in Rosenberg, *World Connecting,* 3.

28. Prebisch, *Economic Development,* 5.

29. UN FAO, *Coffee in Latin America.*

Chapter 26. Past Lives

1. Galeas, *Oligarca rebelde.*
2. Compiled from Galeas, *Oligarca rebelde;* interview with Jaime Hill, Perdita Huston Papers [PHP]; "Relato de Jaime Hill, secuestrado por las ERP," Alianza Republicana Nacionalista, August 27, 2010, www .facebook.com/notes/alianza-republicana -nacionalista/relato-de-jaime-hill-secue strado-por-las-erp-el-perdón-el-resultado -de-la-paz-en/443761842148/; David Ernesto Pérez, "Empresario Jaime Hill . . . ," *La Página,* January 6, 2015.
3. Lindo-Fuentes et al., *Remembering a Massacre,* 195–96.
4. Stephen G. Rabe, *The Most Dangerous Area in the World: John F. Kennedy Confronts Communist Revolution in Latin America* (Chapel Hill: University of North Carolina Press, 1999).
5. Alistair White, *El Salvador* (New York: Praeger, 1973), 95.
6. Tommie Sue Montgomery, *Revolution in El Salvador: From Civil Strife to Civil Peace* (1982; 2nd ed., Boulder, CO: Westview, 1995), 58–59.
7. Durham, *Scarcity and Survival,* 21–30; Russell Crandall, *The Salvador Option: The United States in El Salvador, 1977–1992* (New York: Cambridge University Press, 2016), 22.

8. Crandall, *Salvador Option,* 149.
9. Montgomery, *Revolution in El Salvador,* 48–49.
10. Lindo-Fuentes et al., *Remembering a Massacre,* 5.
11. Montgomery, *Revolution in El Salvador,* 104.
12. Montgomery, 71–73.
13. Crandall, *Salvador Option,* 183–97; Montgomery, *Revolution in El Salvador,* 67.
14. Mark Danner, *The Massacre at El Mozote* (New York: Vintage, 1994), 25–26.
15. Montgomery, *Revolution in El Salvador,* 73–79.
16. "14 Reported Killed in 3 Salvadoran Clashes," *New York Times,* November 1, 1979, A3.
17. Galeas, *Oligarca rebelde.*
18. Romero quoted in Montgomery, *Revolution in El Salvador,* 94–95; more generally, Crandall, *Salvador Option,* 140–43.
19. Oscar Romero, "God Brings the Joy of Salvation to All," December 16, 1979, Romero Trust, www.romerotrust.org.uk/homilies/193/193_pdf.pdf; *Journal d'Oscar Romero,* trans. Maurice Barth (Paris: Éditions Karthala, 1992), 195.
20. Paul Heath Hoeffel, "Eclipse of the Oligarchs," *New York Times,* September 9, 1981. The pseudonymous oligarch "Francisco," the primary source for Hoeffel's

story, was Harold Hill.

21. "Family of Salvadoran Pays for Ad at Bidding of His Leftist Captors," *New York Times,* March 12, 1980, A9.

22. "THE PEOPLE'S REVOLUTIONARY ARMY (ERP) OF EL SALVADOR TO ALL NATIONS OF THE WORLD" [advertisement], *New York Times,* March 12, 1980, A21.

23. Montgomery, *Revolution in El Salvador,* 133.

24. Crandall, *Salvador Option,* 1.

25. Inter-American Commission on Human Rights, Annual Report of 1979–1980, quoting the El Salvador Commission on Human Rights, www.cidh.org/annualrep/79.80eng/chap.5c.htm.

26. Quoted in Crandall, *Salvador Option,* 465–66.

27. Crandall, 476.

28. Richard C. Holbrooke, "Foreword," in Perdita Huston, *Families As We Are: Conversations from Around the World* (New York: CUNY Press, 2001), ix–xiii.

29. Mike Edwards, "El Salvador Learns to Live with Peace," *National Geographic* 188, no. 3 (September 1995): 108.

30. Kelefa Sanneh, "Sacred Grounds," *The New Yorker,* November 21, 2011, https://www.new yorker.com/magazine/2011/11/21/sacred-grounds.

31. Elisabeth Jean Wood, *Insurgent Collective Action and Civil War in El Salvador* (New York: Cambridge University Press, 2003), 88.
32. Claudia M. Harner, "Sustainability Analysis of the Coffee Industry in El Salvador," July 1997, Case #706, INCAE Business School, http://www.incae.edu/EN/clacds/publicaciones/pdf/cen706filcorr.pdf.
33. Sanneh, "Sacred Grounds."
34. Roger Cowe, "Brewing Up a Better Deal for Coffee Farmers," *The Guardian*, June 4, 2005, www.theguardian.com/environment/2005/jun/05/fairtrade.ethicalliving.
35. Sanneh, "Sacred Grounds."
36. William Fox, *An Address* . . . [1791], https://archive.org/details/addresstopeopleo1791foxw/page/n2.
37. Sidney Mintz, *Sweetness and Power: The Place of Sugar in Modern History* (New York: Elisabeth Sifton Books / Viking, 1985; reprint, New York: Penguin Books, 1986), 214.
38. Fox, *An Address*.
39. Julie Holcomb, "Blood-Stained Goods: The Transatlantic Boycott of Slave Labor," *Ultimate History Project*, www.ultimatehistoryproject.com/blood-stained-goods.html.
40. Sidney Mintz, "Response," *Food and Foodways* 16, no. 2 (June 2008): 148–58.

41. Mintz, *Sweetness and Power,* 214, 61.

42. Mintz, *Sweetness and Power,* 16.

43. "Nicaraguan Coffee Available," *New York Times,* March 25, 1987; "History of Equal Exchange: A Vision of Fairness to Farmers," www.equalexchange.coop/story.

44. Elizabeth Anne Bennett, "A Short History of Fairtrade Certification Governance," in *The Processes and Practices of Fair Trade: Trust, Ethics, and Governance,* ed. Brigitte Granville and Janet Dine (London: Routledge, 2013); Colleen Haight, "The Problem with Fair Trade Coffee," *Stanford Social Innovation Review,* Summer 2011, www.ssir.org/articles/entry/the_problem_with_fair_trade_coffee.

45. For example, Gavin Fridell, *Fair Trade Coffee: The Prospects and Pitfalls of Market-Driven Social Justice* (Toronto: University of Toronto Press, 2007), 5.

46. See Geoff Watts, "Direct Trade in Coffee," in Thurston et al., *Coffee: A Comprehensive Guide,* 121–27.

47. For example, Ndongo S. Sylla, *The Fair Trade Scandal: Marketing Poverty to Benefit the Rich,* trans. David Clément Leye (Athens: Ohio University Press, 2014); Keith R. Brown, *Buying into Fair Trade: Culture, Morality, and Consumption* (New York: New York University Press, 2013).

48. Rick Peyser, "Hunger in the Coffee

Lands," in Thurston et al., *Coffee: A Comprehensive Guide,* 86–91.

49. For example, Daniel Jaffee, *Brewing Justice: Fair Trade Coffee, Sustainability, and Survival* (Berkeley: University of California Press, 2007), 165–98; V. Ernesto Méndez et al., "Effects of Fair Trade and Organic Certifications on Small-Scale Coffee Farmer Households in Central America and Mexico," *Renewable Agriculture and Food Systems* 25, no. 3 (September 2010): 236–51.

50. Martha Caswell et al., "Food Security and Smallholder Coffee Production: Current Issues and Future Directions," ARLG Policy Brief # 1 (Burlington: University of Vermont, Agroecology and Rural Livelihoods Group, 2012), 5.

51. "A Blueprint to End Hunger in the Coffeelands," *Specialty Coffee Association of America White Paper,* 2013, https://scaa.org/PDF/SCAA-whitepaper-blueprint-end-hunger-coffeelands.pdf.

52. *The Source* (Weather Films, 2016).

53. Hamilton and Chinchilla, "Central American Migration," 84–86. Two studies of the relation of coffee farming to migration: Daniel R. Reichman, *The Broken Village: Coffee, Migration, and Globalization in Honduras* (Ithaca, NY: Cornell University Press, 2011); David Griffith et al., "Losing

Labor: Coffee, Migration, and Economic Change in Veracruz," *Culture, Agriculture, Food & Environment* 39, no. 1 (June 2017): 35–42.

54. "A Blueprint to End Hunger."

55. *Trade Reforms and Food Security: Conceptualizing the Linkages* (Rome: Food and Agriculture Organization of the United Nations, 2003), www.fao.org/docrep/005/y4671e/y4671e00.htm#Contents.

56. Hannah Wittman et al., eds., *Food Sovereignty: Connecting Food, Nature, and Community* (Halifax, NS: Fernwood, 2010).

57. Huston, *Families As We Are*, 276–78; interview with Jaime Hill, PHP.

SELECTED BIBLIOGRAPHY

Uncollected Manuscripts

Libro de planillas de la Finca de la propiedad de Antonio Flores Torres, 1926–1931, Intercorp, S.V., San Salvador, El Salvador
Papers of J. Hill y Cía., 1902–1950, Las Tres Puertas, Santa Ana, El Salvador
Papers of Otis McAllister, Inc., 1902–1907, San Francisco

Archival Collections

Archives Center, National Museum of American History, Smithsonian Institution, Washington, DC
  Hills Bros. Coffee Inc. Records
  N. W. Ayer Advertising Agency Records
Archivo General de la Nación, San Salvador, El Salvador
  Fondo de Impuestos, Ministerio de Hacienda
  Fondo Judicial, Sección Criminal, Departamento de Santa Ana, 1930–1941

Manchester Central Library, Manchester,
UK
  Marriages and Banns, 1754–1930
  School Diary, St. George's Infants, 1875
  St. George's Infants School Report of the
    Diocesan Inspector, 1875
Massachusetts Historical Society, Boston
  Adams Papers Digital Edition, http://www
    .masshist.org/publications/adams
    -papers/
Miller Center, University of Virginia,
Charlottesville
  Famous Presidential Speeches, https://
    millercenter.org/the-presidency/presi
    dential-speeches/
The National Archives, Kew, Richmond, UK
  Foreign Office (UK), Embassy and Con-
    sular Records of Salvador
Princeton University Library Department of
  Rare Books and Special Collections, Prince-
  ton, New Jersey
  Edwin W. Kemmerer Papers
UCLA Library Special Collections, Los
  Angeles
  Frederic William Taylor Papers
University of New England, Portland, Maine
  Perdita Huston Papers, Maine Women
    Writers Collection
U.S. National Archives and Records Adminis-
  tration, College Park, Maryland
  Records of the Bureau of Foreign and
    Domestic Commerce

Records of the Executive Committee on Commercial Policy

Records of the Foreign Service Posts of the Department of State: El Salvador, 1862–1958

Records of the Interdepartmental Advisory Board on Reciprocity Treaties

Records of the Interdepartmental Committee on Cooperation with the American Republics

Records of the Interdepartmental Committee on Trade Agreements

Records of the Office of American Republic Affairs

Records of Tariff Negotiations with Latin American Countries, 1937–1952

U.S. National Archives and Records Administration, San Bruno, California

Records of the Immigration and Naturalization Service

Periodicals

El Café de El Salvador, monthly journal of the Asociación Cafetalera de El Salvador (Coffee Planters Association of El Salvador), published in San Salvador, El Salvador, from 1929.

The Spice Mill, founded in New York 1878 by Jabez Burns, inventor of an early commercial coffee roaster, considered the first U.S. periodical to focus on the coffee trade.

Tea and Coffee Trade Journal, founded in New York in 1901, edited and published by William H. Ukers, author of *All About Coffee,* after 1904.

Published Government Documents

Atwater, W. O. *Methods and Results of Investigations on the Chemistry and Economy of Food.* Washington, DC: Government Printing Office, 1895.

Bureau of American Republics. *Coffee in America: Methods of Production and Facilities for Successful Cultivation in Mexico, the Central American States, Brazil and Other South American Countries, and the West Indies.* Washington, DC: Bureau of the American Republics, 1893.

Bureau of the American Republics. *Mexico.* Prepared by Arthur W. Fergusson. Bulletin no. 9 of the Bureau of the American Republics. Washington, DC: Government Printing Office, 1891.

Bureau of Foreign and Domestic Commerce. *Merchandising Characteristics of Grocery Store Commodities: General Findings and Specific Results.* Washington, DC: Government Printing Office, 1932.

Bureau of Labor Statistics. *Hours, Fatigue, and Health in British Munition Factories.* Washington, DC: Government Printing Office, 1917.

Department of Commerce. *Coffee Consumption in the United Sates, 1920–1965.* Washington, DC: Government Printing Office, 1961.

England Census, 1871 and 1881.

Inter-American Commission on Human Rights. Annual Report of 1979–1980. www.cidh.org/annualrep/79.80eng/chap.5c.htm/.

Mitchell v. Greinetz. U.S. Court of Appeals, 10th Circuit. July, 24, 1956.

Pan-American Union. *Coffee: Extensive Information and Statistics.* Washington, DC: Pan American Union, 1902.

Prebisch, Raúl. *Economic Development in Latin America and Its Principal Problems.* New York: United Nations, 1950.

Proceedings of the International Congress for the Study of the Production and Consumption of Coffee. Washington, DC: Government Printing Office, 1903.

Smithsonian Institution. *Annual Report of the Board of Regents.* Washington, DC: Government Printing Office, 1896.

United Nations Food and Agriculture Organization. *Coffee in Latin America: Productivity Problems and Future Prospects.* New York: United Nations and FAO, 1958.

United Nations Food and Agriculture Organization, *Coffee 2015.* FAO Statistical Pocketbook. www.fao.org/3/a-i4985e.pdf/.

United Nations Food and Agriculture Organization. *Trade Reforms and Food Security: Conceptualizing the Linkages.* Rome: FAO, United Nations, 2013. www.fao.org/docrep/005/y4671e/y4671e00.htm#Contents/.

Film

The Source: The Human Cost Hidden Within a Cup of Coffee. An Investigation by The Weather Channel and Telemundo. Weather Films, 2016.

Books, Articles, Dissertations, Theses, Websites

Adams, Henry. *The Education of Henry Adams: An Autobiography.* Boston: Houghton Mifflin, 1918.

————. *Letters of Henry Adams.* Vol. 5. Cambridge, MA: Belknap Press, 1982.

Adams, R. L. *Farm Management.* New York: McGraw-Hill, 1921.

Aguirre, Robert D. *Informal Empire: Mexico and Central America in Victorian Culture.* Minneapolis: University of Minnesota Press, 2004.

Altick, Richard D. *Victorian People and Ideas: A Companion for the Modern Reader of Victorian Literature.* New York: W. W. Norton, 1973.

Alvarenga, Ana Patricia. "Reshaping the Ethics of Power: A History of Violence in

Western Rural El Salvador, 1880–1932." Ph.D. diss., University of Michigan, Ann Arbor, 1994.

Anderson, Thomas P. *Matanza: El Salvador's Communist Revolt of 1932*. Lincoln: University of Nebraska Press, 1971.

Armstrong, Robert, and Janet Shenk. *El Salvador: Face of Revolution*. Boston: South End Press, 1982.

Arnold, Edwin Lester. *Coffee: Its Cultivation and Profit*. London: W. B. Whittingham, 1886.

Arrighi, Giovanni. *The Long Twentieth Century: Money, Power, and the Origins of Our Times*. New York: Verso, 1994.

Atwater, W. O. "How Food Nourishes the Body: The Chemistry of Foods and Nutrition, Part II." *Century Illustrated Magazine* 34 (June 1887): 237–52.

Aubey, Robert T. "Entrepreneurial Formation in El Salvador." *Explorations in Entrepreneurial History* 6, 2nd ser. (1968–1969): 268–85.

Backhouse, Roger E. *The Ordinary Business of Life: A History of Economics from the Ancient World to the Twenty-First Century*. Princeton, NJ: Princeton University Press, 2004.

Badger, Anthony J. *The New Deal: The Depression Years, 1933–1940*. New York: Hill and Wang, 1989; reprint, New York: Ivan R.

Dee, 2002.

Balzac, Honoré de. *Treatise on Modern Stimulants.* Translated by Kassy Hayden. Cambridge, MA: Wakefield Press, 2018.

Barkai, Avraham. *Nazi Economics: Ideology, Theory, and Policy.* Translated by Ruth Hadass-Vashitz. New Haven: Yale University Press, 1990.

Baxter, Maurice G. *Henry Clay and the American System.* Lexington: University Press of Kentucky, 1995.

Beckert, Sven. *Empire of Cotton: A Global History.* New York: Alfred A. Knopf, 2014.

Benjamin, Jules R. "The New Deal, Cuba, and the Rise of a Global Foreign Economic Policy." *Business History Review* 51, no. 1 (Spring 1977): 57–78.

Benjamin, Ludy T. "Pop Psychology: The Man Who Saved Coca-Cola." *Monitor on Psychology* 40, no. 2 (February 2009): 18.

Bennett, Elizabeth Anne. "A Short History of Fairtrade Certification Governance." In *The Processes and Practices of Fair Trade: Trust, Ethics, and Governance,* edited by Brigitte Granville and Janet Dine, 43–78. London: Routledge, 2013.

Bernstein, Barton J. "The New Deal: The Conservative Achievements of Liberal Reform." In Bernstein, ed., *Towards A New Past: Dissenting Essays in American History.* New York: Pantheon, 1968.

Bernstein, Michael A. *The Great Depression: Delayed Recovery and Economic Change in America, 1929–1939.* New York: Cambridge University Press, 1987.

Bethell, Leslie. "Britain and Latin American in Historical Perspective." In *Britain and Latin America: A Changing Relationship.* Edited by Victor Bulmer-Thomas. New York: Cambridge University Press, 1989.

———, ed. *The Cambridge History of Latin America.* Vol. 6. Cambridge: Cambridge University Press, 1994.

———, ed. *Latin American Economic History Since 1930.* New York: Cambridge University Press, 1998.

Bethell, Leslie, and Ian Roxborough, eds. *Latin America Between the Second World War and the Cold War, 1944–1948.* New York: Cambridge University Press, 1992.

A Blueprint to End Hunger in the Coffeelands. Specialty Coffee Association of America White Paper. 2013. https://scaa.org/PDF/SCAA-whitepaper-blueprint-end-hunger-coffeelands.pdf/.

Bodnar, John. *The Transplanted: A History of Immigrants in Urban America.* Bloomington: Indiana University Press, 1985.

Boissoneault, Lorraine. "How Coffee, Chocolate and Tea Overturned a 1,500-Year-Old Medical Mindset." Smithsonian.com, May 17, 2017. www.smithsonianmag.com/

history/how-coffee-chocolate-and-tea-over
turned-1500-year-old-medical-mindset
-180963339/.

Bordo, Michael D., Claudia Goldin, and Eugene N. White, eds. *The Defining Moment: The Great Depression and the American Economy in the Twentieth Century.* Chicago: University of Chicago Press, 1998.

Borgwardt, Elizabeth. *A New Deal for the World: America's Vision for Human Rights.* Cambridge, MA: Belknap Press of Harvard University Press, 2005.

Brady, Cyrus Townsend. *The Corner in Coffee.* New York: G. W. Dillingham, 1904.

Brandes, Joseph. *Herbert Hoover and Economic Diplomacy: Department of Commerce Policy, 1921–1928.* Pittsburgh: University of Pittsburgh Press, 1962.

Brinkley, Alan. *The End of Reform: New Deal Liberalism in Recession and War.* New York: Alfred A. Knopf, 1995.

Brown, Keith R. *Buying into Fair Trade: Culture, Morality, and Consumption.* New York: New York University Press, 2013.

Browning, David. *El Salvador: Landscape and Society.* New York: Clarendon Press of Oxford University Press, 1971.

Buckles, Daniel, Bernard Triomphe, and Gustavo Sain. *Cover Crops in Hillside Agriculture: Farmer Innovation with Mucuna.* Ottawa: International Development Research

Centre, 1998.

Bulmer-Thomas, Victor. *The Economic History of Latin America Since Independence.* 2nd ed. New York: Cambridge University Press, 2003.

Burkett, Paul, and John Bellamy Foster. "Metabolism, Energy, and Entropy in Marx's Critique of Political Economy: Beyond the Podolinsky Myth." *Theory and Society* 35, no. 1 (February 2006): 109–56.

Burns, E. Bradford. "The Modernization of Underdevelopment: El Salvador, 1858–1931." *The Journal of Developing Areas* 18, no. 3 (April 1984): 293–316.

Butler, Michael A. *Cautious Visionary: Cordell Hull and Trade Reform.* Kent, OH: Kent State University Press, 1998.

Cabrera Arévalo, José Luis. *Las controversiales fichas de fincas salvadoreñas: Antecedentes, origen y final.* San Salvador: Universidad Tecnológica de El Salvador, 2009.

Caneva, Kenneth L. *Robert Mayer and the Conservation of Energy.* Princeton, NJ: Princeton University Press, 1993.

Cardoso, C. F. S. "Historia económica del café en Centroamérica, siglo XIX." *Estudios Sociales Centroamericanos* 4, no. 10 (January 1975): 9–55.

Carlyle, Thomas. *Sartor Resartus.* 1831; London: J. M. Dent, 1902.

Carpenter, Murray. *Caffeinated: How Our*

Daily Habit Helps, Hurts, and Hooks Us. New York: Penguin, 2014.

Caswell, Martha, V. Ernesto Méndez, and Christopher M. Bacon. *Food Security and Smallholder Coffee Production: Current Issues and Future Directions.* ARLG Policy Brief #1. Burlington: University of Vermont, 2012.

Catto, Henry E., Jr. *Ambassadors at Sea: The High and Low Adventures of a Diplomat.* Austin: University of Texas Press, 2010.

Charlip, Julie A. "At Their Own Risk: Coffee Farmers and Debt in Nicaragua, 1870–1930." In *Identity and Struggle at the Margins of the Nation-State,* edited by Aviva Chomsky and Aldo A. Lauria-Santiago, 94–121. Durham, NC: Duke University Press, 1998.

Ching, Erik. *Authoritarian El Salvador: Politics and the Origins of Military Regimes, 1880–1945.* South Bend, IN: University of Notre Dame Press, 2014.

———. "In Search of the Party: The Communist Party, the Comintern, and the Peasant Rebellion of 1932 in El Salvador." *The Americas* 55, no. 2 (October 1998): 204–39.

Ching, Erik, with Carlos Gregorio López Bernal and Virginia Tilley. *Las masas, la matanza, y el martinato en El Salvador: Ensayos sobre 1932.* San Salvador: UCA Editores, 2007.

Ching, Erik, and Virginia Tilley. "Indians, the Military, and the Rebellion of 1932 in El Salvador." *Journal of Latin American Studies* 30, no. 1 (February 1998): 121–56.

Choussy, Félix. *El café*. San Salvador: Asociación Cafetalera de El Salvador, 1934.

Clarence-Smith, William Gervase, and Steven Topik, eds. *The Global Coffee Economy in Africa, Asia, and Latin America, 1500–1989*. New York: Cambridge University Press, 2003.

Coatsworth, John H. *Central America and the United States: The Clients and the Colossus*. New York: Twayne, 1994.

Coffee: The Story of a Good Neighbor Product. New York: Pan-American Coffee Bureau, 1954.

Cohen, Lizabeth. *A Consumers' Republic: The Politics of Mass Consumption in Postwar America*. New York: Random House, 2003.

———. *Making a New Deal: Industrial Workers in Chicago, 1919–1939*. New York: Cambridge University Press, 1990.

Cole, Wayne S. *Roosevelt and the Isolationists, 1932–45*. Lincoln: University of Nebraska Press, 1983.

Conant, Charles A. *A History of Modern Banks of Issue: With an Account of the Economic Crises of the Present Century*. New York: G. P. Putnam's Sons, 1896.

Coopersmith, Jennifer. *Energy, the Subtle*

Concept: The Discovery of Feynman's Blocks from Leibniz to Einstein. Rev. ed. New York: Oxford University Press, 2015.

Copley, Frank Barkley. Frederick W. Taylor: Father of Scientific Management. Vol. 1. New York: Harper & Brothers, 1923.

Courtwright, David T. Forces of Habit: Drugs and the Making of the Modern World. Cambridge, MA: Harvard University Press, 2001.

Cowan, Brian. The Social Life of Coffee: The Emergence of the British Coffeehouse. New Haven: Yale University Press, 2005.

Cowe, Roger. "Brewing Up a Better Deal for Coffee Farmers." The Guardian, June 4, 2005. www.theguardian.com/environment/2005/jun/05/fairtrade.ethicalliving.

Crandall, Russell. The Salvador Option: The United States in El Salvador, 1977–1992. New York: Cambridge University Press, 2016.

Culbertson, William Smith. Reciprocity: A National Policy for Foreign Trade. New York: McGraw-Hill, 1937.

Cumings, Bruce. Dominion from Sea to Sea: Pacific Ascendancy and American Power. New Haven: Yale University Press, 2009.

Cunningham, Eugene. Gypsying Through Central America. London: T. Fisher Unwin, 1922.

———. "Snake Yarns of Costa Rica." Outing

80, no. 6 (September 1922): 266.

Curtis, William Eleroy. *The Capitals of Spanish America*. New York: Harper & Brothers, 1888.

Dallek, Robert. *Franklin D. Roosevelt and American Foreign Policy, 1932–1945*. New York: Oxford University Press, 1979.

Dalton, Roque. *Miguel Mármol*. Translated by Kathleen Ross and Richard Schaaf. Willimantic, CT: Curbstone Press, 1987.

Danner, Mark. *The Massacre at El Mozote*. New York: Vintage, 1994.

Daviron, Benoit, and Stefano Ponte. *The Coffee Paradox: Global Markets, Commodity Trade, and the Elusive Promise of Development*. London and New York: Zed Books, 2005.

Dean, Warren. *Rio Claro: A Brazilian Plantation System, 1820–1920*. Stanford, CA: Stanford University Press, 1976.

————. *With Broadax and Firebrand: The Destruction of the Brazilian Atlantic Forest*. Berkeley: University of California Press, 1995.

Deutsch, Tracey. *Building a Housewife's Paradise: Gender, Politics, and American Grocery Stores in the Twentieth Century*. Chapel Hill: University of North Carolina Press, 2010.

Didion, Joan. *Salvador*. New York: Simon & Schuster, 1983; reprint, Vintage, 1994.

Dietz, James. *The Economic History of Puerto*

Rico: Institutional Change and Capitalist Development. Princeton, NJ: Princeton University Press, 1987.

Dion, Michelle. "The Political Origins of Social Security in Mexico During the Cárdenas and Ávila Camacho Administrations." *Mexican Studies / Estudios Mexicanos* 21, no. 1 (Winter 2005): 59–95.

Drake, Paul W. *The Money Doctor in the Andes: The Kemmerer Missions, 1923–1933.* Durham, NC: Duke University Press, 1989.

Dunkerley, James. *Power in the Isthmus: A Political History of Modern Central America.* London: Verso, 1988.

Dur, Philip F. "U.S. Diplomacy and the Salvadorean Revolution of 1931." *Journal of Latin American Studies* 30, no. 1 (February 1998): 95–119.

Durham, William H. *Scarcity and Survival in Central America: The Ecological Origins of the Soccer War.* Stanford, CA: Stanford University Press, 1979.

Eckes, Alfred E., Jr. *Opening America's Market: U.S. Foreign Trade Policy Since 1776.* Chapel Hill: University of North Carolina Press, 1995.

Edwards, Mike. "El Salvador Learns to Live with Peace." *National Geographic* 188, no. 3 (September 1995): 108–31.

Eichengreen, Barry. *Globalizing Capital: A History of the International Monetary System.*

2nd ed. Princeton, NJ: Princeton University Press, 2008.

———. *Golden Fetters: The Gold Standard and the Great Depression.* New York: Oxford University Press, 1992.

Ekbladh, David. *The Great American Mission: Modernization and the Construction of an American World Order.* Princeton, NJ: Princeton University Press, 2009.

Eliot, L. E. *Central America: New Paths in Ancient Lands.* London: Methuen, 1924.

Elliot, Robert Henry. *The Experiences of a Planter in the Jungles of Mysore.* Vol. 1. London: Chapman and Hall, 1871.

Ellis, Markman. *The Coffee-House: A Cultural History.* London: Weidenfeld & Nicolson, 2004.

Engels, Friedrich. *The Condition of the Working Class in England in 1844, with Preface Written in 1892.* Translated by Florence Kelley Wischnewetzky. London: Swan Sonnenschein, 1892.

———. *Landmarks of Scientific Socialism: "Anti-Duehring."* Translated and edited by Austin Lewis. 1877; Chicago: Charles Kerr, 1907.

Erb, Claude C. "Prelude to Point Four: The Institute of Inter-American Affairs." *Diplomatic History* 9, no. 3 (July 1985): 250–67.

Fair Trade USA 2016 Almanac. www .fairtradecertified.org/sites/default/files/

filemanager/documents/FTUSA_MAN
_Almanac2016_EN.pdf/.

Farrar, F. W. "The Nether World." *Contemporary Review,* September 1889.

Ferguson, Thomas. "From Normalcy to New Deal: Industrial Structure, Party Competition, and American Public Policy in the Great Depression." *International Organization* 38, no. 1 (Winter 1984): 41–94.

Foster, John Bellamy. *Marx's Ecology: Materialism and Nature.* New York: Monthly Review Press, 2000.

Fowler, William R., Jr. *The Cultural Evolution of Ancient Nahua Civilizations: The Pipil-Nicarao of Central America.* Norman: University of Oklahoma Press, 1989.

———. "The Living Pay for the Dead: Trade, Exploitation, and Social Change in Early Colonial Izalco, El Salvador." In *Ethnohistory and Archaeology: Approaches to Postcontact Change in the Americas,* edited by J. Daniel Rogers and Samuel M. Wilson, 181–200. New York: Plenum, 1993.

Fox, William. *An Address, to the People of Great Britain, on the Utility of Refraining from the Use of West India Sugar and Rum.* London, 1791. https://archive.org/details/addresstopeopleo1791foxw/page/n2.

Fraser, Steve, and Gary Gerstle, eds. *The Rise and Fall of the New Deal Order, 1930–1980.*

Princeton, NJ: Princeton University Press, 1989.

Fregulia, Jeanette M. *A Rich and Tantalizing Brew: A History of How Coffee Connected the World.* Little Rock: University of Arkansas Press, 2019.

Fridell, Gavin. *Fair Trade Coffee: The Prospects and Pitfalls of Market-Driven Social Justice.* Toronto: University of Toronto Press, 2007.

Frieden, Jeffry A. *Global Capitalism: Its Fall and Rise in the Twentieth Century.* New York: W. W. Norton, 2006.

———. "Sectoral Conflict and Foreign Economic Policy, 1914–1940." *International Organization* 42, no. 1 (Winter 1988): 59–90.

Furnas, J. C., and the Staff of the *Ladies' Home Journal. How America Lives.* New York: Henry Holt, 1941.

Galeas, Marvin. *El oligarca rebelde: Mitos y verdades sobre las 14 familias: La oligarquía.* San Salvador: El Salvador Ebooks, 2015. Kindle.

Gallagher, John, and Ronald Robinson. "The Imperialism of Free Trade." *Economic History Review,* new ser. 6, no. 1 (1953): 1–15.

Gardner, Lloyd. *Economic Aspects of New Deal Diplomacy.* Madison: University of Wisconsin Press, 1964.

Gerstle, Gary. *Working-Class Americanism: The Politics of Labor in a Textile City, 1914–*

1960. New York: Cambridge University Press, 1989.

Glickman, Lawrence B. *A Living Wage: American Workers and the Making of Consumer Society.* Ithaca, NY: Cornell University Press, 1999.

Gold, Barri J. *ThermoPoetics: Energy in Victorian Literature and Science.* Cambridge, MA: MIT Press, 2010.

Goldberg, Joseph P. *The Maritime Story: A Study in Labor-Management Relations.* Cambridge, MA: Harvard University Press, 1958.

Gould, Jeffrey L. "On the Road to 'El Porvenir.' " In *A Century of Revolution: Insurgent and Counter-Insurgent Violence During Latin America's Long Cold War,* edited by Greg Grandin and Gilbert M. Joseph, 88–120. Durham, NC: Duke University Press, 2010.

Gould, Jeffrey L., and Aldo A. Lauria-Santiago. *To Rise in Darkness: Revolution, Repression, and Memory in El Salvador, 1920–1932.* Durham, NC: Duke University Press, 2008.

Grandin, Greg. *Empire's Workshop: Latin America, the United States, and the Rise of the New Imperialism.* New York: Metropolitan Books / Henry Holt, 2006.

———. *Fordlandia: The Rise and Fall of Henry Ford's Forgotten Jungle City.* New York:

Metropolitan Books / Henry Holt, 2009.

Green, David. *The Containment of Latin America: A History of the Myths and Realities of the Good Neighbor Policy.* Chicago: Quadrangle Books, 1971.

Grieb, Kenneth J. "The Myth of a Central American Dictator's League." *Journal of Latin American Studies* 10, no. 2 (Nov. 1978): 329–45.

———. "The United States and the Rise of General Maximiliano Hernández Martínez." *Journal of Latin American Studies* 3, no. 2 (November 1971): 151–72.

Griffith, David, et al. "Losing Labor: Coffee, Migration, and Economic Change in Veracruz." *Culture, Agriculture, Food & Environment* 39, no. 1 (June 2017): 35–42.

Grindle, Roger. *Quarry and Kiln: The Story of Maine's Lime Industry.* Rockland, ME: The Courier-Gazette, 1971.

Guidos Véjar, Rafael. *El ascenso del militarismo en El Salvador.* San Salvador: UCA Editores, 1980.

Habermas, Jürgen. *The Structural Transformation of the Public Sphere: An Inquiry into a Category of Bourgeois Society.* Translated by Thomas Burger with Frederick Lawrence. Cambridge, MA: MIT Press, 1989.

Haggard, Stephan. "The Institutional Foundations of Hegemony: Explaining the Reciprocal Trade Agreements Act of 1934."

International Organization 42, no. 1 (Winter 1988): 91–119.

Hahamovitch, Cindy. *The Fruits of Their Labor: Atlantic Coast Farmworkers and the Making of Migrant Poverty, 1870–1945.* Chapel Hill: University of North Carolina Press, 1997.

Haight, Colleen. "The Problem with Fair Trade Coffee." *Stanford Social Innovation Review,* Summer 2011. www.ssir.org/articles/entry/the_problem_with_fair_trade_coffee/.

Hamilton, David E. *From New Day to New Deal: American Farm Policy from Hoover to Roosevelt, 1928–1933.* Chapel Hill: University of North Carolina Press, 1991; reprint, 2011.

Hamilton, Nora, and Norma Stoltz Chinchilla. "Central American Migration: A Framework for Analysis." In *Challenging Fronteras: Structuring Latina and Latino Lives in the U. S.,* edited by Mary Romero, Pierrette Hondagneu-Sotelo, and Vilma Ortiz, 81–100. New York: Routledge, 1997.

Hamilton, Shane. *Trucking Country: The Road to America's Wal-Mart Economy.* Princeton, NJ: Princeton University Press, 2008.

Hanson, Simon G. *Economic Development in Latin America: An Introduction to the Economic Problems of Latin America.* Washington, DC: Inter-American Affairs Press, 1951.

Hargrove, James L. "The History of the Calorie in Nutrition." *Journal of Nutrition* 136, no. 12 (December 2006): 2957–61.

Harner, Claudia M. "Sustainability Analysis of the Coffee Industry in El Salvador." Case #706, INCAE Business School, Alajuela, Costa Rica, July 1997. http://www.incae.edu/EN/clacds/publicaciones/pdf/cen706 filcorr.pdf.

Hart, Albert Bushnell. *The Monroe Doctrine: An Interpretation.* Boston: Little, Brown, 1916.

Hartman, Paul T. *Collective Bargaining and Productivity: The Longshore Mechanization Agreement.* Berkeley: University of California Press, 1969.

Harvey, David. "Revolutionary and Counter-Revolutionary Theory in Geography and the Problem of Ghetto Formation." In Harvey, *The Ways of the World,* 10–36. New York: Oxford University Press, 2016.

Hawley, Ellis. *The New Deal and the Problem of Monopoly.* Princeton, NJ: Princeton University Press, 1966.

Head, Barclay V. *A Guide to the Principal Gold and Silver Coins of the Ancients, from circ. B.C. 700 to A.D. 1.* London: Trustees of the British Museum, 1886.

Helmholtz, Hermann von. "On the Interaction of Natural Forces." Translated by John Tyndall. *American Journal of Science,* 2nd ser., 24, no. 71 (1857): 189–216.

Henderson, George L. *California and the Fictions of Capital.* Philadelphia: Temple University Press, 1998.

Henius, Frank. *Latin American Trade: How to Get and Hold It.* New York: Harper & Brothers, 1941.

Hewitt, Robert, Jr. *Coffee: Its History, Cultivation, and Uses.* New York: D. Appleton, 1872.

Hindman, Hugh D. *The World of Child Labor: An Historical and Regional Survey.* Armonk, NY: M. E. Sharpe, 2009; New York: Routledge, 2014.

Hobsbawm, Eric. *The Age of Revolution, 1789–1848.* 1962; reprint, New York: Vintage, 1996.

———. *Industry and Empire: From 1750 to the Present Day.* Revised and updated ed. New York: New Press, 1999.

———. *Labouring Men: Studies in the History of Labour.* London: Weidenfeld & Nicolson, 1964.

Hoganson, Kristin L. *Consumers' Imperium: The Global Production of American Domesticity, 1865–1920.* Chapel Hill: University of North Carolina Press, 2007.

Holcomb, Julie. "Blood-Stained Goods: The Transatlantic Boycott of Slave Labor." *Ulti-*

mate History Project. www.ultimatehistory
project.com/blood-stained-goods.html.

Hollingdale, R. J. *Nietzsche: The Man and His Philosophy.* New York: Cambridge University Press, 2001.

Hollingworth, H. L. *The Influence of Caffein on Mental and Motor Efficiency.* New York: Science Press, 1912.

Hoover, Herbert. *Memoirs: Years of Adventure, 1874–1920.* New York: Macmillan, 1951.

Horowitz, David. "The Crusade Against Chain Stores: Portland's Independent Merchants, 1928–1935." *Oregon Historical Quarterly* 89, no. 4 (Winter 1988): 340–68.

Houghton, John. "A Discourse of Coffee." *Philosophical Transactions of the Royal Society* 21, no. 256 (September 1699): 311–17.

Howe, Daniel Walker. *What Hath God Wrought? The Transformation of America, 1815–1848.* New York: Oxford University Press, 2007.

Hunt, Rockwell D. "Changes in California in My Time." *Historical Society of Southern California Quarterly* 36, no. 4 (December 1954): 267–86.

Hunt, Tristram. *Marx's General: The Revolutionary Life of Friedrich Engels.* New York: Metropolitan Books / Henry Holt, 2009.

Huston, Perdita. *Families As We Are: Conversations from Around the World.* New York:

Feminist Press at The City University of New York, 2001.

Hyman, Louis. *Debtor Nation: A History of America in Red Ink.* Princeton, NJ: Princeton University Press, 2011.

Igler, David. *Industrial Cowboys: Miller & Lux and the Transformation of the Far West, 1850–1920.* Berkeley: University of California Press, 2001.

Jackson, Kenneth T. *Crabgrass Frontier: The Suburbanization of the United States.* New York: Oxford University Press, 1985.

Jacob, H. E. *Coffee: The Epic of a Commodity.* Translated by Eden and Cedar Paul. 1935; Short Hills, NJ: Burford Books, 1998.

Jacobs, Meg. " 'Democracy's Third Estate': New Deal Politics and the Construction of a 'Consuming Public.' " *International Labor and Working-Class History* 55 (Spring 1999): 27–51.

————. *Pocketbook Politics: Economic Citizenship in Twentieth Century America.* Princeton, NJ: Princeton University Press, 2005.

Jacobson, Matthew Frye. *Whiteness of a Different Color: European Immigrants and the Alchemy of Race.* Cambridge, MA: Harvard University Press, 1998.

Jaffee, Daniel. *Brewing Justice: Fair Trade Coffee, Sustainability, and Survival.* Berkeley: University of California Press, 2007.

James, C. L. R. *The Black Jacobins: Toussaint*

L'Ouverture and the San Domingo Revolution. 1938; rev. ed., New York: Random House, 1963.

Jevons, William Stanley. *The Principles of Science: A Treatise on Logic and Scientific Method.* 2nd ed. London: Macmillan, 1905.

Jiménez, Michael F. " 'From Plantation to Cup': Coffee and Capitalism in the United States, 1830–1930." In *Coffee, Society, and Power in Latin America,* edited by William Roseberry et al., 38–64. Baltimore: Johns Hopkins University Press, 1995.

———. "Traveling Far in Grandfather's Car: The Life Cycle of Central Colombian Coffee Estates. The Case of Viotá, Cundinamarca (1900–1930)." *Hispanic American Historical Review* 69, no. 2 (May 1989): 185–219.

Judd, John Wesley. *Volcanoes: What They Are and What They Teach.* New York: D. Appleton, 1881.

Kapstein, Ethan B. *Seeds of Stability: Land Reform and U.S. Foreign Policy.* New York: Cambridge University Press, 2017.

Kargon, Robert H. *Science in Victorian Manchester: Enterprise and Expertise.* Baltimore: Johns Hopkins University Press, 1977; reprint, New York: Routledge, 2017.

Katznelson, Ira. *When Affirmative Action Was White: An Untold History of Racial Inequality in Twentieth-Century America.* New York:

W. W. Norton, 2005.

Kay, Jane Holtz. *Asphalt Nation: How the Automobile Took Over America, and How We Can Take It Back.* New York: Crown, 1997.

Kemmerer, Edwin W. "The Work of the American Financial Commission in Chile." *Princeton Alumni Weekly* 26, no. 12 (December 16, 1925): 295.

Kennedy, David M. *Freedom from Fear: The American People in Depression and War, 1929–1945.* New York: Oxford University Press, 1999.

Kerr, Derek. "The Role of the Coffee Industry in the History of El Salvador, 1840–1906." master's thesis, University of Calgary, April 1977.

Kessler-Harris, Alice. *In Pursuit of Equity: Women, Men, and the Quest for Economic Citizenship in 20th-Century America.* New York: Oxford University Press, 2001.

Kimeldorf, Howard. *Reds or Rackets? The Making of Radical and Conservative Unions on the Waterfront.* Berkeley: University of California Press, 1988.

Kindleberger, Charles P. *The World in Depression: 1929–1939.* 1973; rev. ed., Berkeley: University California Press, 1986.

Klein, Jennifer. *For All These Rights: Business, Labor, and the Shaping of America's Public-Private Welfare State.* Princeton, NJ: Princeton University Press, 2003.

Koehler, Jeff. *Where the Wild Coffee Grows: The Untold Story of Coffee from the Cloud Forests of Ethiopia to Your Cup.* New York: Bloomsbury USA, 2017.

Kotkin, Stephen. *Stalin.* Vol. 1, *Paradoxes of Power, 1878–1928.* New York: Penguin Press, 2014.

Krehm, William. *Democracies and Tyrannies of the Caribbean in the 1940s.* Toronto: Lugus, 1999.

Kuhn, Thomas S. "Energy Conservation as an Example of Simultaneous Discovery." In *Critical Problems in the History of Science,* edited by Marshall Clagget, 321–56. Madison: University of Wisconsin Press, 1959.

LaFeber, Walter. *Inevitable Revolutions: The United States in Central America.* 2nd ed. New York: W. W. Norton, 1993.

———. *The New Empire: An Interpretation of American Expansion, 1860–1898.* Ithaca, NY: Cornell University Press, 1963; reprint, 1998.

La Garde, Louis A. *Gunshot Injuries: How They Are Inflicted, Their Complications and Treatment.* New York: William Wood, 1914.

Lauria-Santiago, Aldo. *An Agrarian Republic: Commercial Agriculture and the Politics of Peasant Communities in El Salvador, 1823–1914.* Pittsburgh: University of Pittsburgh Press, 1999.

Lauria-Santiago, Aldo, and Leigh Binford,

eds. *Landscapes of Struggle: Politics, Society, and Community in El Salvador.* Pittsburgh: University of Pittsburgh Press, 2004.

Lebhar, Godfrey M. *Chain Stores in America, 1859–1950.* New York: Chain Store Publishing Corp., 1952.

Lenin, V. I. *Imperialism: The Highest Stage of Capitalism.* 1916; reprint, New York: International Publishers, 1969.

————. *Materialism and Empirio-Criticism: Critical Comments on a Reactionary Philosophy.* 1927; reprint, New York: International Publishers, 1970.

————. " 'A Scientific' System of Sweating." In *Collected Works of Lenin.* Vol 18. Progress Publishers: Moscow, 1975.

Leonard, Thomas M. "Central American Conference, Washington, 1923." In Leonard et al., eds., *Encyclopedia of U.S.–Latin American Relations.* Vol. 1. Thousand Oaks, CA: CQ Press / SAGE, 2012.

Lesser, Jeffrey. *Immigration, Ethnicity, and National Identity in Brazil, 1808 to the Present.* New York: Cambridge University Press, 2013.

Leuchtenburg, William E. *Franklin Roosevelt and the New Deal, 1932–1940.* New York: Harper & Row, 1963.

————. *Herbert Hoover.* New York: Henry Holt, 2009.

Levin, Yisrael. *Swinburne's Apollo: Myth, Faith,*

and *Victorian Spirituality*. New York: Routledge, 2016.

Levinson, Marc. *The Great A&P and the Struggle for Small Business in America*. New York: Hill and Wang / Farrar, Straus and Giroux, 2011.

Lieberman, Robert C. *Shifting the Color Line: Race and the American Welfare State*. Cambridge, MA: Harvard University Press, 1998.

Liggio, Leonard P., and James J. Martin, eds. *Watershed of Empire: Essays on New Deal Foreign Policy*. Colorado Springs: Ralph Myles, 1976.

Lindo-Fuentes, Héctor. *Weak Foundations: The Economy of El Salvador in the 19th Century, 1821–1898*. Berkeley: University of California Press, 1990.

Lindo-Fuentes, Héctor, Erik Ching, and Rafael A. Lara-Martínez. *Remembering a Massacre in El Salvador: The Insurrection of 1932, Roque Dalton, and the Politics of Historical Memory*. Albuquerque: University of New Mexico Press, 2007.

Lindsay, Robert Bruce. *Julius Robert Mayer: Prophet of Energy*. New York: Pergamon Press, 1973.

Linebaugh, Peter. "Karl Marx, the Theft of Wood, and Working-Class Composition." In *Stop Thief! The Commons, Enclosures,* and Resistance. Oakland, CA: PM Press, 2014.

Longstreth, Richard. *The Drive-In, the Supermarket, and the Transformation of Commercial Space in Los Angeles, 1914–1941.* Cambridge, MA: MIT Press, 1999.

Lorenz, Edward C. *Defining Global Justice: The History of U.S. International Labor Standards Policy.* Notre Dame, IN: Notre Dame University Press, 2001.

Lundestadt, Geir. "Empire by Invitation? The United States and Western Europe, 1945–1952." *Journal of Peace Research* 23, no. 3 (September 1986): 263–77.

MacDonald, Michelle Craig. "The Chance of the Moment, Coffee and the New West Indies Commodities Trade." *William and Mary Quarterly,* 3rd ser., 62, no. 3 (July 2005): 441–72.

MacDuffie, Allen. *Victorian Literature, Energy, and the Ecological Imagination.* New York: Cambridge University Press, 2014.

Mack, Adam. " 'Speaking of Tomatoes': Supermarkets, the Senses, and Sexual Fantasy in Modern America." *Journal of Social History* 43, no. 4 (Summer 2010): 815–42.

Maier, Charles S. "The Politics of Productivity: Foundations of American International Economic Policy After World War II." In *Between Power and Plenty: Foreign Eco-*

nomic *Policies of Advanced Industrial States,*
edited by Peter J. Katzenstein, 23–50.
Madison: University of Wisconsin Press,
1978.

Marchi, Regina. "Día de los Muertos, Migration, and Transformation to the United
States." In *Celebrating Latino Folklore,* Vol.
1, edited by María Herrera-Sobek, 414–24.
Santa Barbara, CA: ABC-Clio, 2012.

Marroquín, Alejandro D. "Estudio sobre la
crisis de los años treinta en El Salvador."
Anuario de Estudios Centroamericanos 3, no.
1 (1977): 115–60.

Marx, Karl. *Capital.* Vol. 1. Translated by Ben
Fowkes. New York: Penguin, 1990.

Mayo, James M. *The American Grocery Store:
The Business Evolution of an Architectural
Space.* Westport, CT: Greenwood Press,
1993.

McClintock, Michael. *The American Connection.* Vol. 1, *State Terror and Popular Resistance in El Salvador.* London: Zed Books,
1985.

McCreery, David. *Rural Guatemala, 1760–
1940.* Stanford CA: Stanford University
Press, 1994.

McWilliams, Carey. *Factories in the Field.*
1939; reprint, Santa Barbara CA: Peregrine
Publishers, 1971.

Méndez, V. Ernesto, et al. "Effects of Fair
Trade and Organic Certifications on Small-

Scale Coffee Farmer Households in Central America and Mexico." *Renewable Agriculture and Food Systems* 25, no. 3 (2010): 236–51.

Menjívar Larín, Rafael. *Acumulación originaria y desarrollo del capitalismo en El Salvador.* San José, Costa Rica: Editorial Universitaria Centroamerica (EDUCA), 1980.

Meyers, Richard L. *The 100 Most Important Chemical Compounds: A Reference Guide.* Westport, CT: Greenwood Press, 2007.

Mintz, Sidney. "Response." *Food and Foodways* 16, no. 2 (June 2008): 148–58.

———. *Sweetness and Power: The Place of Sugar in Modern History.* New York: Elisabeth Sifton Books / Viking, 1985; reprint, New York: Penguin Books, 1986.

Mirowski, Philip. *More Heat than Light: Economics as Social Physics, Physics as Nature's Economics.* New York: Cambridge University Press, 1989.

Montgomery, Tommie Sue. *Revolution in El Salvador: From Civil Strife to Civil Peace.* 1982; 2nd ed., Boulder, CO: Westview, 1995.

Morgan, Howard Wayne. *William McKinley and His America.* Kent, OH: Kent State University Press, 2003.

Morton, Paula E. *Tortillas: A Cultural History.* Albuquerque: University of New Mexico Press, 2014.

Mosley, Stephen. *The Chimney of the World: A History of Smoke and Pollution in Victorian and Edwardian Manchester.* Cambridge, UK: White Horse Press, 2001; reprint, New York: Routledge, 2008.

Multatuli. *Max Havelaar.* Translated by W. Siebenhaar. New York: Alfred A. Knopf, 1927.

Munro, Dana Gardner. *The United States and the Caribbean Republics, 1921–1933.* Princeton, NJ: Princeton University Press, 1974.

Murray, Alex. " 'The London Sunday Faded Slow': Time to Spend in the Victorian City." In *The Oxford Handbook of Victorian Literary Culture,* edited by Juliet John, 310–26. New York: Oxford University Press, 2016.

Nakamura, Takafusa, and Kônosuke Odaka, eds. *The Economic History of Japan, 1914–1955: A Dual Structure.* Vol. 3 in *The Economic History of Japan, 1600–1990.* Translated by Noah S. Brannen. New York: Oxford University Press, 2003.

Nayyar, Deepak. *The South in the World Economy: Past, Present, and Future.* New York: United Nations Development Programme, Human Development Report Office, 2013.

Newman, Kara. *The Secret Financial Life of Food: From Commodities Markets to Supermarkets.* New York: Columbia University

Press, 2013.

Novak, Matt. "The Great Depression and the Rise of the Refrigerator." *Pacific Standard,* October 9, 2012. https://psmag.com/environment/the-rise-of-the-refrigerator-47924.

O'Brien, Thomas F. *The Century of U.S. Capitalism in Latin America.* Albuquerque: University of New Mexico Press, 1999.

Olson, Paul R., and C. Addison Hickman. *Pan American Economics.* New York: John Wiley & Sons, 1943.

Olverson, T. D. *Women Writers and the Dark Side of Late-Victorian Hellenism.* New York: Palgrave MacMillan, 2009.

Osterhammel, Jürgen. *The Transformation of the World: A Global History of the Nineteenth Century.* Translated by Patrick Camiller. Princeton, NJ: Princeton University Press, 2014.

"Our Phantom Ship: Central America." *Household Words,* February 22, 1851, 516–22.

Owens, Larry. "Engineering the Perfect Cup of Coffee: Samuel Prescott and the Sanitary Vision at MIT." *Technology and Culture* 45, no. 4 (October 2004): 795–807.

Paige, Jeffery M. *Coffee and Power: Revolution and the Rise of Democracy in Central America.* Cambridge, MA: Harvard University Press, 1997.

————. "Coffee and Power in El Salvador." *Latin American Research Review* 28, no. 3 (1993): 7–40.

Palacios, Marcos. *Coffee in Colombia, 1850–1970: An Economic, Social, and Political History.* New York: Cambridge University Press, 1980.

Palmer, Frederick. *Central America and Its Problems.* New York: Moffat, Yard, 1910.

Palmer, Phyllis. "Outside the Law: Agricultural and Domestic Workers Under the Fair Labor Standards Act." *Journal of Policy History* 7, no. 4 (1995): 416–40.

Patenaude, Bertrand M. *The Big Show in Bololand: The American Relief Expedition to Soviet Russia in the Famine of 1921.* Stanford, CA: Stanford University Press, 2002.

Paulsen, George E. *A Living Wage for the Forgotten Man: The Quest for Fair Labor Standards, 1933–1941.* Selinsgrove, PA: Susquehanna University Press, 1996.

Pendergrast, Mark. *Uncommon Grounds: The History of Coffee and How It Transformed the World.* 2nd ed. New York: Basic Books, 2010.

Pérez Sáinz, Juan Pablo. *From the Finca to the Maquila: Labor and Capitalist Development in Central America.* Boulder, CO: Westview Press, 1999.

Perkins, Edwin J. *Wall Street to Main Street: Charles Merrill and Middle-Class Investors.*

New York: Cambridge University Press, 1999.

Phillips, Charles F. "The Supermarket." *Harvard Business Review* 16, no. 2 (Winter 1938): 188–200.

Phillips, Kevin. *William McKinley.* The American Presidents Series. New York: Henry Holt, 2003.

Pictures of Travel in Far-Off Lands: Central America. London: T. Nelson and Sons, 1871.

Pilcher, Jeffrey M. *Planet Taco: A Global History of Mexican Food.* New York: Oxford University Press, 2012.

Pinchbeck, Ivy. *Women Workers and the Industrial Revolution, 1750–1850.* 1930; reprint, New York: Frank Cass, 1969.

Podolinsky, Sergei. "Socialism and the Unity of Physical Forces." Translated by Angelo Di Salvo and Mark Hudson. *Organization and Environment* 17, no. 1 (March 2004): 61–75.

Pomeranz, Kenneth, and Steven Topik. *The World That Trade Created: Society, Culture, and the World Economy, 1400 to the Present.* 3rd ed. Armonk, NY: M. E. Sharpe, 2013.

Prescott, Samuel C. *Report of an Investigation of Coffee.* New York: National Coffee Roasters Association, 1927.

Putnam, George Palmer. *The Southland of North America: Rambles and Observations in*

Central America in the Year 1912. New York: G. P. Putnam's Sons, 1914.

Quin, Mike. *The Big Strike.* 1949; reprint, New York: International Publishers, 1979.

Rabe, Stephen G. *The Most Dangerous Area in the World: John F. Kennedy Confronts Communist Revolution in Latin America.* Chapel Hill: University of North Carolina Press, 1999.

Rabinbach, Anson. *The Human Motor: Energy, Fatigue, and the Origins of Modernity.* New York: Basic Books, 1990.

Racine, Karen. "Alberto Masferrer and the Vital Minimum: The Life and Thought of a Salvadoran Journalist, 1868–1932." *The Americas* 54, no. 2 (October 1997): 209–37.

Rauchway, Eric. *Murdering McKinley: The Making of Theodore Roosevelt's America.* New York: Hill and Wang, 2003.

Reichman, Daniel R. *The Broken Village: Coffee, Migration, and Globalization in Honduras.* Ithaca, NY: Cornell University Press, 2011.

Remini, Robert V. *Henry Clay: Statesman for the Union.* New York: W. W. Norton, 1993.

Report of the College of Agriculture and the Agricultural Experiment Station of the University of California. Berkeley: University of California Press, 1922.

Rhodes, Carolyn. *Reciprocity, U.S. Trade Policy, and the GATT Regime.* Ithaca, NY:

Cornell University Press, 1993.

Riesman, David. "Some Observations on Changes in Leisure Attitudes." *Antioch Review* 12, no. 4 (Winter 1952): 417–36.

Riis, Jacob. *How the Other Half Lives: Studies Among the Tenements of New York.* New York: Charles Scribner's Sons, 1890.

Ripley, George, and Charles Anderson Dana, eds. *The American Cyclopaedia: A Popular Dictionary of General Knowledge.* New York: D. Appleton, 1881.

Rock, David, ed. *Latin America in the 1940s: War and Postwar Transitions.* Berkeley: University of California Press, 1994.

Rodríguez, Roberto Cintli. *Our Sacred Maíz Is Our Mother: Indigeneity and Belonging in the Americas.* Tucson: University of Arizona Press, 2014.

Roediger, David R. *Working Towards Whiteness: How America's Immigrants Became White: The Strange Journey from Ellis Island to the Suburbs.* New York: Basic Books, 2005.

Romero, Óscar. *Journal d'Oscar Romero.* Trans. Maurice Barth. Paris: Éditions Karthala, 1992.

Roseberry, William. *Coffee and Capitalism in the Venezuelan Andes.* Austin: University of Texas Press, 1983.

———. "La Falta de Brazos: Land and Labor in the Coffee Economies of Nineteenth-

Century Latin America." *Theory and Society* 20, no. 3 (1991): 351–82.

———. "The Rise of Yuppie Coffees and the Reimagination of Social Class in the United States." *American Anthropologist,* new ser. 98, no. 4 (December 1996): 762–75.

Roseberry, William, Lowell Gudmundson, and Mario Samper Kutschbach, eds. *Coffee, Society, and Power in Latin America.* Baltimore: Johns Hopkins University Press, 1995.

Rosenberg, Emily S. *Financial Missionaries to the World: The Politics and Culture of Dollar Diplomacy, 1900–1930.* Durham, NC: Duke University Press, 2003.

———, ed. *A World Connecting: 1870–1945.* Cambridge, MA: Belknap Press, 2012.

Rothermund, Dietmar. *The Global Impact of the Great Depression, 1929–1939.* New York: Routledge, 1996.

Rovensky, Joseph C., and A. Willing Patterson. "Problems and Opportunities in Hemispheric Economic Development." *Law and Contemporary Problems* 8, no. 4 (Autumn 1941): 657–68.

Ruhl, Arthur. *The Central Americans: Adventures and Impressions Between Mexico and Panama.* New York: Charles Scribner's Sons, 1928.

Ryant, Carl G. "The South and the Movement Against Chain Stores." *Journal of*

Southern History 39, no. 2 (May 1973): 207–22.

Rydell, Robert W., et al. *Fair America: World's Fairs in the United States.* Washington, DC: Smithsonian Books, 2013.

Sanborn, Helen J. *A Winter in Central America and Mexico.* Boston: Lee & Shepard, 1886.

Sanderson, Michael. *Education, Economic Change, and Society in England, 1780–1870.* London: Macmillan, 1991; 2nd ed., New York: Cambridge University Press, 1995.

Sanneh, Kelefa. "Sacred Grounds." *The New Yorker,* November 13, 2011. https://www .newyorker.com/magazine/2011/11/21/ sacred-grounds.

Schlesinger, Arthur M., Jr. *The Age of Roosevelt.* 3 vols. New York: Houghton Mifflin, 1957; reprint, New York: Mariner / Houghton Mifflin, 2003.

Schlesinger, Jorge. *Revolución comunista: Guatemala en peligro?* Guatemala City: Editorial Unión Tipografia Castañeda, 1946.

Schmitt, Cannon. *Darwin and the Memory of the Human: Evolution, Savages, and South America.* New York: Cambridge University Press, 2009.

Schutte, Ofelia. *Beyond Nihilism: Nietzsche Without Masks.* Chicago: University of Chicago Press, 1984.

Scott, James C. *Against the Grain: A Deep His-*

tory of the Earliest States. New Haven: Yale University Press, 2017.

Scroop, Daniel. "The Anti-Chain Store Movement and the Politics of Consumption." *American Quarterly* 60, no. 4 (December 2008): 925–50.

Seigel, Micol. *Uneven Encounters: Making Race and Nation in Brazil and the United States.* Durham, NC: Duke University Press, 2009.

Sicilia, David B. "Supermarket Sweep." *Audacity* 5 (Spring 1997): 11–19.

Slater's Directory of Manchester and Salford, 1869–1879.

Smith, Andrew F., ed. *The Oxford Encyclopedia of Food and Drink in America.* 2nd ed. Vol. 2. New York: Oxford University Press, 2013.

Smith, Crosbie. *The Science of Energy: The Cultural History of Energy Physics in Victorian Britain.* Chicago: University of Chicago Press, 1998.

Smith, Robert Angus. *Air and Rain: The Beginnings of a Chemical Climatology.* London: Longmans, Green, 1872.

Sochor, Zenovia A. *Revolution and Culture: The Bogdanov-Lenin Controversy.* Ithaca, NY: Cornell University Press, 1988.

Soule, George, David Efron, and Norman T. Ness. *Latin America in the Future World.* New York: Farrar & Rinehart, 1945.

Sperber, Jonathan. *Karl Marx: A Nineteenth-Century Life.* New York: Liveright, 2013.

Squier, E. G. *Notes on Central America.* New York: Harper & Brothers, 1855.

———. *The States of Central America.* New York: Harper & Brothers, 1858.

Stamberg, Susan. "Present at the Creation: The Coffee Break." NPR.org. December 2, 2002. www.npr.org/programs/morning/features/patc/coffeebreak/index.html/.

Steffens, Henry John. *James Prescott Joule and the Concept of Energy.* New York: Science History Publications/USA, 1979.

Stein, Stanley. *Vassouras: A Brazilian Coffee County, 1850–1900: The Roles of Planter and Slave in a Plantation Society.* Cambridge, MA: Harvard University Press, 1957.

Stevenson, Robert Louis. *Treasure Island.* Boston: Roberts Brothers, 1884.

Steward, Dick. *Trade and Hemisphere: The Good Neighbor Policy and Reciprocal Trade.* Columbia: University of Missouri Press, 1975.

Steward, Luther N., Jr. "California Coffee: A Promising Failure." *Southern California Quarterly* 46, no. 3 (September 1964): 259–64.

Stewart, Balfour, and J. Norman Lockyer. "The Sun as a Type of the Material Universe." Part 1. *Macmillan's* 18 (July 1868): 246–57.

Stoetzer, O. Carlos. *The Organization of American States.* 2nd ed. Westport, CT: Praeger, 1993.

Stolcke, Verena. *Coffee Planters, Workers, and Wives: Class Conflict and Gender Relations on São Paulo Plantations, 1850–1980.* London: Macmillan, 1988.

Strasser, Susan. *Satisfaction Guaranteed: The Making of the American Mass Market.* New York: Pantheon, 1989.

Sylla, Ndongo S. *The Fair Trade Scandal: Marketing Poverty to Benefit the Rich.* Translated by David Clément Leye. Athens, OH: Ohio University Press, 2014.

Talbot, John M. *Grounds for Agreement: The Political Economy of the Coffee Commodity Chain.* Lanham, MD: Rowman & Littlefield, 2004.

Tantillo, Astrida Orle. *The Will to Create: Goethe's Philosophy of Nature.* Pittsburgh: University of Pittsburgh Press, 2002.

Tasca, Henry J. *The Reciprocal Trade Policy of the United States.* Philadelphia: University of Pennsylvania Press, 1938.

Tedlow, Richard S. *New and Improved: The Story of Mass Marketing in America.* New York: Basic Books, 1991; reprint, Boston: Harvard Business School Press, 1996.

Terkel, Studs. *Hard Times: An Oral History of the Great Depression.* New York: Pantheon, 1970; reprint, New York: New Press, 2005.

Thompson, E. P. "Time, Work-Discipline, and Industrial Capitalism." *Past and Present* 38 (December 1967): 56–97.

Thompson, Wallace. *Rainbow Countries of Central America.* New York: E. P. Dutton, 1926.

Thorp, Rosemary. *Progress, Poverty, and Exclusion: An Economic History of Latin America in the 20th Century.* Washington, DC: Inter-American Development Bank, 1998.

———, ed. *An Economic History of Twentieth-Century Latin America.* 2nd ed. Vol. 2, *Latin America in the 1930s: The Role of the Periphery in the World Crisis.* New York: Palgrave, 2000.

Thurber, Francis Beatty. *Coffee: From Plantation to Cup.* New York: American Grocer Publishing Association, 1881.

Thurston, Robert W., Jonathan Morris, and Shawn Steiman, eds. *Coffee: A Comprehensive Guide.* Lanham, MD: Rowman & Littlefield, 2013.

Tilley, Virginia. *Seeing Indians: A Study of Race, Nation, and Power in El Salvador.* Albuquerque: University of New Mexico Press, 2005.

Tobey, Ronald C. *Technology as Freedom: The New Deal and the Electrical Modernization of the American Home.* Berkeley: University of California Press, 1996.

Tocqueville, Alexis de. *Journeys to England and Ireland.* Translated by George Lawrence and K. P. Mayer. Edited by J. P. Mayer. 1979; reprint, New Brunswick, NJ: Transaction, 1988; New York: Routledge, 2017.

Topik, Steven. "Historicizing Commodity Chains: Five Hundred Years of the Global Coffee Commodity Chain." In *Frontiers of Commodity Chain Research,* edited by Jennifer Bair, 37–62. Stanford, CA: Stanford University Press, 2008.

Topik, Steven, Carlos Marichal, and Zephyr Frank, eds. *From Silver to Cocaine: Latin American Commodity Chains and the Building of the World Economy, 1500–2000.* Durham, NC: Duke University Press, 2006.

Topik, Steven, and Allen Wells, eds. *The Second Conquest of Latin America: Coffee, Henequen, and Oil During the Export Boom, 1850–1930.* Austin: University of Texas Press, 1998.

Tucker, Catherine M. *Coffee Culture: Local Experiences, Global Connections.* New York: Routledge, 2010.

Tucker, Richard P. *Insatiable Appetite: The United States and the Ecological Degradation of the Tropical World.* Berkeley: University of California, 2000.

Tulchin, Joseph S. *The Aftermath of War: World War I and U.S. Policy Toward Latin America.* New York: New York University

Press, 1971.

Turner, Mary. "A History of Collyhurst, Manchester, to 1900." Submitted for a Certificate of Extra-Mural Education, Manchester University. May 1975. Manchester Central Library, Manchester, UK.

Ukers, William H. *All About Coffee.* New York: Tea and Coffee Trade Journal Company, 1922.

———. *All About Coffee.* 2nd ed. New York: Tea and Coffee Trade Journal Company, 1935.

Underwood, Ted. *The Work of the Sun: Literature, Science, and Political Economy, 1760–1860.* New York: Palgrave Macmillan, 2005.

Vickers, Douglas. *Economics and Ethics: An Introduction to Theory, Institutions, and Policy.* Westport, CT: Praeger, 1997.

Wallace, Alfred Russel. *The Malay Archipelago: The Land of the Orangu-tan and the Bird of Paradise.* 4th ed. London: Macmillan, 1872.

Walvin, James. *A Child's World: A Social History of English Childhood, 1800–1914.* New York: Penguin, 1982.

Watkins, Melville H. "A Staple Theory of Economic Growth." *The Canadian Journal of Economics and Political Science* 29, no. 2 (May 1963): 141–58.

Watkins, T. H. *The Hungry Years: A Narrative History of the Great Depression in America.*

New York: Henry Holt, 1999.

Weinberg, Bennett Alan, and Bonnie K. Bealer. *The World of Caffeine: The Science and Culture of the World's Most Popular Drug.* New York: Routledge, 2002.

West, Paige. *From Modern Production to Imagined Primitive: The Social World of Coffee from Papua New Guinea.* Durham, NC: Duke University Press, 2012.

Whitehead, Andrew. "Red London: Radicals and Socialists in Late-Victorian Clerkenwell." *Socialist History* 18 (2000): 1–31.

Wickizer, V. D. *The World Coffee Economy, with Special Reference to Control Schemes.* Stanford, CA: Stanford University Press, 1943.

Wild, Antony. *Coffee: A Dark History.* New York: W. W. Norton, 2004.

Williams, Philip J., and Knut Walter. *Militarization and Demilitarization in El Salvador's Transition to Democracy.* Pittsburgh: University of Pittsburgh Press, 1997.

Williams, Robert G. *States and Social Evolution: Coffee and the Rise of National Governments in Central America.* Chapel Hill: University of North Carolina Press, 1994.

Williams, William Appleman. *Empire as a Way of Life.* New York: Oxford University Press, 1980; reprint, Brooklyn, NY: Ig Books, 2006.

————. *The Tragedy of American Diplomacy.* 50th anniversary ed. New York: W. W. Norton, 2009.

Williamson, Harold Francis. *Edward Atkinson: The Biography of an American Liberal, 1827–1905.* Boston: Old Corner Bookstore, 1934.

Wilson, Charles Morrow. *Central America: Challenge and Opportunity.* New York: Henry Holt, 1941.

Wilson, Everett Alan. "The Crisis of National Integration in El Salvador, 1919–1935." Ph.D. diss., Stanford University, 1969.

Wise, M. Norton, with Crosbie Smith. "Work and Waste: Political Economy and Natural Philosophy in Nineteenth Century Britain (part 1)." *History of Science* 27, no. 3 (September 1989): 263–301.

Wise, M. Norton, with Crosbie Smith. "Work and Waste: Political Economy and Natural Philosophy in Nineteenth Century Britain (part 2)." *History of Science* 27, no. 4 (December 1989): 391–449.

Wittman, Hannah, Annette Aurélie Desmarais, and Nettie Wiebe, eds. *Food Sovereignty: Connecting Food, Nature, and Community.* Halifax, NS: Fernwood, 2010.

Wolfe, Joel. *Autos and Progress: The Brazilian Search for Modernity.* New York: Oxford University Press, 2010.

Womack, John., Jr. "Doing Labor History: Feelings, Work, Material Power." *Journal of* the Historical Society 5, no. 3 (2005): 255–96.

Wood, Bryce. *The Making of the Good Neighbor Policy.* New York: Columbia University Press, 1961; reprint, New York; W. W. Norton, 1967.

Wood, Elisabeth Jean. *Insurgent Collective Action and Civil War in El Salvador.* New York: Cambridge University Press, 2003.

Youmans, Edward L., ed. *The Correlation and Conservation of Forces: A Series of Expositions.* New York: D. Appleton, 1864.

Zamosc, Leon. "Class Conflict in an Export Economy: The Social Roots of the Salvadoran Insurrection of 1932." In *Sociology of Developing Societies: Central America,* edited by Jan Flora and Edelberto Torres Rivas, 56–74. New York: Monthly Review Press, 1989.

———. "The Landing That Never Was: Canadian Marines and the Salvadorean Insurrection of 1932." *Canadian Journal of Latin American and Caribbean Studies* 11, no. 21 (1986): 131–47.

Zeiler, Thomas W. *Free Trade, Free World: The Advent of GATT.* Chapel Hill: University of North Carolina Press, 1999.

Zencey, Eric. "Some Brief Speculations on the Popularity of Entropy as Metaphor." *North American Review* 271, no. 3 (September 1986): 7–10.

Zimmerman, M. M. *The Super Market: Spectacular Exponent of Mass Distribution.* New York: Super Market Publishing Co., 1937.

———. *Super Market Merchandising: A Revolution in Distribution.* New York: McGraw-Hill, 1955.

———. "The Supermarket and the Changing Retail Structure." *Journal of Marketing* 5, no. 4 (April 1941): 402–9.

ABOUT THE AUTHOR

Augustine Sedgewick earned his doctorate at Harvard University and teaches at the City University of New York. His research on the global history of food, work, and capitalism has received fellowships from the American Council of Learned Societies, the Andrew W. Mellon Foundation, and the Project on Justice, Welfare, and Economics at Harvard, and has been published in *History of the Present, International Labor and Working-Class History,* and *Labor.* Originally from Maine, Sedgewick lives in New York City.

The employees of Thorndike Press hope you have enjoyed this Large Print book. All our Thorndike, Wheeler, and Kennebec Large Print titles are designed for easy reading, and all our books are made to last. Other Thorndike Press Large Print books are available at your library, through selected bookstores, or directly from us.

For information about titles, please call:
(800) 223-1244

or visit our website at:
gale.com/thorndike

To share your comments, please write:
Publisher
Thorndike Press
10 Water St., Suite 310
Waterville, ME 04901